The Social Worker as Manager

A Practical Guide to Success

FOURTH EDITION

Robert W. Weinbach

University of South Carolina

Editor in Chief, Social Sciences: *Karen Hanson*
Series Editor: *Patricia Quinlin*
Editorial Assistant: *Anne Marie Kennedy*
Marketing Manager: *Taryn Wahlquist*
Editorial Production Service: *Whitney Acres Editorial*
Electronic Composition: *Peggy Cabot, Cabot Computer Services*
Manufacturing Buyer: *JoAnne Sweeney*
Cover Administrator: *Kristina Mose-Libon*

For related titles and support materials, visit our online catalog at www.ablongman.com.

Library of Congress Cataloging-in-Publication Data

CIP data not available at the time of publication.
ISBN 0-205-34198-5

Printed in the United States of America

10 9 8 7 6 5 4 3 2   07 06 05 04 03 02

Contents

Preface

This book is organized in a way similar to earlier editions, yet it is very different in some important ways. Once again it was designed to be easy to read, conversational, and full of examples and practical applications. It is also based on the same premises that guided earlier editions. It was written for use in a one-term course in management for BSW or MSW students, but also for those practitioners who, by choice or necessity, now find themselves with significant management responsibilities and can use a little help.

Now more than ever, as organizational charts grow flatter and efficiency concerns result in the elimination of many mid-level managerial positions, management is a part of every social worker's job. By design, the vast majority of what is discussed in this book is applicable to all social workers functioning as managers, that is, for first level administrative supervisors on through executive directors of large public or private, not-for-profit organizations. To a lesser degree, it even addresses management issues faced by those who spend much of their day delivering direct service to clients but who may supervise volunteers, students or clerical staff. I have deliberately not included in-depth discussion of a few topics and issues that are the exclusive domain of, and thus would be of interest to, only a relatively few CEO types who manage very large organizations. I believe that, if needed, this knowledge can better be acquired through narrowly focused workshops, informal mentoring, or other books written exclusively for these individuals. This book is designed to address a much wider audience and to cover topics of universal concern.

What is new and different about this edition? A lot! It still has 12 chapters, but most of them have undergone major updating and revision. There are both new and revised case examples drawn from real-life situations. I have added discussion questions after each case example in response to professors who told me that they use them for small group discussions and thought that some guiding questions would be helpful. There are also new and revised figures to help clarify old content and to illustrate some of the new material.

There is much more content on management ethics. This very important topic is introduced in Chapter 1 and appears again in the context of discussions in several other chapters.

Many of the major headings remain the same, but there are some important changes within them. The five major management functions—planning, staffing, organizing, controlling, and leading are still the focus of the central portion of the book. However, some examples of topics that receive new or expanded coverage in Chapters 4–10 of this edition are:

- Organizational mission, vision, and mandates
- Strategic planning
- Rules, policies, and procedures; tactics; evaluability assessment

- Personnel issues relating to use of volunteers
- Diversity in the workplace
- Job rotation and job enlargement
- "Remote supervision"
- Fairness and consideration as they relate to performance evaluations
- Suggestions for conducting evaluation interviews
- Reprimands, warnings, and contracts; job abandonment
- Informal organizational power
- Professional values and ethics

There is a new Chapter 11 in which other important management tasks are discussed that received much less attention in previous editions. They are: financial management, time management, change management, technology management, staff turnover, and monitoring and evaluation of programs.

Chapter 12 is still designed to summarize and to assist the reader in sorting out his or her own attitudes about a career in management. However, along with minor revisions, it also includes an entire new section on how the intra-personal needs of managers can either contribute to or interfere with their effectiveness.

In order to add all of the new content while still keeping the book at a practical and affordable length, some content from the third edition had to go. The most obvious of these deletions is the "Additional Readings" section at the end of each chapter. I hope that, with the ready availability of electronic searches of computer-accessible data bases as well as such websites as the Social Work Access Network (SWAN) which is maintained at my university, this will present no great inconvenience. Much of the other content that I deleted was either getting out-of-date or somewhat redundant. Some, frankly, I would have liked to keep, but I deemed other new content to be more important for today's manager.

Acknowledgments

Many other people besides those writers and researchers cited contributed to the book's content. Karen Hanson at Allyn & Bacon has once again demonstrated her belief in and support for my writing. The other members of the editorial staff were also very helpful. Among other things, they acquired three thoughtful and helpful reviews of the fourth edition by Arturo Acosta, El Paso Community College; Suzanne McDevitt, Edinboro University of Pennsylvania; and Todd W. Rofuth, Southern Connecticut State University. The suggestions of these reviewers formed the basis for many of the changes and additions that were made, and I am most grateful to them for their help. My colleagues at the University of South Carolina, most notably Michelle Carney, Naomi Farber, Leon Ginsberg, and Terry Tirrito, also provided some valuable critiques and suggestions.

Back in 1990 when the first edition of this book was published, I acknowledged several managers who I had known who had influenced my ideas about management. Some set excellent examples, others left me determined never to repeat or encourage others to make their mistakes! Since then there have been others. Two, Frank B. Raymond III and

Lois Wright, have been especially helpful to me in formulating some of the ideas about management that are reflected in this edition.

Finally, I owe a special debt of gratitude to my wife, Lynne M. Taylor. By sharing with me some of the problems and rewards that she encounters as a manager, she has provided me with a rich source of current examples for my writing. She has also reinforced my belief that there are a wide array of philosophies and approaches to management that can be effective, some of which are very different from my own. I hope the readers of this book will keep that in mind.

Robert W. Weinbach
University of South Carolina

Part I

Management in Perspective

In order to develop a clear understanding of what management is and the context in which it occurs for social workers, we approach the topic from several different angles. In Chapter 1 we attempt to describe management in a way that accurately reflects both its richness and its complexity. We examine what an "organization" would look like without management and why management is essential for any kind of purposeful activity to take place.

In Chapter 2, the concept of the task environment is introduced; it will be central to our discussion of management throughout this text. Having done so, we examine the similarities and differences that exist between for-profit businesses and human service organizations in both the public and not-for-profit sectors and how they affect the management functions of the social worker. We focus on the concept of prime beneficiary and how it explains some of the conflicts that exist between human service organizations and their task environments.

In Chapter 3 we review the legacy of management theory that continues to influence management behaviors today. Classical management theories are examined, along with some of the newer approaches that have evolved in recent years.

1

Definitions and Assumptions

The last years of the twentieth century were a time of uncertainty and change for social workers in the human services. Concern with the rising costs of services in areas such as health care and corrections gave rise to demands for better management at all levels within organizations. Those management activities designed to reduce costs have received special attention. Emphasis on concepts such as managed care and case management should have come as no surprise to us. Human services are multibillion dollar enterprises and getting bigger all the time. They are an integral part of the economy of all nations in the Western Hemisphere. They represent an increasing percentage of the gross national product of Western nations, a fact that has not gone unnoticed by politicians and just plain concerned citizens.

The recent changes occurring in human services suggest the need for a greater emphasis on management within human service organizations and for a study of relevant theory. But for the social worker, there should be another and more compelling reason to study management. We are committed to providing the best possible services to clients. Management, when performed well at all levels, contributes greatly to achieving this objective. Thus it is an important part of social work practice that deserves the careful attention of all present and future social practitioners.

If There Were No Management

A world without management is almost unimaginable. Every human activity involves management. In fact, the human brain is sometimes offered as an example of a full-time manager, managing our respiration, our locomotion, our thought processes, our digestion, and so on—even our dreams and other activities while we sleep. A brain is a special kind of manager. Unlike any other manager, it never really takes a break or slips into another role. It is on-duty 24 hours a day, seven days a week.

Without our brains functioning as managers, we could not breathe or move a muscle. No human organism could exist for more than a few seconds without the brain's management activities. The situation is "manage or die." The same situation exists within organizations. No organization could exist, much less thrive, without management. Management is not a choice; it is a necessity.

Individual social workers cannot choose whether or not they want to perform management functions in their professional roles either. We can choose not to take a "management job" which demands that a high percentage of our time be spent in certain management activities, but we cannot choose to avoid management altogether. Social workers at any level within an organization need to understand management and to perform its functions effectively. We must know how to manage in order to function in our private lives; our professional work requires no less.

People generally enter into personal management activities with little preparation and formal instruction. They learn to manage their checkbooks, their social lives, or their budget through a combination of trial and error and informal tutoring from friends or relatives. They discover that they have to learn to manage because they have learned the consequences of insufficient management or mismanagement of their activities. Unfortunately, many people have "backed into" management in their professional lives in a similar way. They have not seen the importance and inevitability of management and have, therefore, not prepared themselves to perform management activities. Students who are planning for a career as a higher-level administrator in a human service organization readily recognize the need for studying the topic of management. But others who have no immediate plans to become a "boss" or for whom direct client contact is a major source of professional gratification may have more difficulty in understanding why the study of management is relevant to their professional goals.

Some people are convinced about the importance of management only when they have to make management decisions without benefit of existing knowledge. After making bad decisions, they begin to recognize the importance of availing themselves of the vast amount of knowledge that exists to help them perform their management functions.

All of us have worked in or been around organizations where mismanagement has occurred. That is inevitable. No one can be a perfect manager, any more than anyone can be a perfect clinician or community organizer. But think how ineffective an organization would be without *any* management. Try to imagine a human service organization where no one even attempted to perform the functions of management. What would it look like? A few of its more dramatic features might be:

> There would be no mission to differentiate the organization from any other organization. It would have no identity and no real purpose. It would offer no support or assistance to its employees.

> Staff would be hired without regard to their capabilities or potential contributions. They might show up (or they might not) as the mood hit them. If and when they showed up, they would decide what they wanted to do. There would be no guidelines available to tell them what they should be doing or how best to do it. All behavior would be random and independent of the behavior of others. It would have no purpose and would not be directed toward any goal or objective. There would be nothing in place to help staff members upgrade their knowledge and skills. There would be no guidelines or yardsticks to evaluate the quality of their work. Decisions about promotions, compensation, even continued employment would be made in a purely arbitrary and capricious way.

Clients might be offered services, or they might not. There would be no clear-cut responsibility or accountability for any assistance offered. Nothing would protect them from staff apathy, incompetence, laziness or malpractice.

What we have just described is chaos—really, a nonorganization. Without management, organizations as we know them do not exist. Management is inevitable and necessary. It is what makes an organization different from just a place in which people rattle around in random purposeless activity.

What Is *Management?*

Management is often misunderstood. Even the word management itself is used in different ways that connote different images. It is sometimes used as a proper noun (as in "the Management") in referring collectively to a few people who occupy the highest positions on the organizational chart. It is also used frequently as a verb to suggest a wide range of seemingly unrelated activities that consist of virtually anything except direct treatment services to clients. Either misuse of the word can only produce dangerous misunderstandings about this important activity.

Complicating matters even further, the word *management* frequently is used arbitrarily and interchangeably with another term, administration, within the social work literature and elsewhere. Efforts to differentiate the two have usually met with limited success. One recent writer[1] has concluded that, in terms of function, they overlap. The literature in business and elsewhere is replete with attempts to define management, but unfortunately, there is only limited consensus. Based upon the author's review of the work of others and his own biases as expressed in this book, a working definition is provided that should simplify our study. Management is defined as "certain functions performed by social workers at all administrative levels within human service organizations which are designed to facilitate the accomplishment of organizational goals."

Management can be conceptualized as various ways of shaping and exerting an influence over the work environment. Social workers in the role of manager attempt to build and to maintain an optimal internal work environment (often referred to as "climate") conducive to the efficient delivery of effective services to clients. Thus, management is primarily a proactive (rather than a reactive) activity. A work environment can range from highly supportive of delivery of services at one extreme to a destructive environment that actually seems to sabotage delivery of services at the opposite extreme. Of course, both extremes are rare; the work environment usually falls somewhere closer to the middle of this continuum. Management uses a variety of methods to build in sources of support for good service delivery, and to remove or minimize the effects of those conditions that might tend to make the delivery of effective services difficult. It thus promotes productivity.

Some business-oriented definitions of management focus heavily on management's role in promoting economical service delivery. A manager's function is sometimes described as the creation of surplus.[2] The idea is that the output of an organization should exceed its input; it should generate more than the resources required to produce its products or services. The difference is called the surplus. In the corporate sphere, surplus is easily understood—it is profit. The money derived from the sale of a product is expected to exceed the cost in personnel, raw materials, advertising, etc., of producing and marketing the product. Management is used to make the organization function more efficiently, thereby increasing the likelihood that surplus will be great.

The "surplus" concept is not without applicability for social work practice or inconsistent with the definition of management that has been provided. With recent increased emphasis on managed care within the medical and mental health fields of practice, it is becoming increasingly relevant in understanding the functions of management that social workers perform. In fact, in some managed care facilities, a monetary profit can result for the organization if treatment costs are less than standardized reimbursement for a procedure or treatment. This is most likely to happen in organizations that are well-managed.

Even within more traditional clinical practice there may be the assumption that well-managed treatment can and will produce a kind of surplus, to someone, if not to the organization. For example, social workers offering weekly counseling to unemployed clients to help them become financially self-sufficient again are hoping to generate a surplus. Specifically, they hope that their services will result in financial gain to clients (namely wages from employment) that will exceed the cost of the counseling offered. If most human service organizations did not believe that well-managed counseling is effective in generating surplus, it would make more sense simply to calculate the cost of services, stop offering them, and give the money saved directly to clients to help them pay their bills or otherwise alleviate their problems. In fact, in those human service organization settings where counseling services have not been able to document the production of a surplus (for example, the public welfare sector), some social workers and many members of the general public have concluded that this latter approach might be preferable to treatment strategies.

Certain social programs and services may, by their very nature, lend themselves to creation of a "surplus" of one form or another through effective management. Generally, they contain elements of prevention, services designed to preclude a more expensive scenario from happening. For example:

- The cost of well-managed HIV infection prevention programs can be compared favorably with the medical costs of treating AIDS within hospitals.
- The cost of a well-managed, short-term family preservation program is generally less than the cost of long-term foster care for children at risk for abuse or neglect. (Of course, the death of a child from abuse within a home where family preservation services are being offered can quickly shift the balance.)
- A hospital that offers in-home hospice services for terminally ill people may have little difficulty in justifying why these services are less expensive than hospitalization. Of course, the reduction in human suffering in any of these examples is easily recognized by social workers as surplus of yet a different kind.

In other human services organizations, even the best management cannot always generate a surplus in dollars and cents or in human benefits that can be easily documented. By its very nature, social work intervention is often a very expensive, inefficient enterprise. For example, a well-managed program in a family service agency may produce a surplus in human benefits (increased self-esteem, improved family communication, and so on), but these benefits may not be able to be measured. They also are unlikely to represent a financial surplus. Some well-managed programs have as their goal the maintenance of the status quo (for example, avoidance of the recurrence of substance abuse). It would be difficult to assert that the problem definitely would recur without the program. Thus, it would be very difficult to document the production of any kind of surplus. Documenting the value of good social work management in fiscal or human terms can be extremely difficult in many treatment situations for a variety of reasons. It is usually not possible to compute how much our efforts are worth. Sometimes we cannot even prove that we have been instrumental in changes that occurred. Sometimes we cannot even document whether or not any changes occurred.

The constraints on producing and documenting the existence of surplus in some social work settings do not preclude our viewing its production as another way of conceptualizing it as a goal of good management. The practice of good management, either in those organizations and programs where a surplus is relatively easy or in ones where it is virtually impossible, will always increase the *likelihood* that a surplus will be generated. Social workers performing management at all levels can still use the activities of management to contribute to the goal of surplus, even if that goal is unattainable. Also, while an organization or program may not be able to generate a surplus, that does not preclude a well-managed subunit of it from doing so. For example, the training director of a program that of necessity operates at a "loss" or break-even point may produce surplus by designing and implementing an orientation program for new workers that, over time, will more than pay for itself in reduced supervisory demands or costly errors.

The Functions of Management

Management as it has been defined entails a limited list of somewhat overlapping functions. Unfortunately, there is a lack of consensus on what labels should be applied to them. In fact, in the chapters that follow, we will discuss some management activities that can and do fall within two or more broad functions; others, such as those described in Chapter 11, do not quite fit particularly well in any, but are nevertheless critical to our study of management.

The authors of one textbook commonly used in public administration and business and sometimes in social work courses, group its study of functions into five categories: planning, organizing, staffing, leading, and controlling.[3] (We have opted to organize this book loosely around these five functions.) Another author condenses this list to only planning, organizing, and controlling.[4] A third cites the classical management functions as organizing, coordinating, planning, and controlling.[5] A fourth list contains planning, organizing, leading, and controlling,[6] and so forth.

What are the "common denominators" among these lists? All the lists suggest the efforts of a manager to take an *active* role in shaping various aspects of the work environment. They all reflect the manager's responsibility to do more than just let things happen naturally. They suggest attempting to improve on what might happen spontaneously if the manager did not take charge and did not manage.

Unfortunately, the lists all contain words that are sometimes frustrating in their ambiguity and their vagueness. They hint at but do not tell us what a manager really does. They require considerable explanation. When we use these rather general terms in future chapters, we will first provide a working definition of them. Then we will focus on the specific activities, tasks, behaviors, and even attitudes that characterize them. When appropriate, we will even offer a specific menu of vehicles for performing a given management function.

Management as Both a Science and an Art

Management is a science in that there exists a body of empirical knowledge relevant to the practice of management. We will be looking at some of this knowledge in later chapters of this book. Some of it, particularly that related to such phenomena as motivation, group dynamics, morale, and so on, has been derived from the work of researchers in fields such as industrial psychology, education, sociology, and social work. Another sizable body of relevant knowledge has been accumulated in the business field. Certain fields of study, such as organizational theory or social psychology, bridge two or more disciplines. A relatively new phenomenon is the accumulation of a variety of relevant material into a category loosely identified as management theory or some similar term. Social work has recently attempted to define a body of knowledge for the practice of management. Recent years have witnessed the publication of a large number of management books and a successful professional journal with a specific management focus (*Administration in Social Work*).

Social workers who need help in performing the functions of management take and use helpful knowledge wherever they can find it. This is similar to what social workers have done in acquiring needed knowledge for other areas of social work practice, such as human behavior or research, where much of our knowledge is "borrowed" from other fields.

In order to understand the knowledge component of management, it is important to recognize both the nature and the limitations of the knowledge that is available. Knowledge related to management (as in other areas of social work practice) can be thought of as existing in three somewhat overlapping categories: descriptive, predictive, and prescriptive.[7] The mix of management knowledge among these categories is also very similar to that available for other areas of social work practice. Because of the complexity of the problems that social workers encounter and the phenomena involved (that is, human behavior) and because, for ethical and other reasons, our research is often limited to the use of certain designs, the preponderance of the available knowledge is descriptive. Specifically, it consists of observations of patterns that have been observed in the natural setting or in some setting where minimal control was exerted.

When descriptive knowledge begins to accumulate from a variety of empirical observations and there is general consensus among those who interpret and classify these observations, we feel sufficiently bold to begin to make predictions. Predictive knowledge is knowledge that provides an educated guess regarding what will occur in the future in a given situation. It is based upon patterns of what has been observed to occur in the past when similar conditions were present. Predictive knowledge is an extension of descriptive knowledge. It is based on the assumption of probability theory that states that the patterns of what occurred in the past are generally pretty good indicators of what will occur in the future. However, there are no guarantees. Weather forecasters employ predictive knowledge. They base their prediction that there is a 30 percent chance of rain on the knowledge that 30 percent of the times in the past when similar conditions were present, it rained. Their predictive knowledge allows them to be right more often than they are wrong in predicting whether or not it will rain.

People who invest in the stock market also depend on past trends in predicting the direction of the price of a stock. Subjective probability and predictive knowledge are based on studies of the past, not on the laws of mathematics that form the basis of objective probability and of the field of inferential statistics. Frequently, we use subjective probability in making decisions and in anticipating the future without even realizing it. Subjective probability is a "best guess" based on the past and its similarity to the present situation, but it cannot consider all of the variables that exist in the present. These "unknowns" will have the effect of adjusting the "real" probability either up or down (see Figure 1.1).

As social workers, we sometimes predict a legislator's reaction to certain community action tactics or assess the likelihood of further abuse if an abused child is returned to the home. We feel reasonably comfortable with our predictions based on what has occurred in similar situations in the past. Similarly, in the role of manager we can sometimes make management decisions and feel relatively confident that we are right, based on available predictive knowledge. But we are always well aware that past observations do not guarantee future events. Furthermore, in management as well as in other areas of practice, there are many problem areas where our descriptive knowledge is so incomplete or so conflicting that predictive knowledge simply does not exist to help us.

While there is a limited amount of predictive knowledge available for management, there is even less prescriptive knowledge. Again, the parallel to other areas of practice is strong. Prescriptive knowledge is knowledge about how to intervene, to act so that what can be predicted to occur can be changed or avoided. Total prescriptive knowledge for child-protection workers (which, of course, does not exist) would tell them exactly what to say to and do with the perpetrator and the child to guarantee that another instance of abuse would never occur. Prescriptive knowledge for supervisors functioning as managers would enable them to write the perfect annual evaluation (containing useful feedback and constructive criticism) for their supervisees which would guarantee that their maximum productivity would occur. Not likely! Our knowledge does not even approach this level. While researchers hope to ultimately generate prescriptive knowledge in an area of inquiry, getting to that point is often difficult if not impossible.

The knowledge presented in this book will be representative of the knowledge levels most frequently found in management. There will be much more description than prediction and even less prescription in the form of specific "how to do it" suggestions. Because management involves so many different human and situational variables, often we will not be able to say what will work for the reader in the role of manager and what will not. For example, there is no telling just what one or a group of human beings can do to undermine a "good" management decision or even to support a "bad" decision in such a way that it produces a successful outcome!

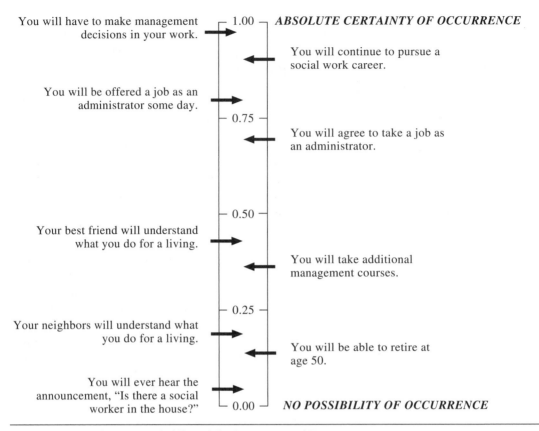

FIGURE 1.1 *Subjective Probability of the Occurrence of Events*

We said that management is both a science and an art. The art factor enters in when we try to apply the best available knowledge to a situation or problem. Knowledge may be the basis for management decisions, but whether they can be successfully implemented or not is to a large degree a function of art factors. What are some of these art factors? They are, for example, personality, intuition, experience, personal loyalties, group confidence, trust, or self-confidence. All of these factors and others, can be viewed as variables that differ in degree and form from one manager to another and from one situation to another. It is the combination of these that allows any given manager to succeed while another may fail. They explain why one manager can make a management decision and gain widespread support while another manager can make the same decision in a similar situation and provoke only resentment and suspicion.

A management decision is often not inherently right or wrong; its success is dependent on the knowledge and skills of the manager, the human beings through which it is "processed" and their relationships with each other and with the manager, and the unique situation in which it occurs. Where predictive knowledge exists, it is the human element that can either increase or decrease the likelihood of occurrence of the predictable event.

(This is why the hypothetical probabilities in Figure 1.1 may be reasonably accurate in a collective sense but seem a little "off" from any one individual's perspective.) As an extreme example, an especially adept and respected manager with the right combination of art factors for a given situation could gain support for a necessary pay cut without jeopardizing morale or causing resentment. In contrast, a particularly hapless manager who is mistrusted by staff as a leader could hire additional support staff and cause a minor rebellion.

The idea that art and knowledge interact to influence the likelihood of success in management should not be new or foreign to social work practitioners. Insightful clinical social workers may know, for example, that confrontation may be appropriate with some clients. But they may also know that they could not "pull it off" successfully because it is so contradictory to their usual helping styles. Similarly, one competent macro-level practitioner may not possess the "art" of working successfully with legislators for passage of a stricter state licensure bill, whereas a colleague might garner their support with ease. Some of the mystery and the intimidation of management dissipates if we recognize that management is just a form of practice and that there are many similarities between it and those other activities more commonly thought of as the province of the social worker. In all areas of practice certain innate abilities and personality characteristics can be supportive of or can present obstacles to the performance of a task. Of course, while some of us may have a "knack" in one area or another, we can also learn to perform any task better. Art in management, as in other areas of practice, is both innate and learned. We will be emphasizing the importance of recognizing the innate and acquiring the knowledge necessary to assist us to learn those skills necessary for successful management practice.

Management Ethics

In the role of manager, social workers often must function in a work environment characterized by limited resources and both internal and external political pressures. This can (and often does) create ethical conflicts. While such conflicts are present in any activity or setting, they take on a particular form for social workers as managers. Management ethics center around the issue of whose rights and needs should take priority over those of others. Often, an ethical conflict occurs because of the necessity of "paying the bills" while still showing compassion for clients or staff. Whatever action or decision a manager makes may benefit one individual or group at the expense of another individual or group. This is a stressful yet inevitable part of management in the human services.

In the role of clinician, a social worker is expected to advocate for the rights and needs of his or her individual client or client system. Ethical conflicts are rare. But in the role of manager the social worker must consider the rights and needs of the individual client or client system, but also those of all clients and client systems presently served by the organization as well as those who might be served in the future. Ethical conflicts are common. Priority given to one individual or group may necessarily have a negative effect on the other. Similarly, if a manager takes action or makes a decision designed to protect the rights and needs of a given staff member, those of the entire staff or of the clients served by that staff member may be negatively affected. Or, if the rights and needs of the entire staff or the clients served by the staff member are given priority, the rights and needs of the staff member may be negatively affected.

Not surprisingly, ethical management often requires taking actions and making unpopular decisions that lead to accusations of "selling out." Because the rights and needs of any one individual or group cannot be consistently given priority over those of others without destroying morale or jeopardizing the organization in some other way, trade-offs and compromises often must be made. And, they may end up pleasing no one.

In performing the functions of a manager, ethical issues occur in many ways. We will examine some of the more common ones in the chapters that follow.

Avoiding Misconceptions about Management

Unfortunately, some social workers hold mistaken ideas about what management is and about whose responsibility it is. These ideas can lead to destructive attitudes and practices. Before we go any farther in our study of management, let us state some important, interrelated assumptions that will be reiterated again and again throughout this book.

Management Is Everyone's Work

In a successful organization, everyone is a manager at least some of the time. If we believe and act otherwise, problems will inevitably occur. Management is not the sole responsibility of a certain elite group of "senior" individuals within an organization called directors, administrators, or (unfortunately, for our purposes) managers. In fact, there has never been any such distinct division of labor whereby managers manage, supervisors supervise, direct-service practitioners deliver services, etc. But with the advent of contemporary theories and practices of management with their emphasis on involvement of workers at all levels in management decision making, such a misconception is even more inaccurate than in earlier times.

If social workers, whose primary responsibility is direct practice with clients or client systems, mistakenly believe that management is what "they" are paid to do, various problems can result. As frustrations occur on the job or things go wrong, as they inevitably will sometimes, a logical response is to blame those high up in the administrative hierarchy. When members of an organization view management as solely the work of certain other individuals, it allows them to project the responsibility for nearly any misfortune or unhappy circumstance on the work of a few higher-level individuals. Instead of sharing in the responsibility for problems and working together toward their solution, others are simply scapegoated. Resentment builds. (Hostility may be further fueled by the fact that higher-level administrators also probably make more money, have a more glamorous title, and enjoy more status in the community than the "nonmanagement employees" possess.) An adversarial relationship, rather than a cooperative one will exist.

People who do not perceive themselves as managers will not bother to understand what managers do or why they do them. They are likely to make accusations that "they" are insensitive to client needs, obsessed with efficiency, out of touch with social work practice, and more. Not surprisingly, staff ignorance and disavowal of that often mysterious activity called management lead to suspicion and assumptions about higher-level administrators. They may be assumed to possess a different and often conflicting set of values and priorities from those of others who do not perceive themselves to be managers.

People who carry the title of director, administrator, or manager must take ultimate responsibility for their decisions and their actions. But they do not have a monopoly on the functions of management, just on certain specific management tasks. Supervisors and other middle-level employees manage too, primarily in their tasks of administrative supervision, but in other ways as well. Even social workers who spend most of their day offering direct services plan, organize, lead, and control and are involved in some of the tasks of staffing. The management activities of all work together to affect the likelihood of successful organizational goal achievement.

Most management is neither the work of only a group of high-level staff nor does it involve activities that are the exclusive province of these elite individuals. Management is a specific group of important functions that are performed by all persons within a work setting. The contention that, like it or not, all staff members "manage" within public social work organizations, private practice, or the not-for-profit-sector does not suggest that all persons in these settings necessarily devote as much time to management or that their management activities all take the same form. In fact, those who carry titles such as director, administrator, or manager usually spend a larger percentage of their time performing management functions than others within the organization. In turn, mid-level managers and supervisors generally spend more of their time in management functions than do those with titles such as case manager, therapist, or group worker. However, even this difference is not as dramatic as it was ten or twenty years ago. Management decision making is increasingly becoming the work of teams made up of people from different levels of the organization rather than of individuals.

Despite the fact that management occurs at all levels within an organization and is increasingly being shared, the specific tasks or activities that fall within the various management functions still tend to differ. For example, organizing is a management function performed by everyone. For the person called director, it might involve (among other things) the task of designing an equitable way to divide staff into working units. A supervisor or team leader might need to organize the work flow of the unit. For a case manager or team of case managers, organizing might entail establishing a menu of client support systems to minimize the time required for in-patient treatment. All three administrative levels need to know how to organize and perform the managerial function of organizing, but their specific organizing *tasks* are different.

The assumption that all staff members manage (or "do management") precludes the notion that only certain persons are held accountable for management within an organization. Individuals within an agency suffering from "mismanagement"—whatever that is—cannot simply blame "the administration" for their problems. They must all go through a period of self-examination and share the responsibility for management difficulties that exist. Because everyone manages, a "we-they" dichotomy is less likely to occur. Although social workers delivering services to clients may lack complete understanding of the specific management tasks of the director, there is no reason why everyone in an organization cannot possess a general understanding of the functions of planning, staffing, organizing, controlling, and leading. Both mystery and suspicion are less likely when we are all perceived as performing similar functions and understand, at least in a general sense, what each of these functions entails.

Management and Services Are Interdependent

Management is an integral part of social work practice. Management decision making at all levels can serve either to support or jeopardize the delivery of effective service delivery. This occurs in both direct and subtle ways. Those decisions that determine how services will be delivered exert a direct effect on the effectiveness services themselves. For example, policy decisions regarding the appropriate use of group services vis-à-vis individual counseling have clear implications for the potential for treatment success with a given client.

Other management influences on service delivery are a little more subtle. Research over the past few decades has also highlighted the importance of management style and organizational climate to service delivery. The attitudes of higher-level personnel toward lower-level staff, as reflected in management practices and decisions, tend to get played out again in the attitudes of direct-service workers toward their clients. Both flexibility and tolerance toward clients occur more frequently in organizations where higher-level management decision making also reflects flexibility than in settings where managers reflect a need for routinization in decisions affecting staff.

The best management practice in human service organizations is probably carried out by those who possess not only a clear identification as social workers but also a clear understanding of the functions of management. Sound management decisions may sometimes appear to be in conflict with practice values. For example, the decision to refer rather than to treat clients diagnosed as alcoholic may appear on the surface to be in conflict with the "right to help" value of the profession, at least as it affects a given client. This decision may, however, be quite consistent with practice values emphasizing that the client is entitled to the best assistance available. It may also be reflective of the economic necessities for survival of the agency that are unknown to staff at all levels. If we can assume that all of us are both social workers and managers, we are less likely to conclude that we operate out of a different value base.

Management is a part of social work practice, and, as such, cannot be separated from services. To believe otherwise can cause problems, such as the erroneous belief that competent direct-service workers can and should insulate themselves from management and go about their business. It can promote the idea that services are good, bad, or somewhere in-between, based only on the skill level of those who deliver them. It can perpetuate the idea among both students of social work and direct practitioners that management is not really social work practice; that, as an activity not requiring face-to-face contact with clients or client groups, it does not contribute to the achievement of the profession's goals. This can lead to statements such as, "I want to be a social worker, not a manager."

Obviously, if we view an activity as outside the mainstream of professional practice (research is often thought of in the same way), we value it less and tend to distance ourselves from it. We begin to believe that management functions derive from a different set of values and ethics that are invariably in opposition to those of the social work profession. We tend to make certain assumptions about the motivation of those who spend large portions of their day making management decisions. This can result in antagonism and unnecessary conflict among those who are really working toward the same goals. Most importantly, it can negatively affect services to clients.

Good Management Requires Both Technical and People Skills

If management were nothing more than the application of technical skills, we could easily train anyone to be a good manager. Once having learned the standard required skills, people could be employed interchangeably to perform management functions. Technical skills are important to effective management. For example, constructing a budget, writing a grant proposal, and developing a flowchart require specific, detailed instruction. Once the skills are acquired, they can be applied in a variety of situations with very few modifications needed. But while everyone can benefit from the acquisition of these skills, they are not in themselves a guarantee of success in management.

An over-reliance on the technical components of management is almost certain to result in problems for managers. Among other things, it can build barriers between managers and co-workers who may not share these skills or have any desire to acquire them. We typically work among a group of professional peers who value and practice effective interpersonal interaction. They expect the same from their colleagues and their bosses.

Co-workers also expect to be treated as knowledgeable colleagues, even though they understand that in any organization there are bosses and there are subordinates. Technical skill or knowledge about a particular management activity is not synonymous with superiority. There is no reason to assume that the expertise, insight, and judgment needed for any given decision are concentrated at the top. In fact, those most knowledgeable about a specific area of knowledge that is needed may be people anywhere in the organizational hierarchy. The manager needs to be able to acknowledge this, to tap that knowledge, and to still maintain the integrity of the organizational hierarchy. This requires the use of interpersonal skills. Sensitivity to the behavior and attitudes of one's colleagues is critical to successful management. We will place considerable emphasis on the interpersonal aspects of management, acknowledging that, although technical skills are useful, they are better acquired in a hands-on training environment than through the reading of a book.

Management is not "anti-people." It cannot be performed by a computer. True, it involves tasks like research design, accurate prediction of future events, and application of the laws of probability to empirical data. But none of these tasks can be performed well without knowledge of and reference to the "actors" within one's work environment. Management decision making is greatly hindered when managers remain isolated in their own mysterious world and relate to other personnel only when absolutely necessary. Skills can be learned, but concepts like personality, art, and style also have important places in the work of management. Management is not simply a necessary evil performed by those who "sort of like that kind of thing." It entails "working with and through individuals and groups to accomplish organizational goals."[8] Thus a successful manager cannot be removed from the rest of the organization and those people who work within it. An identification with social work professional practice and with other professionals at all administrative levels are assets to performing management tasks well.

A word of caution may be in order here. If we were to approach the functions of management from the perspective that it requires interaction skills no different from those that are successful in work with clients, we would also be unsuccessful as managers. Too much emphasis on the interpersonal components of management can quickly antagonize one's co-workers who can start to feel manipulated, "caseworked," or demeaned in some other way. And, there is much scientifically acquired knowledge outside of social work that can make the job of manager easier. We would cheat ourselves as managers if we failed to take advantage of the wealth of relevant knowledge that has been generated by those outside of our profession. This text relies heavily on the work of many people who may never have studied human-service organizations and who certainly would not identify themselves as social workers. Yet some of what they have learned has universal application to management within all work settings. The knowledge and theory of other fields, with a little translation and adaptation here and there, can provide us with valuable insights to assist in our management practices.

While knowledge derived from empirical research conducted within the business sector is not inherently applicable to human service organizations or social work private practice, neither is it inherently inapplicable. Contemporary business literature is often on the cutting edge of management theory. It is both controversial and exciting; it provides the social worker with interesting reading while offering valuable assistance in performing the functions of the manager. We will examine some of these theories and conceptualizations that seem to have particular utility for social workers in their roles as managers.

If we acknowledge that management is more than the application of social work intervention skills to management activities, it follows that a first-rate direct-service social worker may or may not be a good choice for another position requiring that a larger percentage of time be spent in management activities. First, the organization may not be able to continue to take its best direct practitioners and remove them from client contact where their services are needed and valued. Second, success as a direct practice professional is no guarantee of success as, for example, a supervisor. Similarly, success as a supervisor is no guarantee of success at an even higher administrative level.

As we have discussed earlier, the functions of management are the same at all administrative levels, but the tasks and activities required to manage well are not. Repeated misunderstanding of this fact often has led to a tradition in which the best direct practitioners have been picked to be supervisors or mid-level managers. The assumption is that a good practitioner will necessarily be good at management tasks and vice versa. One-to-one, group, community organization and other skills will certainly serve a social worker well in the role of manager. But increased and different management tasks also require knowledge, technical skills and a perspective on events that may differ from those of the social workers in their helping roles.

Similarly, in the past, the most successful supervisors or mid-level managers have been promoted higher in the organizational hierarchy, and the best of these have been chosen to be agency directors. While this can work well, it also can cause real problems. By the time a worker "survives" to become director, this individual may have lost touch with direct practice. Also, an unfortunate phenomenon may occur whereby employees will tend to leave positions where they function well and continue to be promoted until they reach a level where they can no longer function effectively. They will remain there, at great cost to the agency. The understanding that good management is much more than social work practice with staff can help to avoid situations where people leave jobs where they perform well in order to take positions for which they lack the necessary interest, aptitude, and/or skills.

The Presence of Management

We have attempted to describe management in a number of ways. We have operationally defined it as a group of functions performed by social workers at all levels. Now that we know what management is, it might be interesting to see if we can identify how it manifests itself in an organization. Figure 1.2 is a somewhat facetious comparison of life in a prison and life on the job. It is adapted from a joke that appears now and then on the Internet.

Figure 1.2 is written from the perspective of a disenchanted employee. The reader may or may not think it is funny. However, if we look at it seriously for a moment, it seems to underline some points from our discussion to this point. For example, we can see

FIGURE 1.2   *Life in Prison and Life in a Human Service Organization*

- In prison, there is time off for good behavior.
- On the job, good behavior gets you more work.

- In prison, you get three free meals.
- On the job you get to have one meal and to pay for it.

- In prison, you can join programs and quit if you like.
- On the job, you are assigned to progams and cannot quit.

- In prison, you can play games or watch TV.
- On the job, you are reprimanded for playing games or watching TV.

- In prison, family and friends are encouraged to visit.
- On the job, you are not supposed to speak to family and friends.

- In prison, antisocial behavior got you there.
- On the job, antisocial behavior can get you out.

- In prison, there are sadistic guards.
- On the job, there are managers.

CASE EXAMPLE • *The Manager Who Wasn't*

Ramon was hired as the District Director of the state health department. He was the first social worker in the state to hold such a position. He came highly recommended by his boss in another district where he had been a case supervisor for five years. When he took the new job, the organization was in disarray. The district office was notorious for its poor performance. Various errors in judgment by staff had led to several "exposé" articles in the local newspaper. There were threats of loss of federal funding.

Ramon was told by the state director that (within the limits of civil service requirements) he could "clean house." He was told to fire those probationary employees whose poor performance had been previously documented and replace them with new people. He also was given authorization to fill six other job slots that had previously been frozen.

Ramon wasted no time. He fired any staff who he was allowed to fire and replaced them with people he knew to be highly competent. Within two months over half of the staff in his office were people that he had hired. Some had worked with him in his previous job. Others were recommended by friends who he trusted. When he had put together his new staff he called them together for a meeting. He outlined the problems that had previously existed and reminded them that things needed to change. He told them that he had great confidence in them and that he knew that soon the office would be "running like a finely tuned machine." He told them that they knew what they had to do but that he would be available at any time should they need his advice on anything. He wished them good luck. Over the next year, Ramon was true to his word. He was available for consultation, but did little else. He could usually be found surfing the Internet on his personal computer or swapping stories with a supervisor who, like him, had served in the Army. He organized a college football pool and a pool for professional basketball games and gave the best holiday party that anyone could remember.

Despite staff suggestions that a policy manual might be helpful, he told them they did not need one. They were told that they should "just use your own judgment—I trust you." He told everyone when they were hired that they could all expect to receive "outstanding" performance evaluations since he knew they were good or he would not have hired them. And, he kept his word, despite the fact that some staff members clearly were doing a better job than others. When one employee consistently refused to assume her share of the work he refused to deal with her directly, but sent a memo to everyone stating his expectation that they were professionals and should work as a team. He avoided organizing the staff (which consisted of 22 people) into smaller work groups, stating that "you all just need to learn how to work together." When mistakes were made, he reprimanded everyone by a memo sent to the entire staff. He never called staff meetings. Soon staff did not bother to even come to Ramon with problems anymore. They had learned that, while free with advice, he rarely gave them any other kind of support to carry out his recommendations.

The mistakes continued. Staff morale was very low. Two good staff members resigned and were replaced by two of Ramon's friends. Finally, an investigative reporter ran an article on how a manufacturing plant had continued to leak toxic substances into a nearby stream despite frequent calls to the district office. It was revealed that his staff had never even bothered to follow through on the complaints. At about the same time, another feature story told of the 70 percent rise in reports of sexually transmitted diseases in his district. The state director demanded that Ramon meet with him immediately. (Ramon did not know it but the director's cousin was also a long-time secretary in Ramon's office.) The director demanded to know just what Ramon had been doing. She told him that, as best she could determine, he had been a manager in name only. She waited for his response. Ramon had an explanation. He said, "I employ a hands-off

CASE EXAMPLE • *(continued)*

management style. I hire the very best people and just stay out of their way and let them do their jobs." The director reminded him that he was paid to manage and that things needed to improve or he would be looking for another job.

Six weeks later another story hit the newspaper. This one was about an outbreak of food poisoning in a restaurant that had not been checked out despite numerous complaints by the public to Ramon's office. The editor wrote an editorial calling for a full investigation. A week later the state director called Ramon in again. This time she fired him.

Discussion Questions

1. Was it a good idea for Ramon to fire so many staff members and replace them with people he knew? Why or why not?
2. Given Ramon's approach to management, why might a policy manual have been helpful?
3. What are some of the things that Ramon should have done that he failed to do?
4. What are some of the things that Ramon did that are not "good management"?
5. Was it fair that Ramon was blamed for errors made by his staff? Why or why not?

how within the human service organization, managers have attempted to organize and control the activities of others. They have shaped the work environment and to make it conducive to productivity. They have made efforts to minimize distractions and to focus staff attention on organizational goal attainment. Figure 1.2 also makes the point that managers are not always appreciated for their efforts. However, as we shall discuss in later chapters, there are many other sources of gratification for the manager within human service organizations.

Summary

In this chapter we have stressed the importance of management to human functioning in all areas of life, but especially to organizational goal achievement. It is necessary for any kind of constructive activity to take place within an organization. Management was portrayed as a group of important functions performed by social workers at all administrative levels. These functions are intended to enhance worker productivity and, whenever possible, produce a "surplus." We presented the working definition of management that will be employed throughout this book, "certain functions performed by social workers at all administrative levels within human service organizations which are designed to facilitate the accomplishment of organizational goals."

Management is not some mysterious function performed by a limited number of "higher-ups." It is an integral part of practice that is more similar to the other functions performed by social workers than it is dissimilar to them. It employs some of the same knowledge, values, and skills. It is both a technical and a "people" skill. We emphasized that management involves components of both science and art.

Endnotes

1. Kettner, P. *Human Service Organizations* (Boston, MA: Allyn & Bacon, 2002), p. 3.

2. Harold Koontz, Cyril O'Donnell, and Heinz Weihrich, *Essentials of Management* (New York: McGraw-Hill, 1986), pp. 5–6.

3. Koontz, O'Donnell, and Weihrich, *op. cit.*

4. Arthur G. Bedeian, *A Standardization of Selected Management Concepts* (New York: Garland Publishing, 1986).

5. Henry Mintzberg, *The Nature of Managerial Work* (Englewood Cliffs, NJ: Prentice-Hall, 1980), pp. 86–98.

6. James A. Stoner and R. Edward Freeman, *Management* (Englewood Cliffs, NJ: Prentice-Hall, 1989), pp. 11–12.

7. Eugene J. Meehan, *Economics and Policy Making* (Westport, CT: Greenwood Press, 1982), pp. 19–38.

8. Paul Hersey and Ken Blanchard, *Management of Organizational Behavior* (Englewood Cliffs, NJ: Prentice-Hall, 1982), p. 3.

2

The Context of Human Services Management

Although most management activities are designed to positively influence what takes place within an organization, our understanding of management cannot ignore the place of a human service organization within its external environment. In fact, the specific nature of management activities and their potential for success are very much determined by the kind of interaction that exists between the organization and those persons and forces that exist outside its boundaries.

We will examine the external influences that must be addressed by the human service organization with particular emphasis on how they differ from those usually encountered by the corporate sector. By borrowing a few concepts from the business literature, we will identify some of the environmental factors that tend to shape and direct the management activities of social workers.

The Task Environment

Many years ago, a researcher who studied Norwegian manufacturing provided us with a concept that is still useful today in understanding the effect of external influences on social work management. It is also helpful in understanding how some human service organizations differ from others, and how these differences affect the work of the social worker as manager. William Dill identified those parts of an organization's environment that are "relevant or potentially relevant to goal setting and goal attainment." He referred to these as an organization's "task environment."

An organization is believed to be more or less successful in its goal achievement based largely on its capacity to interact successfully with its task environment. Consequently, many of the activities of higher-level managers involve efforts to negotiate support from the task environment or at least to minimize its potential to undermine achievement of the organization's goals.

In a manufacturing corporation, the components of the task environment are easily specified. They include its customers, suppliers of raw materials and resources needed to manufacture the organization's products, its competitors, and regulatory groups that might restrict its ability to operate in the most profitable manner. But, what is the task environment of a human service organization? There are many parallels with manufacturing corporations. Generally, it consists of any persons, organizations, or groups on whom it is dependent for goal achievement and who have the potential to support or to interfere with its efforts. For example, a human service organization's task environment might consist of past, present, and potential clients, other human service organizations, funding organizations like United Way, private insurance companies or HMOs, government programs like Medicaid and Medicare, professional organizations such as the National Association of Social Workers (NASW), the media and, of course, the general public. Both the nature of the task environment and the way it affects management activities within an organization vary widely among human service organizations. There are also differences between human service organizations and manufacturing corporations. For example, in manufacturing corporations, the general public gets involved most often as potential customers. Generally, if the product is a good one, is seen as fairly priced, and is not offensive or seen as contributing to a social problem, the general public will be supportive of the organization. Even those individuals who may not want or have use for a corporation's products generally have no objection to its manufacture. They simply will not buy it.

The general public gets involved with human service organizations sometimes as potential customers (clients). However, many people are required to pay for services that they will never use. Much of human service funding comes from tax revenues, either directly or indirectly. The general public is not always friendly toward human service organizations, particularly those in the public sector. The clients of these organizations are frequently those whom the general public sees as unlike themselves and benefiting from services paid for by the public's earnings. In fact, we all are "on the dole" in some way; that is, we all benefit from some form of entitlement program paid for out of tax dollars. Frequently, we receive more in benefits than we paid in. (Social Security is a good example.) As is often the case, it is the *perception* of human service programs, as benefiting others at their expense, that negatively influences the attitudes of large segments of the general public. This perception represents an important distinction between business and many human service organizations, one that, like other differences that we shall discuss, ultimately shapes the role of the manager.

Different Types of Task Environments

Organizations, based primarily on their functions and goals, operate in a task environment where some of the components of the task environment are likely to be friendly, others less friendly. As we have suggested, many manufacturing concerns have a friendly working arrangement with one task environment, the general public. Unless they pollute the environment, exploit their employees, or otherwise threaten the members of their community, they receive support for their goal achievement. Producing a socially accepted and wanted product, providing employment, and contributing to the tax base are other "pluses" for a manufacturing firm. Sometimes, special concessions are even made in the form of tax incentives, attractive leases, or relaxing of local codes to lure a given industry into an area. As a general rule, they have much to offer to the general public and, therefore, find that it is likely to be friendly and supportive.

The primary threat within the task environment of a manufacturing corporation is often its competitors, those other organizations producing similar products who are forever trying to increase their own "share of the market" and, if possible put them out of business. However, depending on conditions, other components of the task environment may also represent a threat to goal achievement (for example, stockholders, government regulatory commissions, or the media).

Like manufacturing corporations, human service organizations reflect wide variation in the attitudes of their task environment and its components. With the recent increase in privatization of human services, there is also an increasing number of organizations that must deal with competition. Within the public sector, the general public component of the task environment may be an organization's greatest threat, one that is seeking to sabotage the organization's efforts at goal achievement.

Some human service organizations are fortunate enough to work in a task environment where mostly all of its components are relatively friendly. What are their characteristics? More favorable task environments are found in those situations where the organization's services (1) cost the taxpayer little or nothing; (2) are seen as desirable, that is, consistent with the society's predominant values; and, (3) offer services that most people can envision that they (or someone they care about) are likely to use some day. A private adoption agency would be a good example. Costs are borne by those seeking the service; taxpayers contribute nothing. The placement of an unwanted child into a home where the child is wanted (and, incidentally, one that is more likely to be able to provide a higher level of financial support for the child) is viewed by the general public and other components of the task environment as a noble enterprise. And, most people know someone who has been seeking to adopt a child.

An organization that offers in-home hospice services to terminally ill patients and their families would also be expected to operate in a relatively supportive and friendly task environment. It would meet all three of the previously mentioned criteria. Hospice services are less expensive than expenses incurred by hospitalization; tax dollars and expenses reimbursed by private medical insurance are thus minimized. As a society, we value dying at home in the presence of family and other loved ones and in familiar surroundings. Most of us who are realistic also recognize that we and/or those who we love might benefit from hospice services someday. Perhaps, we had a friend or relative who received hospice services and we learned to appreciate them.

In those human service organizations fortunate enough to operate in a relatively friendly task environment, managers can focus upon doing what is necessary to facilitate the flow of work and services. Threats and attacks from the task environment are infrequent. Little management time need be spent on trying to placate and to buffer out the assaults of the task environment—they just do not occur very often. This is not to say that management is less important than in an organization where the task environment is less friendly. But it explains why, within a friendly task environment, management activities may take on different forms than in, for example, a juvenile correction facility where omnipresent cries for tighter security betray the existence of a hostile task environment.

Among other differences, the manager in the organization with the friendly task environment, generally, does not need to spend large portions of the day establishing and enforcing the trappings of bureaucracies (to be discussed in Chapter 3). In the more hostile task environment, these management tasks are more necessary.

Let us now look at a human service organization with a more hostile task environment, the kind frequently seen and experienced by social workers. A county department of social services is a good example. Social workers (at whatever administrative level) involved with a public assistance program almost certainly will encounter a hostile task environment. This is largely because of both the realities and public misperceptions of their work. The organization's employees are dispensing tax dollars collected from wage earners. That is reality. Generally, they are giving funds to persons who are not gainfully employed and who are also victims of public stereotyping that assumes that they are unwilling to work, sexually promiscuous, dishonest, and so on. Toss in the general public's misinformation about the demographic characteristics of welfare recipients and it is no surprise that the general public neither seems to value nor support the work of the public assistance social worker. Judging by the widespread political popularity of various welfare reform legislation in recent years, we can conclude that most Americans would probably vote to discontinue public assistance altogether, were a public referendum held.

Other components of the public welfare organization's task environment are not much more friendly than the general public. Professional organizations may push for tighter licensure requirements and other forms of credentialing that may have the ultimate effect of ostracizing many public welfare employees as "nonprofessionals." Other human service organizations seek to distance themselves, partly out of a need to create a more favorable task environment for themselves. Even individual professionals who work in related areas of practice may be far from supportive. They may be eager to point out that many staff in the public organization "are not really social workers!" They tend to blame public welfare bureaucracies for many of the client problems that they see. They are more likely to describe instances of public welfare "incompetence" than they are to report instances when a public assistance caseworker was effective and highly competent.

Among public social service organizations, even clients often bear resentment toward the organization and the professional staff who are seeking to help them. They may perceive that the bureaucratic structures in place may be designed to discourage them from seeking assistance or to humiliate them. They are often embarrassed and angry at having to request help in the first place; they may resent having their privacy invaded as a prerequisite to receiving it. They may express their hostility directly to social workers or, fearful of antagonizing them, communicate it by denigrating the organization and its staff within the community. Of course, this only serves to make the general public more hostile. It lends support to the perception that the organization is poorly managed. Sometimes, it seems as though the task environment only becomes more favorable toward public social service organizations when an effort to expose fraud is launched, eligibility is rigidly enforced, or the organization takes some other action consistent with the general public's stereotypes and values.

While public social service organizations with programs offering temporary financial assistance present the most dramatic examples of human service organizations that operate within a hostile task environment, their situations are far from unique. Other social work enterprises, while receiving widespread social support on the surface, operate in a task environment that may not be much more friendly. For example, while the deinstitutionalization of persons who are mentally disabled is acknowledged as a worthwhile endeavor, the public rarely welcomes them into their community when a group home is proposed. Similarly, programs engaged in refugee resettlement often encounter public resistance despite public sympathetic statements about the plight of victims of political oppression. Responses of "not in our neighborhood" or "not taking our jobs" are common.

Child-protection services also often experience their share of hostility from the task environment. No one publicly advocates child abuse or neglect and most people believe that public organizations have a right to intervene when it is believed to have occurred. So, why do child protection organizations not have the benefit of a friendly task environment? For one thing, their employees are engaged in investigating and exposing a problem that the general public prefers to believe "does not happen here." They create more work for overburdened county solicitors. They embarrass politicians, clergy, and educators who take pride in the well-being of citizens within "their" community. Caseworkers find themselves working as advocates for children whose credibility and perceptions of events are often questioned. Recent revelations that children have been successfully coached to lie about allegations during divorce custody battles have further weakened their credibility. Caseworkers may find themselves in an adversarial role, pitted against some of the community's leading professionals and citizens with only children's allegations and limited medical evidence (often refuted by other "expert witnesses") on their sides. Even the children whom they seek to protect may be unappreciative of their efforts, especially if they are removed from their homes and moved to a strange setting (foster home). Along with financial assistance workers, child protection caseworkers perform a job that the general public may endorse in a general way, but resent as it is played out and as it impacts them personally. Is it any wonder that they encounter the passive aggressiveness and, in some cases, the overt aggressiveness of a hostile task environment?

It is not surprising that many of the activities of management that occupy the time of social workers in organizations involved in services such as public assistance, deinstitutionalization, refugee resettlement, and child protection are devoted to buffering out or in some way protecting the organization from the hostile task environment. The many bureaucratic controls in the form of policies, procedures, and rules that exist are designed to defend the organization against charges of mismanagement, waste, uncontrolled staff activities, and other phenomena that could leave the organization vulnerable to withholding of funding or other tactics that could halt or curtail the achievement of objectives. These organizations also find themselves operating with uncertain long-range funding. They are left vulnerable to shifting service priorities and needs as perceived by legislators seeking to court public support. In contrast, a manufacturing organization with a more friendly task environment and more predictable funding sources (steady high sales) worries less about protecting itself from the general public or funding sources and can devote more of its management activities to production. Upper-level managers can concentrate on other threats from the task environment, most frequently the competition of other manufacturers or, perhaps, the possibility that its sources of supply might be cut off.

Similarly, managers in a human service organization with a relatively friendly task environment can focus much of their energies on working to improve the quality of services offered.

Improving Relationships with the Task Environment

A hostile task environment promotes a sense of uncertainty within an organization. While a limited amount of uncertainty is inevitable and possibly even desirable, too much of it is stressful and debilitating. No one can work well in an organization whose task environment is constantly watching, waiting for a mistake or a sign of weakness. For those human service organizations that lack the good fortune of having a friendly task environment, a social worker's management tasks must be devoted in part to negotiating with the hostile environment in order to improve relationships. The goal is to decrease the vulnerability of the organization at the least possible cost in terms of compromise of professional values, loss of autonomy, and service effectiveness. Because a task environment that is essentially hostile is not likely to reverse itself spontaneously to become more friendly, the only realistic way to negotiate successfully with it is to increase power over it. Several methods for accomplishing this are cited in the business literature.[1] Most have applicability to the functions of the social work manager. We will suggest how some of these might work and assess their relative costs.

Acquiring Prestige.   The organization that can become recognized for its first-class products or services has an easier time dealing with its task environment. Develop a reputation as being the best and environmental resistance diminishes. Medical treatment facilities such as Johns Hopkins University Hospital, The Mayo Clinic, or Roswell Park Memorial Institute meet far less hostility from their task environment than do other organizations, in part because they are acknowledged as very good at what they do. Of course, what they do, namely medical treatment and research, makes acquiring prestige relatively easy, too. These activities generally are more valued than are, for example, public assistance or child protection. That is the problem with acquiring prestige—it is much easier for those organizations that begin with one or more of the criteria for a relatively favorable task environment. It is far more difficult for those whose task environment is most naturally inclined to be hostile. Acquiring prestige, in the usual sense of the word, may be an unattainable goal for most public, tax-supported human service organizations and for other organizations that offer unpopular services to those who are stigmatized within a society.

While a reputation for first-class services may be a less attainable goal for a public assistance organization than for a cancer research institute, there is one way that even an organization that offers unpopular services to unpopular people can increase its power over a hostile task environment—good management. The general public may not embrace the services or the clientele of a human service organization but may grudgingly acknowledge the inevitability and need for its existence. A well-managed, efficient organization that does a good job of demonstrating that it is financially accountable for the funding that it receives will face less hostility from its task environment (especially the general public) than will one that has a reputation for slack management. A reputation for good management, which is especially difficult to attain while "giving away tax dollars," is a worthwhile goal for a human service organization. It will help to make the general public less critical and more supportive, even if the services remain largely resented.

Acquiring prestige, particularly for those organizations offering services valued by the general public, is a relatively "inexpensive" way of negotiating with the task environment. First-rate, professional services are in the best interest of client and organization alike; they do not generally cost more than poor services. They also result in increased prestige. In delivering services that are less popular with the general public, management that emphasizes efficiency and accountability can positively influence an organization's reputation, causing it to approach prestige as we have described it. Also, good management requires no more effort than poor management. But acquiring prestige can still have other costs. There are times when demonstrating the kind of management that our society values and rewards hurts staff morale or results in staff turnover. For example, rigid adherence to unfair eligibility requirements for public assistance or total compliance with laws relating to due process that results in leaving a child in a potentially dangerous home environment are just two examples of tight management that may conflict with social work values. Professional staff may respond with anger and resentment. A manager must then assess whether the benefits of a potentially friendlier task environment are worth the cost. It might be useful to weigh the benefits that might accrue to present and future clients from the existence of a more friendly task environment against the human and organizational costs.

Contracting.   Contracting is a special kind of cooperation with the task environment. Contracting is designed primarily to make interaction with the task environment more predictable and, therefore, potentially less threatening. It is most often used to increase the power over those components of the task environment that provide the customers (in our case clients) or personnel needed for the organization to function. Contracting is a strategy that is well-known to the profit sector and is becoming increasingly familiar to many organizations within the human service area. In business and manufacturing, a corporation might sign long-range leases for facilities or contracts for supply of those raw materials that are needed to manufacture its products. It may even contract with various marketing outlets to guarantee purchase of a certain number of its products. Contracting of this nature increases certainty. It also results in fairly predictable manufacturing costs.

How do human service organizations contract to increase control over the task environment? Beginning in the mid-1970s, Title XX of the Federal Social Security Act provided reimbursement to state public welfare organizations that purchased services for their clients from other human service organizations. Services were bought by one organization from another. Costs were fixed and both organizations were able to operate with more certainty. One gained assurances regarding availability of services; the other, a fixed market for services.

A common form of contracting used by human service organizations today are Employee Assistance Programs (EAPs). Organizations agree to provide services such as substance abuse treatment and marriage counseling to employees of a corporation or other organization for an agreed upon amount of money. The corporation can project its costs. It generally pays a negotiated fixed cost to the organization for a certain number of hours of services or for providing specified services as needed to a certain number of its employees. The organization in turn is guaranteed a sizable number of pay-for-services clients, a source of both guaranteed client input and of funding.

Contracting with another organization, like acquiring prestige, may be relatively inexpensive as a method to increase control over the task environment. However, even though it involves a reciprocal agreement, it often requires some loss of autonomy in decision making for the organization providing services. In some respects, the purchaser often buys more than just services. For example, if an organization has a contract to provide services to a manufacturing corporation's employees under an EAP contract, it generally cannot refuse to see a client referred for services, sometimes even if professional staff do not see the need for treatment. The corporation may also have the right to have input into decisions relating to diagnosis, the nature of treatment, when an employee can or cannot return to work, and so forth. The corporation, paying for treatment, may also feel that it has a right to know more about the nature of the client's problem than the social worker feels should be shared. This can create ethical dilemmas.

Another dangerous situation can occur if an organization becomes too dependent on contracts such as EAPs. Most contracts are put out for bids periodically and an organization can easily lose its contract to a competitor if the other organization promises to offer more for the same amount of money or to offer the same services for less. Awarding of contracts is supposed to be performed in a fair and unbiased manner, but that does not always happen in the real world. Political issues and personal friendships can be deciding factors in who receives the contract. Although, it is generally regarded as unethical, some individuals who have administered contracts for an organization have been known to leave the organization to go into business for themselves. Miraculously, the contracts have followed them, leaving the organization in a situation where it is overstaffed and short on revenue. Most managers are aware of the dangers of overdependence on contracts. They are reluctant to commit too large a percentage of organizational activities to programs and services that are contract-funded. They also plan for contingencies (Chapter 4) in which contracts may be lost.

Many social work students have experience with contracts of a different nature. In situations where an organization has difficulty hiring trained staff, it often contracts with potential employees (students). The organization may offer a stipend or paid field experience to a student nurse or social work student in exchange for a commitment to one or more years of employment. As in the earlier examples of contracting, the contract is mutually beneficial to the organization and to that part of the task environment that is not, by nature, supportive of it.

Organizations that have bought work commitments from students usually risk relatively little in terms of loss of autonomy. They may not have to hire new graduates with whom they have contracted if they later decide they do not want them or need them as employees. If they do hire them, they usually can still fire them if they do not work out well following a probationary period. Of course, the up-front cost in dollars to provide the stipend of the student cannot be ignored in deciding whether this type of contracting is worth the cost. Guaranteeing the presence of an employee may be expensive, especially for one who may come to work "kicking and screaming" and seeking a way out of a commitment. In the last years of the Twentieth Century we witnessed a new trend—contracting of government organizations with the private, for-profit sector to provide human services. For example, some states have contracted with corporations within the private sector to provide correctional services for juveniles and adults. The corporations then may turn around and hire professionals such as social workers to provide the services that clients receive.

Contracting, in one form or another, is likely to occupy an increasingly larger portion of time spent by social work managers. It can be an effective method of reducing both costs and uncertainty. It should be noted, however, that contracting is not always useful for ameliorating the hostility of the general public toward certain programs and services. Like acquiring prestige, it can work best in those situations where the services offered are seen as "desirable" and thus the organization already enjoys a reasonably favorable task environment. It is not usually as effective for those organizations which, because of the programs and services they must offer, must work in the most hostile task environments and face attitudes of the general public that are especially threatening to goal achievement.

Co-opting. Most everyone knows about co-opting. Children usually learn early in life that they can reduce opposition to a request by a parent if they can bring the parent "on-board" and allow the parent to take partial ownership in it. ("Mom, remember that great idea you had about going out for pizza once a week?") Doctoral candidates writing a dissertation or Master's students writing a thesis usually learn to co-opt their advisors, if they hope to finish. They meet regularly with them, get plenty of advice, and include the advisors' suggestions in their work. Their final document is likely to be approved since the advisors see many of their own "brilliant" ideas and suggestions incorporated into it.

How do organizations co-opt a potentially hostile task environment? Co-opting involves bringing a potentially hostile or threatening portion of the task environment "into" the organization. Co-opting is not merely skillful manipulation or a kind of political ploy. Sometimes it is beneficial to the organization in other ways. It provides a fresh perspective to the organization (from its potential enemies) that may not be available among its natural "friends." But it also increases control over the task environment. The idea is that if the boundary lines between the organization and its environment can become somewhat blurred, hostility will dissipate. Why would the task environment want to oppose decisions and activities into which it had input?

One common method of co-opting the task environment is to place a political opponent or otherwise outspoken critic within the community on an advisory board or board of directors. Most boards consist of a mixture of people who have knowledge and/or skills to contribute, those who contribute their names, and those whose goodwill has been courted by the offer of input into planning and decision making. The "names" generally are a "plus" for the reputation of the organization. But they can also cause problems; a "star" on a board can result in some bad decisions if other members are "starstruck" and routinely defer to him or her regardless of what they believe to be best for the organization. The third group in particular represents a frequent target of efforts to co-opt. For example, conservative opponents of educational programs may have valuable knowledge about the transmission of sexually transmitted diseases. But their presence on a human service organization board is often more related to the belief that they will be less vocal in their

CASE EXAMPLE • *Co-opting That Backfired*

Latesha was the new director of a shelter for battered women in a conservative rural community. She was the only professional social worker on a paid staff of six. The organization had been established only three years earlier by a retired social worker and two other women who themselves had been victims of spouse abuse.

Ever since its establishment, the shelter had faced a hostile task environment. It was housed in an old home that had been donated by one of its founders. There had been complaints to the local zoning board by several neighbors seeking to get the organization to either move or close. Two local politicians had stated that they saw no need for such an organization. One stated in a town meeting that "there is no such problem here." Even the local United Way chapter seemed to be delaying in responding to the shelter's request for financial assistance. One United Way employee confided to Latesha "off the record" that there were some board members who feared that contributions might suffer if the shelter was given any United Way money.

Latesha knew that she had to do something to weaken the local opposition to her agency. She decided to attempt to co-opt some of those who had been most openly hostile to make them more sympathetic to the work of the shelter. She created an advisory board, but carefully made sure that three of its five members could be counted on as friends who had been supportive of the shelter in the past (including one of its founders). But for the other two members (who quickly accepted the invitation to join the board) she chose one of the two politicians who had been highly critical of the shelter and a prominent, local minister who also had stated his doubts about the need for such an organization on several occasions.

The first two times that the Board met, the politician (an attorney) and the minister were most cordial. They said little and seemed

genuinely interested in what the other members and Latesha had to say. However, during the third meeting, the minister began to tell the others what his true feelings were about battered women—"most of them probably provoked it." The politician clearly agreed. Before long, both men began to dominate discussion and seemed to become more bold in their statements. Latesha anxiously looked to the other Board members to challenge what they were saying. They looked at the table, but said nothing. They clearly were intimidated.

During the next few months the politician and the minister argued convincingly against most of Latesha's plans for expansion of services. They frequently recommended a variety of changes that would actually weaken the agency's programs. Another Board member consistently supported them. (She learned later that his wife was a paralegal who worked in the politician's law firm.) When she dared to go against the recommendations of her advisory board, Latesha was criticized by people in the community who always seemed to find out about the Board's recommendations. An uncle who attended the minister's church told Latesha that he had even criticized her from his pulpit. He reminded his parishioners that, "I know for a fact that those people, unless we stop them, have every intention of violating the sanctity of the family anyway that they can."

Finally, in desperation, Latesha decided to expand her board by adding four more members who she hoped would be more friendly to the shelter. The newly constituted board was more supportive. Soon, the minister and politician both resigned, but not before writing an angry "letter to the editor" stating that Latesha had "stacked the board to promote her own liberal agenda." It was several years before the shelter was no longer threatened with efforts to close it down.

CASE EXAMPLE • *(continued)*

opposition to certain HIV prevention programs if they are allowed input into the health organization's policy-making than if they are allowed to criticize the program from the outside. Similarly, the invited presence of vocal opponents of entitlement programs on a county welfare organization's advisory board may also be reflective of efforts to co-opt. They are more likely to have been invited to join the board because they may represent a threat to the organization than because they have important contributions to make to its operation.

The addition of a potential adversary to an organization's board can be costly. Even one obstructive person, particularly if the individual is politically powerful and tends to command deference on the part of others, can seriously jeopardize an organization's potential for goal achievement and/or divert its focus away from professionally sanctioned objectives. Two or more such additions from a hostile task environment can paralyze the work of an organization. A shift away from professional values and ethics can even occur. Co-opting by giving potential adversaries input into important decision making should be approached with extreme caution.

A potentially less costly method of co-opting a part of a hostile task environment is used when an organization makes use of volunteers drawn from families and groups that represent obstacles to goal achievement. Because volunteers can make a real and valued contribution and they are not generally in a position to influence policy, this tactic is frequently used. But, as we shall discuss in Chapter 5, there are inherent dangers in the use of volunteers too. Cost-benefit analysis of any form of co-opting and projections about the likelihood of its success should be undertaken before it is attempted.

Other Ways to Increase Control over the Task Environment.   The business literature suggests other approaches that would also seem to have some utility for the social work manager who is seeking to create a more friendly task environment. These include expanding alternatives, diversification, and coalescing.[2] Expanding alternatives, in business, includes using many different suppliers for raw materials. If the supply is disrupted from one supplier, more can be purchased from another. In human service organizations, this might translate as development of different client referral sources and networks, and development of working relationships with universities to create sources for new staff, etc.

Diversification, if you are a manufacturer, means manufacturing a variety of products so that if, for example, demand for one product drops, demand for another can balance it off and/or the corporation can shift its resources into the manufacture of the more profitable product. In human service organizations, we might similarly create more certainty and leave ourselves less vulnerable to a reduced need for services if we were to offer a variety of programs. It is hoped that some of these would generate wide public acceptance and would also "carry" the organization if support for other services erodes or they must be discontinued. However, "some businesses and manufacturing concerns have run into trouble when they did not "stick to the knitting." The same thing can happen in human service organizations that diversify too much. The organization can lose its identity, its niche, and develop a reputation for trying to be "everything to all people." Thus overdiversification may result in a loss of prestige!

Coalescing can be an extremely costly method of increasing control over a hostile task environment. It is often a "last resort" tactic of survival. In business, the environment (often the competition) is brought in and shares in the profit, often through a "friendly takeover" or merger. Autonomy, jobs, and influence of certain individuals generally suffer. While relatively rare in human services, coalescing does occur. For example, two or more state organizations that offer similar programs and services have been forced to merge because state legislators concluded that wasteful duplication existed. Other coalescing arrangements, that are not a result of legislative coercion, may promote efficiency, but at a cost. The creation of certain "umbrella" organizations is a type of coalescing that results in some loss of autonomy but one that can reduce a considerable amount of uncertainty and hostility within the task environment. This tactic can result in a new organization with considerably more clout for negotiating with the task environment than that possessed by any of its smaller elements.

Comparing Human Service Organizations and Businesses

We have pointed out the fact that businesses are far more likely to operate in a task environment with a supportive public-at-large than are most human service organizations, particularly publicly supported ones. We have chosen to explore this phenomenon in depth because it goes a long way toward explaining why many of the activities of social workers, when they are managing, must be devoted to buffering hostility from outside the organization. In Chapter 3 we will see how the task environment faced by most human service organizations contributes to the proliferation of bureaucratic activities.

Other similarities and differences between businesses and human service organizations also help to explain the role and functions of social work management. As we look at some of these, it should be remembered that it is becoming increasingly difficult to make many generalizations about either human service organizations or about businesses that will apply across the board. Large public organizations, such as state departments of social services, for example, are less similar to private psychiatric organizations, hospitals, or long-term care facilities (many of which are really corporations) than they are to many businesses. Many for-profit treatment organizations and private practices bear close resemblance to businesses in their goals, indicators of success, etc. Many so-called not-for-profit organizations really have " profits," but they hide them in salary increments, lavish fringe benefits, and other methods of profit sharing. Historically, fiscal concerns have been less a driving force in human service organizations than the need for high-quality client services. Business and manufacturing organizations were profit-driven; human factors became relevant only as they related to the "bottom line." Businesses have become more sensitized to the need to "humanize" in order to be successful. At the same time, human service organizations have been required to operate in an environment that emphasizes efficiency and cost cutting. The difference between them is no longer so distinct. Social workers still find employment in more traditional nonprofit service organizations, but increasing numbers are working in organizations where the cost of services is of paramount concern. Consequently, no simple comparison between businesses and human service organizations is possible. Few generalizations are possible. Yet it is still a valuable exercise to examine the issues and how they play out within various work settings.

Equity and Efficiency

As already suggested, a business or corporation exists to make a profit. Consequently, it is "efficiency driven." Any activity that will reduce the cost of production of a product has the potential to increase profit ("surplus" as we described it in Chapter 1). If, after a reasonable time, efficiency methods cannot generate a profit, the product will be dropped from the manufacturer's line, or, in the case of a large conglomerate, the manufacturing division may be sold, usually at some tax advantage to the corporation. The decision is purely an economic one; there is no place for a product that cannot contribute to profit and that may even affect the profitability of the company's other products by consuming valuable resources of the organization that are needed elsewhere. Sentiment and concerns over fairness rarely enter into the decision to drop a product or division. When they do, they usually are prompted by either a need to either retain good public relations or to respond to the demands of another component of the task environment, organized labor.

In contrast, managers within human service organizations must always attempt to balance efficiency and equity. Large public bureaucracies or small for-profit private psychiatric organizations cannot ignore efficiency. They must pay utility bills, salaries, and address other fiscal issues. But they must also meet professional obligations to provide quality client services. They cannot afford to develop a reputation for being overly preoccupied with efficiency or with profit. The decision to discontinue a service that is costly and represents a financial drain on resources will sometimes have to be made, but not without a good deal of soul-searching and justifying not usually required in a business enterprise. For example, the decision to refer out rather than to treat people who are sexual abusers of children or mothers who are crack cocaine addicted would be a simpler one if a human service organization were just a business. Treatment of either group is unpopular, expensive, and the success rate does not justify the drain on resources required. It would certainly not enhance the image of the organization within the community. A social work manager may have to make the decision and implement a policy to not offer treatment, but only after carefully factoring in professional ethics and values. Having made the decision to no longer offer treatment in these situations, the manager can anticipate some criticism both within and outside the organization.

Sometimes, for professional and ethical reasons, a human service organization will also do what a business would rarely, if ever, do—operate at a loss. If, for example, the more efficient use of group services for treatment of victims of sexual abuse is not viewed as professionally sound, individual treatment may continue to be offered despite the fact that client fees in no way pay for all of the cost of treatment. In fact, many human service organizations, by their very nature, regularly operate at a loss, at least in the financial sense. Human services are very costly and, frequently, very inefficient. Organizations often charge more for services than what the client is willing or able to pay or what an insurance company or other third party payer is willing to reimburse. Of course, they cannot do this on a consistent basis and continue to exist.

Client needs, social responsibility, and professional ethics often dictate more loudly to social work managers than do demands for efficiency, or at least they should. Managers must compromise by making some concessions to efficiency when required, especially when the survival of the organization is at stake. Simultaneously, because we are social workers we listen to our professional conscience and "stonewall" many demands for efficiency that we see as ethically unacceptable. This is one of the most difficult tasks of the manager in a human service organization. It occurs at every level in some form or other and often leaves manager feeling as if they in no-win situations. Managers are vulnerable to criticism whether they opt for efficiency or for equity. Business managers, possessing a much clearer set of priorities, usually have a much easier job of decision making—they know that opting for efficiency is the defensible and popular decision to make, at least among their stockholders and most other components of the task environment.

Consumer Dependency

A business or manufacturing firm actively courts the dependency and trust of its customers. A company that produces a product that can keep a large share of the market for its products is the envy of its competitors. Customers buy the products again and again and will "accept no substitutes." Businesses and manufacturers love to hear comments like "my family has always bought Chevrolets and I would not own any other car," unless, of course, they are trying to sell a competitive product. Advertising dollars are often devoted to promoting the idea of repeat sales.

The reason why both customer dependency and customer trust in business are so desirable is pretty obvious. Having a customer "locked in" to a product is a real advantage to the corporation. Knowing that they can count on a certain number of repeat sales allows manufacturers to predict accurately the sales cycles and market for a product. Costly inventories will never get too large. A challenge for management sometimes entails determining how a product can be improved to attract new customers while sufficiently retaining its identity so as not to lose those whose dependency provides a cushion of certainty for the organization. But long-term dependency of customers is much more a blessing than a management burden; it can make a manager look good while others are more vulnerable to the ebb and flow of the fickle customer.

In contrast, professionals within not-for-profit human service organizations do not generally seek to promote long-term client dependency; it would be contrary to social work values. In fact, while a business sees dependency as an indicator of success, an individual social worker is likely to see it as a clear warning that services may be ineffective and that goal achievement is not being accomplished. What business would offer a product that its employees hope will soon not be needed? It would not survive long if they did. Yet in human service organizations, we value such treatment approaches as crisis intervention that are designed for brief client exposure to the organization. If successful, they will result in a client never having to return for more help. We often are skeptical of those social workers who seem to favor long-term treatment; we may wonder just who is dependent on whom. We seek to promote client self-sufficiency, beginning termination procedures sometimes when clients would prefer to continue to be seen, but when in our professional judgment we think that they are ready to function on their own. By not promoting dependency among our clients, we lack the relatively certain and predictable market for our "product" that often is present within businesses.

There would be more certainty and more predictability in long-term client dependency. For example, it might appear desirable to know that "Ms. Johnson has Tuesday at 10:00," is always on time, and always pays for her counseling in cash. Her guaranteed presence might be preferable to that of a new client who feels ambivalent about coming, may not show up or show up just once or twice, and who resents the organization's fee structure. Some social workers might rather see clients like Ms. Johnson; they know and like her and may receive personal gratification from the realization that Ms. Johnson has not made an important decision in her life since 1995 without first discussing it with them. But professional values regarding dependence must take precedence over the comforts of Ms. Johnson's weekly presence.

Increasingly, financial considerations also argue against client dependency. With recent emphasis on managed care, professional staff must increasingly place greater emphasis on case management designed to achieve client self-sufficiency. If, for example, an HMO will reimburse the organization for six counseling sessions, it might be impossible to offer long-term counseling to clients. Higher-level managers also have had to adapt. They now must devote more of their time to outreach activities designed to seek new clients who will never establish a relationship of long-term dependency on the organization or its services.

Both professional values and concerns over reimbursement for services both argue against promoting client dependency in human service organizations. They create increased uncertainty. This uncertainty requires management activities at all levels that are designed to keep uncertainty at a tolerable level where staff can comfortably go about the work of the organization. All organizations face some uncertainty. But within many human service organizations, offering services that are designed to be unneeded by a given client after a short period of time presents unique management challenges for the social worker as manager.

In proprietary organizations that are publicly owned, in private practices, and in similar types of human service organizations that seek to make a profit, client long-term dependence may be viewed as either undesirable or desirable. If clients have insurance that offers limited benefits, they may not be allowed to stay in treatment as long as they might wish or even need. Clients who wish to remain (and who can pay for it or have good long-term coverage) may get their wish. Unoccupied beds and/or open treatment time cost money. In such settings, professional values about client dependence may be in direct opposition to the fiscal needs of the organization. Social workers can get caught in an ethical conflict between values and fiscal necessities in their role as manager. Any decision regarding client discharge or termination can leave someone unhappy. In such situations, the best a social work manager may be able to do is sort out one's own allegiances and priorities and strive to make difficult decisions in a consistent and defensible manner.

Attitudes toward Competition

In business or manufacturing, the competition is a major component of the task environment. It is always waiting for a marketing error or a bad product decision so that it can move in and take a larger share of the market. What is more, competition is inevitable—part of the American free-enterprise system. If you are well-managed and produce goods or services and a profit results, competition will quickly pop up to try to share in the benefits. Rarely in our nation's history has a monopoly been allowed to exist. As soon as a monopoly starts to look too self-serving, competition is encouraged or even enforced.

The inevitable presence of competition in business and industry results in a variety of management activities designed to gain an advantage. Competition keeps an organization "on its toes." Stale, old approaches to situations and problems can cause an organization to lose ground quickly. Competition provides a driving force to business that requires it to be dynamic and planful.

Historically, the specter of competition has been less important for most human service organizations (once again, those in the profit sector and certain health care providers always have been notable exceptions). Client waiting lists and service gaps, which no one organization can see itself clear to fill, were often typical of many human service organizations. They were more frequently seen than the highly competitive outside environments known to the business sector. In nonprofit organizations we might have been delighted if another organization opened up to take away a few of our clients—we were probably overloaded anyway. Who feared competition? We welcomed the help.

This happy or unhappy situation (depending on how we wish to view it) is rapidly changing. Today, in most human service organizations, there is competition for funding, programs, and even clients. Developing efficient referral networks and implementing inter-organization coordination remain important management activities at several levels. Getting another organization to take a referral through some reciprocal agreement is still desirable in many situations. But an increasing amount of the time of higher-level managers is now devoted to attempting to successfully compete with other organizations in the public and private sectors that offer the same or similar services.

Overall, the relationship with other related organizations in the human services sector remains generally cordial and congenial, if occasionally a little strained by the tensions of competition. But in an era of competition for limited funding and demands for accountability, social work managers must provide leadership in keeping an organization flexible and responsive. They must remain knowledgeable about the needs of potential clients but also must have an awareness of shifting sources of financial support.

Marketing Strategies

Competition naturally increases the need for good marketing. Both business and human services advertise and seek out potential customers/clients. Both have limited financial resources available for this activity, but they may employ them quite differently. In business, marketing research is used to determine if there are large groups of people with sufficient interest and enough money to purchase a product. Then and only then is the product manufactured. If the market potential for a product is small, the product is usually not produced. Similarly, human service organizations sometimes conduct needs assessments before they offer a service to be sure that there is a need and that potential clients will use the service if it is offered. But the resemblance to business may end at the point of evaluating the results of the research. Human service organizations, seeing that a large number of potential clients exist, will likely offer the service if sufficient funding is available. But, and this is an important difference, they may occasionally offer a service even if only a relatively few potential clients indicate an interest in it. If they do, it will be offered at a fair price, or even free. This occurs when the need of the few is great. Once again, a professional value (in this case, the necessity of helping those in need) takes precedence over efficiency or marketing principles.

A manufacturer would be unlikely to produce a product that can be used by only a few people, no matter how badly it is needed by them. If it did, the cost of the "specialty" item would likely be very high to recoup the high cost of manufacturing the product. The only time it might offer the product at a loss is when the public relations benefits of doing so might be great. Drug manufacturers have received sharp criticism from social workers and others because of their refusal to manufacture "orphan" drugs for persons afflicted with very rare diseases. From a business perspective, their manufacture makes no sense, unless manufacturing them would foster an image of social consciousness. Generally, it is unrealistic to expect people with a profit-driven orientation to make decisions that detract from the "bottom line." However, in some human service organizations, we will sometimes devote great effort and time to seeking out and serving small numbers of clients with relatively rare problems, often at a financial loss. Such marketing strategies would be considered irrational to those in the corporate sector. The offering of services with potentially few clients may become less frequent in the future as human service organizations must focus more on cost effectiveness.

Available Technology

As was suggested earlier, although management decisions in any environment are usually made based largely on descriptive or, perhaps, predictive knowledge, technology levels may differ markedly between manufacturing and human services organizations. A manufacturing plant is likely to have many of its employees engaged in simple, repetitive tasks. The product of their work is predictable. For example, add two ounces of blue dye to the plastic compound and a toy of the desired hue will result. Or, grind a metal replacement part to within a certain tolerance as measured by a micrometer and it will be acceptable. Thus, workers operate in an environment of "reasonable certainty." No comparable level of technology exists for the social work practitioner. Cause–effect knowledge is simply not available for most forms of practice intervention, primarily because of the complexity of the human behavior that we often are trying to influence. For example, we cannot predict with reasonable certainty that a typical social work response of "how do you feel about that?" or "thank you for sharing that" to a client description of a difficult life experience will result in new insights or otherwise alleviate a problem. It could result in a quizzical look, a fit of laughter, an obscene gesture directed at the social worker, or any one of an infinite number of other behaviors. Similarly, a social worker's professional judgment that an HIV education program will reduce the rate of anonymous sex may be correct, but it also may not. Still another practitioner's use of confrontational strategies to attempt to change a client's living conditions may produce landlord responsiveness, but the response may take many different forms. Some of these would be advantageous to the client but others might make life more difficult for the client.

An organization whose services must be performed without much cause–effect knowledge requires different management activities than one where more cause–effect knowledge is available. In human service organizations, we often cannot know what is the "right" (that is, effective) way to intervene with a client or client group. Thus, a supervisor in a human service organization will need to nurture a work climate conducive to the exercise of professional judgment and discretion, one in which some risk-taking is perceived as necessary and desirable. Manufacturing supervisors, in contrast, would be more likely to emphasize and enforce conformity. They would attempt to create an environment in which it is clear that deviation from the "right" way of doing something will not be tolerated.

Consumer Interaction

A business or corporation that manufactures a product has one primary occasion to interact with consumers—when consumers face the decision to buy or not buy a product. They vote on the desirability of the product by their decision. It reflects their evaluation of the product itself, of how it is displayed, of how well it was advertised, and so forth. The consumer never sees those within the organization who manufactured the product or who made management decisions relative to its manufacture and marketing. They may write a letter to complain if dissatisfied with a product or even bring suit if it causes them some harm, but generally their interaction with the organization that made it is confined to its purchase or non-purchase.

Consumer feedback in human service organizations is likely to be different. It tends to be more direct and frequent. Face-to-face contact with the "producer" of services is inevitable. In a manner similar to others who offer a service (e.g., plumbers, painters, etc.), social workers come face-to-face with the critical consumers (clients) who expect something of value in return for (in some cases) the money or the time that they have spent. However, while a plumber or a painter has a reasonably solid yardstick to fall back upon to resolve criticisms and conflicts with the consumer (the sink drains or it does not; the painting is finished or it is not), the human service provider frequently lacks agreed-upon indicators of satisfactory service. Dissatisfaction may result from one or more conditions or factors that are unrelated to the quality of services offered. For example, clients may simply take a dislike to a competent social worker, not choose to invest sufficient energies in change objectives, or (consciously or unconsciously) sabotage intervention in other ways. Any of these may produce unsuccessful intervention which may in turn result in consumer dissatisfaction with the organization and its professional staff.

Determining whether social work intervention is effective is very difficult. Seeing consumers face-to-face when they are unhappy with their state in life, and when they sometimes project the blame onto those who would try to help, is not pleasant. In human service organizations, management tasks frequently involve sorting out a wealth of client evaluations of services. The manager must find ways to receive and process useful feedback but also to recognize and to diffuse anger and other negative consumer reactions that may be neither valid nor constructive.

Evaluation of Success

In addition to processing consumer feedback, management requires ongoing evaluation of many other aspects of organizational functioning. A business that manufactures a product has available good, clear indicators of success—sales and earnings. Managers can devote most of their evaluation time to identifying factors that either contributed to, had no influence on, or diminished sales and earnings.

In human service organizations, as was suggested in the previous discussion, success and failure in service delivery are not easily operationalized or documented. In business, success is assumed to have occurred if the customer buys a product, takes it home, and does not ask for a refund. If the customer buys it again, this is an even greater indication of success.

In human service organizations, managers spend an inordinate amount of time just documenting whether success occurred. Their findings are very tentative and are arrived at from a variety of evaluation criteria that are much "softer" than those available in business or industry. Sometimes, for example, it can not easily be determined if clients have really made the progress that we think they made. Direct practitioners may use single-system research to evaluate their work with clients where some objective measurement of success is available. Frequently, however, treatment involves less easily demonstrated objectives such as improved family communication, better self-esteem, or development of community leadership. Then some very elusive indicators of success must be employed. Most of these would make a business person very uncomfortable. In the role of manager, social workers sometimes must evaluate organization programs (a task discussed in more detail in Chapter 11) by focusing on, for example, their structure (facilities and personnel), or impact (presence of long-term permanent change).[3] Another popular method of assessing effectiveness, Differential Program Evaluation[4] examines a program with respect to its stage of development. All of these evaluative focuses result in management tasks that differ somewhat from those required by the business or manufacturing organization. Because of their "softness," they are also often regarded suspiciously by members of an already hostile task environment.

The Prime Beneficiary Issue

Another major difference between the business/corporate sector and most human service organizations goes a long way toward explaining the unique context of social work management. It is so important to our understanding that we will give it special in-depth attention. In their classic 1962 study, Blau and Scott first introduced the concept of prime beneficiary.[5] They identified four categories of individuals as potential beneficiaries of any organization:

1. The members
2. The owners
3. The clients or customers
4. The public-at-large

While more than one of these groups may benefit from an organization's activities, Blau and Scott suggest that there is (or should be) only one *prime* beneficiary for an organization. An organization is expected to be most accountable for its actions to that group. Any benefits that accrue to other beneficiaries are usually viewed as cost since they usually result in fewer benefits for the prime beneficiary.

For some organizations, identification of the prime beneficiary is quite simple. For example, in "mutual-benefit associations" such as social clubs, credit unions, buying services, or other organizations where members share equally in costs and benefits, the membership is clearly the prime beneficiary. For most businesses and manufacturing corporations that are either privately or publicly owned, the prime beneficiary is the owners or stockholders. Service organizations, including most human service organizations, *should* regard the client as their prime beneficiary. A police department or public utility would have as its prime beneficiary the public-at-large.

The right of owners to be the prime beneficiary of a business or industry is rarely challenged by the public in our society. It may be threatened if, for example, the business or industry is viewed as engaging in "price-gouging" (for example, an "excessive" rise in food prices following a drought or flood, dramatic rises in gasoline prices during a crisis in the Middle East, or exorbitant prices for portable generators or other emergency supplies during a natural disaster. It may also be threatened if a business or industry engages in environmental pollution, destruction of natural resources or labor exploitation. But, short of these relatively unusual occurrences, the right of a business to make a reasonable profit is usually acknowledged by the public. We do not expect a business to operate at a loss, and we expect its managers to make decisions that will contribute to the production of a profit. Managers need not apologize for their actions. Owners demand profits.

The legitimized prime beneficiary of a business or manufacturing corporation (owners) has a right to "call the shots." Owners have invested their savings with the hope that they will grow; they also run the risk that the investment will diminish or be lost. Neither the business nor the corporation nor its owners are there to perform a public service. If there is any public service taking place, it is generally viewed as an investment in community relationships. It is hoped that the good will generated will ultimately result in increased profit.

The presence of a clear-cut and societal sanctioned prime beneficiary (owners) puts a business or manufacturing corporation in a position that is envied by most human service organizations. There is only one master to please. As long as sales and profit figures are good, the prime beneficiary is pleased with the organization. There is general agreement between the business and its prime beneficiary about what is a desirable goal. Business managers can work to improve efficiency, knowing that if they can, the prime beneficiary will be pleased.

A characteristic of most human service organizations is a lack of consensus about who should be the prime beneficiary. Consequently, much of a manager's time may be spent in trying to find ways to address client needs while not ignoring other groups and individuals who think their interests and priorities should be of paramount importance. This requires some skill and diplomacy. One author has noted that, "managers are confronted almost daily with the need to satisfy different and sometimes competing values and stakeholder interests."[6]

The lack of consensus about who is the prime beneficiary creates an ongoing tension within many human service organizations. In the public sector, the social work manager may spend great amounts of time trying to gain acceptance for the client as being the prime beneficiary. Members of the public-at-large, because they contribute money through the tax structure to support organization services, may think, logically, that they should be the prime beneficiary.

Social workers employed in a state in-patient psychiatric hospital regularly have their activities shaped by a lack of consensus regarding just who is the prime beneficiary. To the professional social worker, the organization is there to treat and to serve the patients. The patients' best interests should always take precedence over other factors. They are the prime beneficiary. How would such a perception affect one's daily activities? Treatment staff would take the position that a patient should be released when, in their judgment, discharge is a more therapeutic alternative to continued hospitalization. Occasional errors in judgment, present in all professional decision making, would be both tolerable and inevitable. Operating from this perspective, a social work manager might, for example, devote considerable effort to try to make the physical environment more home-like, less threatening or oppressive, and thus more conducive to treatment.

The public-at-large, viewing itself as the prime beneficiary, may take a very different attitude about the same organization and what it should be doing. While paying lip service to treatment goals, it may express opinions that belie its real priorities. It may demand protection and react with outrage when a former patient is released "prematurely" and engages in violent or embarrassing behavior. (One wonders, sometimes, whether premature is not synonymous with "prior to death" as evidenced by the comments of some members of the public-at-large.) It may see no reason to spend public funds to make hospital settings more "friendly." Security would be a high priority. The public might advocate building walls to separate patients from the community rather than bridges to it (sometimes, even literally).

Social workers employed in correctional settings see even more extreme examples of the same phenomenon. Members of the public-at-large, believing themselves to be the prime beneficiary, want what they see as their right. They are likely to insist on punishment for crimes and protection of the public from possible future offenses. In contrast, professional staff, who view the prisoner as the prime beneficiary, would probably view rehabilitation as the principal mission of the organization. This basic disagreement in perception explains, at least in part, the position taken by both advocates and opponents of early release programs or even of capital punishment. If correction is being provided by a for-profit organization through a contract with state or local government, things can become even more complicated. Then owners or stockholders would be a third group which might claim the position of prime beneficiary. Their primary concern would be likely to be efficiency of operation; they would demand efforts designed to make a profit.

In public child-protection organizations, members of the public-at-large pay the bills through the tax structure. But their right to "call the shots" takes a slightly different form. As the prime beneficiary, they believe that they have a right to shape and control the actions of employees of the organization. They may believe that their definition of who is a client, family, or even a community should be the accepted one. While not denying the need for child protection and not beyond a reaction of rage and charges of incompetence when a child is severely injured or killed, they are equally likely to fight against "precipitous" removal of the child from the home or investigations that may embarrass the family and/or the community. In contrast, social workers viewing the child as the client and thus the organization's prime beneficiary are likely to see their functions as child protection and child advocacy and to view their responsibilities to parents or to the community as secondary.

It is not surprising that a similar conflict is also played out in many other settings in which social workers are employed and where funding does not come from tax revenues. Sometimes disagreements about who should be the prime beneficiary may not be quite as dramatic as in mental health, corrections, or child protection, but the lack of consensus over the identity of the prime beneficiary exists nevertheless.

Many other social workers labor in settings where a lack of consensus regarding the prime beneficiary is inevitable. There is a prevailing belief in Western nations that "they who pay the fiddler get to call the tune." In those human service organizations that receive primary funding from tax revenues, or private contributions (for example, those who receive a major share of funding from United Way), members of the public are likely to view themselves as the prime beneficiary and will demand a say in how, when, where, and to whom services will be delivered. For those organizations that are designed to make a profit (e.g., many nursing homes, private psychiatric facilities, or those that have contracts with state or local governments), tension over the issue of who is the prime beneficiary (the client, owners, or managers) is almost inevitable. The owners or stockholders cannot simply be ignored. The issue becomes especially problematic in private psychiatric facilities or hospital corporations when a patient or client is viewed by professional staff as ready to go home, but still has days left under insurance coverage. Perhaps, there is not another patient awaiting admission. As we noted earlier, empty beds or empty cells do not generate profit. So, should the patient go home, despite a loss in revenue to the organization? Or, what if the reverse situation is true? Suppose that, in the professional judgment of a social worker, a patient needs to remain hospitalized for health reasons or for the protection of others, but insurance coverage has run out and other patients with coverage are waiting to be admitted? There is no easy answer to these ethical dilemmas. Social workers in the role of manager cannot simply pretend that fiscal concerns are unimportant and go about their business as if the interests of patients are all that matters. An organization that fails to respond to the demands of the various groups that view themselves as the prime beneficiary will soon cease to be an organization.

Especially in those organizations where employees are unionized or have organized to protect their interests in some other ways, another interesting phenomenon may exist. Is the prime beneficiary the clients or the members (employees) of the organization? Individuals themselves may struggle over the answer to this question. The issue can produce conflicts for the manager over, for example, whether staff should work evenings and weekends when clients are most available for services or whether overtime pay or compensatory time should be awarded for work performed after 5 PM. If managers naively assume that professionals just naturally adhere to the belief that the client is the prime beneficiary and that self-interest should always be of lesser importance, they will continue to be puzzled by many staff activities. To some staff in highly unionized settings, particularly those at lower administrative levels, their own interests may sometimes take precedence over those of the clients. This is a reality that a manager cannot afford to ignore.

Misuses of the Prime Beneficiary Concept.   The concept of prime beneficiary is helpful in understanding the feeling of being "caught in the middle" that a social work manager often experiences. While it can help to explain a manager's problems, an absence of consensus on who should be the prime beneficiary is never a valid excuse for poor management. Some managers have attempted to justify inattention to the demands of the public-at-large or of employee labor unions on the grounds that they have done their job by concerning themselves primarily with their prime beneficiary—the client. They have run a very inefficient, but client-centered organization and have reacted with indignation when accused of mismanagement or under-management. Especially in the public sector but in other settings as well, managers need to remind staff and themselves of who the prime beneficiary should be, while negotiating (and sometimes compromising) with those groups who think they ought to be the prime beneficiary.

Social workers as managers should not use the presence of tension over who is the prime beneficiary as a convenient alibi for a lack of sensitivity to client needs and demands. Some managers have done a good job of courting the favor of either the public-at-large, its owners or stockholders or even its professional staff. But they have accomplished this at the expense of needed client services. The "creaming" approach to client selection—choosing only those clients where the potential for demonstrated success is high—is a good example of a way in which managers court the favor of the public. Another way is through strict adherence to rules and policies that assure maximum payments from insurance companies or other third parties. Either practice demonstrates an approach to management that can be considered fiscally sound. But it may also be inconsistent with a social worker's professional ethics and values. A focus upon pleasing a prime beneficiary other than the client can result in services that are insensitive and unresponsive to client needs.

Managers who use the concept of prime beneficiary (whether they call it that or not) to justify a myopic focus on either meeting the needs of clients or on pleasing some other constituency do not fully understand the role of the social work manager. Good social work management is often an ongoing balancing act in which trade-offs are inevitable and in which satisfaction with management decisions on the part of all (and sometimes any!) parties cannot always occur. A good manager can derive satisfaction from maintaining the balance. In some situations where it seems like the best decision will end up pleasing no one, this may be the only source of satisfaction for the social worker as manager.

Accountability Implications of the Prime Beneficiary Question.   Social workers often find themselves walking a narrow path. In their role as managers, they recognize the need to be accountable, but to whom? Should they demonstrate efficiency and effectiveness to clients or to the public-at-large? Efficiency relates to cost of services, usually relative to the costs of those organizations or organizations that offer similar services. Effectiveness relates to an organization's ability to demonstrate that it does what it says it does and the degree to which it accomplishes its goals.

As was suggested earlier, many social workers recognize that human services are, by their very nature, not very efficient. Counseling services, for example, usually are very costly in comparison with the benefits that can be documented. Effectiveness of social work intervention is not easy to prove. For example, can a social worker really document that counseling has resulted in improvement in Ms. Gonzalez' self-esteem? How much? Can the social worker claim credit for any improvement that occurred, or were other factors such as the birth of her grandchild the real reasons for change? Or, is it possible to even say with certainty that her "having to see a social worker" has not been a negative contribution to how she feels about herself?

The accountability emphasis that preoccupied and struck fear in the hearts of social work managers in the 1970s and 1980s stressed responsibility to the general public. Many social workers believed that the focus of the "age of accountability" was not sufficiently concerned with client welfare. They feared, among other things, that concerns over efficiency would dominate organization activities and that professional standards would become less important than the economics of "people processing." An "anti-efficiency" climate developed in some organizations.

Demands for fiscal accountability arose in the early 1970s, in part in response to what was perceived as social workers' failures to reduce welfare caseloads during times of relatively generous funding for social services during the Lyndon Johnson administration.[7] Waste and inefficiency in human service organizations were exposed with glee by John Ehrlichman and others who announced that social workers and others would "have to make an honest living"[8] in the future.

The presence of inefficiency and even ineffectiveness within human service organizations was not totally the imagination of a vindictive group of federal officials. A lack of accountability over the years had resulted in some services and practices for their delivery that were dubious. The emphasis on accountability and, in some cases, the application of business evaluation methods were not without some value. As organizations tightened up, the social worker's prime beneficiary, the client, sometimes benefited. Those organizations that really were delivering effective services in an efficient manner had little problem in demonstrating accountability. Those that were not were forced to improve their management methods or risk loss of funds. While undoubtedly some good organizations were evaluated out of existence and some good but inefficient services had to be discontinued, in retrospect the accountability focus may have been more beneficial than harmful. Those managers who were able to look beyond the threats of accountability and to see demands for it as opportunities to improve efficiency and effectiveness made changes within their organizations, many of which ultimately were beneficial to clients.

The rapidly rising cost of health care in the last two decades of the twentieth century produced another dramatic example of the ethical issues that human service managers can face when there is a lack of consensus as to who should be the prime beneficiary. Health insurance companies, threatened with reduced profits and losses, cut benefits and instituted a variety of health care cost containment measures that culminated in what is referred to collectively as managed care. Social workers and other health care professionals who viewed patients as the prime beneficiary cried "foul" and predicted the demise of responsible, medically sound treatment. Did the HMOs and other health insurance providers have a legitimate claim to being the prime beneficiary (since they paid most of the bills)? Did that give them a right to, for example, limit reimbursable days of hospitalization to the average length of hospitalization for a particular procedure? Did they have a right to allow non-medically trained bureaucrats to make such determinations? Perhaps, but perhaps the people whose employers paid for their health insurance or who paid for it directly, that is, the patients, could also claim prime beneficiary status and thus to the best care available.

While managed care has not been as disastrous as many professionals predicted it would be, it has undoubtedly resulted in a reduction in quality of medical and psychiatric treatment for some patients. Like other developments that have exacerbated the tension between different groups who believe they have the right to be the prime beneficiary, it has made the working lives of managers more difficult. It has produced numerous ethical dilemmas as managers attempt to "serve two (or more) masters." One of them is almost certain to be dissatisfied. This has resulted in a lack of job security and even firings for some higher-level managers. Others have simply chosen to leave because of dissatisfaction with the inevitable compromises, thus putting even greater strain on those who remain.

Summary

In this chapter we have examined the context of human services in order to better understand what sometimes makes role of the social worker as manager different from that of other managers. For example, the presence of a task environment that is not always friendly, and sometimes quite hostile, suggests why the tasks of management in social work take certain directions that would seem illogical to many people in business or industry. Ways to try to make the task environment more friendly were discussed.

We reviewed the ways in which businesses are similar to and how they differ from human service organizations and how these differences shape the actions of their respective managers. We singled out an old but still very serviceable concept, namely prime beneficiary, to explain an especially important difference. The lack of consensus regarding who is the prime beneficiary presents problems and occupies much of the energies of the social worker as manager, particularly in public and nonprofit private organizations, but in an increasing number of other settings as well. We looked at a related issue, accountability, and at the special problems faced by manager in addressing it. Social workers as managers must demonstrate effectiveness and efficiency to the public-at-large and/or to owners and stockholders that regard themselves as the organization's prime beneficiary. At the same time they must address the needs of consumers, the group that social work professionals regard as the prime beneficiary of human service organizations.

Endnotes

1. Peter M. Blau and Richard W. Scott, *Formal Organizations* (Scranton, PA: Chandler Publishing Company, 1962), pp. 194–206.

2. James D. Thompson and William J. McEwen, "Organization Goals and Environment: Goal Setting as an Interaction Process," *American Sociological Review,* 23 (1958): pp. 23–31.

3. Ruth E. Weber and Norman A. Polansky, eds., *Social Work Research* (Chicago: University of Chicago Press, 1975), pp. 185–187.

4. Tony Tripodi, Phillip Fellin, and Irwin Epstein, *Social Program Evaluation* (Itasca, IL: F. E. Peacock Publishers, 1971), pp. 41–60.

5. Blau and Scott, *op. cit.,* pp. 42–44.

6. Richard L. Edwards, Philip W. Cooke, and P. Nelson Reid, "Social Work Management in an Age of Diminished Federal Responsibility," *Social Work,* 41 (1996): p. 473.

7. See, for example, Daniel P. Moynihan, *Maximum Feasible Misunderstanding: Community Action in the War on Poverty* (New York: Free Press, 1969), pp. 75–101.

8. See, for example, John Ehrlichman, *Witness to Power: The Nixon Years* (New York: Simon & Schuster, 1982), pp. 207–241.

3

Historical Origins of Current Management Theories

To understand the so-called "new management" theories and practices that are prevalent today, it is helpful to examine those earlier theories whose successes and failures were the impetus for their evolution. However, there is a second reason to study the history of management theory. As social workers, we know that change in human behavior is slow and difficult. While few current social work managers today would admit to heavy reliance on, say, scientific management or administrative management theories, their behavior as managers suggests that earlier theories are alive and well, and continue to be a major direct influence on their behavior. Earlier conceptualizations of workers and of the role of managers continue to have an unmistakable imprint on management within human service organizations. It is worth our time to examine them in some detail.

In our examination of historical approaches to management we will attempt to identify both what they have to offer today's social workers as managers and where they fall short of their needs. With relatively few exceptions, management theories were based upon research conducted within work settings where efficiency was emphasized. It was viewed as a desirable means to an even more desirable end—profit. As we discussed in Chapter 2, human service organizations may reflect some very basic differences from organizations in the "for-profit" sector. But these differences are not nearly as distinct as they once were and, even if they persist, they do not preclude our learning from the work of those who have studied management in the business sector. Past, present, and emerging business management theories all have great importance for social work managers charged with demonstrating the efficiency and effectiveness of programs and services.

In the early and middle Nineteenth Century, when family businesses and cottage industries were the norm, there was little interest in the development of a systematic body of knowledge relating to management. The coming of the industrial revolution to North America produced a new phenomenon, namely the large-scale business or manufacturing organization. Individuals found themselves working with hundreds and sometimes thousands of other employees in the production of goods and services. An impersonality, heretofore unknown, characterized many working relationships.

The growth of large and complex businesses and industries prompted the arrival of a new kind of specialist—the manager. The manager's role was neither that of worker nor owner. Managers neither helped to make a product with their own hands nor stood to gain directly from its sale. They were paid to oversee and support the work of others and were evaluated on their ability to perform these tasks. In some large organizations, some managers had no direct dealings at all with workers who produced a product; they performed only higher-level management tasks, such as supervising lower-level managers. Those who found themselves in roles as managers at any level often had little preparation for their new roles. They stood to benefit from the development of a systematic body of knowledge to help them perform their work.

The discussion that follows provides a brief overview of some of the best-known, identifiable management theories that evolved during the past century. Each reflects a "school" or philosophy of management that is based upon certain assumptions about what motivates people, the correct role for a manager to play, and how organizations should work. They provide a rationale (other than instincts) for making management decisions and for taking action when there is no cause-effect knowledge or empirical research available to guide us.

Scientific Management

The earliest identifiable theories of management, collectively labeled *scientific management,* really had their origins in the apprenticeship methods of the Nineteenth century. Frederick W. Taylor (1856–1915), an engineer by profession, is the name most often associated with scientific management, although the scientific management label was first applied to his theories in 1910 by Louis Brandeis.

Taylor was heavily influenced by the work ethic that was prevalent in his time. Scientific management was based on a number of assumptions about people and their behavior in the workplace. Taylor assumed that workers are motivated primarily by economic concerns. They act rationally. They prefer simple tasks, and they require and want guidance and supervision to help them with their work. What they are really seeking in their work is financial security and a stable work environment that guarantees good, regular pay.

If one subscribes to this view of human beings, certain management principles and behaviors follow. The work of the manager should involve the design and application of better ways to increase worker productivity. To accomplish this, scientific management relied heavily on methods of reward such as incentive pay, commissions, and piecework (pay based on number of units of work produced). All of these methods provided financial incentives to workers under the belief that, because of the presence of these incentives, they would devote more of their time and effort to production. If someone works primarily to earn money, that person will work harder if more money is offered as a reward. It makes sense, particularly if your perception of human beings is that of Frederick Taylor, that is, "economic man" (sometimes referred to as "machine man").

Because workers, managers, and owners all tend to benefit when efficiency and productivity increase, proponents of scientific management argued that conflict within an organization ought to be minimal. If conflict existed it was only because of a lack of scientific knowledge and management expertise. Again, there was a compelling logic to this line of thought, given Taylor's basic assumptions about people. Why would any rational, economically motivated worker not want to be productive, contributing to organizational profit as well as to one's own financial well-being?

Scientific management theory, because it believed that employees wanted work to be simple and financially rewarding, placed great emphasis on the selection and careful training of workers. It emphasized careful division of labor with "hands-on" workers performing simple tasks and managers relieving them of the responsibility to think and make decisions. All workers do their own specific tasks. Because their work is so uncomplicated, employees quickly learn to do it correctly and become increasingly more productive. Managerial and worker roles are clearly differentiated. The assembly line, first widely publicized for its efficient production of Model T and Model A Fords, was one of the applications of scientific management theories. It relied heavily on strict adherence to the principle of division of labor.

A phrase that is commonly remembered as critical to an understanding of scientific management is the "one best way." If one assumes that people are rational and that their motivation is uncomplicated, it is only logical to conclude that a best way to bring them to full productivity can be identified. The role of managers was to discover that way through a combination of their own scientific research and the application of the scientific studies of management performed by others. Scientific management assumed that the best way (often the most efficient way) exists; it must be found. Managers aspired to making management a science based upon an accumulation of knowledge about the best way to perform tasks. A popular application of the scientific method to the business sector was time-and-motion studies that sought to identify and eliminate waste and to increase the quantity of worker output.

Limitations of Scientific Management

Scientific management theory relied heavily upon research. Taylor once wrote, "Under scientific management you ask no one. Every little trifle—there is nothing too small— becomes the subject of experiment. The experiments develop into a law: they save money."[1] Thus, Taylor and his followers conducted studies that seemed to lend empirical support to the positions that they advocated. Later theorists sought to discredit their findings based in part on the researchers' methods.[2] It was pointed out that Taylor and his followers generally did not use a control group when "testing" for the effectiveness of the application of scientific management principles. It was also suggested that the findings were influenced by what later became known as the Hawthorne effect,[3] a measurement bias that is introduced by the presence of the researcher. The findings of his research and the theories that they produced suffer in their scientific credibility because Taylor himself was a convincing salesperson. When he conducted research, his personality and charismatic presence may have had more to do with a rise in worker productivity than did the management methods he employed.

Other criticisms of scientific management focused on the basic assumptions about people on which it was based. Some critics saw it as condescending and insulting to workers, viewing workers less as individuals, than as interchangeable parts. Taylor was also accused of a lack of sensitivity to the possible long-term physiological and psychological damage that can occur to an individual who, day after day, must perform repetitive tasks. This accusation may be a little unfair, as at least one author points out.[4] Taylor was not totally insensitive to human needs or to the potentially damaging effects of routinized tasks on the worker. His writings reflect a beginning understanding of group dynamics and their influence on productivity. His emphasis on individual motivation through economic incentives was probably more designed to overcome group influences on worker behavior than an indication of Taylor's naiveté about them.

The "one best way" focus of management met opposition from both contemporaries and later critics. Employees and managers of his day were use to making decisions based upon "art" factors such as instinct, experience, and tradition. Therefore, they resented what they saw as an effort to develop a body of scientific knowledge that might suggest that some current practices were simply wrong. Identifying what Taylor believed to be the "best way" had the potential to limit their available options as managers. Later, criticism was leveled at the idea that there could ever be a single way to perform management functions that would be universally best in different situations and with people who differed markedly from each other.

Critics also questioned Taylor's contention that conflict was unnecessary within organizations if managers just did their jobs well. Especially as unionization spread, organized resistance to Taylor's methods grew. Workers often argued that they were not sharing equally with owners in the profits of their productivity. They began to resent the constant pressure to produce more and more without commensurate rewards. Labor union leaders argued that scientific management methods were used to undermine the limited progress that had been made by workers.

In fairness to Taylor, his conception of human beings, particularly his ideas about economic motivation, may not have been as far off-base for his time as they might appear to be today. Many of us have grown up with the belief that our work should be interesting, challenging, varied, and should be something we genuinely enjoy, at least some of the time. Workers in the late nineteenth and early twentieth centuries often had quite different expectations for their jobs than what we might have today. Many of the workers of Taylor's time were recent immigrants who came to the United States primarily to better their economic lot in life. They were inclined to see their jobs as a means to escape poverty, to get a financial start that would put them on the road to prosperity. They wanted financial security first (having often had little in the past) and were less inclined to expect or seek higher-level need gratification. They were not looking for a career; they wanted a job that would pay well and offer job security. In short, Taylor's perception of "economic man" may have been largely accurate (if a little over-generalized), given many of the workers that he encountered. It would be a mistake to precipitously judge his assumptions and methods based on our understandings of the dynamics of human behavior as they exist in the twenty-first century.

Current Applications of Scientific Management

On the surface, given the many criticisms of scientific management that have been made, it would seem that the theories would offer little to social workers today in their roles as managers. However, Taylor and his colleagues made major contributions to management;

many of which are still valid and useful. We must remember that scientific management was a major departure from management practices of the pre-Industrial Revolution era. It was a first step in the right direction. Prior to the era of scientific management, managers operated and made decisions based upon precedent, their instincts, and impulse. There were no principles of management or any other conceptual framework available to assist them. Only profit, and whatever promised to produce it, guided management decision making. As a result, workers were often abused and made to feel powerless. Managers often appeared to be arbitrary and capricious in their handling of individual employees. Scientific management was at least based upon certain assumptions and principles; it offered a more objective approach to management and to the treatment of workers.

The search for the one best way, the belief that people are motivated by money, and other assumptions of Frederick Taylor did not disappear with his death in 1915. Social workers in the role of manager continue to see the presence of scientific management ideas, sometimes in the management of others and occasionally in their own management practice. These are not always inappropriate. For example, there are occasions when there is a best way and there are times when financial considerations are powerful influences on staff behavior. Scientific management theory contributed many insights into organizational behavior that remain relevant today.

Administrative Management

Another approach to management was also taking shape during the first half of the twentieth century. The theories collectively referred to as administrative management evolved from the writings of Henry Fayol (1841–1925) and others. Fayol was a French industrialist (mining) who believed that there are certain management principles that are universally appropriate for higher administrative levels in different settings. He first published his observations in 1916, but they were not generally known in the United States until the 1940s when they were widely discussed among management theorists.

Fayol has been widely misunderstood. While it was probably never his intention that his 14 management principles be perceived as rules or laws, a common misunderstanding of them is that they were meant to be quite rigid. Such supervisory principles as "span of control shall not exceed eight" (no one should supervise more than eight people) or [sic] "one man—one boss" were assumed to be prescriptive, yet they really were more descriptive, general suggestions. Unfortunately, they are what is generally remembered about administrative management while the broader principles of Fayol are less well-known.

Fayol believed that good management could be taught. He took the position that persons who applied his principles could be successful in performing the tasks of the manager. His list of managerial functions (see Chapter 1) consisted of planning, organizing, commanding, coordinating, and controlling. He observed, as we have noted earlier, that management is not confined to the workplace. We engage in management in all human activities. But, Fayol argued, people can be taught to do a better job of management wherever they manage if they adhere to his basic principles. These principles are outlined below:

1. *Division of work.* Fayol believed that specialization will produce more and better work without increased effort.

2. *Authority and responsibility.* For Fayol, authority (the right to give orders and expect obedience) is closely related to responsibility. Responsibility is a natural consequence of authority. A manager not only possesses but also encourages others to accept responsibility.

3. *Discipline.* Fayol saw discipline as part of the "contract" between workers and employers and as absolutely essential for the smooth functioning of an organization.

4. *Unity of command.* Fayol believed that an employee should receive instructions and be accountable to only one boss. Any other situation undermines authority and causes major problems for the organization.

5. *Unity of direction.* Fayol believed that a group of activities that are designed to achieve the same objective should have one plan (and one leader).

6. *Subordination of individual interest to the general interest.* Fayol believed that such human characteristics as selfishness and laziness could produce an organization in which self-interest would take precedence over the best interests of the organization unless supervision, certain agreements, and firmness and the example of superiors precluded it.

7. *Remuneration.* Fayol believed that it should be fair and, whenever possible, satisfactory to both employer and employee. He advocated some innovative (for his time) methods of compensation such as bonuses and profit-sharing.

8. *Centralization.* Fayol viewed centralization as always present (to a greater or lesser degree) within an organization. However, he thought that the balance between centralization and decentralization should vary based largely on the characteristics of managers and their subordinates. He believed that a manager's job was to achieve the most appropriate balance between them given the uniqueness of the situation.

9. *Scalar chain.* Fayol believed that strict adherence to the chain of command could cause problems, especially when prompt communication is required. He suggested that organizations sometimes need to create shorter, more direct routes ("gang planks") that are much more efficient for communication flow, even if they do not coincide with the chain of command.

10. *Order.* Fayol believed strongly that everything and everyone in an organization needs to be in its proper place. He placed great emphasis on matching employees to appropriate positions, so that, employees would find themselves in a job where they could make their greatest possible contributions.

11. *Equity.* Fayol viewed fairness as being more than justice based on convention. He stressed the need for common sense and kindliness in making decisions that would be perceived as fair.

12. *Stability of tenure of personnel.* Fayol observed that prosperous firms tend to be stable; they tend to have relatively little staff turnover. He noted the high cost of training new personnel, especially managers, and, therefore, advocated job security through such methods as the granting of tenure or permanent employee status. However, he also recognized the problems that could result if too large a proportion of an organization's employees were tenured and became secure in their jobs.

13. *Initiative.* Fayol recognized the importance of managers promoting initiative among employees of an organization. But he believed that this must be balanced by respect for authority and discipline.
14. *Esprit de corps.* Fayol valued harmony within an organization. He believed it should be promoted by managers, for example, by not splitting up work groups or by not insisting on written communication among employees when verbal communication would be more efficient and would be more likely to produce positive interpersonal relationships.[5]

It might seem logical to conclude that Taylor's scientific management and Fayol's administrative management theories were rivals that were also incompatible. In fact, they were neither. For one thing, Fayol's principles were designed primarily to assist administrators in performing higher-level management functions. Taylor's approaches focused on ways for managers to positively affect the productivity of individual workers. Both contributed to management theory, but from a slightly different perspective. Actually, their insights are quite complementary. They shared (along with advocates of the bureaucratic model) very similar beliefs about human beings and, especially, what motivates them.

One of the theorists who took some of Fayol's ideas and developed them a little further was Mary Parker Follett. She relied heavily on the idea of universal management principles, but her writings are based on different experiences and, therefore, have a somewhat different emphasis. Follett knew and understood government and business administration. She also understood the importance of psychological and social factors in the practice of management. While not trained as a behavioral scientist per se, her writings reflect more the need for a manager's sensitivity to human individuality than do those of Fayol or most other writers identified with administrative management theories. Not surprisingly, the social work manager is likely to feel more at home with Follett's work than with the others. Her insights are more compatible with our profession's emphasis on the needs of the individual than those of the other theorists.

Limitations of Administrative Management

As suggested above, much of the criticism of Fayol and those who extended his work was based on a misunderstanding of just how rigidly his principles were designed to be enforced. If mistakenly viewed as laws, it is not hard to discredit them. It was pointed out, for example, that in real life the principles did not always work for the manager. In addition, the limits of each (the situations in which they fail) were not defined. Also, the literature rarely discussed the consequences of noncompliance with the principles.

While the principles are logical, they are not always factual in the real world of work. One writer, Herbert Simon, went to great pains to demonstrate the lack of consistency of some principles with others. He demonstrated that, in some situations, compliance with one principle would require the violation of a second one.[6]

Although critics of administrative management may have been somewhat unfair in their attacks, advocates of administrative management probably did rely too heavily on the 14 principles. Management cannot be based on 14 or even 400 principles. Overemphasis on principles can result in a situation in which managers pay insufficient attention to some very important situation variables, especially the unique human beings affected by management activities and the unique person who is the manager. Follett reflected a beginning recognition of the importance of these, but her insights still fell short of those needed by the social work manager of the twenty-first century.

Current Application of Administrative Management Theory

While the 14 principles of administrative management have their limits, they are still worthy of our study today. They are far more valuable than misleading. In fact, adherence to them will result in management decisions that will be sound far more often than not. Many of the ideas implicit in this and other current texts are consistent with them and probably evolved from them, at least indirectly.

The reader will also note that Fayol's five functions of management are reflected in current literature. We might argue that organizing and coordinating are not discreet functions. But the management functions specified by Fayol constitute a rather complete description of management activities in any environment, whether personal or professional.

The idea that management can be taught may be administrative management's most relevant contribution to current management theory. It is consistent with the social work value which contends that people can change, that they can learn to function better if given a chance and some assistance. It would be most unfortunate if we still adhered to earlier attitudes about management which held that good management practice is a gift, given to some and not to others. Because all social work practitioners are managers, as we contend throughout this book, such a belief would not bode well for many of us. However, believing that we can learn to become better managers not only provides justification for the study of management, it suggests that we can become successful in our roles as managers through study and skill building.

Bureaucratic Management

The third component of what is collectively referred to as classical management theory, *bureaucratic management,* is quite familiar to most social workers. Bureaucracies are very much in evidence within the human services. They are often favorite targets for criticism when we feel frustrated in our ability to offer services to our clients. It is even a fairly common practice among those who are not social workers to use large social welfare bureaucracies, such as large state psychiatric hospitals or public welfare organizations, as examples of everything that can go wrong when bureaucratic principles dominate within an organization.

As with the two theories discussed above, one name is most frequently associated with bureaucracies—Max Weber (1864–1920). While Weber's writings began to appear at the same time that scientific management and administrative management theories were taking shape, translation and widespread implementation of his ideas did not occur in the United States until after World War II. The bureaucracy, as conceptualized by Weber, still remains a dominant model in many organizations today.

To Weber, the bureaucracy was the ideal organization for twentieth-century needs. Above all, he believed that it promised a high degree of both efficiency and control. A bureaucracy is really an organizational design, one specifically constructed along certain principles that are believed to promote efficiency. These principles are familiar to anyone who has ever worked in a human service organization. They are logical and, at this point, time-honored and time-tested. For example, bureaucracies are usually characterized by:

1. *A vertical organizational hierarchy.* The person on the top is the boss; power decreases at each respective lower level of the hierarchy. Everyone's behavior is monitored by somebody else.
2. *Well-defined guidelines that limit functions.* Rules and policies are widely used. There is also use of methods such as procedure manuals, and even decision-making rules to govern and control behavior when no other formal guidance exists. The idea is that they will function within organizations much as habits work for individuals.
3. *Promotion and other rewards based on demonstrated technical competence.* "Do your job well and you will be rewarded," often with promotion to the next level in the organization's hierarchy.
4. *Formal, rigid communication channels.* There is strict adherence to the chain of command in communication (and in other activities).
5. *Job security for full-time employees.* "Do your job and you can not be fired."
6. *Division of labor.* People have very specific jobs to do. They know exactly what their job entails and so does everyone else. Use of detailed job descriptions.
7. *Emphasis on written documentation.* "When in doubt, always put it in writing."

A bureaucracy is very logical. Its strict adherence to rather impersonal, unresponsive principles makes it a natural for many human service organizations. Organization around bureaucratic principles makes it possible to retain control over large numbers of people and their activities. A bureaucracy offers a high level of certainty to employees who might otherwise have difficulty navigating their way within a large organization. Adhere to rules, policies, and procedures (you can look them up if you have to) and you can be rather certain that you will be rewarded with job security and promotion. Please your immediate supervisor and you will be okay.

Since many social welfare programs receive financing from federal sources and the federal government is itself a highly structured bureaucracy, it is not surprising that bureaucracies also occur at the state and local organization levels. Bureaucracies interact well with other bureaucracies. (They interact less efficiently with organizations that are structured around other principles.) Internal rules and other controls can easily be tailored to meet federal guidelines and requirements. This promotes even more certainty—it increases the likelihood that funding and reimbursement will be forthcoming.

Bureaucracies are even credited with providing a desirable level of certainty to clients. Client advantages of bureaucracies include uniform treatment (no favorites) and protection of clients from discrimination by those who might try to withhold needed services to which they are entitled. The impersonality of a bureaucracy can work to assure clients that they will be treated no differently from anyone else and that they will get all that they are entitled to, assuming that they meet all eligibility requirements.

Higher-level administrators, those most responsible for the long-range survival of the organization, find bureaucracies to be an especially useful way of dealing with a hostile task environment. If, as in the case of public assistance, the primary enterprise is the distribution of tax dollars to those often stereotyped by the general public as lazy or unworthy, managers need all the protection from the task environment that they can muster. It is not surprising that bureaucracies have evolved in organizations that live under constant assault from a hostile task environment. A bureaucracy can insulate and protect itself from criticism. It does this through the use of organizational principles that promote and communicate to the task environment a sense of control and accountability. Careful and rigid adherence to federal guidelines, documentation, voluminous record keeping, close monitoring of everyone's work, rules that control behavior even when the supervisor is unavailable—these and other bureaucratic methods minimize embarrassing mistakes and keep criticism by the general public down to a tolerable level. An organizational structure that promotes efficiency and the reduction of errors (e.g., in eligibility determination) is far less likely to risk critical attack from a hostile task environment than one based on principles of individualization of clients, flexibility, or professional judgment in decision making. A bureaucracy is ideally suited to silencing those critics who are eager to accuse an organization of overly zealous distribution of public funds and publicly supported services. When challenged, a record of strict adherence to rules can be presented in the form of statistics, records of correspondence, and other data.

Limitations of Bureaucratic Management

Anyone who has ever experienced the frustrations of working in a bureaucracy is well aware of the limitations of bureaucratic principles. While bureaucracies are logical, rational, and would, on the surface, seem to have high potential for promoting efficiency, sometimes just the opposite occurs. We will mention some of the most commonly acknowledged flaws; the reader can undoubtedly add to the list.

Job Descriptions.   In bureaucracies, the responsibilities of all jobs are supposed to be fully described. However, this is often not realistic in the real world of human services and, to a lesser degree, even in business or manufacturing. What if, as so often happens with client services, there is a need for a service that falls within no one's job description? Ethically, it is difficult to deny a person in need because the needed services are not anyone's responsibility. For example, a social work bureaucracy or bureaucratic health care organization tightly structured into spheres of confidence might not have been able to address the current needs of AIDS patients or their families in 1983 or even in 2003. The nature of our work as social workers is constantly evolving along with the needs of our current clients and those that we will serve next year. The manager who relies too heavily on job descriptions fails to recognize both the inevitability of some overlap in function and the need for some flexibility to meet the ever-changing demands for services.

"Put It in Writing."   This principle also seems like a good idea but it sometimes can cause problems. While designed to promote efficiency, it can result in a very inefficient use of time. Effort and resources (secretarial, clerical supplies, data storage capacity) that

could be used for client services frequently are expended in the support of unnecessary documentation and record keeping. The "memo barrage" that frequently is seen in bureaucracies presents a clear example of this kind of waste. Employees have been known to exchange dozens of memos or e-mail messages in a work week with another employee whose office is 10 feet from their own! They could have gone over, talked directly to the co-worker, and completed the communication in two minutes or less, but bureaucratic principles discourage this type of behavior.

Promotion Based on Proven Competency.   This principle has a compelling logic; but it is also flawed. As we suggested earlier, different knowledge skills, motivation, and abilities are needed for different jobs. There is no guarantee that a good direct-practice worker will be successful as a supervisor or that a good planner will be equally competent as the administrator of a community-based organization. Sometimes the principle results in people being promoted out of jobs where they perform well and into other jobs where they struggle.

Stability.   Bureaucracies are best suited to relatively stable, unchanging environments. This, of course, is not characteristic of most human service enterprises. Bureaucracies have a way of breeding conformity and stifling creativity. The reward system promotes behavior according to the book; this behavior may or may not be consistent with the needs of changing situations. Frequently, the heavily bureaucratized organization seems to be populated by survivors, namely those willing to learn and comply with the rules and to "make no waves." Those who seek new and better ways of doing things and who agitate for change in order to adapt to new situations inevitably find themselves at odds with the bureaucratic power structure. They remain frustrated or go to work elsewhere where they believe that their flexibility will be more appreciated.

Job Security.   Like tenure in an academic setting, job security theoretically should provide workers with the freedom to do their work without danger of losing their job. Sometimes increased productivity is the result. There are some very able civil service employees whom, we would all agree, deserve know that their job is secure. Their security helps them to do their jobs well. However, there are those who have been awarded permanent employee status based upon evaluation of a brief probationary period and who have later proven to be a liability to their organization. Job security *can* promote good job performance, but it can also result in apathy, complacency, and a feeling of invulnerability for those who lack the necessary dedication and motivation to perform well. Bureaucracies can become overpopulated with the latter, particularly if work conditions and rewards are so limited that the more marketable and more creative employees tend not to stay around long.

Continued Growth.   Bureaucracies seem to want to grow and to become increasingly inflexible. A written guideline, when reinforced by tradition over time, seems to take on even more controlling force. Even solutions to problems and structures that were intended to be only temporary soon become institutionalized. For example, task forces (designed to address a specific problem) are a common approach to the solution of problems in bureaucracies. They seem especially well suited to those situations where involvement of all persons who have an interest in solving the problem is logistically impractical and would be an inefficient use of their time. However, in bureaucracies, task forces often become committees. Committees seem to be self-perpetuating, always identifying additional work that needs to be done or issues that need to be discussed. Sometimes a committee seems able to meet for thirty minutes to produce nothing tangible other than a time and place for the next meeting. Unfortunately, lack of productivity rarely leads to the termination of a committee.

Of course, task forces are not the only "temporary" structures that tend to "live on" in bureaucracies. This is why bureaucracies often grow so large. Programs also sometimes exist long after a need for their services has dissipated. Because of vested staff interest and the overall tendency of bureaucracies to grow rather than to diminish, some social programs have remained and continued to drain needed funds long after they could have been phased out. For example, the drastic reduction in influx of Southeast Asian immigrants into the United States in the late 1980s as a result of declining immigration quotas had little immediate effect on the size and scope of many programs in state bureaucracies that were created to address an earlier need. The frequently discussed but rarely required "sunset provisions" provide for programs to be terminated at a given time unless a convincing new demonstration of need can be provided. They are an effort to address the tendency of programs in bureaucracies to exist beyond the point where they are no longer needed.

Goal Displacement.   We would be remiss if we did not mention one other problem that seems to pervade most bureaucracies. Just the sheer size of many bureaucracies makes it difficult to retain a focus on an organization's goals and objectives. Vehicles that were originally designed to achieve goals and objectives more efficiently (for example, having one's records up to date), can quickly become goals themselves. The goal (effective service to clients) becomes forgotten. This specific type of goal displacement is what is referred to as a "means-end displacement." Means-end displacements are common in bureaucracies. They often occur subtly and incrementally over time. They may go unnoticed until someone (usually an outsider) calls attention to them. They can be extremely detrimental to the goal achievement that social workers hope to promote in their role as managers. Persons immersed in meeting the requirements of their job may be unaware of their presence and may even resist "changing the rules" to regain a focus on what was the original goal or objective.

Current Applications of Bureaucratic Management

We must acknowledge that the bureaucracy is not the ideal organization envisioned by Max Weber. It may result in over-conformity, it may promote mediocrity, and it may, in fact, promote inefficiency. Other than that it's not bad!

The continued widespread use of bureaucratic methods in many human service organizations cannot be totally in error. Bureaucracies can and do work effectively for the delivery of human services. The fact that certain undesirable phenomena tend to occur naturally within bureaucracies does not negate their value. Their existence, however, underlines the need for alert and skilled management on the part of social workers. The social worker as manager must be adept at deriving the benefits from a bureaucratically oriented organization while using specialized knowledge and skills to prevent the problems that can readily occur.

A bureaucracy can be a very effective vehicle for coordinating activities within organizations that must, of necessity, be large and/or possess a variety of functions. Problems in bureaucracies occur when bureaucratic methods are allowed to feed on themselves and to hamstring the service functions that deserve top priority. A bureaucratic structure imposed on an organization that is small and uncomplicated and that does not need the tight control and accountability benefits that the model offers can similarly result in problems. Bureaucracies work best in those situations where tasks are fairly routine and standardization of their performance is generally desirable if not necessary.

Not surprisingly, few social workers have many good things to say about bureaucracies. But most of our negative experiences with bureaucracies have occurred when principles were used inappropriately or over-zealously applied—over-bureaucratization given the needs of a situation. Skilled social work managers who understand the merits and the shortcomings of the bureaucratic model can make decisions that will minimize these abuses of a very serviceable body of theoretical knowledge.

Common Shortcomings of the Classical Management Theories

In addition to the problems noted above, four common problems can be seen in the scientific, administrative, and bureaucratic approaches to management. We will discuss each of the four in greater detail in other contexts within this book and only briefly mention them here. All three classical management theories tend to ignore (1) the power of group norms on individual behavior, (2) the degree of individual differences that exist among people, particularly in regard to their motivation, (3) the irrational side of human beings that results in their doing things that are not always in their best interests, and (4) the existence of a very powerful force, namely the informal organization, that may bear little resemblance to what appears on a tidy organizational chart. Limited attention to these factors results in a great amount of false confidence regarding what behaviors will succeed for the manager. If one views people as relatively simple and easily understood, various prescriptive approaches to management will result. Classical theories tended to ignore the complexities of human behavior. Later concepts, based more on those ideas closer to social work's understanding of behavior (multiple causation, systems theory, etc.), were less presumptive. They focused more on general descriptions of patterns of behavior and did not presume to be able to demonstrate 100 percent success in influencing it.

Responses to Classical Management Theory

Taylor, Fayol, Weber, and other classical theorists saw managers as rational people capable of possessing the necessary knowledge to make the right decisions. Managers identify the various available alternatives and project the consequences of each. Then, based upon previously identified priorities, they decide and act. It all sounds perfectly logical. The idea is to seek out the perfect solution (referred to in the literature as "optimizing").

CASE EXAMPLE • *Means-End Displacement in a Bureaucracy*

When she was promoted to Child Protection Supervisor, Arlene set out to do a good job. While employed as a worker in the same public organization, she frequently had been frustrated when she had to pick up cases from other workers who had been reassigned or who left the organization. She inherited case records from workers who were months behind in their recording. As a result, she did not know what work had been done with her clients and she felt that continuity of service suffered badly. She determined that, as a supervisor, this type of irresponsibility would not be tolerated.

Arlene received excellent support from the district director when, as a new supervisor, she implemented strict new rules about case recording. The director had recently received a call from an angry and prominent citizen who wanted to know why his brother-in-law was being "harassed" by a caseworker about how he disciplined his child. The director called for the case record and was unable to either understand or defend the caseworker's actions because there was no record of an investigation. The district director agreed with Arlene that her new rules were in the best interest of defending the organization from outside criticism. How could anyone not support the implementation of rules that promised to provide better client services while also saving higher level managers from embarrassment?

Arlene clearly communicated the new rules to her workers. A minimum of a 100-word summary must be placed in the record for each telephone contact or in-person interview with clients or other persons contributing relevant information about the alleged abuse incident. All recording must be completed within 72 hours of the contact. "Adherence to recording rules" would be a component of semi-annual employee evaluations.

Within a short time, most workers in Arlene's unit were in compliance with the new recording rules. However, gradually over a period of three years, a means-end displacement

occurred. New workers had learned the importance of timely compliance with the rules. One individual who provided good services was denied a merit raise because her records were not up-to-date and she complained loudly about the amount of record keeping required. Others, whose records were up-to-date but whose client services were of only marginal quality, were rewarded with good semi-annual evaluations. Over time, most staff became aware that complete, up-to-date records were perceived as evidence of competence. They spent a considerable amount of time counting words in their records. Certain cliché phrases occurred regularly to pad a case note to the required 100-word minimum. One very good worker left the organization because she felt that she no longer had time to conduct thorough investigations because of heavy paperwork requirements. Others who were less conscientious simply made fewer collateral calls to avoid having to write notes in the record. Useful calls that contained important information were often described by workers as "providing no relevant information" so that there was no requirement that a summary be written for the record.

Things got worse. The director expressed pleasure with Arlene's rules. She now felt that she was in a much more defensible position when complaints from the community occurred. She rewarded Arlene with public compliments and high evaluations. Other supervisors, perceiving the high value placed on Arlene's methods, implemented even more demanding rules for recording within their work units. An implicit message was sent out at all levels of the organization—a good worker is one whose records are up-to-date; an incompetent one does not comply with the recording rules. Employees who could accept this definition stayed on and were rewarded for their attention to rules. Those who could not, because they saw other child-protection tasks as a higher priority than record keeping, soon left. Before long, the professional

CASE EXAMPLE • *(continued)*

community learned of the organization's emphasis on record keeping; some very good potential employees did not bother to apply.

Finally, the district director retired. The new director was dismayed to observe that the need for record keeping had become an unhealthy obsession. What had begun as an appropriate means to an end had become the end for many workers. Record keeping had taken on a higher priority than services themselves. The director moved quickly to regain an organization focus on professional services.

Service priorities were outlined and it was made clear that, while timely and complete recording is desirable, this should never take precedence over protection and service needs of children.

The new director's reminder of the appropriate place of recording as a means to an end (services) brought relief to some employees and produced anger and anxiety in others. Some of those who had fared well in the earlier environment were able to adjust their priorities. Some simply resigned.

Discussion Questions

1. What was the problem that Arlene identified? Why was she correct in attempting to do something about it?
2. What about the new rules made it likely that a means-end displacement would happen?
3. How did the staff responses to the new rules affect client services?
4. What could Arlene have done to help to avoid the means-end displacement?
5. What are some other means-end displacements that can occur in a large bureaucracy such as the one in which Arlene worked?

Based chiefly on a recognition of the complexity of human behavior, those writers who have been especially critical of the classical theorists held a somewhat different perception of managers. They viewed managers more as pragmatists, making acceptable decisions based on limited information and with the knowledge that even good decisions cannot guarantee success. As opposed to the optimizing of the classical theorists, Herbert Simon[7] viewed managers as "satisficing," that is, searching until they find an acceptable solution, one that is good enough rather than optimal. The term "bounded rationality" was used to describe managers' approach to decision making. Because they can not consider all possible alternatives and can not fully understand all the variables involved, limits (boundaries) are placed around the amount of information that will be processed prior to making a decision.

We make decisions using bounded rationality every day of our lives. If, for example, we need to buy a used car, we first identify the most important criteria that must be met. It must cost under $4,000, get at least 25 mpg, seat four or more people, be any color but red, and so on. Many cars would qualify. Obviously we cannot afford to examine every car in the Western Hemisphere that might meet our criteria in order to be able to identify the best one overall. We never would be able to make a decision because new ones would keep becoming available, some would be sold, etc. A reasonable approach to the decision of which car to buy would be to go to five or ten local dealers who are regarded as relatively reputable, see what they have, and choose among those cars that meet our criteria. This is satisficing through the use of bounded rationality. Optimizing would be more than just costly; it would be impossible. Any effort to seek the best car would only leave us incapable of making any decision. Whether we like to admit it or not, even more important decisions in life—for example, selection of a college, a career, or even a partner—also tend to be made through a process of satisficing. Any other approach might result in the decision maker becoming immobilized and unable to ever make a decision.

There are several identifiable "schools" of management theory which seem to address the perceived shortcomings of classical management theory. There is considerable overlap among them and a lack of consensus in the literature as to exactly how they relate to each other, which school is a variation of which other one, and so on. We will briefly mention several. They are those most frequently discussed in the management literature. We will identify only the more important concepts usually associated with them and note the major contributions of each to our current study of the management functions of the social worker.

The Modern Structuralists

Structuralist writers describe the organization as heavily influenced by its outside environment. This is consistent with much of our discussion in Chapter 2. As we noted, managers, particularly those at the higher levels, spend much of their time addressing the demands and pressures of an ever-changing task environment.

Structuralist theorists also assume that there is inevitably a lack of goal congruence among persons who work in an organization. Some employees, but certainly not all, share the goals formally espoused by the organization. Others have their own quite different goals and agenda. This, necessarily, results in conflict. The inevitability of conflict, it is proposed, need not be destructive or unhealthy for the organization. Lewis Coser has suggested that conflict has many positive functions, including the identification and solution of problems that exist.[8] An important function of managers at all levels, the structuralists suggest, is the control and management of conflict to keep it at a tolerable and productive level. Insights into conflict within organizations and the inevitable stress between the organization and its external environment are important contributions to our study of management. They help us to better understand the importance of managers and their role in relation to these phenomena.

Human Relations

Those theorists generally associated with human relations theories of management stress the complexity of human motivation. They especially focus on the ways in which levels of productivity, attitudes toward one's work, and various behaviors on the job are socially determined—that is, influenced by group norms. Social needs, largely ignored by people like Taylor, Fayol, and Weber, are viewed as important influences. They are used to explain, at least in part, why people in organizations behave in ways that appear irrational given the classical theorists' limited perception of what motivates people. The contention that non-monetary factors can influence behavior would explain, for example, why a person might decline a promotion in order to avoid having to supervise those people who are their best friends. Taylor would have been puzzled by such a decision.

Human relations theorists also depart drastically from classical writers in their attitudes toward specialization. Simple tasks are not regarded as necessarily better. Instead, more complex and integrated (with those of others) work is seen as more consistent with human social needs. The production line is viewed as a demeaning, stultifying way of organizing work that tends to make people hate their jobs and to devalue productivity.

Unlike the structuralist theoreticians, human relations writers do not see conflict as inevitable within organizations. They note that it occurs frequently but that sensitive and responsive management can prevent much of it and resolve the rest, primarily through creating an environment that promotes open communication and trust.

Human relations theorists based their understanding primarily on empirical research that studied the behavior of persons in formal organizations. Their theories formed the basis for the field of industrial psychology and contributed a major component to our understanding of systems. There was a heavy emphasis on problem solving and decision making that were based on a manager's understanding of both the rational and the more irrational (that is, social, affective) determinants of human behavior within organizations.

The contributions of the human relations management theorists are, of course, very consistent with the social work knowledge base and with our professional values. In fact, many schools of social work rely heavily on content taken from human relations research, particularly in discussing the influences of the organization as one of several social systems that impact on individual behavior.

Contingency Approaches

Another loose grouping of ideas about management became identified as the contingency school of management. It was also largely a response to the classical emphasis on optimizing and, specifically, to the "one best way" approach of scientific management. In contrast, contingency approaches to management argue that there is no one best way or no correct decision that will work for all situations. Different situations require different decisions and managerial behaviors. Managers will, however, make good, acceptable decisions if they have the sensitivity to make a valid assessment of the needs of a situation and have some skill in decision making.

Contingency theories of management seem quite relevant to social work management needs. They are also consistent with other areas of social work practice. In management or in treatment situations, we rarely find ourselves in identical situations. A managerial response that works well in one situation is by no means certain to work in another situation any more than a successful treatment intervention in one situation will produce the same results in another situation. We make most of our decisions in a "one time-only" environment. As in other areas of social work practice, we make managerial decisions that affect professionals who are definitely not interchangeable parts. Contingency approaches to management emphasize decision making that considers the individual person affected and the likely impact of the decision on that person's behavior. Contingency theories, of course, may be less appropriate in those relatively rare situations in human service organizations where we must make the same decision again and again. In such a situation, we may know from experience what will work and what will not work. Overall though, contingency approaches to thinking about management have much to say to the social work manager. Their basic concepts are woven throughout much of the content of the chapters that follow.

Participative Management

Another identifiable approach to management is based heavily on the application of the democratic process. While there are certain techniques associated with participative management,[9] it is probably better understood as an application of a manager's belief that human beings are more productive, more loyal, and are more trustworthy if they are granted a role in decision making in areas that affect them and their jobs. Participative management is believed to promote consensus between individual goals and the goals of the organization. It is also believed that it is easier to promote a desirable "team" atmosphere by requiring groups rather than individuals to examine issues and make decisions. Organizations that employ participative management methods often use labels such as "Quality Assurance Team" or "Executive Management Team" for their decision-making groups.

A prerequisite for participation in group decision making is that individuals must have knowledge, experience, and/or expertise that they can contribute to a decision. If not, they should not be involved. Consequently, the degree of involvement of employees in management decision making will vary, depending on the decision to be made or the problem to be addressed. Even the type of involvement will vary—an employee's role may be simply to share a perspective in regard to one decision but may include a vote in another. However, certain areas of decision making are generally off-limits to all employees not specifically charged with their responsibility (for example, expenditure of funds in another organizational unit; evaluation of individual staff competence).

The inclusion of staff members (not normally involved in certain decision making) into the decision making process can do wonders for morale, it is argued. This approach is based on certain assumptions about human beings—for example, that they are more likely to support a decision when they have been involved in the decision making. It does not work when staff members perceive their involvement as merely "token" or little more than a manipulative attempt to co-opt them by acting out a charade by pretending to care what they think or pretending to want their input. Participative management theorists insist that employee involvement in decision making should be genuine, based upon strongly held beliefs about the higher nature of people.

Most of the criticisms of participative management are based on observation of its misuse or overuse and the consequences that have ensued. An additional criterion for its successful use often is overlooked. Knowledge, experience, and/or expertise may not be enough to include a person in decision making. The individual should also express an interest in being part of the decision making and its outcome. The concept of "zone of indifference"[10] is relevant here. It is based on the assumption that we all have many areas of our life where we really do not have much investment in a decision one way or the other. The decision is within our zone of indifference. In such situations, we would rather that someone just go ahead and make the decision for us. For example, some students may have a strong preference regarding whether a course requires a term paper or an examination. They might appreciate input into the decision of which will be required. But for others, the decision is within their zone of indifference. They would really rather the professor just tell them what the course requirement is so they can use their time and energies preparing to meet it.

Critics of participative management note that many managers who employ it underestimate the scope of their employees' zone of indifference. The manager may inappropriately tend to ask for a vote on decisions where staff just do not care about the decision. For example, they might ask employees to debate and vote on whether monthly or weekly calendars should be ordered or the color of new office carpet that should be ordered. In some cases, where individual preferences of just a few employees may be especially strong, it is their individual wishes, not the preferences of the entire work group, that should be sought. A vote of the entire group is neither desirable nor necessary and time spent in trying to achieve it is likely to be resented.

Participative management is also misused in situations where other influences of which the manager is aware—for example, some political necessity—limit the decision that can realistically be made. If a certain decision must be made anyway, why involve others in it? The manager might be fortunate and staff might arrive at the inevitable decision. Successful co-opting will have occurred. But they might also vote for another alternative. They may then become angry, frustrated, and resentful of the time that was wasted when, ultimately, their decision was not implemented. There response may be, "Why did you ask us if you knew what you had to do in the first place?" Correctly applied, participative management is used only in those situations where any reasonable group recommendations can at least be seriously considered and, ideally, implemented.

Another criticism often leveled against participative management methods is that they tend to confuse (some would say corrupt) the role of the manager. If used to excess, group decision making can make a manager feel and be perceived like more of a chairperson than a leader. Managers might even be perceived as abdicating their leadership responsibilities. Most importantly, their ability to possess the required respect to make necessary but unpopular decisions may be weakened by too much participative management. The question is, "What is too much?" There is no easy answer to this question. However, when participative management approaches begin to be viewed as more a burden than a blessing by managers and/or their co-workers, a manager should consider if it is not time to cut back on unnecessary collaboration. However, this too can cause problems. It is easier to grant input into decision making than it is to take it away. Staff may secretly welcome the opportunity to avoid participating in decisions that are within their zone of indifference or are otherwise burdensome. But they still may express some concern that the manager is making more unilateral decisions.

Participative management can create an environment of uncertainty that can interfere with morale and productivity. When a manager takes major responsibility for decision making, decisions tend to follow a pattern based on the manager's priorities, values, style, etc. Staff can learn to predict the behavior of the manager. This affords fairly good certainty for them; they know what to expect in most situations. But if a decision is delegated to a work group, many different and unpredictable results can occur. This can produce anxiety among staff.

Politics, friendships, hidden agenda, power groups, and other dynamics and forces that operate within groups can produce some surprising decisions. These dynamics and forces can sometimes even take priority over organization needs or client services. The result is that employees and even clients are sometimes subject to decisions that may be based more on, for example, loyalties to others in the group than on what is rational or sound or even the will of the majority. The group process sometimes precludes irrational decision making; sometimes it promotes it.

Participative management methods can be very appealing to the social worker as manager. It sets aside the organizational hierarchy to tap the best available knowledge for decision making and problem solving. Knowledge and experience are widely distributed in most human service organizations. The greatest knowledge in an area (for example, a particular intervention technique or computer technology) is as likely or even more likely to be found with a newer, lower-ranking employee than with a higher-level administrator. Some of those people may have gained knowledge during prior employment elsewhere. They may feel insulted and constrained when their input is not sought in areas where they have knowledge and expertise. Their involvement in decision making and problem solving can help to create a greater climate of mutual respect within human service organizations.

A note of warning is in order. Many social work managers state that their philosophy of management is participatory. (It is difficult in our democratic society to be opposed to it.) But a much smaller percentage actually practice it. Some may try it initially and then retreat from it when they find themselves having to live with decisions that they find difficult to implement or enforce or when their authority or control begins to feel threatened.

A statement of a belief in participatory management has been known to get managers hired. Search committees usually are pleased to hear it. But within a short time after the manager is hired, all traces of participation in decision making may have vanished (along with the "open-door policy"). When this happens, staff often feel angry and betrayed. They might feel less resentment if assurances of regular employee input into decision making had never been made in the first place.

The same three variables that are so important in other management decisions—the manager, the other people involved (staff), and the situation—need to be considered before deciding to implement a policy of participatory management. Participative management can work, but only in certain situations involving certain staff and certain managers. For example, there are some managers who should never attempt it (they have too strong a need for control). Others, for whom it is just a logical extension of their style and personality, use it with great success. Some staff, for whatever reasons, cannot be trusted to make good decisions; others do an extremely conscientious and competent job when asked for their input. Some situations may not allow for the time needed for group decision making; others are well-suited to it. If a manager does decide to give participative management a try, it is probably a good idea to do it in an incremental way, that is, a little at a time, stopping periodically to evaluate how it is working before going further.

Variations on Participative Management

Ironically, approaches to management that emphasized wide worker participation in decision making initially were not well accepted in the United States. They were given a second look and more careful consideration in the 1970s and 1980s, largely because of their successful application in Japan. The so-called Japanese management, Theory Z, and other related concepts are applications of participative management ideas originally developed in the United States, where they had met with a lukewarm reception by North American industry. But financial success has a way of getting the attention of the for-profit sector.

The effectiveness of Japanese management techniques was seen most dramatically in the success of the Japanese automobile industry. During the past several decades, U.S. car sales have been drastically hurt by the import of Japanese automobiles. Import quotas were set and heavy import taxes were levied to limit foreign car sales and to drive foreign car prices up to a point where U.S. cars would be able to compete. It soon became apparent that North American car buyers really preferred Japanese cars largely because they perceived them to be better made. There were fewer flaws and defects. Quality control was better; Japanese workers seemed to care more about the quality of the product they produced. They did not, for example, deliberately drop bolts into inaccessible door panels to annoy future car owners as U.S. workers were known to do or allow cars to leave assembly lines with known mechanical defects. Such behavior was unheard of among Japanese workers who viewed their job as a career, had considerable input into decision making that affected production, received rewards and extensive fringe benefits tied to the quality of their work, and generally took pride in their association with their employer. The 1980s and 1990s were years of experimentation with the application of Japanese management techniques within U.S. industry and, to a lesser degree, within human service organizations. At this point, the verdict is not yet in on the effectiveness of these new-old methods when applied to North American workers.

Quality Circles. Probably the best-known of the Japanese management methods is the use of quality circles (known as quality control circles when they were first discussed earlier in the United States).[11] As a means of solving problems, these methods have been credited with helping to change the meaning of "Made in Japan" from a connotation of shoddy product quality in the 1950s to one of high quality in later years. A quality circle is a voluntary group led by a supervisor and consisting of fewer than 15 (seven or eight is ideal) workers. The group might meet one hour per week at a regular time (during regular work hours) to discuss problems that have been identified. Circle leaders are trained in step-by-step problem-solving methods. The circle members discuss possible solutions to the problem and decide on the best one. If it can be immediately implemented, it will be. If it can not be implemented without higher-level approval, a presentation to sell it to the next level is developed. The emphasis is on developing solutions to problems, not simply complaining about them. In turn, higher-level management assumes a position of receptiveness to ideas and to solutions that are proposed.

Problems for quality-circle work must be production-related (work flow, product defects, etc.). Such areas as salary, promotions, grievances, personalities, or anything outside of the group's work responsibilities are not discussed. The group leader (supervisor) must be a good facilitator. The leader must be comfortable in stepping out of and back into an authoritarian role. Leaders must be able to create a group climate of trust where even "half-baked" ideas can be proposed by the most timid of members without fear of ridicule or reprisal. Leaders must be able to give recognition to the group for solutions that work while not blaming group members for solutions that do not work. Clearly, quality circles require the type of manager, staff, and work situation also conducive to other forms of participative management. The social worker as manager needs to know about the use of quality circles and to be sensitive to the presence of situations where they can be appropriately and productively employed.

Total Quality Management (TQM).   One approach to management with origins in participatory management has been implemented in a sizable number of human service organizations. It is referred to as Total Quality Management (TQM) or some similar term (e.g., Continuous Quality Improvement or Total Quality Control). TQM and its variations owe much of their theoretical underpinnings to the work of W. E. Deming.[11] His fourteen principles, while clearly designed for the business and manufacturing sector, recently have been adapted to a wide variety of human service organizations.

TQM is largely a response to the shortcomings of an earlier management model called Quality Assurance (QA). QA focuses on outcome measures, that is, indicators of service effectiveness in organizations like hospitals and public welfare or mental health centers. It is characterized by case audits and the evaluation of staff's clinical activities. While there is nothing essentially wrong with emphasizing the clinical effectiveness of social workers and other professionals, QA offers little help in understanding all of those other activities that occur within human service organizations and which contribute to overall goal achievement. Therefore, it was criticized for its narrowness of focus.

Besides its greater attention to all of the activities of an organization, TQM differs from Quality Assurance in a number of other important ways. Consistent with the general principles of participative management, TQM is initiated by the leadership within the organization, not imposed by outside authorities or funding organizations as QA often is. It also employs a more equal distribution of power for decision making than does QA. The customer (client in our work settings) plays an important role. A basic premise of TQM is that quality of products (services in human service organizations) should be defined by the needs and wishes of the customers (clients). Heavy emphasis is placed on knowing what they need and want. TQM entails knowing who clients are, being able to anticipate their needs, translating needs into services that are responsible to them, and designing a system that efficiently delivers needed services.

TQM is based on several basic assumptions or tenets. There is the belief that what constitutes quality is dynamic, never fixed. It is also determined to a great extent by the process used to produce it. Quality thus requires a total organizational commitment, from the chief executive to the lowest ranking member of the organization's staff.

TQM emphasizes continuous improvement and the elimination of defects within an organization and its activities. While (like QA) it acknowledges the importance of service outcome measurements, it really focuses most heavily on the process of service delivery. In doing this, TQM relies on graphs and statistical analysis to monitor activities and to provide accurate data for decision making. Use of control charts, flow charts, bar graphs, pareto charts, histograms, fishbone diagrams, run (trend) charts, and scattergrams is common. At the same time, such common attributes of organizations as numerical quotas, slogans, and targets are eliminated. There is an effort to remove anything perceived as a barrier to staff's pride in their work itself.

TQM has been described as "holistic." Ersoz has identified seven elements that all must be present for an organization to function effectively as a system. She notes that if any of the elements (organizational philosophy, vision, strategy, skilled personnel, resources, reward system, or organizational structure) are absent, the system will be jeopardized in predictable ways.[12]

It should not surprise us that TQM has received an enthusiastic response from many social workers in their roles as managers. Like other management models that have elements of participative management, it has a democratic flavor that is consistent with our professional value system. It is very consistent with both "client-centered treatment" and the practice principle of "beginning where the client is." It also involves a problem-solving process which is systems-oriented. It is designed to empower staff at all levels of an organization, as well as its clients.

Summary

This chapter has presented an overview of management theory that has influenced the behaviors of managers during the late nineteenth and the twentieth centuries. By understanding the principles and ideas that have been and continue to be influential, we have gained a perspective on how we have arrived at some of the current ideas presented in this and other management books.

Each of the respective theories has left a rich legacy. To some degree, all continue to affect how managers think, how they perceive situations and people, and why they respond to situations in the ways they do. All the theories that we examined had a compelling logic for the times in which they were developed. None are totally obsolete or have nothing to offer us. The classical theories may have been based on a different perception of human beings and their motivation, but they increased objectivity within organizations, suggested some still-useful management principles, and proposed many ways to increase worker productivity. Later theories offered better insight into social and psychological influences on behavior while stressing the limits of what a manager can know and process in order to make decisions. We have not finished with any of the theories examined in this chapter. Their influence will be seen again and again in the chapters that follow.

Endnotes

1. Taylor, F. W. "The Principle of Scientific Management" in *Classics of Organizational Theory,* 2nd ed., J. Shafrity and J. Ott, eds. (Chicago, Dorsey Press, 1987), p. 75.

2. David Whitsett and Lyle Yorks, *From Management Theory to Business Sense: The Myths and Realities of People at Work* (New York: American Management Association, 1983), pp. 221–241.

3. Ibid., pp. 221–241.

4. Ibid., p. 223.

5. Daniel Wren, *The Evolution of Management Thought* (New York: Ronald Press, 1972), p. 218; Claude George, *The History of Management Thought* (Englewood Cliffs, NJ: Prentice-Hall, 1972), p. 113.

6. Herbert Simon, *Administrative Behavior* (New York: Macmillan, 1976), pp. 20–44.

7. Ibid.

8. Lewis Coser, *Functions of Social Conflict* (New York: Free Press, 1956), pp. 151–157.

9. Alfred Marrow, *The Failure of Success* (New

York: American Management Association, Inc., 1972), pp. 83–102.

10. Chester Barnard, *The Functions of the Executive* (Cambridge, MA: Harvard University Press, 1938), p. 167.

11. Walton, M. *Deming Management at Work* (New York: Perigee Books, 1990).

12. Ersoz, C. J. "TQM: Health Care's Roadmap to the 21st Century," paper presented at the New Paradigms in Health Care Conference, Erie, PA, 1992.

Part II

The Functions of Management

In Chapters 4 through 10 we will examine those functions (planning, staffing, organizing, controlling, and leading) that comprise the majority of the work of the manager. It is helpful to envision them as ways to positively influence the activities that go on within organizations and in their environments. They are designed to increase the likelihood of organizational goal attainment and, thus, the delivery of effective services.

We will devote more discussion (Chapters 5 through 7) to the function of staffing than to any other management function. While all of management requires "people skills," staffing activities like hiring and deploying a diverse staff, enhancing their professional development, evaluating their work performance, making personnel decisions, or identifying and using individual and group motivation afford social workers an opportunity to directly apply their knowledge of human behavior. Therefore, on the surface, tasks related to staffing should be "second nature" for social workers. Yet, paradoxically, social workers often find staffing tasks to be among the most stressful. We will examine why this occurs and what can be done to make the staffing function of management easier.

The functions of management overlap somewhat. When we get to controlling (Chapter 9) and leading (Chapter 10), we will be taking a second look at some management tools that we discussed earlier in the context of other functions of the manager. This "overlap" is consistent with the role of manager. Sometimes we use the same behavior or activity to perform two or more management functions simultaneously. It should be remembered that the five functions are just ways of trying to help us to conceptualize the complex work of the manager by breaking it down into smaller parts. The break is not always a clean one. If we think of management as influencing, it is understandable that we often find ourselves trying to influence the best way we can and worrying later (if at all) which management function or functions we were actually performing.

4

Influencing by Planning

Within organizations, planning is critical to the creation and maintenance of an organizational climate in which staff will want to work and will devote most of their activities to the work of the organization. There should be nothing mysterious about planning. It involves the use of some very natural and familiar structures and activities. We use them every day in both our personal and our professional lives.

Planning requires both an understanding of past events and the capacity to envision the future. In order to plan successfully, the social worker as manager must be able to learn from past mistakes. Lessons learned are a valuable asset for future planning and for avoiding a repetition of mistakes.

In many ways, good planning is more a "people" skill than a technical skill. It involves a careful matching of plans to the needs of situations, but also to the personalities of managers and their subordinates and co-workers. Thus planning requires a good understanding of people and their needs. It also requires a high level of self-awareness.

What Is Planning?

Planning is nothing more than taking action to influence future events. When we talk about the planning functions of social work managers, we are talking about those structures and activities that are used to help shape what will happen in the future within an organization. Plans are designed to take us from where we are today to where we hope to be tomorrow, and to avoid costly detours along the way.

Planning is necessary because managers cannot afford to leave too much to chance. A human service organization manager cannot, for example, assume that a general commitment to quality client services on the part of staff will necessarily result in goal attainment. In fact, experience tells us that activities tend to get sidetracked within organizations unless someone puts into place certain vehicles designed to keep them on track. In the process of planning, managers use a variety of activities and structures that are designed to increase the likelihood that the organization and its staff will move in an orderly, unified way. Plans help to coordinate an organization's activities and to help them to remain focused on goal attainment.

We have deliberately not used the word control in describing planning. Yet planning and control (a function of the manager described in more detail in Chapter 9) are very closely related. In fact, some types of plans that we describe in this chapter (for example, policies and budgets) are also included in later discussions as methods of control. Chronology is important in understanding the relationship between planning and controlling as management functions. Planning is decidedly future-oriented. It has been described as "selecting from among alternative future courses of action."[1] It is also defined as "a rational approach to pre-selected objectives."[2] Among other things, it entails deciding in advance just what needs to be done, what are the best ways and times to do it, and who is the best choice to do it. Planning attempts to structure individual and group activities in such a way that they are both productive and supportive of each other.

In contrast, control (Chapter 9) is more present-oriented. It is designed to enforce the standards that have been set by planning and, therefore, is best accomplished when appropriate plans are already in place. But planning does not end when control begins. Planning is a continuous process; it requires ongoing monitoring and revision as needs and conditions change.

It requires both human and material resources to create plans and to put them into effect. Like other management functions, planning *should* generate a surplus, that is, it should contribute more to improved client services than it takes away from them. It should thus be worth the effort and cost involved. For example, good planning can make a positive contribution to the organizational climate by fostering such desirable environmental conditions as teamwork, confidence, certainty, or trust, factors that all help positively affect staff morale. In turn, improved morale can positively affect the services offered to clients. Unfortunately, planning can also produce negative results. Like any other management function, it can be inefficient, that is, it can result in a net loss to clients if not performed well. For example, over-planning or planning that focuses on trivia[3] can be destructive of teamwork, confidence, certainty, or trust, and thus of morale. And, if staff morale is low, staff may waste more time in nonproductive activities on the job, call in sick more frequently, or even quit their jobs, necessitating costly retraining of new workers. Thus planning might actually decrease the likelihood of good service delivery within the organization.

The Planning Menu

Within human service organizations, there exists a considerable amount of misunderstanding about exactly what is meant by the terms used to describe different types of plans. We all use them, but all too frequently we may have something quite different in mind than does a colleague who uses the same term. And, that can cause serious problems. In the discussion that follows we will use terminology that is applied fairly consistently in the business literature and less consistently within human service organizations.

We will discuss nine major types of plans. They are: missions, goals, objectives, strategies, policies, rules, procedures, programs, and budgets. Each takes on a rather distinctive character when applied to human service organizations. Figure 4.1 provides a summary definition of each. The discussion that follows expands on these definitions and suggests the most appropriate use for each type of plan.

FIGURE 4.1   *The Planning Menu*

1. Missions—statements of why the organization or its subunit exists and what it does. They should be legitimized by the task environment.
2. Goals—broad statements of what an organization or program hopes to accomplish.
3. Objectives—specification of the accomplishments that will signify that goals have been achieved; operationalization of goals.
4. Strategies—specific plans of action designed to achieve goals. They involve deployment of resources.
5. Policies—general statements or understandings that are designed to guide or channel thinking, decision-making, and behavior. Policies may be written, but often they are not.
6. Rules—specific requirements that are designed to standardize behavior and decision making and to eliminate the use of judgment and discretion.
7. Procedures—structure provided to influence the nature and (especially) the chronology of events.
8. Programs—packages of goals, policies, rules, procedures, and (sometimes) strategies assembled in a unique manner to facilitate the achievement of a goal or objective.
9. Budgets—projections of future income and expenditures expressed in dollars and cents.

Missions

The *mission* of an organization represents the broadest type of plan. Social work managers may not be involved in formulating the mission of an organization; they inherit it when they take a job within the organization. An organization's mission may be referenced when some other plan (for example, a new goal or program) is being considered. Then there may be discussion of whether or not the new plan is consistent with the organization's mission. An organization thus may be either supported or restrained from moving into an area of service or from serving a new client group by reference to its mission.

The necessity for societal legitimization of a mission is important in understanding how a mission affects all other plans within human service organizations. Unless a society sees a mission as desirable and appropriate for that organization and thus legitimizes it, the organization will fight a never-ending battle with its task environment. That is why mission statements are often stated in such a way that hardly anyone within the task environment would wish to disagree with them.

It is important to understand the difference between a mission and a mandate. A *mandate* is what the organization is required to do because of ethical constraints, accreditation requirements, even laws. Mandates also can be gleaned from the informal communication received from members of the organization's task environment. In contrast, a mission is what the organization *wants* to do and, hopefully, what its task environment has legitimized it to do.

Many organizations have composed idealistic phrases, for example, "every child adoptable" or "building healthy families" which may appear on the organization's stationary and/or logo. While these may provide some general indication of an organization's mission, a mission statement can and should do much more. It should provide legitimization for all activities within the organization.

A mission statement should be relatively concise and matter-of-fact, yet thoughtful. It should describe the social problem that the organization seeks to address, what its leaders believe to be the cause of the problem, and the organization's response to the problem. Thus, it indirectly suggests the values and intervention philosophies of the organization's staff, the "organizational culture," and the activities that are appropriate for people within the organization.

The process of clarifying and stating the mission of an organization is a very valuable exercise. It establishes the organization's niche in the human services community—the "claim" it stakes out for itself. It identifies what is unique about the organization, any competitive advantages that it might have, and how it proposes to relate to other organizations. It also identifies the critical elements of the organization's task environment (its stakeholders) and, if different from those of its staff, how they define the problem and think it should be addressed. This informs people within the organization as to what kind of relationship with the task environment can be anticipated, that is, how much tension and hostility is likely to be encountered.

Mission statements are not designed to inspire staff or to get them to engage in heroic and unselfish acts, just to clarify what they do and keep them on focus. Inspiration, if it is present, is more likely to come from a *vision statement,* which is designed to be an inspiring, attractive glimpse into the future. It goes beyond what people in the organization do, focusing instead on where the organization hopes to be some day.

Goals

Organizationwide goals are the outcome toward which activities of persons in an organization are (or should be) aimed. Examples of organizational goals might be, "to provide meaningful daytime programs for the frail elderly" or "to increase services to people of color"). Either statement represents an end to which other management activities (for example, organizing, staffing, controlling, leading) might appropriately be directed. Thus, any management decision should be able to be evaluated with reference to organizational goals. We might ask, "Will the decision produce results that will enhance the likelihood of goal attainment?" or "Will it contribute to their attainment more than other decisions might?" While this is an unrealistic approach to all of a manager's decision making, it demonstrates the ways in which goals can shape a variety of management activity.

Goals are not meant to be written in stone. As conditions and needs change, they should change with them. Social workers employed at all levels can have input into planful (usually incremental) goal changes.

Sometimes there may be a rather dramatic shift in an organization's goals. It can occur when an organization is especially successful in its goal achievement. This desirable phenomenon, which involves a conscious abandonment of one goal and its replacement with another, is called goal succession (as opposed to goal displacement, discussed in Chapter 3, which is an undesirable and inadvertent goal shift). Unfortunately, goal succession is a relatively rare phenomenon in human service organizations, where our goals often are only theoretically attainable. But it does occur. In the 1940s and 1950s, the March of Dimes had as its goal the finding of a cure or method of prevention for poliomyelitis ("polio"). The development of an effective vaccine all but eliminated new cases of the disease; the goal of the organization was essentially accomplished. Stripped of a viable goal, the March of Dimes had to choose between going out of existence or finding a new goal. As we know, it chose the latter, and now the organization is devoted to the goal of elimination of birth detects. The new goal is sufficiently like the old one that it seems natural and appropriate for this organization, which has always stressed fundraising for research, to enhance the health of children. But, given the current state of genetic knowledge, it is not likely to be attained in the foreseeable future. The shift in goals at the March of Dimes meant that an effective, well-managed organization was kept in place and remained viable. Of course, the shift in goals also necessitated major changes in other types of plans and in other managerial functions aimed at attainment of the new goal.

A less favorable organizational goal switch, *goal abandonment,* can occur if an organization has to admit defeat, that it has no hope of goal achievement. Usually this will occur because of some outside factor such as the total elimination of funding available to support the achievement of the goal. Another goal may be substituted if, for example, grant funding becomes available to support attainment of some other, equally desirable goal.

Objectives

Objectives make it possible to determine to what degree goals have been accomplished. They often include time deadlines for their accomplishment. Examples of objectives that might correspond to the goals in the previous discussion might be "to design and implement by the end of the current year a program of music and art activities for people who attend the adult day care center program" or "to increase the number of people of color served by the organization by 25 percent within the next 18 months."

Objectives are used by managers at all levels, not just by those planning for the total organization. They are formulated by employees who work primarily in direct services to clients, by supervisors, and by work groups and units of all sizes and varieties. A well-known method of integrating the activities of all persons within an organization is known as Management by Objectives (MBO).[4] This method relies heavily on planning by objective-setting at all levels and has been employed within human service organizations with mixed results. MBO is characterized by written objectives (referred to as targets) for each employee. Targets are supposed to be measurable; they should also be realistic, but challenging. They contain statements of how and when something is to be done. There is ongoing assessment of progress toward achievement of objectives. Targets are supposed to be negotiated, not assigned, by supervisors.

With MBO, integration of objectives within the organization is accomplished by selecting targets for individual staff that, if accomplished, will provide the means whereby the individual at the next higher level (the supervisor) will be able to accomplish objectives. Actually, the target-setting begins at the top levels. Each successive supervisor (moving down the hierarchy) works with those below to set targets that will assist in the achievement of objectives. In theory, at least, it makes for a tight organization in which goal displacement is not as likely to occur. It is also very useful for building more objectivity into the manager's task of employee evaluation; evaluation is based almost exclusively on an assessment of the attainment of each individual's negotiated objectives.

MBO, when used effectively, illustrates just how useful objectives can be in performing the task of planning. They can be a powerful influence in shaping the course of activities in a human service organization as they occur at all levels. A primary task of the social worker as manager is to remind others of objectives in a subtle and sometimes not-so-subtle way. Like all plans, their mere presence alone does not guarantee productive activity. Ideally, objectives of individuals and work groups are consistent with and contribute to the achievement of the objectives of the organization (at least that's what many of the classical management theorists believed). In the real world this is not always the case. Then social workers as managers need to do what they can to move organizational objectives and individual and group objectives closer to congruence. This is done through a combination of emphasis, restatement, and reminder of objectives and of what each person should be doing to contribute to their achievement.

A well-functioning organization requires a clearly stated mission and carefully articulated goals and objectives. Yet this is not always the case. Sometimes social workers find themselves in an organization that seems to have just developed from its grassroots beginnings, addressing human needs as they have emerged and pursuing available funding. Evaluation of the agency and its programs is virtually impossible, since one cannot determine if objectives are being met if there are no well-articulated objectives. Then, an important task of managers is evaluability assessment,[5] a process whereby the mission, goals, and objectives of the organization are identified and specified using an inductive process. It entails describing clients being served, identifying and specifying the services that they are receiving, and also identifying and specifying what other "maintenance" (that is, non-service) activities characterize the organization. These descriptions then are used to create the previously unwritten mission statement, goals, and objectives of the organization and its programs. Since some activities clearly will not be consistent with these plans, they are modified or deleted.

Strategies

The word *strategies* seems to imply a kind of purely intellectual type of plan. We tend to think of chessboards and complex cognitive exercises. The word also has certain military connotations. We have images of generals surrounding a topographical map, deciding how, when, and where to deploy their infantry, armor, artillery, and air power to defeat the enemy. The image is not totally inaccurate in describing strategies as a type of plan employed by the social worker as manager. What are the elements in a military strategy? A general plan of action is developed. It entails a carefully integrated deployment of resources (always limited), committed in such a way as to attempt to defeat an opponent.

Do human service organizations really do this? Yes. Do we really have enemies or opponents? Yes. They may be within the organization, outside of it, or anywhere within the organization's task environment. Our opponent might be, for example, public ignorance of sexually transmitted diseases, community apathy about child abuse, community resistance to a group home for people with chronic psychiatric problems, political intervention in the agency's budget allocations, inefficient use of professional staff, or employee burnout. For large government programs the opponent might be a little more general, like institutional ageism, racism, or sexism, inferior housing, overcrowded prisons, or even poverty within a nation of wealth. When we identify an opponent, resources available to do battle with it are always limited. We must hold some back, set priorities, and select and carefully expend those that we believe will do the most damage to the enemy. We develop plans to do this; they are our strategies. We might, for example, develop a strategy to improve our poor public image as an agency with the local press. It might involve a coordinated plan of expenditure of our version of troops, tanks, and artillery. There could be staff time devoted to public speaking or part of our printing budget could be used to develop a public relations brochure. We might commit time to review carefully a case record of a relative or friend of the local newspaper publisher that might help us to better understand why the paper is so hostile toward the agency. Whatever the strategy, it would involve the careful exploration of options and costs and the coordinated use of resources prior to committing them.

Strategies seem especially appropriate when designed to attain an objective that involves the elimination or reduction of an existing problem (enemy). But they can also be used to plan in situations where there is no identified opponent currently present. A social work supervisor could, for example, develop a strategy aimed at maintaining professional staff members' interest in expanding their direct treatment skills. It might involve the use of tangible and intangible rewards for participation in continuing education, granting of release time, use of case staffings in staff meetings, and other resource commitments that would reinforce positive attitudes toward ongoing learning. Another manager might develop a strategy to prevent loss of senior professional staff to some other organization. The strategy might involve development of enhanced employee fringe benefits, a new system of awards and recognition or a profit-sharing plan. In either example, the strategy is designed to prevent an "enemy" from ever gaining a foothold. While human service organizations may sometimes lack the obvious opponents of the corporate sector (competitors), real and potential enemies abound everywhere. A manager who identifies enemies can use strategies as plans to defeat them.

Strategies are more than just *tactics,* which tend to be less comprehensive, more short-term, and more reactive than strategies. Strategies can be a creative use of a social worker's interpersonal skills. They often entail networking and dialogue with key players within the task environment. They also frequently employ a certain amount of deception and the presence of hidden agenda. This does not mean, however, that "anything goes" when strategies are used. A strategy must be legal and consistent with our professional code of ethics. It also must be morally defensible. In order to be successful in, for example, improving the organization's relationship with its task environment, it should also be politically acceptable to all parties concerned. Of course, it should also be workable, that is, there should be no logistical obstacle to its being employed.

Strategies, like the other types of plans that we are discussing, are no stranger to the social worker. In our personal lives, we might develop a strategy to obtain a graduate degree or even to get the attention of another person to whom we are attracted. Professionally, we might develop strategies to promote family involvement in treatment of our clients through deployment of resources (transportation, telephone calls, etc.) to assist relatives to be able to participate in treatment sessions. We might develop social-action strategies to reduce exploitive rent rates charged to members of a community. Somewhere, perhaps because of their military associations, strategies have gotten a bad name in social work practice. They are sometimes seen as manipulative, deceptive or "sneaky." But they should be thought of as just another of the useful planning tools of a manager. Strategies can increase the likelihood that clients can be better served.

Policies

Probably the most frequently misunderstood plan is a policy. Most of the confusion centers around how a policy differs from a rule, the type of plan that we shall examine next. As Figure 4.1 stated, policies are "general statements or understandings which guide or channel thinking and action in decision making."[6] To understand policies we will need to look at the full meaning of several words in this definition.

The word *general* suggests that policies are not meant to give specific instruction as to what a staff member is to do or not do in a given situation. Rather, policies set broad guidelines for decision making. Policies are used for situations where the specific unique nature of a situation cannot be anticipated. An organization may, for example, have a policy against promotion from within (hiring a current staff member as a high-level administrator when a vacancy arises). If the choice of a policy (rather than a rule) to address this issue—which is related to some future need for decision making—was a conscious, deliberate one (as it should be), we can infer something about the intentions of the manager who made the policy. The manager wanted others to know about a strong preference that exists in the agency. But being unable to anticipate all future hiring decisions relating to higher-level administrators and the variables involved in each, the manager deliberately left open the possibility that there might be some rare instances when hiring from outside might not be the best decision. The manager did not want to tie the hands of some future manager and force that person to make a decision that would *not* be in the best interest of the organization and the clients it serves. Thus, policies must be general. They are broad enough to cover most situations, even those that have never occurred before and may never occur again.

The phrase "statements or understandings" in the definition of policies suggests the variety of ways in which policies are communicated. Policies can be written and assembled into a single document. (In fact, the "Policy Manual" in many organizations contains more of other types of plans—usually rules and procedures—than it does policies.) Memos are another common written way of communicating a policy from a boss to a subordinate. Policies are also found in job descriptions or in motions passed within business meetings and recorded in their minutes. Certain words usually are a tip-off that a policy has been formulated. When we see "generally," "expected," "should," or some other word that is designed to communicate the normal expectation, a policy probably has been intended.

Policies are also communicated verbally in both formal and informal ways. Orientation sessions contain many policies. Other policies are communicated by supervisors or administrators in staff meetings. Others are learned through verbal communication that occurs in the coffee room, over lunch, or in myriad other informal ways. They can come from persons on the same level, from above, or even (less frequently) from below.

Many policies are simply implied by the actions of others, usually superiors. Certain patterns of behavior and decision making are observed consciously or even unconsciously over time and are perceived as policies. Managers' preferences or philosophies are gleaned from their behavior and copied by other staff, further solidifying a policy. The dangers of this type of policy communication should be apparent. Managers who do not want their behavior copied need to be abundantly clear that they are not implying a policy. There are situations where the behavior of a manager and the kind of decisions made are right for the manager, but not for other staff. Unless this is communicated, overly zealous staff members may perceive a policy, act on it, and respond with resentment if later criticized for their actions.

The phrase "guide or channel thinking and action in decision making" in the definition of a policy is especially important. Policies are an effort to shape the way others think and act. They attempt to use the valuable experience of the past by communicating to the less experienced employee what has usually been the right decision in the past and, therefore, is likely to be the right one in the future. Even more than that, employees are expected to make a certain decision or think and act in a certain way most of the time. Implicit in this is the idea that a decision that is not consistent with policy may require justification.

Policies are meant to constrain (and they can become frustrating). But they are also meant to help workers, facilitating certain types of decision making and freeing us up to use our energies in other areas. Policies have been equated with social roles and, more specifically, with role expectations. They perform similar functions. Social roles make moving into a new situation easier; so do policies. Both tell us what is generally acceptable practice in a situation and when our behavior could get us into trouble. Similar to role expectations, policies are sometimes not even noticed until they are violated. For example, we may be unaware that a greeting to fellow students whom we pass on the sidewalk is an expectation of our role of student or friend until some person goes by without speaking. Then we start asking how we might have offended that person. Similarly, we may be unaware that there is a policy that support staff are not invited to staff holiday parties until we invite one and observe the discomfort and consternation of the other professional staff. Both role expectations and policies can save us time, effort, mistakes, and embarrassment.

Policies are made by individual managers at all levels. Particularly in those organizations where participative management principles are employed, policies also are made by work groups based on the democratic process and by the principle that "the majority rules."

Policies are designed so that they contain some flexibility. It is assumed that there will be exceptions made to policies in some situations. In fact, people are *expected* to make exceptions to policies if the conditions warrant them.

Some managers mistakenly insist that a policy is no longer a policy once an exception is made. They may base this on the realities of our current age of litigation in which, even the perception of a double standard my be grounds for a lawsuit. The thinking goes, "if I make an exception in one situation, it may be impossible to use the policy to deny making an exception in another." But the situations are almost always different—that is why a policy (and not a rule) was developed in the first place! While the manager must be concerned with equitable treatment of staff and clients, this in no way means that an exception to a policy causes the policy to cease to exist. On the contrary, many good policies have been refined over the years to the point that not only the general policy but also the likely situations in which exceptions should be made are now communicated to staff. The exceptions have further refined and clarified the policy, but they have not erased it.

Is there a point where the number or percentage of exceptions to a policy becomes so great that the policy no longer exists? Probably. Just where that point is (10 percent? 20 percent? 30 percent?) is a matter of judgment for the manager. It is probably safe to say that when a policy is no longer a helpful shortcut to decision making for employees and when it begins to require too much thought to be able to consider all desirable exceptions before implementing it, its effectiveness as a plan disappears. It is time to consider substituting a new, perhaps, a broader policy or to acknowledge that no policy can be written that would adequately address the needs of the situation.

Policies are especially popular in human service organizations, and for good reason. They are flexible. Because they are designed to allow and even to encourage exceptions, they leave room for the exercise of professional discretion in decision making. Given the knowledge and education level of most human service professionals and the many unique situations in which they find themselves, policies can be very useful. There are many gray areas of decision making in social work practice in which there is no decision that is right 100 percent of the time. Then, policies are helpful. They tell us what will usually be the right decision or course of action, but allow for exceptions. They allow us to consider, for example, individual client welfare, professional values, political, ethical, economic and morale issues, and to employ common sense.

Let us look at a few policies often seen in human service organizations. In micropractice organizations that offer direct counseling or therapy to individuals, families, or groups, a common policy relates to accepting gifts from clients. It might be fairly precise, such as: "Social workers should not accept a gift from a client that is of any significant monetary value." This policy is stated in such a way that it makes it clear that gifts from clients are generally discouraged (employees are certainly not expected to solicit them), but that (as with all policies) some exceptions are permitted and even expected. It communicates the criterion to be applied in most cases for determining if a gift should be accepted—that is, "significant monetary value." But as a policy (not a rule) it implies that rare exceptions may be made, at the discretion of the social worker. The word "significant" in the policy statement is deliberately vague. To anyone but a statistician it is open to a (limited) range of interpretations. To a staff member, it probably suggests something in the $5 or $10 range, or even less. The term "significant," while usefully vague, clearly conveys the message that employees should not subsidize their income through receipt of gifts from clients.

The use of a policy with its implied potential for exceptions makes it possible for a staff member to exercise professional discretion when a client offers a gift. For example, what if the client wants to give to a social worker an especially nice piece of pottery or a hand-made quilt made in occupational therapy? It might have a fair market value of over $10. The social worker, if a policy were not, by definition, flexible, would have to refuse the gift. The decision might be the correct one, or it might not be. Perhaps, the client would be offended or perceive the refusal as arrogance. A good treatment relationship might be endangered. But because a policy (and not a rule) was in effect, the social worker could make an exception, exercising professional judgment as to what is best overall for the client and for the treatment relationship. In another situation, the same worker might refuse a gift of very little monetary value from a client when, in the worker's professional judgment, the giving of the gift is designed to manipulate the social worker or to resist the establishment of an appropriate and productive social worker–client treatment relationship. A policy would allow the social worker to refuse the gift.

Another policy commonly seen in human services might relate to "moonlighting" (outside employment). Realistically, it is impossible within most human service organizations to forbid an employee from taking an evening job or from having a business on the side. However, policies sometimes exist to discourage certain types of behavior that would result in bad public relations for the organization. Such a policy might be unwritten, or a vaguely written policy might exist, e.g., "Outside employment should not be in conflict with the goals and mission of the organization." The policy would, therefore, make it clear that bartending within the community served by the alcohol treatment center is not desirable behavior. The question of the ownership of low-income rental property within the same community might also be forbidden by such a policy. Professional discretion on the part of the employee (owner) would be needed to determine at what point the role of landlord might have a negative effect on work within the organization, its image, and that of its professional employees.

Clearly, a manager cannot simply take the position that what employees do after work hours is their own business and nobody else's. Protection of the organization may require a policy to provide guidance as to which type of activities are generally acceptable and which are not. If the policy proves to be ineffective because employees consistently use poor judgment, some other type of plan (for example, a rule or procedure) may be required.

Policies are appropriate and useful in many situations, especially when people can be depended upon to use good common sense and professional judgment. A major problem with the use of policies is that they tend to be confused with rules. We will look more at this phenomenon in the discussion that follows.

Rules

In contrast to policies, *rules* are used to *disallow* the exercise of discretion. Rules specify the required decision or action for a situation. They are used most frequently for help in decision making in those situations that tend to recur regularly in the same way within an organization and when there is a right or wrong decision to be made. Rules either require or forbid a particular behavior. Implicit in rules is the idea that those persons who violate them are subject to some kind of sanction (Chapter 12) or punishment.

When managers choose to use rules for performing a planning function, they are making a statement to other staff. They are saying that "only this is acceptable" and/or that "this is not acceptable." Rules are very useful in those situations where it has been determined that the consequences of any action other than the desired ones cannot be tolerated. A rule would be used, for example, when noncompliance might result in legal action against the organization, when severe financial loss might occur, when there might be severe harm to the community image of the organization, and, of course, when there is the possibility of a violation of professional and ethical standards for treatment of clients. Rules are frequently used to forbid a behavior (for example, sexual involvement with clients or business dealings with them) that might potentially result in all of these negative consequences and more.

Rules are more commonly used in large public bureaucracies than in smaller private organizations or in private social work practice, but they are seen in all human service organizations. Generally, we see more rules in organizations with more hostile task environments, fewer in those with more friendly task environments. This makes sense, since rules can be used to avoid giving those already critical of the organization and its functions even more reason to find fault.

In large federal bureaucracies, rules may be tailored to enforce compliance with federal requirements. A public assistance organization is likely to have rules regarding the frequency of mandatory home visits. A child-protection division will have rules for timely investigation of alleged incidences of child abuse. Noncompliance in the first example would risk federal reimbursement for benefits paid out. In the case of the child-protection division, a lawsuit or even the death of a child creates a specter that just cannot be allowed to occur.

A smaller organization may have a need for rules that might be unnecessary in larger organizations. For example, a small private practice may have the rule that "No more than two employees may be on vacation at any one time." The need for adequate professional coverage necessitates the rule. In a larger bureaucracy with many more staff, a less rigid approach to approving vacations (a policy?) might suffice. The reverse situation may also exist. A rule that "All lunch breaks must occur between 11 AM and 1:30 PM" may be needed in a large public services organization; it may be unnecessary in the small private practice.

Rules can be laid out in great detail. They can also cover several different but related situations that require different correct courses of action. No matter how many contingencies rules are designed to cover, they must be enforceable. If a rule is unenforceable, it is worse than no rule at all. An unenforceable rule soon becomes a joke, sometimes along with its creator. If a rule is found to be unenforceable or if it is enforceable but there is found to be a need for exceptions to it, by definition it is no longer a rule. It has become, in effect, a policy. This is probably all right; but then it should be made clear to everyone that a policy is now in place. Remember that rules are designed for those situations in which there is only one correct course of action and when no exceptions are envisioned or can be tolerated.

Rules sometimes end up as policies but, as suggested in our discussion of policies above, policies can become rules too. Sometimes social managers have chosen to switch to rules when they originally thought that policies were best-suited to the needs of the organization. But they learned that the exercise of professional discretion led to abuses and/or more problems than would hard-and-fast rules. Employees may have sought the loopholes provided by policies rather than constructively using them as guides for action, as intended. In such cases, rules probably should be substituted for policies, effectively removing decisions or behaviors from the realm of professional discretion.

If we all fully understood the differences between rules and policies and always understood the manager's intentions correctly, there would be far fewer problems in human service organizations. Unfortunately, this is often not the case. The terms rule and policy often are used as if they were interchangeable, which, of course, they are not. Managers also may fail to make themselves clear as to their meaning and or intentions—is it a rule or a policy? Sometimes, even if managers clearly communicate which of the two they intend, the receiver of the communication may not choose to hear correctly or may not receive the message accurately for some other reason. If one or both is confused about the difference in meaning, situations can become chaotic.

There is no shortage of real-life examples of confusion over policies and rules. Here are a few:

- A rule may be in effect that "employees may not accumulate over 30 days' leave." An employee who perceived this as a policy fails to take vacation time because she is trying to get caught up on work and to see a client through a crisis. The employee becomes outraged when her pay stub reveals that she has lost four days of leave time.
- A social worker knows about the rule that requires that "complete medical coverage information must be collected and recorded during the initial patient contact." But he perceives it to be a policy. He fails to get the details of the client's health coverage as required because he does not want to appear to be disinterested in the client's problem. The client never returns for a second interview and leaves the state with no forwarding address. The worker is furious when given a written reprimand by his supervisor.
- A social worker is aware of a policy that limits the size of treatment groups to eight clients, but she perceives it as a rule. She refuses to admit the son of a prominent local politician into the smoking-cessation group that she leads because the group already has eight members. She later is reprimanded by her supervisor for using poor judgment.
- A supervisor is aware of the policy that "social workers should use computers only for official business." Treating it as a rule, he demands that a social worker work overtime to reimburse the organization for the ten minutes that she used to send an e-mail to a friend in another agency since only a small portion of the message was work-related. The social worker complains to the supervisor's boss and the supervisor is required to back down on his demand for reimbursement.

Like any of the other forms of plans, rules have both advantages and disadvantages. Like policies, they can be timesavers for employees and for the manager. With a rule in place, very little if any direct supervision may be needed. For the person bound by a rule, no real thought is required. Just comply and you will be correct. Thus rules have a way of freeing up the time and cognitive processes of employees so that they can better devote them to other decisions where they are needed (for example, in deciding whether an exception to a policy is indicated).

Rules rarely apply to only one individual. They are impersonal. Thus, they are not perceived as designed to limit or humiliate any one individual. While nearly everyone finds some rule annoying or insulting, most people recognize the need for rules. They provide even more certainty than policies. One can be faulted for making an exception to a policy without adequate justification or for not making an exception when one was indicated. But abide by a rule and you are safe. It is also possible to use a rule to make an unpopular decision; it is more difficult to do the same thing with a policy. For example, it is possible to say "I wish I could make an exception, but we have a rule that forbids it."

Because of their rigidity and the fact that they are designed to disallow the use of discretion, rules sometimes are resented as condescending, or a form of "one-up" game played by professional staff. They can be an unpleasant reminder of rank and power differentials that exist within organizations.

Some rules are inevitable in any organization. Some tasks must be done the only correct way; some decisions cannot be left to individual judgment. The social worker as manager should view rules as useful planning methods of choice for some situations. But, because they are often sources of resentment among professionals, they are best reserved for situations where policies would leave just too much room for judgment.

Procedures

Plans that are designed to influence the sequence or chronology of events are called *procedures*. The use of procedures is most appropriate for situations where the best results are achieved (or results are best achieved) when a step-by-step method is followed. Procedures are rarely used in shaping the sequence of events in individual social work treatment or in macro-level social work practice. For example, we don't usually have the kind of knowledge available to prescribe the best order of methods to use in counseling a client who has just sustained a personal loss or in influencing the power structure to support legislation to provide funding for psychiatric aftercare services. Our clients are not interchangeable parts to be worked on using a "correct" chronology of behaviors in the way that an automobile mechanic might rebuild a fuel pump or an automatic transmission. There never could be a cookbook approach to all types of social work practice that details the chronology in which social work methods should be used. However, as more and more social workers assume the job of case managers, procedures are likely to become more prevalent.

For performing certain tasks, procedures can be useful planning tools for the social worker as manager. They can serve to standardize activities within human service organizations. This can have real advantages for both staff and clients. For example, we might use a procedure for the intake of new clients that will assure that data on the client are available and have been collected in a logical sequence prior to a staffing conference (social worker performs intake history, then medical work-up, then psychological testing). Or we might design and implement a procedure for applying for vacation time that will assure that all the right people will be notified that a particular employee will not be at work January 3 through January 7, and that those who need to plan for the employee's absence farthest in advance will be notified first, those who need little warning will learn of it last, etc. Similarly, a case manager in a hospital may be more likely to comply with managed care requirements if procedures for discharge planning are developed and enforced.

Unlike policies—where exceptions are implicit; and rules, where they are not—procedures seem to run the gamut from very flexible to very rigid. Some procedures are quite loose and are meant to serve as general guidelines for shaping the sequence of events. Others are meant to allow no flexibility. Because the intent of procedures can vary so much, managers need to make their intentions abundantly clear when they are presented and clarified to staff. If it is intended that exceptions will occur, it might be useful to give examples of when they might be appropriate and what criteria might be used in determining when an exception will be acceptable to the manager. If no exceptions will be tolerated, this also should be made explicit.

Like rules, procedures sometimes can be viewed as insulting by some professional staff. They prescribe the right sequence of events to perform tasks and suggest that other sequences are incorrect. When considering the use of a procedure we should ask, "Does it really matter in what order the events occur?" If it doesn't matter, procedures may be viewed as an unnecessary harassment and should not be used. If it does matter, use them. Procedures can be very helpful for shaping the outcomes of organizational behavior.

Programs

Most social work practitioners have a thorough understanding of what a program is within a human service organization. But we may not think of a program as a planning tool of the social worker. A program is a complex system. It is a type of plan that is really a component of an organization, a more or less self-contained package with its own goals, objectives, policies, procedures, and rules, and frequently its own budget. It may even have its own mission but, if it does, it should be supportive of the organization's mission.

An organization usually has many programs that are supposed to interact supportively or at least cooperatively with each other. Sometimes managers find themselves immersed in the difficult and thankless task of trying to coordinate the various programs that exist within an organization. Competition (especially for resources) among the programs can be fierce. The manager may have to assume the role of peacemaker. For example, a manager may need to find ways to reduce the resentment expressed toward an unfunded new program by staff who are aware that it will almost certainly cause a drain upon their own needed financial and staff resources. Some conflict between programs is almost inevitable, even if there is no competition for resources. Frequently, there is overlap in some aspect of two or more programs. For example, one program treating substance abuse and another offering treatment for family violence may both need to offer similar services to clients. This can produce turf protection issues that a manager must try to resolve.

For the social worker as manager, programs are more easily understood and used if there exists an understanding of systems theory and concepts. For example, a manager, tuned in to the systems concept of "interface," can anticipate the effect of a new program on all other components of the supra-system, and can thus head off many potential problems before they occur.

In the business literature, programs are often described as time-limited. This is logical, because they are regarded rather naturally as packages put together to address a need or eliminate a problem. In social work, we often use programs to confront problems that can be alleviated somewhat but that will not ever go away completely. We are not so presumptive as to believe that any program will meet all the needs of the victims of child abuse or will be 100 percent effective in eliminating the consequences of a lifetime of discrimination or economic or psychological deprivation. Therefore, while some of our programs are time-limited, many are not, and probably should continue indefinitely.

Others began as time-limited and perhaps should have been eliminated, but, bureaucracies and people's vested interests being what they are, still continue to exist (Chapter 3).

A program that continues to exist primarily for self-serving reasons rather than for client service contributes little to goal attainment and is an example of a misuse of a plan. A program that is of little use can also be very demoralizing for the staff associated with it. No one can feel very good about work that is of little value or about pretending to address a need that no longer exists. Managers need to be sensitive to the different situations that require time-limited programs and those that do not. Sometimes, in addition to setting up and monitoring programs, managers need to make unpopular decisions as to when a program should be terminated. This is a decision that managers find very distasteful because it may involve the loss of jobs for friends and colleagues.

A program can have a wide influence on the future course of events within an organization. Social work practitioners who deliver client services cannot help but have their behavior shaped by programs. In their role as managers, social workers make frequent use of programs for planning.

Budgets

We do not often think of a budget as a planning document. But a budget is really little more than a projection of future income and expenditures expressed in dollars and cents. When we make up budgets, whether for the management of our personal finances or for an agency's upcoming expenditures, we are anticipating what financial resources are needed to support the various activities that we hope will achieve our objectives. We then allocate limited resources, which, in turn, constrain the scope of the various activities. When managers construct budgets, they are using them for planning; when they use existing budgets to set limitations on activities within an organization they are controlling (Chapter 9).

There are different types of budget that are used by managers. We will describe the general characteristics of a few of them. They vary in specificity and in the amount of flexibility that they contain. They also vary in the degree to which they hold components of an organization (usually programs) accountable for what is done with the money that is allocated to them.

The *line-item* budget is probably the most commonly used type of budget. It contains many different lines, each reflecting some category of expenditure (for example, salaries, office supplies, postage, professional travel, insurance, building rental, and so forth) for the organization. It is inclusive, that is, every dollar that is projected to be spent is contained in one of the categories. A grand total appears at the bottom right, reflecting the total (usually annual) budget. Sometimes one or more additional columns may be added at the right to reflect projected expenses (line by line) for one or more future years. The numbers in this column are usually based on projected income and the likely effects of inflation on costs. A line-item budget simply states how much money is allocated for the next year for the various expenses incurred in operating the organization. Little or nothing about it suggests the mission of the organization or the specific focus, goals, or objectives of its various programs.

If different programs exist within the organization, the line items may be broken down by programs (*program budgeting*). Each program would then have its own column in the budget with a dollar amount on each respective line. Thus, if there are five programs and line one in the budget is salaries, there would be a dollar figure in each of the first columns reflecting the amount of salary money budgeted for each program. If different programs share an expense such as rent, the dollar amounts in the "rent" line often would be pro-rated to reflect the percentage of the building actually used by each respective program. Program budgeting provides easier monitoring of programs and thus for more accountability than simple line-item budgeting. Programs are expected to stay within their respective budgets. Because a manager knows the exact amount received and spent by a given program, it is possible to calculate the program's cost effectiveness ratio at the conclusion of the year.

Accountability is also a focus in another approach to budgeting known as *zero-based budgeting*. It requires that an organization or its programs start "from scratch" each year and justify why it needs each dollar that it requests for the upcoming year. Unless a request is justified, it is assumed that it is unnecessary, whether or not it was budgeted in the past. The goal is to eliminate those budget allocations that in the past went unchallenged because of the rationale that "we had money for it last year" or because "everyone has a line item for it." Zero-based budgeting is similar in philosophy to the so-called sunset provisions that now govern the continuation of many social programs. They require that a program is funded for a specified time, after which it is to be discontinued unless it can demonstrate anew that it is needed. As is the case with zero-based budgeting, the past is no guarantee of the future.

In using budgets to perform the planning function of the manager, it is useful to be aware of the dangers of constructing budgets that are too rigid or too detailed. Especially in our areas of work, we rarely can predict the exact financial support needs of our various enterprises a year or more in advance. Rigid budgets that disallow transfer of funds from one area to another or do not permit carryover of funds into the next fiscal year can sometimes run at cross-purposes to goal attainment and client services. They promote a "spend it or lose it" mentality that results in some organizational units wasting money while others lack sufficient support to be as effective as they might. This undesirable phenomenon is even more likely to occur when next year's budget allocation relies heavily on evidence of full expenditure of monies earmarked for the previous year. When staff either are not allowed to turn back or are discouraged from turning back unneeded funds that might be needed elsewhere, budgets can detract from delivery of effective services rather than promote them. Thus flexibility is a desirable quality in budgets used for planning.

Types of Planning That Occur
Within Human Service Organizations

The planning menu presented in Figure 4.1 and discussed in the previous section includes the most common vehicles for influencing future events. Some are best suited to the type of long range planning that occurs at the top levels of an organization with limited input from those persons farther down in the organizational hierarchy. Others are used at all levels to influence the daily behavior of others and still others can be used for the personal planning of social workers as managers. Let us look briefly at three different types of planning that illustrate these different usages.

Strategic Planning

Currently, the best-known and most widely used method for long and intermediate range planning within the human services is strategic planning. It has been defined as, "a disciplined effort to produce fundamental decisions and actions that shape and guide what an organization is, what it does, and why it does it."[7] A manager engaged in strategic planning is most concerned with the first types of plans on our planning menu—missions, goals, objectives, and strategies. A detailed description of the strategic planning process is well beyond the scope of this book. It is the subject of whole textbooks and of numerous instructive seminars and workshops. We will mention just a few of the features that set it off from other planning models designed for use at the higher levels of an organization.

In general, strategic planning can be seen as a response to both the threats and the opportunities within an organization's task environment. It is designed to increase the autonomy and control of the organization by enhancing its value and importance to the task environment. Unlike some other planning models that focus on problems and seek to alleviate their causes, strategic planning uses a more positive approach. It requires formulating a vision of the future for the organization that is more desirable than its present situation and developing strategies to take it there.

Strategic planning is ideal for those organizations where tension exists because of a lack of consensus over who should be the prime beneficiary. It produces decisions that are both pragmatic and politically sensitive enough to assure the survival of the organization.

Strategic planning is a team activity that entails clarifying the boundaries of an organization (its mission and mandates) and assessing both its internal and external environments. This includes an honest, careful examination of strengths, weaknesses, opportunities and threats. Current forces and trends are identified and there is speculation about how they might impact on the organization and achievement of its objectives. For example, strategic planning in the early twenty-first century is likely to include identification of such forces and trends as technological changes, privatization of services, or the need for human diversity in the work setting. It might also wish to consider trends such as managed care, welfare reform, tax cuts, government deregulation, or other indicators of growing public impatience, as well as threats of additional acts of terrorism, economic recession, or the need for increased spending for national defense.

Strategic issues, for example, challenges relating to the organization's mission, services, sources of funding, clientele, structure, or management, are identified. However, rather than being described in negative terms, they are articulated as challenges that must be handled either by taking immediate action, as part of the usual planning cycle, or simply by monitoring until such time as further action is required. When action is required, strategies are formulated to meet the challenges.

Strategic planning is ongoing, not a one-time activity. When first introduced some years back, it met with considerable resistance on the part of helping professionals. It can be time-consuming and staff may resent it unless there is a reasonable expectation that the results of it will be implemented. It does not work well when an organization is in crisis or if the staff really prefer to follow the vision of a charismatic leader rather than to struggle with the planning process themselves. However, when there is a commitment to it on the part of leaders and other staff and it is undertaken with the necessary skills and resources (planning is expensive in terms of staff time and research needed), strategic planning can be very beneficial to an organization, especially one that must exist and prosper in a potentially hostile task environment.

Planning to Influence the Day-to-Day Activities of Staff

For social workers who are supervisors or other mid-level managers, planning most often entails setting up plans that will increase the likelihood that subordinates will do what is in the best interest of the organization. We want to increase the likelihood that they will make decisions and engage in activities that will contribute to achievement of organizational or program goals. Consequently, the types of plans on the planning menu most likely to be used are policies, rules, and procedures and, less frequently, strategies, programs, and budgets.

Which type of plan a manager chooses to use and how it is written are often a function of the requirements of the situation. Many policies, rules, and procedures are written so as to comply with federal, state or local guidelines relating to such areas as timeliness of services offered, confidentiality of records, or requirements for client participation in certain types of decision making. Or they may be dictated by the requirements for reimbursement by HMOs or other health insurance organizations.

When there is more flexibility allowed, other factors enter into a manager's decisions about the type and wording of plans to be used. They include whose decisions or actions he or she is attempting to influence as well as his or her own preferences and style. Some managers, based on their needs and those of subordinates, rely heavily on rules and rigid procedures; others rely more on policies and more flexible procedures. That is why one manager can view a need to influence a decision or activity and conclude that one type of plan would be best (for him or her and his or her staff), but another manager might arrive at a different conclusion. Here are some situations where a type of plan is needed to influence future staff behavior. Which one would be most appropriate?

1. Paperwork must be completed in a timely manner in order to guarantee federal reimbursement for services.
2. The organization's copier should be used for only work-related copying.
3. Employees attending professional conferences should attend conference sessions.
4. Staff need to be compensated in some way when they must work evenings to deal with client emergencies.
5. Staff need to know who to ask for advice when their supervisor is unavailable.
6. Children of staff should not be able to disrupt work activities.
7. Staff need to know how to file a grievance against another member of the staff.
8. Staff need to know when to deny services and refer potential clients elsewhere for assistance.
9. Staff need to follow the correct sequence of activities to make clients eligible for Medicaid.
10. Staff should not engage in any form of sexual harassment. (Hint—Is an exception ever desirable?)

Contingency Planning

There is one type of planning that we all do. It is called contingency planning. It is planning that is usually performed privately by individual managers and is used to help us make better decisions and take more appropriate actions should the need arise. It involves anticipating some potential event or change and planning in advance how we will react to it.

Even some of the most frightening change scenarios become less formidable if we have anticipated them and thought through (in an earlier, less emotional moment) what would be the best courses of action should they occur. Contingency planning involves asking ourselves, "How will we respond or what we will do if _____ occurs?" For example, what if we must take a 10 percent budget cut, or what if we do not get that big federal grant renewed for next year, or what if we must reorganize into case management teams? What if we no longer receive referrals from a primary referral source or what if we no longer qualify for third-party payments? What if a senior staff person takes another job or what if a client decides to sue? Contingency planning is a kind of insurance. We carry malpractice insurance to protect us from the $5 million lawsuit or some other "worst case scenario." But we also carry insurance in the form of contingency planning to avoid another scenario—being caught off guard. We need contingency planning to ensure that, if some event occurs (even a good one), we will not have to make important and sometimes irrevocable decisions without adequate thought or, perhaps even worse, become so immobilized that we cannot make them at all.

Guidelines for Use

How much contingency planning can and should a manager attempt? That is a difficult question. Everyone would agree that there is some need to plan for contingencies. But we could spend our entire day, evenings, and sleepless nights planning for contingencies and still not cover all events that might occur. There would be no time left for carrying out our other functions as managers (and as people). Over-planning for contingencies is as dangerous as under-planning because contingency planning is costly. Some happy medium must be struck.

Because we must plan and because we cannot and should not plan for all contingencies, it is logical to focus most of our planning energies on those possible future events that (a) would require important adjustments and carefully considered decisions and (b) appear to have a reasonable likelihood of occurring. It might, for example, make sense to consider the probable needs of a situation should we have to sustain a 5 or 10 percent cutback in funding or, if there are reliable rumors on the horizon, even a 20 or 30 percent cut. But the likelihood of a 75 percent cut is so unlikely and would be so disruptive to even the existence of the organization that contingency planning around it is not a productive use of our time. Certain "doomsday" scenarios may occasionally need to be considered. But most human service organizations have enough realistic threats to occupy most of the contingency planning time of managers without planning for an event that is highly unlikely.

Managers will sometimes have access to information about possible changes on the horizon (favorable or unfavorable ones) that suggests the need for contingency planning.

However, this information may have the potential to be very destructive to morale or otherwise cause the preoccupation of other staff members if shared with them. The decision as to whether to share negative (and sometimes even positive) information about what may occur is a difficult one. On the one hand, foreknowledge of a potential change can sometimes help staff to prepare and to adjust to it gradually. However, there is another compelling argument against sharing information about impending problems—if it is shared, staff members can devote great amounts of time and energy to something that may never materialize.

As a general policy, it is probably best if managers do not discuss a hypothetical future situation with subordinates until the likelihood of occurrence of that situation is almost certain. The decision of just how likely the occurrence of the event must be to suggest sharing knowledge about it is strictly a judgment call. It would depend on a manager's assessment of the likely impact on productivity and goal achievement of the knowledge, the time required to prepare for it, and many other factors. No formula can be applied. Open contingency planning can be dangerous. It may be more costly to such factors as staff morale than a lack of warning and preparation for change. Sometimes staff and the organization (including clients) are better off not knowing what *might* occur, especially if it is too early for them to need to begin doing much about it anyway. It generally is best to plan for contingencies privately, or, if we need help in thinking through a plan, by not involving subordinates and/or those likely to be directly affected by a possible future event. Persons at the same level, particularly those not directly involved, are a safer source of assistance in developing and evaluating our contingency plans.

The likelihood of an event, the cost versus the benefits of planning, and the severity of the consequences of not having planned for it should all be considered before contingency planning is undertaken. These are "situational factors." As with all managerial activities that we have discussed and will discuss in this book, the individual needs and personalities of the manager and of other personnel should also play a part in deciding if and when contingency planning should take place. As managers, some of us can function well in an environment of considerable uncertainty. We know that we will react calmly and quickly when a change occurs or a decision must be made and don't need to plan too much for events that may never materialize. Others of us are quite the opposite. We have little tolerance for uncertainty and need to spend more of our time in anticipation of and preparation for possible future events so that we can handle them should they occur. Most of us fall somewhere between these two extremes.

Work groups also tend to vary in their need for contingency planning by managers. Some adapt rather quickly and thus need minimal preparation. Others are easily thrown into a state of chaos when changes occur and need to be reassured that managers have anticipated and already made preparations for changes before they become realities.

There is one more important variable that can greatly affect how contingency planning is and should be performed. The above discussion has been predicated upon the existence of the usual hierarchical organizational structure that is present in most human service organizations. In those organizations that rely on participative management methods, contingency planning may occur very differently. It is likely to be much more open. For example, it is unlikely to be done privately by managers with little or no input or consultation from subordinates. Instead, potential events and situations may be common knowledge and the focus of discussions by many people within the organization at many

CASE EXAMPLE • *Open Contingency Planning*

Sheryl was the Director of Casework Services for a large state agency. She understood the importance of contingency planning. She did not understand the importance of not discussing her contingency plans openly.

One of her case supervisors, Jo, informed Sheryl that she was pregnant, would be quitting work in three months, and would not be returning after her baby was born. Sheryl began to plan for Jo's resignation. Shortly after her meeting with Jo, Jim, a competent caseworker with 10 years' experience working under Jo's supervision, asked for a conference with Sheryl. He wanted to know if he could have Jo's job as supervisor when she left. Sheryl told him that she had already considered her options and decided that he was the best choice for the job. Jim was obviously very pleased at hearing this news. He revealed that he had recently received another job offer and was considering leaving, but that he would now stay. He no longer felt that he was "career-blocked." Learning this, Sheryl felt even more convinced that her plan was a good one. She felt good about herself and enjoyed the obvious happiness that she brought to Jim. She was even more gratified to learn that he intended to take a short course at his own expense to prepare for the job of supervisor. The conference was extremely enjoyable for both parties.

As the euphoria of the conference began to fade, Sheryl began to have some second thoughts about having shared her plan with Jim. She recalled a favorite warning of a previous administrator who had often his staff to "never respond to a question about a hypothetical situation." As she thought even more about the possible consequences of her openness, Sheryl felt even more unsure about what she had done. True, if everything went as planned, no harm might he done by her candor and Jim would be better prepared for the job. However, many other possible events could occur, and virtually all of them would cause her to regret having promised him the job. Sheryl began to speculate.

If Jo left as planned, several negative events could occur. Jim, a good caseworker, might give indications prior to her leaving that he was not a good choice for the job of supervisor. Even if Sheryl's perception of Jim remained unchanged, another social worker might be hired before Jo left who would be a better choice for the job. Or, other valued workers who Jim told of his selection might threaten to leave if he got the job, either because they aspired to it themselves or because they did not want to work under him.

Any change in the situation that would result in her no longer seeing Jim as the best choice would leave Sheryl in an untenable situation. If she kept her word and gave him the job, she might not have the best person in the position and would not be operating in the best interests of the organization. This would antagonize and possibly result in the loss of some good staff.

If Sheryl were to select someone other than Jim for any reason, he would be humiliated, furious, and would feel double-crossed. He might promote the idea that Sheryl could not be trusted. He might resign or file a grievance with the agency. At best, Sheryl would be seen as indecisive, even by those who would agree with her decision to select another supervisor.

Jo might not decide not to leave after her baby was born. She might decide to take a brief maternity leave and then return to work. Then there might be many other negative consequences of Sheryl's conference with Jim. Jim would be disappointed and might resent Jo when she returned to work. Those caseworkers who had looked forward to Jim getting the job would also be disappointed at Jo's return, although they may have been satisfied with her supervision in the past. Jo would eventually learn of Sheryl's plan to replace her with Jim, and she would wonder if Sheryl didn't actually

CASE EXAMPLE • *(continued)*

prefer Jim in the job. All of these phenomena could harm Jo's effectiveness as a supervisor, especially in her relationship with Jim.

If Jim didn't leave when Jo returned, he might cause problems. He would certainly expect to get the next available supervisory job, a choice to which Sheryl might prefer not to feel obligated. Other good workers who might aspire to supervisory jobs might now assume that they were no better than second in line and might decide to take a job in another agency where they might assume that chances for promotion would be better.

Discussion Questions

1. Why would it have been unwise for Sheryl to wait until Jo resigned before thinking about how she would replace her?
2. If she wanted help in her contingency planning, with whom should Sheryl have discussed her ideas?
3. What should Sheryl's response have been when Jim asked her his question?
4. Once she realized her mistake in telling Jim about her plan to promote him, is there anything that Sheryl could have done to reduce the likelihood of future problems?
5. What is the only scenario in which Sheryl's discussion with Jim would not lead to problems?

different levels. Contingency plans may be developed by managers with lower-level staff, rather than for them.

Regardless of how contingency planning is conducted, it is a necessary task for the social worker as manager. Without it, organizations are unlikely to be able to absorb and adapt to the many changes that seem to characterize our profession.

Summary

In this chapter we examined the management function of planning and emphasized why it is important for reducing uncertainty within organizations. Managers plan in order to influence the future decisions and activities of both other people and themselves. Planning is a rational procedure that recognizes the danger in leaving the future to chance. We defined and described the different types of plans that exist within organizations—missions, goals, objectives, strategies, policies, rules, procedures, programs, and budgets.

Planning occurs at all levels of an organization. We briefly described one popular method of planning at the organizational level, strategic planning, and emphasized how it differs from other planning models. Then we looked at how managers use plans (especially policies, rules, and procedures) to shape the daily decisions and activities of their subordinates. Finally, we discussed a type of planning that all people do in both their personal lives and on the job, contingency planning, and offered some practical guidelines for its use.

Endnotes

1. Harold Koontz, Cyril O'Donnell, and Heinz Weihrich, *Essentials of Management* (New York: McGraw-Hill, 1986), p. 73.

2. Ibid.

3. Grover Starling, *Managing the Public Sector* (Belmont, CA: Wadsworth, 1993), pp. 210–211.

4. See, for example, Rex A. Skidmore, *Social Work Administration* (Englewood Cliffs, NJ: Prentice-Hall, 1995), pp. 53–54, or Koontz, O'Donnell, and Weihrich, *op. cit.,* pp. 102–113.

5. Yvonne A. Unrau, Peter A. Gabor, and Richard M. Grinnell, Jr., *Evaluation in the Human Services* (Itasca, IL: F. E. Peacock, 2001), pp. 67–70.

6. Koontz, O'Donnell, and Weihrich, *op. cit.,* p. 79.

7. John M. Bryson, *Strategic Planning for Public and Nonprofit Organizations* (San Francisco, CA: Jossey-Bass, 1995), pp. 4–5.

5

Creating and Managing Staff Diversity

We now turn to a second management function, staffing. The term staffing is really a misnomer. For those social workers not given hiring responsibilities, staffing is likely to involve primarily the skillful deployment of existing staff (some of whom may possess more job security than we have) and efforts to help them blend into an effective team. Whether hiring new staff or making the most productive use of those already employed, social worker as managers can benefit from an understanding of some of the issues that relate to the many forms of human diversity that are found in human service organizations, and the effects that their presence can have on the work of the organization.

Issues That Affect Hiring

When a manager is involved in hiring a new employee, a number of issues cannot be ignored. We will mention a few of the most important of these.

Involvement of Others

The selection of a new staff member is not and should not be a unilateral decision by any one individual. Input can be gleaned from a number of sources (there is no shortage of advice available for personnel decisions). But how much influence it should have in the final decision to hire or not hire a potential employee? Whose input should be sought and how should it be used?

Politically, it may be impossible to ignore the wishes of a high-level administrator or powerful board member who wishes to be involved. Frequently, this person's wishes in regard to a staff vacancy will be consistent with the manager's perception of what is needed. But this also may not be the case, and often for good reasons. It should be remembered that, whoever makes the final choice from among applicants (it may be a personnel specialist). Others may have a valuable perspective to add to the decision. An executive director, for example, must be especially concerned with the long-range planning for and survival of an organization. He or she may be thinking "a little farther down the road" than, for example, a supervisor who is more focused on the immediate needs of a work unit. Board members may have strongly held beliefs about the kind of image they wish the organization to project into the community and may, therefore, have specific ideas about the qualifications and style of employee who would be most consistent with that image. Both the power and the perspective of high-level administrators and, when desired, board members suggest the need for some vehicle for their input into hiring decisions.

Frequently a potential supervisor will wish to meet and interview applicants, even if someone else is actually doing the hiring. Applicants may also insist on knowing under whom they will work. That is certainly a reasonable and wise request. Even if a face-to-face meeting is not used, the general preferences of the potential supervisor would provide valuable input to whomever will make the hiring decision. One question for which there is no easy answer is, "Should a supervisor have to approve the hiring of a new employee?" A rule that requires approval of the supervisor (or a policy that expresses a strong preference for it) can help to create a good beginning working relationship between a supervisor and a new employee. But such a rule or policy can also cause problems. What if a prospective employee is just what the organization needs, but the supervisor (for whatever reason) votes "no"? For example, a particularly competent and hardworking applicant might threaten a supervisor who is only marginally competent. A veto or implied veto by anyone other than the person charged with making the hiring decision can be dangerous. A policy requiring input (sometimes including a recommendation) is fairly common in human service organizations, and may be preferable. It recognizes the fact that a potential supervisor has a stake in the hiring decision and has a valuable perspective to offer. But it still allows the person doing the hiring to overrule the supervisor, when necessary, to make a decision that is in the best interests of the organization.

The input of potential co-workers may be important but usually is even more limited. If a "search committee" is used, they may be involved in screening applicants and recommending a "short list" of people for the person making the hiring decision to consider. But few organizations (even those that employ participative management methods of decision making) allow future peers to have the final decision on whether or not to hire a job applicant. Potential co-workers may have a valuable perspective to contribute (the needs of the work unit), but they are likely to lack a good understanding of the overall personnel needs of the organization. There also are just too many subjective and self-serving reasons why they might dislike a good applicant or might favor one of dubious knowledge and skills. For example, future co-workers might vote not to hire a person, who might tend to "show up" the existing staff. Or they might vote to hire one whom they perceive as a potentially affable co-worker but who is not what the group really needs.

Future worker compatibility is an important consideration in selection of a job applicant. Generally, a work style that would easily mesh with that of the group would be an advantage. The new hire would adjust quickly and with little disruption to the group. Of course, if the group is not noted for its productivity and good approach to its work, the manager may wish to "shake up" the group by hiring someone who might be sufficiently different to raise the level of the group's performance.

Even potential subordinates generally are interested in meeting people who might become their new boss. This is understandable. However, their interaction with potential supervisors or higher-level administrators is generally limited to what is really just a social courtesy. They should not be treated as if they are invisible when an applicant interviews for a job, but they also should not have a "vote" as to who should be hired. However, such meetings can be very valuable for job applicants who wish to "size up" potential subordinates as part of assessing whether or not they want the job.

Available Compensation

A number of other concerns and constraints help to narrow the number of acceptable choices to fill a staff vacancy. An obvious one is the salary and benefits package that can be offered. The needs of the job and the preferences of other staff may suggest the need for a graduate-school educated, experienced professional. But the amount allocated for salary in the budget may indicate that it may be more realistic to think of hiring someone with lesser academic credentials or whose experience can justify only an entry-level position. While persons employed in human services tend to exhibit an above-average level of dedication, they will not generally work for less than the salary range dictated by the market, unless they have another major source of support. However, it is not unheard of for those in human services to take a particularly challenging or professionally gratifying position when they could have made much more money elsewhere. If there is time, it may be worth seeking the optimal employee, knowing that a lowering of sights may be necessary if none can be found who will work for the remuneration offered. A permanent position that offers good benefits and job security versus one that is "soft" (funded by grant or contract money that may disappear) sometimes also can make a lower-paying job more attractive.

Accreditation Requirements and Professional Organization Standards

Professional standards may leave the manager with little choice regarding hiring decisions. In recent years, an increase in certification and licensure requirements for practice have removed some of the judgment from these decisions. Accreditation guidelines of, for example, the American Hospital Association (AHA) or the personnel standards of professional organizations like the National Association of Social Workers (NASW) have different degrees of enforceability. (The NASW standards have suggested salary ranges based upon credentials.) But the desire for good-standing dictates the need for conforming to the wishes of these groups whether they actually can threaten the existence of the organization or can do little but impose a more symbolic "slap on the wrist." No organization that depends on its professional reputation to hire new personnel or to receive client referrals can afford to regularly ignore the personnel standards set by outside organizations and, in some cases, even the legislative and judicial arms of government.

Organized Labor

In those growing number of organizations where labor unions are established and powerful, additional requirements may further limit who can be hired and under what conditions. For example, an organization may be required to hire a recently laid-off former employee or one who has been demoted before hiring a new person. Even the salary and benefits offered may be dictated by the current contract between the organization and the labor union. Other issues such as seniority cannot be ignored.

Labor unions are not the only form of organized labor that can influence hiring decisions. State civil service requirements must be considered when applicable. Scores on a standardized exam may dictate that one potential employee should be hired over another.

Other groups such as state employee associations, while generally less powerful than labor unions or civil service requirements seem to be gaining more "clout." They will occasionally serve as advocates for current employees seeking a job. Especially if an employee has achieved "permanent employee status" or a similar form of tenure, this may serve to give that employee an advantage in competing for a position. If not hired for it, at least some explanation to the employee association may be required.

Legal Requirements

Federal restrictions play an important role in hiring decisions (as well as in issues relating to retention, promotion, and so forth). Over the past three decades we have seen an evolution of constraints that have been designed to counteract forces of discrimination in hiring and other personnel practices.

Affirmative Action.   In the United States, the Equal Pay Act of 1963 was designed to prevent discrimination based on gender. Title VII of the Civil Rights Act of 1964 was another step in the direction of nondiscrimination; it required that organizations with 15 or more employees must specify and justify hiring criteria. In 1968, Executive Order 11246 (revised later as Executive Order 11375) was a major milestone in the increasing role of government in personnel matters. It became generally known as "affirmative action."

The influence of the presence of affirmative action legislation on hiring practices has tended to ebb and flow with the attitudes and priorities of subsequent presidential administrations. During the Carter administration enforcement in the courts became quite vigorous. Several landmark decisions provided support; some challenges to it were also successful. During the Reagan and George H. W. Bush administrations, affirmative action experienced a period in which enforcement in the courts was frequently not in evidence. In the early twenty-first century a number of successful challenges and opposition by various interest groups (including conservatives and labor unions) seem to threaten its continued existence. Nevertheless, social workers as managers need to understand the basic thrust of affirmative action and what it means to their staffing function. Both as a social worker concerned with the problems of discrimination and social justice and as a manager seeking to comply with federal guidelines in order not to put an organization in legal and financial jeopardy, we must be prepared to address affirmative action concerns.

Affirmative action goes one step beyond the concept of nondiscrimination. It requires that organizations that have federal sources of funding (as is true of most human service organizations) must initiate steps to correct employment inequities that exist. Specifically it requires the development and implementation of a plan to grant preferential treatment in hiring and other personnel actions to women, people of color, and other groups in order to increase their representation in an organization. This is sometimes accomplished through the use of quotas, a method that opponents find particularly offensive. Other criticisms leveled center around the potential within affirmative action plans to create a situation that some charge is reverse discrimination. In fact, in one sense, that is exactly what happens. There is an underlying belief to affirmative action that the end justifies the means—short-range preferential treatment of certain groups at the "expense of" white males is thought to be necessary to correct the under-representation of women and other diverse groups in many areas of the current workplace. Certainly the lack of voluntary movement toward a more diverse workplace prior to affirmative action would seem to lend credence to this belief.

Not surprisingly, affirmative action often has met with considerable resistance. Those charged with enforcing it sometimes have seemed to look the other way or have accepted compromises that allowed for statements of intent and half-hearted efforts rather than actual implementation of plans. Various other means of getting around affirmative action also have been tried. A popular one has used a "clear the decks" approach in which reasons were sought to judge women, people of color, and others who apply for a job as not qualified so that white males could be hired.

Central to an understanding of affirmative action legislation is the difference between the concepts of fully qualified and best qualified. The former means that persons are judged to meet the justified requirements of a job or not; the latter involves an additional rank-ordering of all those who are fully qualified. Traditionally, hiring the person judged to be the top applicant for a job opening has been an unchallenged practice. But under affirmative action guidelines, this cannot always be done. The only appropriate criterion is fully qualified. Qualifications for a job must be carefully studied to be certain that they are really needed and not sex-linked, culturally linked, or unnecessarily discriminatory toward a particular group. If they pass this test, all fully qualified applicants are reviewed, but preferential hiring is given to certain groups over white males. The fact that a white male might appear to have additional, desirable, but not required qualifications (for example, an additional graduate degree) cannot enter into consideration. (A woman or African American with the "bonus" could be chosen over other similar applicants without it.)

The shift in emphasis from best qualified to fully qualified is a departure from what, to many people, has been a very logical and time-honored approach to employment decision making. To them, it represents a government's infringement on a manager's assessment of what is in the best interests of an organization. Defenders of affirmative action would reply that a more heterogeneous work force *is* in the best interest of the organization, as well as of the society as a whole. Some social workers who favor professionalization with its emphasis on advanced credentialing find themselves in conflict. They also favor affirmative action, which sometimes will not allow "credit" for the advanced credentials that, historically, have been more likely to be held by white males.

Other Relevant Legislation.   Other, less controversial legislation during recent decades also influences who managers may or may not hire. For example, Section 402 of the Vietnam Era Veterans Readjustment Assistance Act of 1974 requires organizations who receive federal funds to take actions to employ and advance certain qualified disabled veterans and veterans who served during the time of the Vietnam War.

The 1990 Americans with Disabilities Act (actually signed into law by President George H. W. Bush in 1991) requires all programs, services, and activities within similar organizations to be accessible to all employees. The definition of persons with disabilities is rather broad (for example, it includes people with cancer in remission, epilepsy, heart disease, diabetes, mental illness, alcoholism, and even disfiguring scars or a noticeable limp). What the ADA means, in effect, is that managers cannot simply fail to hire people with certain disabilities because a job for which there is an opening requires that they perform certain functions that they cannot perform without some special accommodations. If otherwise qualified, they cannot be discriminated against. The accommodations simply may have to be provided, so long as they are reasonable. There remains considerable disagreement about what is "reasonable," that is, how much should it cost the organization, change its physical structure, affect other employees, and so forth. The ultimate impact of the ADA on hiring practices is yet to be determined. It continues to evolve through a series of legal challenges. For example, in 2001 a professional golfer successfully used it to be allowed to use a motorized cart in order to compete with other golfers on the Professional Golf Association (PGA) tour. Opponents of the Supreme Court decision, while not denying the golfer's disability, argued that he should not be allowed the accommodation since walking from hole to hole is a requirement of the game as defined by the PGA and the court ruling effectively changed the rules of professional golf.

Advertising Requirements

Legislation designed to prohibit discrimination can also require that certain procedures must be followed for advertising job openings and for screening applicants. Standards vary. They may require, for example, that all qualified applicants must be interviewed or that a job opening must be advertised for a certain length of time and/or an announcement must appear in one or more widely circulated state or national publications. Sometimes a job must be advertised within an organization before it is allowed to be advertised elsewhere.

Jobs that are learned about by word-of-mouth can be dangerous for an organization. Because such practices can easily lead to charges of discrimination through networking, it is usually necessary to require that job announcements are widely disseminated and that all evidence of a fair and open search is available for review. Charges of jobs being "wired" to hire a white male acquaintance (or just to a friend) can be particularly damaging to an organization that is committed to the values and ethics of social work.

We have only scratched the surface of the list of the many constraints that operate and must be considered when staff members are hired. Social work managers need to learn what they can and cannot do (both legally and ethically) if they are in the position to hire staff. Even if the actual interviewing and hiring are performed by personnel specialists or managers at another level, every social worker needs to become sensitized to the fact that hiring decisions involve much more than simply choosing the best-liked job applicant or the one who appears to be the best qualified. Both social work values related to fairness and nondiscrimination and the legal best interests of the organization require it.

The Staff Menu

Staff (and managers) all are unique; thus, an approach designed for the "typical" employee is likely to fail. We will examine the various types of staff within organizations with this in mind. When we review various employee categories, we will limit ourselves to some very broad generalizations that usually (but not always) characterize members of that group. The categories give us an initial insight into what we can generally expect in the way of knowledge and other attributes of an employee and help to suggest how those with various backgrounds might be appropriately deployed. They will in no way substitute for the kind of firsthand knowledge of any one employee that will make possible an individualized approach to personnel management. As we did when we discussed planning in the previous chapter, we will consider the various types of staff as a kind of menu (see Figure 5.1). Managers sometimes can consider the pros and cons of different staff types and then select from the menu the one that promises to best meet their specific personnel needs.

Professionals

In social work practice, when we think of agency staff, we are most likely to think of professionals. In beginning social work practice books, there is usually a discussion of social work as a profession. Two of the most widely used quotations in our literature[1] are used to present the issue of whether social work meets the criteria of a profession. We will not take time away from our study of management to get involved in the never-ending debate on whether or not social work is a profession. For our discussion, we will assume that we qualify for the label professional, based on the fact that we meet most, if not all, of the usual criteria that are applied.

FIGURE 5.1 *The Staff Menu*

1. Professionals—People who, through extensive formal preparation in a program of advanced study, have acquired a specialized mix of knowledge, values, and skills as well as credentials that allow them to perform certain highly skilled work. Other criteria often must be met for one to be considered a professional, e.g., maintenanace of certain ethical standards, decisions not based on self-interest, etc.
2. Preprofessionals—People who aspire to become professionals and who have met most (but not all) of the prerequisites for becoming professionals. Because they lack the required academic degree or some other credential, they are not allowed do some of the same work that professionals can do. Most preprofessionals eventually complete the requirements to become professionals.
3. Paraprofessionals—People who have undergone specialized education and training that has prepared them to perform some of the tasks once reserved for professionals. They generally do not aspire to become professionals.
4. Indigenous nonprofessionals—People who lack the formal education and credentials of professionals and, except in rare instances, of paraprofessionals. However, they have life experiences and/or a cultural identification that makes them especially well-suited to relate to certain clients and their problems.
5. Support staff—People who are unskilled or semi-skilled employees who perform certain needed tasks within an organization, e.g., secretaries, custodians, maintenance workers, etc. They do not offer direct services to clients, but facilitate the work of others who offer them.
6. Volunteers—People who, for a variety of reasons, offer their time and services without pay. They can be used to perform a wide variety of tasks within an organization dependent upon their education, experience, and willingness and the needs of the organization.

They generally include:

1. Mastery of a body of knowledge through advanced education.
2. The presence of expertise (skills) derived from that body of knowledge.
3. Adherence to a common code of ethics.
4. A service ideal that emphasizes client well-being over self-interest.

What do these criteria tell the social worker as manager about what to expect from human service professionals? What do they say about how managers can best use their attributes to contribute to the attainment of organizational goals and objectives? The manager *should* be able to expect a high level of commitment to clients and their welfare. This is logical since, as we have already suggested, human service professionals contend that the client should be the prime beneficiary (even though this is often challenged). As professionals, they should already have been socialized to certain values and ethical behavior that should be consistent with those fostered by the organization.

Professionals should be able to perform their jobs with less supervision than other staff. They are likely to want to use the knowledge and skills that they have acquired in situations that require professional judgment. They may resent requirements for mindless obedience to rules and procedures. They may seek opportunities for further professional development and for receiving the kind of intellectual stimulation that can be obtained from regular contact with other like-minded professionals. They can also be expected to be critical of certain ways in which things are done in the organization, particularly if these practices are perceived to conflict with professional ethics and standards. It is probably a cliché, but educated professionals really are the "backbone" of an organization. As long as they view the organization and their jobs positively, they are a valuable asset. But they can also quickly represent a threat to an organization and its stability if they become bitter and cynical about the organization and its activities. Managers will experience great difficulty in doing their jobs unless they have the support, trust, and respect of their fellow professionals.

Professionals seem to be vulnerable to role strain from many directions. One source is the discrepancy between client role expectations and professionals' perception of their roles. A common misconception is that professional social workers provide tangible assistance in the form of cash or commodities or that at least they are supposed to provide specific and effective solutions to problems. To many clients, "How do you feel about it?" or some other professionally acceptable response designed to help clients find answers for themselves can be viewed as inappropriate for one who claims to be so knowledgeable. An "if you know, why don't you tell?" reaction can reflect client frustration and rage that can be very stressful for professionals. Credentials can be challenged, and professionals can be made to feel as though they are on the defensive.

Professionals can also experience role strain when having to work alongside others who do not value or accept their professional credentials. Social workers employed in medical or psychiatric settings often feel that their work is not valued and that they are not viewed as "real" professionals by physicians and staff trained within other disciplines. Role strain may also be felt by social work educated professionals in their relationships with social work staff who have less professional education. Professionals tend to believe in the value of professional education within their discipline. They generally have invested a considerable amount of time and money in acquiring it, and they may be resentful of those who seem to be performing the tasks that they were prepared to perform without benefit of the same preparation.

Particularly for those professionals working in highly bureaucratized settings, there is likely to be conflict between organizational requirements and professional values and priorities. Paperwork, rules, procedures, and attention to lines of communication and authority can be especially maddening to professionals who see these as interfering with rather than facilitating delivery of services to clients. Professionals may perceive that their professional autonomy is being restricted and that use of professional judgment is not valued, or is even discouraged.

The advent of managed care has brought a new kind of role strain for many professionals in the health care field. Frequently, determinations regarding how much and what kind of treatment is needed or if it is even needed at all are made by people who lack professional preparation in the health care disciplines. Professionals can become enraged that persons who, in their opinion, lack their professional knowledge and skills can nevertheless exert great influence over what can and cannot be done for their patients.

Relationships with supervisors can also result in role strain for professionals. Unlike the role of supervisors in business or industry, supervisors of professionals have a heavy responsibility for the educational development and emotional support of those they supervise (Chapter 6). This can inappropriately evolve into the role of counselor or therapist, creating additional role strain for the professional who may not want to be "treated." But how do you tell the person who writes your annual evaluation to "back off" and stay out of your personal business? This problem is especially likely to occur if the supervisor has begun to miss the experience of direct client contact and wants to get involved in a more treatment-oriented relationship with the supervisee. Even if the assistance is welcomed or even sought the respective roles can become blurred, making it difficult for both parties to have a clear understanding of their roles and interfering with their ability to meet more appropriate role expectations.

If the supervisor happens to be from another discipline where the expectations of the supervisory role are different, even more severe role strain can develop. For example, a social worker may be supervised by a registered nurse or vice versa. In treatment teams such as the interdisciplinary ones created for case management within some medical settings, professionals can find themselves getting types of supervision that they neither want nor need and not getting what they have been educated to expect and depend upon. Or, if the team concept is carried to its extreme, the absence of a supervisor with any firsthand knowledge of one's work can represent a still different problem.

Preprofessionals

Preprofessionals aspire to be professionals and may even be working toward becoming professionals, but fall short on one or more professional criteria (usually course work, research, or clinical experience). They have not yet completed all requirements for the entry-level professional degree or have not received some other credential that the profession requires for full status. Preprofessionals may have had their formal education interrupted and have yet been able to go back to complete requirements, or they may simply have not yet passed some examination and need to work while they wait until it is offered again.

Students, technically, cannot be considered preprofessionals since they are not considered staff. Yet social work students completing their field work experience are a lot like preprofessionals in many respects. However, they generally are not paid for their work and are not expected to carry as heavy a workload as preprofessionals. Medical residents are paid, but they also work longer hours and take other forms of abuse that regular, paid preprofessionals would not endure.

Because of accreditation standards, licensure requirements, and various other client "safeguards" that are in place within many human service organizations, preprofessionals vary in the amount and type of work that they are allowed to perform. Frequently, preprofessionals carry workloads comparable to those of professionals—they just cannot do certain things and they get paid less. Their lack of full credentials and supervisory needs may put additional drain on the time of professional staff.

Preprofessionals can "shake up" an organization. Because they are still learning they may ask many questions, some of which professional staff may struggle to answer. They can contribute fresh perspectives and ideas; this is especially useful in relatively stable settings where staff turnover is low, behaviors have become routinized, and traditional ways of doing things are likely to go unchallenged. Preprofessionals, by questioning the way work is done, often initiate needed changes. Of course, they also can easily threaten the manager and other staff who have slipped into certain behavior patterns that lack a logical rationale.

Paraprofessionals

Unlike preprofessionals, *paraprofessionals* generally do not aspire to become professionals (although they sometimes later change their minds). They usually have completed a relatively short, specialized course of study and have a degree or certificate to prove it. It may have been from a two-year or technical education institution or it may have been offered by a private, for-profit organization that specializes in job training and placement. Some have simply undergone a course of instruction provided by the organization where they have been hired after selecting them for their "potential."

Normally we refer to the preparation of paraprofessionals as training; the formal preparation of professionals is called education (see Chapter 6).The training of paraprofessionals prepares them to perform certain limited tasks and duties. They are not assumed to be qualified to do all that a professional can do—just some of the simpler, more routine things. Their decision making usually is limited too. Most all professional disciplines now use paraprofessionals to perform some of the work that professionals once performed. Physicians have their paramedics and medical technicians, lawyers have paralegals, nurses have nursing technicians, and so forth. They free up professionals to do the more interesting, challenging jobs that may require the professional's advanced education.

In the human service professions we have seen a growth in use of paraprofessionals (sometimes called technicians or case-aides) in recent years. Emphasis on cost-saving in some organizations has led to de-classification or downgrading of many positions that previously required professional credentials. As this has occurred, managers have observed that paraprofessionals indeed can handle many tasks that had been believed to require a professional degree. Undoubtedly, increased use of paraprofessionals in some organizations has cost the jobs of professionals. But professionals who have not lost their jobs have sometimes welcomed their presence. For example, social work paraprofessionals have been used to take intake histories, complete forms, transport clients, or do some other job that professionals regard as time-consuming and not especially consistent with their professional education.

Indigenous Nonprofessionals

A third type of nonprofessional, first widely used in the 1960s and 1970s, is the *indigenous nonprofessional.* A frequent criticism of human service agencies during that time was that they were staffed by persons (usually Caucasian, upper middle class) who were out of touch with and unable to understand and relate well to many clients. At the same time, the consumer movement also was demanding greater client input into organizational decision making. Indigenous nonprofessionals began to be hired, not because of any formal training or professional skills, but because of certain life experiences and/or demographic characteristics. Hiring them was a way to both head off criticism and bring organizations in closer touch with those being served.

In recent years, indigenous nonprofessionals have been hired primarily because of their cultural affiliation with client groups and/or life experiences with problems that clients are experiencing. Because of their similarities to clients, they may be better able to communicate with them and will be more readily accepted and trusted by them than, for example, professionals who may have lived very different lives. Indigenous nonprofessionals who have had similar problems (for example, mental illness or substance addiction) can appreciate the difficult process of overcoming them. They can't be accused of not knowing what it is like. If they have overcome the problem they also can serve as a role model while giving valuable help to those still struggling with it. Often, their credibility is much better than those who have never "been there." When they challenge or confront a client or client group, they are usually not resented as an "outsider" who cannot possibly understand. However, they also sometimes have less patience with clients than a professional might have. They beat the problem, and may have difficulty understanding why others cannot.

Indigenous nonprofessionals also are likely to understand and have access to the informal and formal power structures that exist within the community. They can be invaluable resources for community organization tasks because they know just who to contact and how to approach them to get a job done.

There are obvious political reasons why managers hire and use indigenous nonprofessionals. They have been used to gain acceptance and credibility within a community and to attempt to improve an agency's image. While there is nothing inherently wrong with using them for these purposes, their most valuable contribution is as instruments for change. If indigenous nonprofessionals are given little real input into decisions and if their activities are tightly controlled, they can quickly become resentful. They may actually harm the image of an organization within the community, especially if they begin to perceive themselves as little more than "tokens" or "window dressing." But if used appropriately and given meaningful roles, they help an organization to stay "in touch," serving as a communication channel between an organization and its clients. They can be instrumental in promoting timely changes that will ensure that services offered are those that are needed and wanted and that they are delivered in a way that increases the likelihood that they will be used.

Support Staff

A social worker usually does not need to be convinced of the importance of good support personnel. Secretarial and other clerical staff can keep work flowing smoothly or they can seriously impair the functioning of others. They can present an image of competence or dedication to visitors and clients or one of disorganization and disinterest. The work of custodial and maintenance staff can likewise reflect either pride in an organization or apathy.

In their role as managers, social workers know the importance of hiring and keeping good support staff, but they frequently are frustrated in their efforts. Human service organizations often are notorious for their low pay for all staff, but particularly those who lack much formal education. They can become training grounds for entry-level support staff who, if they are competent, frequently move on to private, for-profit settings that can offer far better pay and fringe benefits. Yet some very good support staff members remain despite better offers. The task for the manager often is to identify the benefits and rewards that are helping to keep these long-term good workers and to try to build in more of them.

One advantage that we have is that a human service organization may be able to offer job security to a member of the support staff that is not available in the profit-oriented private sector. In the latter, if business deteriorates, support staff are often the first to go. Funding cuts may result in loss of support staff in human service organizations too, but usually every effort is made to save the jobs of loyal workers in these positions.

Human service organizations sometimes can offer more status to support staff than can businesses or manufacturing organizations. They also may be treated with a little more sensitivity and respect. They may occupy positions of considerable power that are not reflected in their official slot on the organizational hierarchy. For example, a competent senior member of the secretarial staff represents continuity and a source of knowledge and experience that others turn to as professional staff come and go. And that can be good for self-esteem. Such individuals also are often privy to a considerable amount of information and insight into office politics that keeps their job interesting and makes them a valuable resource. In the past, these "perks" were much less likely to exist in a for-profit corporation where higher-level staff often regarded them as "just secretaries" and often were condescending in their treatment of them. However, newer approaches to management have emphasized a more egalitarian approach to all employees. The status of support staff seems to be improving in most all organizations.

Much of the work performed by support staff is unstimulating and repetitive. If a manager can find ways to introduce variety into their day, staff members will find their work more pleasant. But that may not be possible. Then staff will find their own ways to keep the job interesting. On the surface, it may appear that support staff waste a considerable amount of time. But the time spent in socializing and other technically nonproductive activities may help to relieve boredom, thereby keeping a basically good worker around. The social worker as manager may want to carefully assess the cost-benefit ratio of establishing rigid controls to reduce this behavior. It may not be a good idea, unless the behavior represents a serious loss of efficiency for the organization or presents a bad image for it. Elsewhere in this book we will discuss the dangers of the use of rigid controls designed to limit the behavior of staff.

Volunteers

Some organizations depend heavily on the use of volunteers and have used them for many years. For example, adult Red Cross volunteers, teenage candy stripers, and other volunteers have long been an integral part of patient services within hospitals. Other organizations only recently have begun to use volunteers, a decision influenced in part by the recent national emphasis on volunteerism. Despite a recent increase in the number of women involved in paid employment, the number of individuals active in voluntary activities continues to grow. Both young adults and elders in particular are reflecting a greater involvement in volunteerism than ever before.

There are many benefits to the social work manager in the use of volunteers. The most obvious of these is that volunteers can perform important jobs at minimal costs. They can provide many services, thereby freeing up paid staff to do other work. However, they are not "free," even in a financial sense. They require orientation, training, and supervision. They may be given free meals, uniforms, or reimbursement for various expenses. They generally are rewarded by such ceremonial occasions as holiday parties, volunteer recognition dinners, and other "perks" that can get quite expensive.

Some of the benefits of using volunteers are more subtle. In a way similar to indigenous nonprofessionals, volunteer staff can increase credibility for the organization within the community. They can provide a valuable communication link to consumers. They can help to avoid some of the barriers that an overly professionalized organization sometimes seems to construct. A client entering a human service organization and seeing a volunteer who is also a part of the community can provide a kind of legitimization for the organization. Volunteers also can do something that paid staff often cannot. They can offer "unhurried attention, one-to-one caring and community input in planning."[2] Finally, some contracts and grants from federal, state, and even private sources may require citizen involvement if certain programs are to be funded. Volunteers can help to meet these requirements, thus making increased funding possible.

Many of the same characteristics that can make volunteers assets to an organization also can represent hidden costs. Because they are not paid, volunteers often are more difficult to control than are paid staff members. They are not financially tied to the organization; other organizations probably would welcome their services. Some volunteers may be retired professionals. If so, they may find it difficult to adjust to their new role, often trying to get others to do things "the way we always did it." Volunteers who lack professional education have not been socialized to the same values and ethics as professional and even nonprofessional staff. Even if well-oriented and trained, some may never "get the message." For example, they may not fully understand the importance of confidentiality. A curiosity about what goes on in the organization sometimes can become excessive and can cause problems. Interest in client problems may exceed the need to know. Sensitive and confidential client information may be shared with others outside the organization. Even internal problems among paid staff that should not be discussed outside the building can become common knowledge if volunteers choose to discuss it in the community. A manager can quickly come to regret the use of a volunteer when that volunteer's lack of professional values or just good judgment causes problems for the organization.

Over the years, managers have learned from experience that selection of volunteers is equally important as the selection of paid staff. Most of the same issues must be addressed. For example, what methods or sources will be used for recruitment? Personal referrals from paid staff or current volunteers may work well but it may also produce a volunteer group that lacks important diversity. Advertising in the newspaper, on bulletin boards, or in other public places may attract people who clearly would not be appropriate for the work of the organization and for its clients. Having to turn down potential volunteers is an unpleasant task and one that can be damaging to the organization's reputation in the community.

Screening of volunteer applicants requires being alert to other potential problems. Background checks are necessary, since volunteers will be working with clients and representing the agency. Criminal records, driving records, employment history and health status all are relevant and must be investigated. However, investigating them can become expensive and may bring up ethical and legal questions and issues. Applicants may resent them, but a good potential volunteer will understand why they are necessary and will be happy to cooperate. A person who resists them may just have something to hide!

It is sometimes hard to understand volunteers and why they offer their services. People volunteer for many different reasons. They may be "good" reasons or dangerous ones. A manager may struggle to understand the complex motivation that prompts individuals to volunteer their time and talents. The reasons for volunteering often reflect a mixture of personal need-meeting and altruism. Sometimes it is hard to identity the primary motivator. Some volunteers may enjoy the intellectual stimulation that a professional work environment provides. Others may gain considerable gratification from the teamwork required to work toward a common goal. Others seek primarily the social interaction that a work environment can provide. Others seem to want to encourage clients to adopt their personal values. Still others perceive that volunteering is an obligation that should be a part of their religious faith.

Altruistic reasons for volunteering may also include just a strong need to help others or a wish to contribute something to the community. Volunteers also may hold a conviction that they should work toward some social change. Some people volunteer because they have a need to keep busy, or are simply happier when they are productive. Others may wish to share what they have learned over the years. Sometimes volunteers wish to do a kind of "penance" by doing for others what they were never really comfortable in doing for those close to them. Even alleviating personal guilt in this way is not necessarily bad for an organization. Volunteers, just like paid staff members, can be so emotionally involved in their work that the objectivity needed for doing the job is lacking. This is why, for example, hospice organizations generally will not use volunteers who have recently lost a close friend or relative to cancer or a similar illness.

Especially when potential volunteers are first interviewed, it is important to try to determine just what it is that the volunteer is seeking. An assessment must be made as to whether their presence would benefit the organization in the achievement of its objectives or impede it. In short, is there a "match"?

The complexity of the motivation of volunteers (about the only thing that we can be sure of is that they are not doing it for the money) can limit what they can and will do. Generally, volunteers want to do what *they* want to do (jobs consistent with their motivation) and will strongly resist or simply refuse to do anything else. Unlike a paid employee, they don't have to do the less pleasant job that has to be done. If pushed hard enough, they will simply leave. (For the volunteer who hasn't worked out well, a manager or volunteer supervisor sometimes may deliberately provoke such a response.)

Some tasks are, by their very nature, appealing to volunteers. Others are not as much fun and have fewer takers. For example, in a hospital setting, there is usually no shortage of volunteers to read to patients, deliver flowers to them, or just visit with them. More strenuous or less rewarding jobs such as assisting in rehabilitative therapy are less vigorously sought. Fortunately, the complex needs that drive people to volunteer result in widely varying volunteer preferences. Some jobs, where the needs of both patients and clients are very great, are not outwardly attractive for the volunteer, but there may be a good match. Volunteers, once they become aware of the intangible rewards that they hold for them, may resist doing anything else. For example, hospice volunteers or volunteer "brothers" or "sisters" of AIDS patients report a great feeling of satisfaction derived from their work.

Managers who fail to recognize the complexity of the motivation of volunteers and who simply assign them to needed tasks as if they were paid staff may soon find that they have difficulty recruiting or keeping volunteers. Most communities have an effective volunteer communication network—the word gets out fast!

The roles of volunteers in human service organizations vary widely. They might offer professionally supervised direct individual or group services to clients, participate in citizen action groups, serve on advisory boards of public or private agencies, take part in self-help or mutual aid groups, or do any number of clerical and semi-skilled or even un-skilled jobs that need to be done. The nature of the task or tasks will determine the amount of training, education, and supervision that will be required. All volunteers require orientation to the organization. They need to learn its policies, rules, and so forth.

Larger volunteer programs often require a staff member assigned full-time to oversee the volunteer program. Even volunteer programs with only one or two members still need a person clearly designated to supervise them and to coordinate their work with that of paid staff. Happy and productive volunteers are those who know what they are doing as a result of appropriate training and a clear job description. They also require regular support, gestures of appreciation, and feedback by a designated person. The job of volunteer supervisor is a fairly common role for a social worker. It requires the knowledge and skills of a manager. Paid staff members need to be prepared for what to expect from volunteers. They need guidance in how to use them productively and appropriately. Volunteers require written contracts and job descriptions. They also require an advocate who understands them and can defend them, if required. Their contributions need to be regularly acknowledged. A volunteer supervisor must also provide regular evaluation of their work and support for improving their performance. Personnel records must be kept for documentation of their contributions to the organization, but also for possible personnel action, such as dismissing a volunteer if it has been demonstrated that he or she represents a liability rather than an asset to the organization and its clients. (Yes, volunteers can, and sometimes should, be fired.)

In deciding whether to use volunteers or how to use them, managers must be able to see beyond their obvious financial advantages. As we have suggested, volunteers can be a real asset or a liability to an organization. They can either do wonders for public relations or they can be a major source of embarrassment. Before choosing to use volunteers, several questions should be addressed. These include:

1. Are there tasks that lend themselves to the needs and interests of available volunteers? Are these tasks easily defined?
2. Can volunteers be recruited who will appropriately meet the needs of the organization?
3. Will volunteers be accepted by paid staff as valuable team members, or will they be resented or be allowed only token participation? Will there be a tendency to put down their work as of lesser value than that of paid staff?
4. Is there sufficient available paid staff time for training, staff development, education, and supervision of volunteers?
5. Can the organization tolerate the uncertainty and unevenness of service that volunteers sometimes bring? Would absenteeism or high volunteer turnover be a problem?
6. Will paid staff reflect tolerance of a wide range of volunteer demographic characteristics and motivation or do they have narrow attitudes about just how a volunteer should look and act?
7. Will paid staff accept and even welcome input and suggestions from volunteers? How will they receive volunteer efforts to change the way things are done?

The presence of some conditions that would seem to argue against the use of volunteers should not necessarily preclude their use. These conditions may not be permanent or unchangeable. For example, paid staff can be helped by managers to change some of the beliefs and attitudes that might otherwise sabotage the productive use of volunteers. Sometimes only their presence will convince some of those who are most resistive and prone to be resentful of them. While managers cannot afford to cause too much disruption in the work environment at any one time, a little incremental change often can be desirable. The experimental use of one or two carefully chosen volunteers (two is better for mutual support), placed where their potential for success is high, sometimes can be a good first step in the development of a viable volunteer program.

There is every reason to believe that volunteers will become an even more integral part of the staff of human service organizations in future decades. Managers need to be sensitive to areas where volunteers can contribute to achievement of organizational objectives. Managers also need to be aware that, as a group and as individuals, volunteers have both unique assets and liabilities.

Creating the Best Mix of Staff Types

We have briefly discussed some of the categories of staff that exist within human service organizations and their similarities and differences. There is no formula or recipe for providing the exact proportion of each staff category that is best for all organizations or even for any given organization. Even if we could obtain that kind of knowledge, just about the time we were successful in achieving the optimal mix, the needs of the organization would change and we would have to make staffing changes anyway. Nevertheless, managers will make better staffing decisions if they recognize and understand some of the issues that influence what is a good balance of different staff types in an organization.

The Professionalization Issue

Professionalization of an organization entails ongoing efforts to upgrade the credentials of staff. On the surface, it would seem like a good thing and often is. In recent years, social workers have become concerned by efforts to declassify positions in some organizations, especially within the health fields. They have fought these changes which seem to represent a step backward for professionalization. But is professionalization of an organization an undeniable "plus" for the organization and its clients? Just how many professionals are best and how much professionalization is desirable? Can professionalization become nonproductive or cause more problems than it prevents? Before managers attempt to upgrade or even maintain the current credential level of staff, they should recognize both the pros and the cons of such efforts.

The most important question to ask is, "In this work environment, who would benefit most by professionalization?" This question is best answered with reference to a concept that we mentioned earlier, prime beneficiary. Of course, based on our social work values, the client or client groups served should be regarded as the prime beneficiary within human service organizations.

Often there are benefits to staff when an organization professionalizes. It can lead to higher status and rewards and to a greater pride in being affiliated with the organization. However, professionalization can also cause problems for staff. Just as physicians have found in recent years, professionals are assumed by the general public to possess vast amounts of cause–effect knowledge. They should not make mistakes. As a result, mistakes tend not to be tolerated; they can land a professional in court facing a malpractice suit. Those with less claim to professional status are usually less vulnerable. It appears that there has been a direct correlation between social work's limited achievements at gaining recognition as a profession and the presence and threat of malpractice suits. The point is, even for staff, professionalization is probably at best a mixed blessing. It should not be regarded as universally desirable.[3]

What could be bad about the delivery of services by highly educated professionals using a single standard of quality regulated by a professional organization? It would seem difficult to argue that professionalization is anything but good for the client. If a manager is fortunate enough to work in an organization that can pay the cost of highly professionalized service delivery, why not?

The problem sometimes can lie in too much of a good thing. An overly professionalized organization actually can create barriers to client services while it should facilitate them. Frequently, professionalization carries with it some undesirable baggage. Professionals and other staff who are encouraged to look and to act like professionals may provide assurance of competence and objectivity to clients, but their behavior also can tend to accentuate differences between clients and staff and to weaken the staff's perceived ability to relate to clients and their problems. Particularly when cultural and social class differences already exist, a highly professionalized organization can seem to create even more distance between the organization and those whom the organization would serve. Some of the symbols of professionalization (for example, attractive offices, the latest technology, efficient receptionists, white coats) can serve to underscore differences between how clients live and how staff function.

Managers must decide what is best for their work situation. Specifically, they must ask what level of professionalization will best facilitate the efficient and effective delivery of services. The answer will give clues as to the directions that they should take. In some organizations, a highly professionalized work environment is desirable. In others, more casual, laid-back approaches that emphasize human similarities between client and staff and that suggest a dedicated but sometimes fallible approach to helping may be preferable.

Other Forms of Diversity in the Workplace

A dramatic change is occurring within organizations in the twenty-first century. The workplace is becoming much more multicultural than it was only a decade or two ago. There are still paid and volunteer staff. Staff still differ in their educational preparation, general job classifications, or attitudes toward the organization. But other differences are often equally if not more important for managers if they hope to understand the complexity of human behavior within organizations.

Types of Diversity

Rosenor[4] has identified two different categories of diversity—primary and secondary. Primary forms of diversity are those that cannot be changed. They do not reflect a "choice" of individuals. Primary types of diversity include age, ethnicity, physical ability or disability, and sexual orientation. Secondary types of diversity reflect (more or less) choices that the individual has made. Thus they are, at least in theory, alterable—one should be able to change them. In fact, we know that for various reasons many of them often are nearly impossible to change. Examples of secondary types of diversity are marital status, parental status, and religious affiliation.

Social workers generally understand diversity and its importance in understanding human behavior. In our professional education we have been taught to appreciate and to value diversity and to celebrate the richness that it brings to a society and its institutions. However, like any change that is positive, increased diversity within an organization brings with it some potential problems. The social worker as manager needs to be able to anticipate these and to be able to shape the work environment so that it will at least minimize them. This is not something that comes naturally to us; we have to sensitize ourselves to cultural and other forms of diversity and to learn how to work with them.

Diversity among Subordinates

Longres identified what may be the greatest potential problem of diversity, increased conflict. In discussing an issue within social work education he observed that, "Diversity is not an inherent good . . . nor is an inherent evil. Diversity is simply a fact of social life. It leads to richness, as we so often hear in the social work literature, but it also inevitably leads to conflict."[5] Asamoah made a similar observation regarding the effects of diversity within organizations. She said, "Although the mix of cultures, genders, lifestyles, and values can be stimulating and potentially beneficial to the organization, it can also lead to conflict.[6] We noted in Chapter 3 that management theorists over the years have had different attitudes about conflict. Some classical theorists saw it as unnecessary if an organization is well managed. Later writers believed that it was unavoidable, but that it could be contained within reasonable limits and even used productively. A difficult task for the manager is determining when diversity-related tension is present, but also when it represents healthy stimulation for the organization and when it represents unhealthy conflict.

How can managers know when diversity has become more a problem for the organization than an asset? There are a number of warning signs that can be observed if we are sensitive to them. They indicate that the organizational climate for diversity is not favorable and will continue to foster conflict. For example, the manager might observe that:

- There is a disproportionate amount of staff turnover among certain groups, such as women or people who have a disability.
- There is difficulty hiring people from certain groups; they even may agree to take a job and then change their minds.
- Staff seem comfortable making jokes or slurs that denigrate the appearance, customs or beliefs of diverse groups.
- Staff seem to avoid tasks that require them to work with people who are different from themselves.
- Frequent mistakes occur that seem to be a function of staff misunderstandings related to cultural differences.
- Staff complain to supervisors about cultural differences of co-workers (for example, dress, hair styles, speech accents, religious jewelry) that do not affect client services.
- Members of certain groups are not invited to informal social gatherings or, if they are, they are made to feel unwelcome.
- Members of certain groups avoid staff meetings or other meetings. When they attend, their comments and contributions are disregarded or "discounted" by other staff.

Managers can help to avoid many problems by developing cultural sensitivity themselves, supporting its growth among others, and modeling how it is practiced. For example, managers need to be aware of certain days that are of great religious significance to staff who are Jewish, Moslem, Hindu, and so forth. They should make other staff aware of their importance and the need to respect them as we have been taught to do for the more familiar Christian holidays such as Christmas or Easter. They also should take great pains not to schedule important meetings or other events that would interfere with staff participation in their religious celebrations or observances.

Religious observances are only one area of many where important differences exist within a diverse workplace. One's body language, touching, or even the presence or absence of eye contact can have very different meanings among different cultures and different other groups. Certain behaviors or a poor choice of words can easily offend or miscommunicate to a staff member. Managers need to learn what is flattering, insulting, humiliating, and so forth in order to convey accurately what is meant in social interaction. It is equally important that they sensitize other staff to cultural differences and that they understand that attention to them is an expectation of their jobs.

One major problem that occurs because of diversity within organizations is a tendency on the part of staff to view the behavior of co-workers differently than they would if they were more like themselves. Generally, the interpretation is a negative one. Historically, this has been a problem faced by women in male-dominated work settings. It has undoubtedly contributed to the "glass ceiling" experienced by many women who have sought to move into higher level management positions within male dominated organizations. For example:

- He is assertive; she is aggressive.
- He is a perfectionist; she is nitpicky.
- He is demanding; she's just bitchy.
- He is overworked; she must have PMS.
- He is persistent; she doesn't know when to quit.
- He stands by what he believes in; she is stubborn.
- He is a consummate politician; all she knows how to do is socialize.
- He says what he thinks; she's opinionated.
- He knows how to get things done; she's manipulative.
- He's a charmer; she is seductive.
- He is work focused; she is antisocial.

As human service organizations become more diverse, others besides women are subject to misreading of their behavior. When this occurs, managers should make every effort to point it out and to emphasize that such interpretations are not acceptable.

Diversity and Professionalism

As diversity increases within organizations, there is also likely to be conflict related to professionalism. Social workers as managers are likely to face complaints of staff who view cultural differences (for example, dress, speech, or personal hygiene) as "unprofessional." In these situations, the manager can probably safely assume that many of the complaints are likely to be a form of *ethnocentrism,* that is, a tendency to judge others' behaviors and tastes in the context of one's own culture, life experiences, and values. If this is what they represent, it is incumbent on the manager to help the complainants to understand why they may be offended by cultural differences and to see that professionalism can come in many packages.

While pointing out ethnocentrism to staff is a difficult task that requires considerable tact, it is probably not half as difficult for the social worker as manager as having to confront a staff member whose differences may indeed be obstacles to forming useful professional relationships with clients. Ideally, we would like to believe that cultural differences should not matter, but in extreme situations they can and do matter. For example, a professional who regularly uses "four letter words" or other language that is the vernacular in his subculture but that is offensive to some of his clients may never be able to develop a therapeutic relationship with them. Or, another professional who insists on wearing the native garb of her ancestors may have a hard time being recognized as a competent professional by her clients who expect to see modern, Western-style business attire.

In both of the above examples, the differences probably *should* not matter to clients. But what if they do? What if clients frequently cannot look beyond the cultural differences to see the knowledgeable professional who seeks to help them? It is not our responsibility as managers to help our clients become more tolerant of cultural differences (although it might be a goal of their treatment). In such instances, the manager may need to discuss with the professional staff members the ways in which cultural differences might be impacting on their effectiveness as professionals. If work effectiveness is impaired by cultural differences, performance evaluations (Chapter 7) may have to reflect this fact and assistance will need to be offered to correct deficiencies. Even done tactfully, this can produce anger or even charges of discrimination. However, once again, we must recall that it is our clients, not our staff who are supposed to be the organization's prime beneficiaries. Unpleasant as it may be, the manager has a responsibility to do what is necessary to assure that they receive the best possible services in a way that maximizes the likelihood that they can benefit from them.

Diversity among Managers

What if we as managers are different from most other staff members in one or more ways? Managers' own demographic characteristics as well as their life experiences can affect their capacities to manage effectively. A recognition of who we are and how we are likely to be perceived by others within an organization allows us to understand and to anticipate some of the problems that may arise. It helps explain why people react the way they do to us as managers. It can help us understand how sometimes success comes so easily in our role as manager and why, on other occasions, staff responds with resistance, suspicion, resentment, and other less-than-desirable responses to perfectly appropriate management behaviors. Understanding of human variables that affect management may also provide social workers as managers with hints as to how they might overcome some of the personal animosity that invariably exists within organizations where human beings must interact.

Demographic characteristics of the manager undoubtedly influence a person's capacity to manage. That is not the way it should be, but it is. In organizations, as in any social system, it makes a difference whether we are, for example, male or female, gay or straight, younger or older. It matters whether we are members of a diverse group or not or whether we have physical or other disabilities that may make us appear to be different or similar to other staff. Social workers are well aware of the fact that a person's perceived membership in a subgroup affects the ways in which others react to that person. In our professional education, we devote a considerable amount of course time to examining discrimination and its effects on the social functioning of human beings. We seek better ways to help clients who are victims of discrimination.

A manager's ability to function (to manage) is likely to be affected by discrimination. For example, a manager's identity as a woman or a man or as white, African American, Latino, Native American, or a member of some other group can affect the way staff

CASE EXAMPLE • *A Diversity Dilemma*

Louise learned from a friend that Henry, the long time executive director of, Second Chance, was retiring. Second Chance is a not-for-profit organization that offers residential treatment and follow-up for troubled adolescents at nine different locations around the state. It employs more than 100 people and has an active volunteer program. Louise had been a mid-level manager for more than eight years. At the urging of friends and co-workers, she applied for the job. She went through two sets of interviews, first with the search committee composed of three board members and then with the entire board. She was a little surprised, but delighted, when she was offered the job two days later. She readily accepted.

During her interviews with board members, Louise learned that there was concern about the vacant position of Director of "EXSELL," a large program within the organization that was designed to find employment for female adolescents who were deemed ready to return to the community. The position had been vacant for three months. Henry had not filled it or even advertised for it, choosing instead to serve as its acting director himself. He explained to the board that it made no sense for him to select someone in such a key position since it would be his successor who would have to work closely with the person hired. The board did not want to force the issue with Henry, but they had made it clear to Louise that filling the position would be the first priority for the new executive director.

Henry was very gracious and helpful to Louise both before and after she started her new job. He had lunch with her several times and made himself available by phone every afternoon for questions and suggestions. He carefully stayed away from the office in order not to undermine her in any way and he was complimentary of the changes she told him she planned to make.

Louise began to advertise the director of EXCELL position on her third day on the job. Within two weeks she had identified five applicants who seemed to meet the job qualifications and, with encouragement from the chairman of the board, she closed the search. During the two weeks that the position was advertised, she had noticed what she believed to be a potential problem. While about 30 percent of clients served and 25 percent of paid staff were people of color, of the four program directors and nine residential home administrators, only one was African-American and one was Native American. She brought this to Henry's attention when they had lunch again and was surprised by his defensive response. "I hope you are not suggesting that I have practiced discrimination. That's just the way things happened. This organization is as strong as it is because I have always hired the best people I could get for the job without regard to whether they were white, black, yellow or green!"

Partly because she felt badly about offending Henry after he had gone out of his way to be so helpful and partly because she greatly respected his judgment, Louise asked if he would review the applications of the finalists for the position and give her his assessment of their applications. He agreed to do it and even apologized to Louise for "over-reacting."

Two days later, after Henry had a chance to study the applications, they met again. He handed Louise the files and said, "This one is a no-brainer. This one (Alene) is clearly your best choice. I have known her for years and have always wanted to hire her for Second Chance. She is well-liked, experienced, competent, and very knowledgable. You can't go wrong if you hire her." Louise thanked him for taking the time to review the files and for his opinion. But she said nothing else.

Over the weekend, Louise agonized over the decision she would have to make. She read over Alene's application again and again, looking for some problem. There was none. Alene would clearly be a great asset to the organization. Her references were outstanding and everything that Henry had said appeared to

CASE EXAMPLE • *(continued)*

be true. But when she had interviewed Alene, they had not hit it off especially well, although she was not sure why. She also had confirmed that Alene was white.

Two of the five finalists for the position were African-American. Louise read and re-read their files. The references for one woman (Ronessa) were especially strong. One former supervisor who Louise knew and respected described her as "very bright, a quick study, and has the potential to become an outstanding manager." However, Ronessa had been a supervisor for only two years (the minimum job requirement), had never written or administered a grant, and clearly lacked the breadth of experience and knowledge that Alene possessed.

Louise was committed to the principle of Affirmative Action. She also understood the value of diversity in the workplace and had already sensed some dissatisfaction among African American and other minority staff about the fact that they occupied most of the lower level jobs in the organization and so few of the upper level management ones. Yet she also recognized that, if she hired Alene, she would be bringing on board someone able to assume all responsibilities of the job immediately, no one would question Alene's experience and abilities, and Henry would be pleased. After a sleepless weekend, she made her decision—she would hire Ronessa, even though she anticipated that Ronessa might not be able to do the job initially as well as Alene could and that she would need to commit some of her own

time to mentoring Ronessa and helping her to develop as a manager.

To her relief, when she informed them of her decision at their next meeting the board members were supportive. One or two seemed to agree with her about the need for more diversity at the higher management levels. The others may have just been unwilling to oppose her—she was still in her "honeymoon period." Henry was another story. When she told him over the phone, his only response was, "It's your call. You will have to live with the consequences of your decision." He once again urged her to come to him if he could be of help. However, four out of the next five times that she called with a question, he did not return her call. She stopped calling. Soon afterward he moved to a warmer climate, but they continued to exchange holiday greetings. Three years after Henry moved away, a board member confided to Louise that Alene had also applied for the executive director's job (at Henry's urging) and that Henry had been angry when it was offered to Louise instead.

Louise did not regret her decision. While there were times that Ronessa made mistakes related to her inexperience and Louise occasionally wished that she had someone in the job who could function more autonomously, she continued to see evidence that her decision had been a good one overall for the organization. She also took great satisfaction in watching Ronessa develop into a very competent manager.

Discussion Questions

1. Why was the lack of diversity at Second Chance a problem that needed to be addressed?
2. Why did Henry's response to the situation suggest that he did not understand Affirmative Action or the desirability of diversity?
3. Was it a mistake for Louise to ask Henry to review the job applications for the EXCELL director's position? Why or why not?
4. What costs and benefits were involved in hiring either of the two finalists for the job?
5. How might the fact that Alene had also applied for the executive director's job have caused problems for Louise if she had hired Alene instead of Ronessa?

members relate to him or her. Initially, this can be either a benefit or a liability, dependent in part on whether he or she is perceived as similar to or different from other staff members. Over time, it is almost always the latter.

Discrimination is basically a neutral word. It simply means that it is possible to notice difference. As practitioners, as managers, and as staff relating to higher-level managers, social workers need to recognize differences in people and to relate appropriately to these differences. Recognition of difference is essential for good practice and for good management, a point that was stressed in earlier chapters. As managers, it allows us to appreciate the special attributes of staff and to use them most effectively. It also is essential that staff discriminate in their relationships with managers; that is, that they be able to recognize the characteristics of managers that make them unique as human beings and learn how best to relate to them. However, as we know, discrimination is more likely to have negative consequences than positive ones. There is a big difference between recognizing differences and appreciating them (positive discrimination) and recognizing differences and, based on them, making erroneous stereotypes, and treating people in less desirable ways (negative discrimination). This latter form of discrimination is the one that social workers see most often and the one that they endeavor to confront and to eliminate.

The manager cannot afford to engage in negative discriminatory behavior toward staff. It is professionally unethical and puts the organization at risk for legal action. It is also just poor management that will inevitably destroy trust and the manager's effectiveness in performing management functions.

We know that staff of all kinds suffer from many forms of negative discrimination. Are social workers as managers also victimized by negative forms of discrimination directed against them? Definitely. Articles and entire books are devoted to the problems of women and racially and ethnically diverse managers,[7] topics that we will only briefly address in this text. To better understand the negative forms of discrimination that affect managers, it is useful to examine two related terms, prejudice and stereotype. Prejudice has been defined as "interpersonal hostility that is directed against individuals based on their membership in a minority group."[8] It relates to a negative feeling or attitude about people based on their group membership—for example, because they are old, homosexual, African American, female, have a disability, and so on. A stereotype is closely related but slightly different. It results from a cognitive (rather than emotional) function. It is really a cognitive breakdown. A stereotype can be viewed as a standardized, overgeneralized mental picture representing an uncritical judgment based on group membership. A stereotype denies or fails to recognize individual difference.

Traditionally, we have tended to believe that the negative forms of discrimination (treating others in a less desirable way based on their perceived membership in particular group) have occurred because people hold prejudices that cause them to engage in stereotyping. Levin and Levin dispute this notion, suggesting instead that negative discrimination provides its own rewards (economic, social, psychological), and that we use stereotypes and prejudices to justify practices of negative discrimination.[9] Their position has a certain compelling logic within our study of management. Hasn't it been profitable for white males to treat women or other racially or ethnically diverse people as second-class citizens within organizations? Are such stereotypes as "women don't make good managers" or "an African-American person can't supervise a white person" only a rationalization for discriminatory practices that benefit white males? Perhaps. Whether discrimination results from or results in prejudice and discrimination is an interesting philosophical question, but not one that is especially critical to the social worker as manager. What is important is the understanding that who one is can affect how well one is able to perform the functions of manager. As managers, we need to be able to recognize the prejudices, stereotypes, and, most importantly, the behaviors of other staff (discrimination) that can impinge on our ability to manage and to be able to minimize their effects.

Forms and Consequences of Discrimination

Historically and to this day, managers have been hindered by several types of undesirable treatment if they were female or a member of certain ethnic groups or held some other form of group membership. Both subordinates and superiors have treated them in ways that have hindered their ability to manage. Being a woman or a member of a racial or ethnic group (and sometimes even a white man) can present certain problems for the social worker as manager. Being a member of more than one such group (and who is not?) can result in even greater jeopardy. We will examine some different forms that discrimination based on a manager's demographic characteristics can take.

Forms of Discrimination That Affect Managers

Usually when we think of discrimination we think of a type of behavior that excludes or denies people access to something to which they are entitled. The obvious forms of denial, such as discriminatory pay scales and limited access to promotions, have especially affected women and others in both human services and in all other sectors of the job market. Social workers' ability to manage undoubtedly is affected by the rewards that they receive (or don't receive) and their perception of their potential for upward mobility. But the denial of access that can most directly affect people's capacity to perform their management functions is the denial of needed information. If, for example, superiors or subordinates do not provide to a woman manager the details of a particularly messy situation that exists within an organization, they can hinder her ability to make good management decisions that relate to it. The shutting off or limiting of information may be deliberate and designed to hinder her ability to function as a manager. It may also be paternalistic, seeking to "spare" her based on stereotypes about her "sensitivity" or "tendency toward emotionality." Or it may result from her lack of membership in the "old boys' network" where valuable information is exchanged over a round of golf or at informal males-only social hours after work on Friday afternoons.

The lack of informal social contacts with manager–peers and other staff can be particularly problematic for a woman or a member of a racial or ethnic group. Of course, male social workers in an organization where they feel socially cut off by a predominately female staff can experience the same type of information shortage. Managers need good information (and a lot of it) to do their job. Formal communication by way of memos and other such vehicles are not enough to be "on top of" situations and to be able to engage in sound decision making. Managers need both formal and informal information; social isolation tends to deny them access to the latter.

Social workers as managers face a similar problem as do other staff—perceptions of their management behaviors based on their demographic characteristics. They may be doing or saying exactly what other managers are doing or saying, but will it be perceived in the same way? For example, because of the persistent negative stereotypes of women as disorganized, inefficient, and emotional, interpretations of the same behavior may be much more negative for women than for men. Similarly, older managers who become angry at staff incompetence may have their warranted and appropriate reprimand of a staff member dismissed as simply another sign that they are getting "old and irritable." African-American managers may have their appropriate enforcement of rules and procedures interpreted as indicating that they are meeting some intrapersonal need to exert control over white staff. A white male manager's concerned efforts to orient a new female staff member to her job responsibilities may be perceived as paternalistic or condescending or, even worse, as an effort to become inappropriately familiar with her.

Staff will inevitably engage in some stereotyping based on the characteristics of the manager, whatever those characteristics are. Unfortunately, the stereotypes are almost always accompanied by negative types of discrimination. They may result in managers being taken less seriously than they should be or in certain erroneous assumptions about them that can only result in problems in interaction with staff. Whenever superiors, peers, and subordinates relate to the social work manager as a member of a group and fail to individualize the person who is that manager, trouble is waiting to happen. Some other examples of dangerous and erroneous stereotypes based on a manager's group membership that staff may have might include:

- The manager (female) doesn't really need the job and will become pregnant and leave soon.
- The manager (physical handicap) got the job to meet affirmative action requirements.
- The manager (white male) was not the best-qualified for promotion and got the job through the "old boy network."
- The manager (older employee) will not be able to handle the pressure when the workload gets heavy.
- The manager (younger employee) is not assertive enough to supervise older subordinates.
- The manager (Latina) was hired to placate the community, and probably knows nothing about management.
- The manager (a former beauty pageant winner) is not very bright and was hired for her appearance.
- The manager (Native American) has a problem with alcohol.
- The manager (gay male) is an activist who will embarrass the organization in the community.
- The manager (a retired military officer) is rigid and insensitive.
- The manager (Jewish) will show favoritism to other Jewish staff.
- The manager (Northern male) is rude and aggressive.
- The manager (Southern male) is ignorant and a "redneck."

No matter what diverse characteristics managers possess, staff will inevitably hold some stereotypes about them. Stereotypes can encourage behavior that can harm one's capacity to manage and have the potential to erode the trust that we have emphasized as so important to good management. Managers *should* be able to fulfill their role expectations as managers without having the motivation for their behavior erroneously interpreted by staff. But once again, what should exist is not necessarily the way things are.

"Positive" Stereotyping of Managers

All of our examples of stereotyping to this point have been negative. Of course, less frequently, erroneous stereotypes based on the characteristics of the manager can be positive. For example, the older manager initially may be assumed to be very knowledgeable and experienced; the retired military officer may be assumed to be a good leader; the woman or Native American manager may be assumed to be especially competent to have "beaten the odds" against moving up in the organization, the Asian manager may be assumed to be especially intelligent, or the white male may be assumed to be well qualified to supervise the all female staff. A younger manager may be assumed to possess a high energy level; supervisors with 15 years' experience must really know their jobs, and so forth. These stereotypes can work to the manager's advantage, at least in the short run. But what if the manager doesn't live up to the stereotype? Individuals may not possess the attributes that they were assumed to have; their strengths as managers may lie elsewhere. Stereotypes (even the positive ones) can result in disappointment and disillusionment when they are found to have little basis in reality.

Social workers as managers must help staff members see beyond the demographic characteristics of themselves as managers. This is not to suggest that good management necessarily involves baring one's soul to staff or revealing more personal information than the manager wishes to reveal. It does suggest, however, that managers should be open about themselves as managers, their philosophies of management, their style, and even, on occasion, what they perceive to be their weaknesses and strengths. Staff seek an environment of certainty in which to do their jobs. They want to know what they can expect from the manager in the way of behavior; they should not have to rely on assumptions that may be based on stereotypes about the manager's demographic characteristics.

Letting staff members see and recognize the uniqueness of one's self can reduce some of the liabilities faced by managers who tend to be victims of stereotyping, prejudice, and discrimination. The social work manager of the twenty-first century must assume that, for example, being a manager and a woman or a manager and a member of a racial or ethnic group will continue to create special problems. Fortunately, a large amount of empirical research is being conducted that should provide both insight and assistance in dealing with these problems.

Another Way of Viewing Diversity

Sometimes it is helpful for the manager in promoting diversity through hiring or in working with existing diversity within an organization to look beyond job descriptions or demographic characteristics. Often people are influenced in their work by factors that seem to transcend their educational achievements or their gender, ethnicity, cultural affiliation, and so forth. As we have emphasized throughout this chapter, any categorizing and stereotyping of human beings is a potentially dangerous and misleading activity. However, there is still some value in looking at another way of categorizing staff that has been discussed in the business literature for many years.

Alvin Gouldner's research suggested that paid staff tend to fall into one of two categories. He called one group "locals" and the other "cosmopolitans." He proposed three criteria for determining whether a staff member is a local or a cosmopolitan. They are (1) the object of the individual's loyalty, (2) their primary reference group, and (3) their degree of commitment to skills.[10]

What is a local, according to Gouldner? A local owes primary loyalty to the organization. The local's primary reference group is the person who appears as one's immediate supervisor on the organizational chart, whether or not the supervisor was educated in the same discipline. Locals have a relatively low commitment to the skills of their discipline. If, for example, a promotion were offered that would change their job to require primarily supervision of other staff rather than use of their professional skills, locals would eagerly accept it in order to move up within the organization.

Cosmopolitans reflect the opposite characteristics. Their primary loyalty is to their profession and to its values. For example, if a conflict were to arise between the demands of the organization and their professional values or ethics, they would take a position consistent with the latter. Their primary reference group is their fellow professionals. A colleague's opinion of his or her work would be more important to a cosmopolitan than that of a supervisor who may have been educated in another discipline. Cosmopolitans are highly committed to professional skills and demonstrate a desire to use them. For example, they would not be interested in a promotion to an administrative position where they could no longer practice the skills that they learned as part of their professional education.

The local/cosmopolitan typology is, of course, an oversimplification of the real world. Critics of it have pointed out that the two types do not seem to describe some staff within organizations. For example, some people seem to have some characteristics of both locals and cosmopolitans. Some have characteristics of neither. They seem to be self-serving, lacking in loyalty to anything but themselves, not valuing the opinions of anyone else, and have little commitment to either professional skills or to moving up within the organizational hierarchy.

Despite the exceptions to the Gouldner typology, many staff members *do* tend to look and act like locals and cosmopolitans. Cosmopolitans are not necessarily more desirable employees than locals or vice versa. Both have a contribution to make. Both also represent risks and potential problems for the manager. Locals are likely to do what they are told without much questioning; they want to please their immediate superiors. They are not likely to debate the professional ethics of what needs to be done to meet the requirements of the organization. They usually will not object if asked to perform a task that is outside their job description or what they claim as their professional area of expertise. Locals tend to make a career within a single organization; they are not likely to leave as long as promotions and other rewards occur on a fairly regular basis. They can be depended on to speak well of the organization within the community and to try to cover for its potentially embarrassing mistakes. They tend to respect such bureaucratic features as "put it in writing" or the chain of command, and they pay close attention to rules and procedures that, they believe, are there for a reason.

On the negative side, locals sometimes can be *too* agreeable and compliant. They don't speak up or offer valuable criticism, even when it is needed. Their deference to those in authority can make life easy for the manager in some ways, but it also cheats the manager of the negative feedback that is needed. Managers who are especially insecure or in need of validation for their decisions have a tendency to surround themselves with locals who are almost always complimentary of what they do. A mutual admiration society can develop. Managers get a distorted idea of their skills and abilities and, making matters worse, start to discount the opinions and advice of those (cosmopolitans) who are even mildly critical. Before long they listen to nobody but locals, who may lack a kind of professional conscience. Because of a lack of commitment to professional skills, locals may not have much interest in continued professional growth and are less likely to remain current on emerging knowledge in their field than are cosmopolitans (but they know the current policies, rules, and procedures manual!).

What do cosmopolitans offer to an organization and to a manager? They provide a needed critical perspective on the activities of persons and activities within an organization. They insist on adherence to professional standards. In human service organizations, they often provide needed advocacy for clients and the protection of their rights. They offer fresh new ideas that emanate both from their contacts with professionals outside the organization and from their efforts to continue to practice and upgrade their skills. They are not preoccupied with moving up in the organizational hierarchy and never lose sight of the primacy of client needs. They are less likely to slip into means-end displacements than are locals. They keep a better focus on goals and objectives, but they may question them from time to time.

As with locals, the negative contributions of cosmopolitans to organizations are really just the other side of their positive contributions. Cosmopolitans sometimes can be annoying in their self-righteousness. They may seem to challenge and question a little too much, sometimes failing to accept the realities of politics, fiscal limitations, and a need for efficiency as valid reasons to work in an organization that is less than perfect. They may share their criticisms of the organization with community members. They may have little respect for authority and tend to ignore the administrative hierarchy and the chain of command. In service to clients, they may frequently take an "end justifies the means" attitude that tends to ignore rules and procedures and makes overly liberal use of exceptions to policy. They may advocate for change based on new ideas and approaches to practice, sometimes even if there is nothing essentially wrong with the way work is currently being performed. There may be a tendency on their part to think that conditions are better elsewhere. Because they are not committed to a career within the organization, cosmopolitans tend to be highly mobile. If they become too unhappy, their colleagues within the professional community will help them to find work elsewhere. They may give adequate notice about leaving or they may not, especially if they are very unhappy with the organization.

They may exert considerable influence over other cosmopolitans, instigating them to the point of leaving with them or at least making them more dissatisfied with their work than they had previously been.

A staff consisting of either all locals or all cosmopolitans could be a disaster. The two types tend to complement each other—both offer needed attributes and perspectives. Clearly, some mix of the two (and of less pure types) is desirable.

What factors influence the mix that would be optimal for a given organization? Generally, those organizations that are dependent on adherence to rules and procedures for funding and reimbursement and that must work in a relatively hostile task environment function best with a majority of staff who are locals. A public welfare organization, for example, could not tolerate too many cosmopolitans (and would not attract them). Neither would a state correctional facility. In contrast, a private adoption agency or private psychiatric clinic might require (and attract) a majority of cosmopolitans. A certain amount of natural selection takes place—people tend to want to work in settings that value their attributes. If they don't perceive that they are appreciated, they leave to find another place to work where what they have to offer is more consistent with the needs of the organization. Managers should not be alarmed to observe that they have a preponderance of locals or cosmopolitans on their staff. It is likely to be the product of the natural selection process. Of course, if they clearly have the wrong majority, they will have a problem.

Rapid changes that occur within human service organizations can create a special problem of the "wrong mix" for some managers. They may find themselves with a mix of locals and cosmopolitans that was ideal under previous conditions but is now no longer well-suited to the needs of the organization. For example, many hospitals have recently reorganized. Some mid-level social work management positions have been eliminated and a "flatter" organizational chart has resulted. Social workers have been reclassified as case managers. They now no longer "belong" to social work units per se; they are organized into interdisciplinary teams housed in various units (services) within the hospital. They often find themselves working on a team alongside nurses and other professionals, all with the same job description and sometimes even the same pay scale. Their supervision, if any, is performed more often by people from other disciplines than by social workers. A blurring of professional roles and identities has occurred.

Traditionally, medical social work has attracted people who tended to be more cosmopolitan than local because of the way that activities were organized. The unique contributions of social workers were acknowledged; their professional identities were protected and fostered. Lines of supervision, job descriptions, and job titles all reinforced the idea that their primary identity was not with the hospital or with other disciplines; it was with their profession. However, that has changed. Reorganization has helped to redefine social work roles and responsibilities in ways that the job of social worker now seems better suited to locals. Hospitals have on their staff a preponderance of cosmopolitans, but they may not be what is most needed. Social work managers such as directors, faced with this situation, have the task of attempting to either (a) change the system in order to help cosmopolitans to better meet their needs or (b) use attrition and subsequent hiring of new staff to help to create a mix of locals and cosmopolitans (more locals) that may be more appropriate to the current needs of the organization.

As a conceptual model that is not always consistent with the world as it actually exists, the local/cosmopolitan typology is of limited use. However, along with other similar typologies of staff, it contributes (with the staff types discussed earlier in this chapter and the diversity issues that were examined) to our understanding of why people act the way that they do within organizations. Unfortunately, the local/cosmopolitan typology does a better job of identifying and explaining real and potential problem areas for the social worker as manager than it does of suggesting ways to address those problems.

Summary

In this chapter we began our look at the staffing function of the manager. Special emphasis was placed upon a manager's need to create and maintain diversity in ways that will increase the likelihood of organizational goal attainment. We first examined those factors that must be considered in hiring new staff. Then we examined the categories of staff frequently seen in human service organizations. We presented their general characteristics as well as the advantages and liabilities that each can bring to an organization.

We noted that the modern workplace also is characterized by an increase in human diversity. While it can add richness and unique perspectives to an organization, it also can result in problems. We examined some of those problems and how they can negatively affect the work climate of an organization. We looked at diversity issues as they relate to staff and how diversity among managers may also affect their ability to do the job of manager. Finally, a categorization of staff (local/cosmopolitan) that has been around for a long time was "resurrected" to illustrate one of the many other conceptual models available to the manager for assistance in understanding staff behavior.

Endnotes

1. Ernest Greenwood, "Attributes of a Profession," *Social Work,* 2(3), (July 1957):55; Abraham Flexner, "Is Social Work a Profession?" Proceedings of the National Conference of Charities and Correction (Chicago: The Hildman Printing Company, 1915), pp. 576–590.

2. Robert Clifton and Alan Dahms, *Grassroots Administration* (Monterey, CA: Brooks/Cole, 1980), p. 113.

3. Robert Weinbach, "Accountability Crises: Consequences of Professionalization," *Journal of Sociology and Social Welfare,* IV(7), (September 1977):1011–1024.

4. M. Loden and J. B. Rosenor, *Workforce America! Managing Employee Diversity as a Vital Resource* (Homewood, IL: Irwin., 1991).

5. John F. Longres, "Can We Have Our Cake and Eat It Too?" *Journal of Social Work Education, XXXII* (2), (Spring/Summer, 1996): 159.

6. Yvonne Asamoah, "Managing the New Multicultural Workplace" in *New Management in Human Services,* 2nd Ed. Leon Ginsberg and Paul Keys, eds. (Washington, DC: NASW Press: 1995), p. 116.

7. Roslyn Chernesky and Marcia Bombyk, "Women's Ways and Effective Management," *Affilia,* III (1988):48–61; B.A. Stead, ed., *Women in Management* (Englewood Cliffs, NJ: Prentice-Hall, 1985); A. Herbert, "The Minority Administrator: Problems, Prospects and Challenges," in *Social Administration: The Management of the Social Services,* Vol. 1, Simon Slavin, ed. (New York: The Haworth Press, 1985), pp. 212–224.

8. Jack Levin and William Levin, *The Functions of Discrimination and Prejudice* (New York: Harper & Row, 1982), p. 65.

9. Ibid., pp. 81–89.

10. Alvin Gouldner, "Cosmopolitans and Locals." *Administrative Science Quarterly,* 2 (1957-58):281–306 and 444–480.

6

Promoting Work Performance

No matter what credentials and life experiences employees bring to the organization, they will start to change beginning with their first day on the job. As social workers, we are well aware of the influence that the organization, work groups, and other systems have on the knowledge, attitudes, and behaviors of people. As managers, we have a responsibility to assume an active role in shaping the changes that inevitably take place so that they are in a direction that is consistent with the needs of the organization and its clients.

Understanding Motivation

We have all probably heard someone remark in disgust that, "He has no motivation." The speaker may have been a teacher, a parent, a volunteer coordinator, or an agency administrator. The remark provides a bit of therapeutic ventilation for the speaker, but it is not an accurate description of reality. It might have been more accurate for that person to have said, "I cannot seem to identify what motivates him," or "I have not yet been able to use my knowledge of his motivation to increase his productivity." The point is, everyone is motivated by something. People with no motivation at all would not survive for long. They would not get out of bed, would stop eating, and would soon die. We frequently become frustrated as managers because others do not seem to share the same motivators that *we* possess or because of our inability to understand and work with motivators that are different from our own.

Throughout this book we have emphasized that the knowledge and skills required to perform the management functions of the social worker often are similar to those needed for the performance of other roles of the social worker. Effective use of the knowledge of motivation is a "people skill" that is certainly an asset to the counselor or therapist or to the macro-level practitioner. It is equally valuable to the manager.

Classical Theories of Motivation

There is no shortage of studies of human motivation. It did not take long for managers and students of organizational behavior to notice that workers do not all seem to be equally driven or motivated by the same needs and forces. This realization came in part as a response to the scientific management theories of Frederick Taylor and others (see Chapter 3). Taylor's theories, the reader will recall, were dependent on a belief in the existence of "economic man," that is, the belief that money is the primary motivator of workers. The eventual recognition of the limits of Taylor's theories led other theoreticians to the conclusion that Taylor's belief about motivation was at best an overgeneralization and at worst a gross misunderstanding. Subsequent beliefs about motivation tended to emphasize the diversity of needs and forces that influence an individual's behavior. We will look at a few of the better-known conceptualizations of motivation to see what each has to say to the social worker as manager.

Maslow's Hierarchy of Needs

One of the more familiar theories of motivation is attributed to Abraham Maslow.[1] It has great utility for the social work practitioner, but it is also frequently misunderstood. Maslow's needs hierarchy is generally illustrated by a pyramid containing five categories or levels of needs. They are, in ascending order, physiological, safety, social, esteem, and self-actualization. The choice of a pyramid to illustrate the various need levels is a reflection of Maslow's belief that many persons find themselves stalled at the first (physiological) level, fewer are functioning at the second (safety) level, fewer yet at the third level, and so on. In fairness to Maslow, his hierarchy was developed at a time (around 1945) when this may have been a more accurate description of the distribution of workers and their motivation than is probably true today. We now believe that most people have their most basic needs already met and that many more than just a few persons are motivated by a need for self-actualization. Thus, some students of organizations suggest that an upside-down pyramid might be a more accurate portrayal of people today.

The five levels reflect what Maslow believed were the primary motivators seen among individuals. Persons who have not satisfactorily acquired the basic necessities of life (food, clothing, shelter) are motivated by offers that promise to help meet their physiological needs. Having met these most basic of needs, people might "graduate" to the safety-need level. Here, motivators take the form of protection from threat or danger or loss of what has been acquired.

For individuals who have met their safety needs and have thus reached the third (social) level, needs reflect a preoccupation with the question "What do others think of me?" Affiliation and acceptance are primary motivators at this level. Belonging is of utmost importance, and the promise of being able to fit in is a powerful influence on behavior. At the fourth (esteem) level, the important question is more likely to be, "What do I think of myself?" An individual at this level is driven by a need for self-esteem. Recognition, status, and prestige are important, but only because of their potential for enhancing what is most sought, namely self-confidence and a good feeling about oneself.

The fifth level (self-actualization) is the highest need level. It involves the use of one's talents, creativity, and the opportunity for working to full potential. A person operating at this need level would have satisfactorily met lower-level needs; thus, appeals to lower-level needs would not be productive.

The idea that people are motivated by different needs, or that the needs are hierarchical in nature, was really nothing new. Maslow's major contribution was the conclusion that human beings are only motivated by *unmet* needs, specifically by the need above the highest one in the hierarchy that has already been adequately met. Of course, implicit in the idea of adequate need fulfillment is the recognition that what is "enough" for one person may not be "enough" for another. People tend to have different thresholds for their need gratification. Some require relatively little in order to move on to the next higher level. Others appear to be fixated at one level and never seem to be able to meet that need. For example, some of our grandparents who lived through the Great Depression or World War II seem to exemplify persons for whom safety needs will always be a major motivator. They may find it virtually impossible to understand why people would choose a potentially dangerous profession for their life's work or why they would give up job security in order to take a new position that is more challenging or less structured.

Social workers have usually encountered Maslow's needs hierarchy somewhere in their education or work. It is a useful way of explaining client behavior. For example, it helps to explain why a client who lacks the basic necessities of life (one who is operating at the physiological need level) might derive limited benefits from insight therapy or counseling efforts aimed at promoting personality change. How could appeals to higher-level needs be expected to motivate a person who has not yet progressed beyond the first need level? Conversely, the Maslow conceptualization would also explain why an affluent client in a private residential care setting might be more enticed by the affiliation with others afforded by a Friday night bingo game (an appeal to the third need level) than by the possibility of winning the $10 grand prize. After all, a satisfied need (according to Maslow) is no longer a motivator.

Application of the needs hierarchy concept to the social worker's management activities is readily apparent. One employee might be operating at one need level; another may be at another level. It is not inconceivable that all five levels might be represented among the members of a single work unit. It is incumbent on managers to know their employees well enough to assess accurately for each employee which needs have been adequately met and which (the next higher level) have not and, therefore, are a potential source of motivation. For example, managers should be reasonably certain that employees are operating at the highest (self-actualization) level before offering them new work responsibilities that will require more creativity and innovation. Similarly, managers should be reasonably certain that employees are operating at the social need level before offering to move them from a quiet, isolated work environment into one where there is much more expectation for social interaction.

Maslow's theory, not unlike others that are conceptualizations of human motivation, is, of course, a bit of an oversimplification. Which one of us does not feel that, upon different occasions, any one of the five levels represents our need of the moment? Social needs may seem to predominate today but self-actualization may be more important next week.

Some critics of Maslow—for example, Lawler and Suttle[2]—concluded that there was little to document even the existence of a needs hierarchy. They saw only two distinct types of needs, biological and non-biological, with non-biological needs emerging only after biological needs were met. Other researchers[3] noted that, as people move on through the life cycle, higher-level needs predominate. This may occur as a result of career progression or even maturation, rather than as a result of gratification of lower-level needs. Negative changes in our life situation such as losses (for example, losing a job, loss of a significant other, and so forth) can also send us "back down" the needs hierarchy to a level that had previously been gratified. Even if we acknowledge that there are many exceptions to Maslow's theory or believe that it is flawed, it still offers us some basic insights worthy of reflection. Specifically, if we accept the idea that a satisfied need is not a motivator and that only unmet needs immediately above the highest level gratified are potential sources of motivation, we will be more likely to avoid costly mistakes that can damage individual and group morale. We will offer rewards that appeal to workers' current need levels and not to needs that are already met or that they do not yet experience.

Herzberg's Job Enrichment Theories

Frederick Herzberg is one well-known theoretician who argued that persons who are motivated by a need for self-actualization are hardly rare. In fact, his approaches to job enrichment[4] developed in the 1950s and 1960s are a response to the belief that workers generally tend to be more productive when efforts are implemented to build self-actualization potential into their jobs.

Herzberg proposed that for the individual, work contains certain factors called *hygiene factors* and certain other factors known as *motivators*. Hygiene factors include, for example, high salary, job security, status, good working conditions, or fringe benefits. They are, of course, very nice to have. If not present, they can make an individual feel dissatisfied with a job. But, and this is the important point, their presence is no guarantee that an employee will be highly motivated. They are not motivators; they are only potential satisfiers or dissatisfiers (if not present).

The second group, motivators, appeal to people's need for self-actualization. They include, for example, challenge, interesting work, freedom, responsibility, and potential for growth. Thus, they are factors that are intrinsic to the nature of the work itself.

Herzberg developed job enrichment workshops that sought to provide assistance to employers who wanted to build more motivators into their employees' jobs. Sometimes, Herzberg seemed to suggest that these should be built in even at the expense of hygiene factors. Not surprisingly, labor unions have not always eagerly embraced job enrichment. Generally, their efforts have been directed at gaining more of what Herzberg dismisses as hygiene factors for workers.

Job enrichment is not very applicable to highly mechanized organizations, or certain jobs that are necessarily dull and repetitive. But Herzberg never really suggested that job enrichment is for everyone or all work settings. He acknowledged that some jobs, by their very nature, require routine task performance. For work that has little potential for building in motivators, others had previously proposed other methods. One of these is *job enlargement*. It entails a limited expansion of an individual's job responsibilities. How might job enlargement work in a human service organization? Consider the housekeeping staff in a large public agency. Carpets must be vacuumed, wastebaskets must be emptied, recylables must be collected and so forth, usually every day. Job enrichment could probably not be applied to make this challenging, stimulating work with high potential for recognition, feelings of achievement, growth or advancement. But there is still the potential to make the job a little more attractive. It could be enlarged to include decision making about the purchase of cleaning supplies or about the frequency with which recycling containers will be emptied.

A related approach called *job rotation* entails building variety into a job wherever possible to relieve boredom and other associated problems. In our example, this might be done by rotating custodial staff among floors or departments at regular intervals. In this way, the tasks may not vary, but at least there is a "change of scenery" every so often and the opportunity to interact with different people. If some settings are regarded as more difficult or less pleasant than other settings in some other way, job rotation also ensures that no one person will be "stuck" with them more than any other workers.

Would Frederick Taylor have seen the need for job enrichment or even job enlargement or job rotation? Probably not. They would be seen as unnecessary work for the manager, since Taylor thought that people were primarily motivated by money. But in the modern workplace we often see people and situations that seem to support the need for them. For example, we may see co-workers who are not productive despite the presence of a variety of hygiene factors. Job security, relatively high pay, and the best fringe benefits in the world might not be enough to help a social worker "catch fire" in a job that is dull and repetitive and that seems to offer no challenges or no outlet for creativity.

We have also seen dedicated, highly productive professionals who work for low salaries, sharing a work cubicle with another professional, and with virtually no hygiene factors present. They love their work and speak highly of it. We might speculate that their job is probably rich in challenge, freedom, opportunity for professional growth, and/or other motivators as described by Herzberg.

What is the message to the social work manager? Many of the professionals and paraprofessionals with whom we work might be expected to seek gratification for their self-actualization needs. After all, few people who pursue financial wealth choose to enter social work or many other of the helping professions. And most have adequately met their other lower level needs. As managers, we may be in a position to engage in a little job enrichment, even if we cannot do much about including more of the hygiene factors that we all would like. Building in more motivators requires time and thought and the support of superiors.

Job enrichment may appeal to the needs of many professionals, but the manager cannot assume that even all professionals necessarily seek responsibility, challenge, autonomy, etc. Some do not. For them, opportunities for self-actualization may be more resented than welcomed, especially if they appear to be offered instead of such benefits as raises or other hygiene factors.

There also are some people who have a strong need for self-actualization, but they may not seek to gratify it through their work. They may paint, cook, restore old cars, or make furniture as an outlet for their creativity. If so, they may seek nothing more than good pay from their job—enough to support the costs of their creative outlet. They would not likely be spurred to new heights of productivity by efforts to enrich their job. The only enrichment they may want is through their paycheck! Unless they are careful, managers can easily err in interpreting and responding to a professional staff member's motivational

CASE EXAMPLE • *Motivation Misread*

Lamar was bright, energetic, and upwardly mobile. At 28, he was the director of a large employee assistance organization (EAP) that employed a staff of 24 and had EAP contracts with several large manufacturing firms. He was successful and respected in the social work professional community

Lamar's organization was only four years old. Initially, he hired three other social workers to provide services. All were personal friends who Lamar knew well and respected. As the demand for services increased and as new contracts came along, Lamar continued to take an active part in all personnel matters and in decisions related to assignment of staff. While he no longer knew his staff as well as he once had, he believed that he was a good judge of character and continued to handle all personnel matters himself.

It didn't take Lamar long to notice Bruce, a recent MSW graduate. Several senior staff had praised Bruce's attitude and his work. Not only was he exceptionally well-liked, he was also highly productive. He volunteered to take on new cases for other staff who were feeling overworked. He came to work early to get together informally to discuss his work with other staff. He never seemed too busy to listen to others or to just allow co-workers to vent their frustrations. Lamar found himself wishing he could hire 10 other social workers just like Bruce—people with Bruce's high motivation, cooperation, and dedication. Lamar was not surprised when Bruce's employee evaluations (completed by his supervisor) were the best that he had ever seen.

As a manager, Lamar knew the importance of rewarding his staff for their good work. He knew that someone as good as Bruce would be very marketable elsewhere, and he did not wish to lose him to another organization.

Lamar called Bruce in for a conference to discuss his future with the organization. He began by complimenting him on his high evaluations and the other favorable comments that had been made by coworkers, clients, and corporation personnel officers. He told Bruce that he really appreciated his work and his positive attitude toward it, and he assured him that it would not go unrewarded. Bruce clearly savored all the praise. Lamar went on to describe the other two EAP contracts that he had bid on and hoped to receive. He volunteered that, while he could make no promises, Bruce was the current front-runner to be the coordinator for the next contract received. This would be a promotion that would entail considerably more money, status, and the supervision of four or more new staff members. Bruce's response to this information was, "I'm not sure that I'm ready for that!" Lamar dismissed his reaction as humility, or, perhaps, just a way of Bruce fishing for another compliment. Lamar had little doubt that an achiever like Bruce would jump at the chance for a promotion when the next coordinator position became available.

A new major EAP contract was signed in August. It was scheduled for full implementation on January 15th. The staff was informed about it in early September. Three other staff members immediately applied for the coordinator job, but Bruce did not. Lamar asked for his letter of application and received it a week later. During October and November, plans proceeded for the new EAP. During that lime, Lamar began to receive complaints about the quality of Bruce's work. Bruce seemed far less enthusiastic; he took several sick days with no evidence of suffering from any medical problems. What had once been the organization's most highly motivated employee now looked no better or worse than any other staff member. When by December 1st Lamar had to make a decision on the choice of the new coordinator, he could not in good conscience support the selection of Bruce. He chose another applicant.

Not one to avoid the unpleasant tasks of management, Lamar called each of the applicants who was not selected (including Bruce)

CASE EXAMPLE • *(continued)*

into his office to announce and to explain his decision before it became public knowledge. While he didn't relish this task with any of the three, he especially dreaded it with Bruce because of their earlier conference. His concerns proved unfounded. Bruce seemed genuinely relieved. He confided to Lamar that he very much liked just what he was doing and had no desire to supervise others. Shortly afterward, Lamar again began to receive rave notices about the quality of Bruce's work.

Discussion Questions

1. Why was it a mistake for Lamar to continue to handle all personnel matters himself after his organization had gotten so large?
2. What clues did Lamar miss that might have told him that a promotion for Bruce would not be a good idea?
3. What did Lamar ultimately learn was Bruce's greatest need?
4. What about the possible promotion may have caused Bruce to "sabotage" his receiving it?
5. Why did Bruce not say he was just not interested in the coordinator job when Lamar first discussed it with him?

needs. Or, they may accurately assess an employee's motivation, but naively assume that the workplace is the only place workers choose to meet their needs. Not all employees perceive their job as central to their identity or to their need gratification. This is okay. Many staff members who think of their work as "just a job" nevertheless make valuable contributions to organizational goal achievement and client service. They ought to be rewarded and supported along with the self-actualizing professionals whom we are naturally more inclined to value and to support through methods of job enrichment.

McClelland's Needs Theory

David McClelland viewed individual motivation a little differently from either Maslow or Herzberg. His early research suggested that there are basically three different organizational "types"[5] whose behavior suggests the type of need that is predominant for each. McClelland's conceptualization is an appealing one for social workers who have likely seen clients, co-workers, professors, and relatives or friends who seem to be very good examples of the three types.

According to McClelland, people tend to be motivated by a need for (1) power, (2) affiliation, or (3) achievement. Whereas Maslow's theory suggests that people can gratify a predominant need and move on to another; McClelland's theory views people as more fixated. Their predominant need is, in effect, insatiable.

People motivated by a need for power are likely to move toward positions and situations that promise control and influence over others. They enjoy exercising power and never seem to get enough of it. As personality types, they are outspoken, forceful, and demanding; these characteristics frequently are revealed in their interactions with others. Friendships are pursued as devices to be used to acquire more power rather than as a source of pleasure or gratification in their own right.

People with a strong need for affiliation have an approach to human relationships that is almost 180° different from that of the power-motivated individual. Their activities seem to be aimed at being loved and at avoiding rejection. They enjoy all kinds of friendly interaction and are extremely uncomfortable when interpersonal conflict occurs. They do not seek to have power over or to control others, because to do so might damage a friendship or get in the way of forming yet another one. Persons with a need for affiliation are inclined to be nonjudgmental and giving, but, of course, they give primarily in order to receive. Their need is readily apparent in the extremes to which they will go in order to be liked and to avoid offending others.

Individuals driven by a strong need for achievement crave success, but never really believe that they have achieved it. They fear failure more than anything, and it is this specter that drives them on when, by most outside assessments, they have "made it." They often have some unattainable ideal for a definition of "real success" that guarantees that they inevitably fall short, but they keep trying.

As we observed in our discussion of Maslow's needs hierarchy, examples abound of persons who seem to reflect indications of the presence of two or more of these needs simultaneously. But that does not negate the value of McClelland's conceptualization for our examination of motivation and its utility to the manager. If we assume that, at least for a sizable number of staff members, one of the three needs predominates, certain implications emerge.

As people, we might find one or more of the types less than pleasant to be around. But all three have the potential to make important contributions to organizational goal achievement and to client services. As we suggested in our discussion of the merits of locals and cosmopolitans in Chapter 5, it is indeed the unfortunate manager who finds himself or herself with all one type. But a reasonable mixture has the potential to constitute a very effective work group. Thus, it is critical that managers recognize the existence of each of these types and that they tailor their work incentives for them accordingly.

What are the contributions of each to the organization? People with a strong need for power can be expected to work hard in a position that grants them control over their own activities and the activities of others. However, if their motivation is particularly transparent, others over whom they have power may quickly grow to resent them. If placed in a position of authority, the manager had better be prepared to monitor their activities closely to be certain that they are not unnecessarily heavy-handed or abrasive in their interaction with peers and subordinates. The high morale of a work unit is, after all, preferable to attempting to gratify the need for power of one or a few individuals.

People high in need for affiliation have a different contribution to make to an organization. They generally have acquired excellent social skills. These skills can be useful both within the organization and outside it for creating a more favorable task environment. Their diplomacy can be a real asset. They will work extra hard and display a high level of motivation in activities that promise the reward of close friendships and pleasant social interaction. But they may also be virtually unable to function if the environment is too hostile or if conflict is unavoidable.

Individuals with a high need for affiliation will often make sacrifices and give much of themselves in order to please superiors and to help out when needed. In client treatment, for example, they might welcome telephone calls at home or not resent unexpected five o'clock walk-ins from clients. The negative side to this is that excessive dependency (actually it is more like interdependency) can easily occur with clients and other staff because of their strong affiliation need. They might have difficulty in saying no when "no" is the correct response, given organizational or client needs. Their need to give and to receive can occupy great amounts of time and effort that can interfere with efficiency. They can be resented by co-workers who become weary of their never-ending efforts to be liked. Social workers as managers can prevent many of these negative phenomena by recognizing a worker's need for affiliation and by providing situations for its gratification that do not jeopardize collegial relationships or client services. They can be prevented from engaging in too much nonproductive social interaction by limiting their need to interact with others. However, it generally is better to understand and use individual motivation than it is to frustrate it. Any unnecessary structure that prohibits the development of friendships is likely to be deeply resented by people who are motivated by a need for affiliation. The secret (as with the other two types as well) is to find activities that benefit the organization and its clients while at the same time meeting their need.

Staff members who possess strong needs for achievement are, like the other two types, a mixed blessing for the manager. They are likely to work hard at tasks that promise individual recognition or some tangible indicator of their success. But the manager may experience frustration at their incessantly critical approaches to their own and others' achievements. They are likely to accomplish much that is good for the organization while attempting to meet their needs, but they may also demand an unreasonable amount of achievement from subordinates and co-workers. This can be useful as a source of relief for the manager in that it allows someone else to play the "heavy" for a while. But it can also cause real morale problems. Co-workers quickly resent it. While it is tempting for managers to relinquish their role as leader (and to look undemanding and lax by comparison), allowing an achievement-oriented staff member to play boss is dangerous. It can suggest weakness on the part of the manager and can undermine the manager's authority and ability to manage.

McClelland continued to do research and to refine his theories of motivation during the many years since he first published his conceptualization of the three primary motivators. In the 1980s he suggested that there may be another group of motivators—avoidance motives—that may also provide the primary impetus for a person's behavior on the job. He noted that, for example, an obsession with fear of failure, fear of rejection, fear of success, and fear of power seem to be accompanied by behavior not generally seen in individuals who do not possess them. McClelland concludes, however, that evidence for avoidance motives being distinctly different from "the big three" has not been found. In fact, critics have suggested that avoidance motives may be little more than the "other side of the same coin." Perhaps they are not an additional predominant need at all. At least it could be argued that fear of failure may be the same as need for achievement and fear of rejection may be the same as need for affiliation.

McClelland's theories are useful to the manager in assessing individual staff motivation and in promoting appropriate and productive behavior. They also have at least one other practical use—as a mirror. A manager's need for self-awareness is no less than that of a therapist or a community worker. It is useful for managers occasionally to ask, "Are my behaviors and decisions based on organizational needs, management principles, and other appropriate criteria? Or are they perhaps a function of my own predominant need?"

Other Factors That Affect Motivation

Thus far we have viewed motivation from the perspective of some of the theorists who have studied it. Specifically, we have assumed that motivation derives primarily from the needs of the individual. As social workers, we cannot underestimate the importance of individual human needs and the drives for their gratification. But we know that certain motivators (in addition to individual needs) tend to affect the behavior of professionals and other staff within organizations.

Human behavior is complex and often unpredictable, unless we view it as more than just the product of individual motivators. We will now examine some other influences on the behavior of staff within organizations.

Professional Values and Ethics

One of the objectives of professional education is the socialization of students. It is expected that those who complete professional programs will have inculcated the values and ethics of that profession.[6] Our professional values are what we as a professional believe in. Our ethics are what we as a professional will and will not do. It is these values and ethics that then help to guide both the decision making and the behavior of the practitioner.

Generally, professional values serve as positive motivators, that is, they influence professionals to do what we believe to be consistent with them and to resist doing things in those relatively rare situations when the demands of a situation might require a behavior that appears inconsistent with them. Professional ethics generally shape behavior in a little more negative way. They keep professionals from doing or even thinking about doing some things. Professionals simply will not do something that their profession has defined as unethical, such as, having intimate relationships with clients, sexually harassing coworkers, and so forth.

The motivation of staff members to perform or not to perform a requested task or to devote more or less energy to its completion can be affected by whether or not they perceive the task's completion as consistent with their professional values and ethics. Staff members are likely to be highly motivated if a manager's requests and their own professional values and ethics are complementary and mutually reinforcing. For example, a policy that appears to be consistent with, for example, clients' rights to self-determination (a professional value) is likely to meet with enthusiastic compliance. However, resistance to some other policy can be anticipated if that policy appears to impinge on clients' rights to self-determination.

In those situations in which a manager must ask a professional staff member to enforce a decision that appears (from his or her perspective) to be in conflict with professional values or ethics, some explanation by the manager often can help. For example, what if an applicant for counseling must be denied services because the applicant lives just outside a certain geographical area or because the applicant's underlying problem is one that is not consistent with the mission of the organization? A professional might view this as insensitivity or rigidity since it seems to constitute a failure to help a person who clearly needs assistance. Unless an explanation is offered, the worker would be reluctant to deny services to the applicant. Thus professional values can become an obstacle to doing what must be done (from the organizational perspective). However, if the manager makes the extra effort to explain the origin of the agency policy and how it can actually lead to the provision of services to a greater number of clients (an outcome consistent with professional values), motivation for compliance is less likely to be jeopardized and may even gain support.

Professional values may also be supportive of desirable staff behavior in another way. Staff who are aware of funding cutbacks, time constraints, or other stresses that jeopardize client service delivery may set aside self interest, at least in the short run. As professionals, they believe that as prime beneficiaries of the organization, clients should not have to pay a price for conditions beyond their control. They would try to do whatever is required in order to avoid shortchanging client services. An appeal to professional values by the manager may result in professional staff "going the extra mile," for example, they might forego a cost of living pay increase in order that a particular program could continue. However, no professional is likely to continue to respond to this type of appeal if it is made too often or if it begins to be perceived as a device to increase efficiency at staff expense. The manager should be perceived as advocating for the best interests of staff, not as exploiting staff members through too frequent appeals to professional values.

Influences of the Work Group

Professionals and other staff possess various individual needs. Professionals also have their professional values and ethics that they have acquired through their educational and work experience. But when staff enter a work group, the influence of the group often becomes a powerful motivator. Social work managers need to understand how group pressures can influence work performance. They need to be able to create a climate where group norms will foster rather than undercut behavior that is desirable for the organization and its clients.

Virtually all staff are part of one or more work groups. As a member of a group, a person is expected to adopt certain behaviors and attitudes that are consistent with those of other members. These attitudes and behaviors affect what goes on within one's own group. They also affect how one relates to other groups, to the individuals within them, and to bosses and subordinates. Relationships with other groups and individuals within them can run the full range from cooperation to a counterproductive, overt antagonism.

Competition and Conflict.   No matter how well a manager organizes the activities of a work unit and no matter how much the manager attempts to foster a spirit of cooperation among staff, some competition among groups is inevitable. It is not always dysfunctional. Some competition promotes a sense of identity and promotes group loyalty in individuals.

But, as we have probably all witnessed, excessive competitiveness can also result in antagonism, wasted energy, and the absence of teamwork and cooperation.

Social workers usually are familiar with both the benefits and the costs of competition. The classic studies of conflict performed by Sherif in a children's summer camp[7] are often cited. On the positive side, Sherif concluded that the presence of competition between groups (as long as it remains close) promotes task-oriented behavior, greater structure, and demands for conformity and loyalty. These can be very beneficial to the organization. The costs of this kind of competition were also identified. Hostility increases between groups along with decreased communication and stereotyping of members of the other group. These are not helpful to the organization, which requires teamwork and cooperation.

Competition among staff members, while inevitable, can and should be kept at a tolerable level where it has the potential to support rather than to sabotage work productivity. Competition is most likely to degenerate into nonproductive conflict if individuals and groups perceive a situation in which the gain of one is necessarily accompanied by the loss of the other individual or group. This situation has been described as a "zero-sum game."[8] A zero-sum game means, literally, that a conflict situation exists in which the net gain for individuals involved in competition must equal zero—one side can gain only if the other loses the same amount. Zero-sum games do exist. Budgeting situations in homes or in organizations are good examples of zero-sum games. If there is only so much money to spend, spending an amount for one activity means that there is that much less available for another activity.

Not all situations in which there is competition are zero-sum games. In fact, much of the antagonism that exists between groups within organizations may occur because persons perceive the existence of a zero-sum game even though one does not exist. The responsibility of the manager is frequently to acknowledge the existence of a zero-sum game when it is there and to attempt to reduce competition by helping staff to recognize when it is not. For example, professional staff may be in competition for the assigned services of secretarial staff. Clearly, a secretary assigned to work exclusively for one group is not going to be able to work for another. This is a zero-sum game situation, and any manager who suggests otherwise is likely to insult the intelligence of staff and to risk his or her own credibility. Conflict may be expected.

As we have noted, a zero-sum game is often assumed to exist when it is not really present. For example, it is not unusual for professionals in two different service units of a human service organization to act as though there is a limited amount of praise and recognition available to be dispensed by the manager. Proceeding on this assumption, staff may spend a considerable amount of time trying to discredit the work of those in the other unit. In such situations, managers need to stress the lack of a zero-sum game. They should help staff to see that a good job done by one reflects positively on, and therefore benefits, all members of the organization as well as those clients who they serve.

As was noted in Chapter 5, increased diversity among staff almost invariably produces an increased amount of conflict. Some authors have stressed the positive functions of conflict.[9] For example, it can make staff more involved in activities and less apathetic on the job and can spotlight issues and areas of legitimate professional disagreement. It can also reveal professionals at their worst, more concerned with winning an internal struggle than in objectively doing what is in the best interest of clients or of the organization. Even if we are firm believers in the benefits of conflict, we must concede that too much conflict or conflict over the wrong issues can be debilitating within human service organizations.

A manager will, at some time or other, conclude that conflict is excessive. It is preoccupying staff and diverting the valuable energies of those who should be applying them toward organizational goal attainment. When internal squabbles interfere with good decision making and when personal loyalties take priority over the best interests of both the organization and clients, the manager must intervene to reduce conflict.

One possible method of conflict reduction involves the identification of a common goal that transcends individual or group interests and the repeated reminder of the existence of that goal. If the manager can find a goal that everyone wants (not always an easy task if conflict is intense), conflicts will sometimes be set aside. For example, the manager might remind staff of the need to complete and submit a grant application that, if approved, would result in a new needed program. A strategy to achieve this goal could then be developed, one that requires staff to work cooperatively toward its attainment.

A second tactic for conflict reduction involves the identification of a common enemy. This approach is not new to students of political science or of world history. It was used by Adolph Hitler to help unify German factions after World War I. Frequently, in human service organizations, it is not necessary to fabricate a common enemy or to vilify some outside group that represents a threat. Budget cuts and other threats by a hostile task environment can quickly make internal conflict appear trivial if the manager can make staff aware of the threat. A common theme of managers on such occasions is, "This is no time for internal bickering," as it clearly is not. (When is a good time?) If no such acute threat or common enemy exists, a skillful manager may still be able to help staff recognize that most social work practice occurs within a chronically hostile task environment whose members like nothing more than to point out internal conflict within the helping professions. As we stressed in Chapter 2, the task environment is rarely supportive of our efforts. This is a reality that can sometimes be turned to the manager's advantage in helping to reduce internal conflict and to free up staff energies to be directed toward goal achievement. It can serve as an impetus to force interaction and to begin negotiation between warring factions or at least to help conflicting parties see that "the enemy" stands to gain the most from continued conflict.

Group Cohesiveness.   An understanding of cohesiveness and how it varies among work groups is necessary to understanding how group membership impacts on the behavior of staff.[10] Work groups range from very loosely structured ones with ambiguous boundaries to clearly identified, cohesive ones. The latter is characterized by clear boundaries and intragroup loyalties.

Cohesiveness, as we are using the term here, relates to a number of identifiable factors that may be present within work groups to a greater or lesser degree. It refers to the sense of group solidarity that is present. It also refers to pride in group membership and the social desirability of belonging to the group. Employees tend to be more satisfied with their work when they are part of a cohesive work group. They are also more likely to reflect a high commitment to achievement of group goals.

The cohesive work group that is working toward organizational goal attainment is usually characterized by pleasant, cooperative relationships where members eagerly assist each other when needed. People volunteer to help because there is a belief that what benefits one benefits the group and, ultimately, benefits all of its members. A member does not want to let the group down or to withhold information that might assist attainment of group goals. Loyalty exists, both to peers and to group leaders. There is a respect for the knowledge and competence of others in the group. Interest in and enjoyment of most (but certainly not all) of the work is readily apparent to the outsider. A relaxed, informal atmosphere prevails in which people speak up and feel comfortable to disagree. But members listen to others' points of view and give them consideration. They disagree over positions on issues, not over personalities. Hidden agenda and memories of past personal grievances do not surface when disagreements occur.

Some groups tend to promote cohesiveness simply by the way that they are organized. For example, small groups are more likely to be cohesive than large ones, and groups that were formed for a common purpose and have existed for long periods of time are generally more cohesive than ones that have been more recently constituted. Other times, managers need to try a little harder to promote group cohesiveness, since it did not occur naturally.

Let us assume that the manager has determined that there is general agreement between group norms and organization goals. What can be done to promote greater group cohesiveness and, indirectly, to promote desired behavior on the part of group members? For a start, it might help to enhance members' awareness of the compatibility between at least some of their group norms and organizational goals. This can be done by enthusiastic support, reward, and commendation for group efforts and by reminding staff members of just how their collective work is contributing to the organization's goal attainment. Managers can also communicate clearly that they value and will reward cooperation and that they take a dim view of interpersonal conflict that jeopardizes individual and group productivity. They can emphasize that they expect staff to evaluate ideas and group members' positions on issues from an objective position based on professional values, and not based upon their attitudes toward the individual who presents the ideas or their previous interaction with that individual.

Social workers as managers can also influence activities within work groups in several other ways that will help to promote cohesiveness. They can assign work and structure tasks in such a way that their completion will necessitate cooperation; members will have to work together cooperatively to get the job done. For example, the task might depend on expertise and perspectives that are not available within any one member but that exist only if two or more members are involved.

Working together and common experiences can help workers get to know and appreciate each other's contributions, abilities, and knowledge. They can provide experiences to share and memories about which to reminisce. Of course, cohesiveness will be enhanced only if the collaboration is viewed in retrospect as positive and productive. If the experience of working together left one or more group members with the impression that other members are incompetent, do not carry their fair share of the work, or cannot be depended upon, confidence in coworkers will be eroded and the attractiveness of belonging to the work group may actually be diminished. The message to the manager is clear—

work to set up tasks that require cooperation and collaboration and that are likely to leave a *positive* taste for the participants, that is, tasks that have a high probability of successful completion.

As a manager, the social worker at any level of practice is likely to have input into decisions or even total authority over how work groups will be structured and how they may be periodically reorganized. Cohesiveness is most likely to thrive when groups remain reasonably stable. Time is required for confidence in co-workers and for desirable social bonds to develop. A "revolving door" work group with unnecessary transfers of staff in and out of the group can be destructive of cohesiveness.

If the manager is involved in the formation of new work groups, the richness that diversity can offer (Chapter 5) may be of paramount concern in selecting group members. However, cohesiveness seems to develop less quickly in groups where members perceive themselves to be dissimilar to other members than where differences in experience, values, and demographic characteristics are not as readily apparent. Since a fairly homogeneous group (or at least one that is perceived that way by its members) is desirable for promoting cohesiveness, managers need to point out similarities among group members. Especially if a work group is very diverse in its composition, the manager may need to remind group members of what they share in common with other members whenever the opportunity arises.

Up to this point, we have discussed the desirability of promoting group cohesiveness. It would seem, on the surface at least, that work group cohesiveness is universally desirable as a way of advancing productivity. Not quite. In the same way that conflict sometimes can be desirable, cohesiveness sometimes can be undesirable for an organization. *If* group values and goals are consistent with organizational values and goals, cohesiveness is desirable. Unfortunately, this is not always the case. For example, there are some work groups that are highly cohesive, yet part of their cohesiveness is based on shared values that promote minimal standards of work performance, antagonism toward other groups, and a hostile, passive-aggressive approach toward the manager. Or a group may be highly cohesive when, for example, needed changes are being resisted or when there are efforts to overthrow an administrator or sabotage an unpopular program. In short, cohesiveness is a desirable attribute of work groups, but only if there is agreement between group values and goals of the organization. If this is not the case, efforts of the manager may have to be directed toward breaking up work groups or otherwise attempting to weaken group cohesiveness.

Supporting Growth

Most professional staff want to become more proficient at their jobs and to take on additional responsibilities. They are motivated to succeed because of a combination of individual needs and group influences. But they need help, and providing that help is the work of managers. While many factors promote desirable growth among employees, we will focus upon the two most powerful influences available to managers within human service organizations—supervision and continuing education.

Supervision and continuing education send a good message. By providing them, managers tell their staff that they value and are willing to commit necessary time and other resources to promote more effective work performance. They are emphasizing the importance of learning to do more, to do it better, and to do it more autonomously.

In earlier chapters, we have referred to how the social worker as manager should contribute to the creation of a desirable work climate. Supervision and continuing education can provide the knowledge necessary for workers to do their job within such a climate—one of reasonable certainty. It is impossible for anyone to know everything that is needed in order to approach every decision and task confidently. But supervision and continuing education help to reduce the number of decisions for which workers feel lost and unprepared to a tolerable minimum. Prepared workers will rarely find themselves totally without the knowledge necessary to make an intelligent decision or to perform a task.

Growth through Supervision

A manager at any level in the organization needs to understand what supervision is and to be aware of some of the options available for providing it. There are many good texts that prepare the reader for the job of social work supervisor.[11]

One problem that is frequently encountered in understanding supervision is the different functions that are encompassed under the term "supervision." The social worker who is a direct service practitioner is most likely to envision supervision as a process designed to provide workers with insights and assistance in working with specific cases. This is commonly referred to as case supervision or clinical supervision and, perhaps more appropriately, as case consultation. While, as we shall see, this is a legitimate area of supervision and a necessary one, we really cannot understand supervision as managers unless we broaden our understanding to include many other interactions between supervisors and workers that have only an indirect impact on practice intervention. There exists another whole group of supervisory activities that more closely resembles our focus of study—management. It includes the use of management functions as applied to subordinates to shape, support, and enhance the individual's job performance.

Traditional Supervisory Roles

Confusion over case supervision and administrative supervision permeates our literature. Kadushin[12] helped to differentiate supervisory roles by dividing the functions of the supervisor into three slightly overlapping activities: administrative supervision; supportive supervision; and educational supervision. He addressed a related area, consultation, in another text.[13] These four roles provide a workable overview of supervision as a means of enhancing growth.

Kadushin's description of *administrative supervision* comes closest to what we are referring to as management. It involves such important functions as work assignment and task supervision, overseeing, communicating, serving as a buffer between higher-level administrators and workers, and matching of workers to tasks.

The second role that Kadushin describes, *supportive supervision,* spotlights a major difference between the role of the social work supervisor and supervisors in many businesses and industries. The type of job stresses and tensions inherent in many human service organizations (for example, in child protection, investigation of charges of family violence, or work with the terminally ill) often dictate that much of the supervisor's time is spent in providing psychological support to a supervisee. With this support, workers can continue to function on the job without being overwhelmed by various stresses that exist within their work.

The third major role described by Kadushin, *educational supervision,* also represents somewhat of a departure from how business or industry defines supervision. The role of teacher or mentor usually is not emphasized in a manufacturing plant. If anything, such a role may be perceived as inappropriate in that it might compromise the objectivity required to perform the major supervisory function, which is administrative supervision. But it, along with the related task of networking, are viewed as important to growth of staff within the human services.[14] The supervisor is expected to take on the role of educator, partly by facilitating continuing education for a supervisee, but also by providing direct instruction and introducing supervisees to what they need to know to succeed.

Finally, a supervisor is also expected to provide specific advice and direction for working with individual cases or dealing with problems relating to some form of practice intervention—*case consultation.* As a case consultant, the supervisor recognizes that some particularly difficult situations may require the assistance of a senior professional with more experience and/or a different perspective. Sometimes, if the supervisor lacks the knowledge or skills to provide case consultation for addressing some problem, an "expert" may be brought in from the outside either for a one-time consultation or on a regular basis. Or, another employee of the organization who has the necessary knowledge and skill might be asked to provide it.

Alternative Supervisory Methods

The word "supervision" usually tends to connote a one-to-one type of relationship with a senior person with similar credentials. However, in making provisions for the supervision necessary for employee growth, there are several viable options to the traditional supervisor–supervisee model. Each option should be seriously considered; each may offer time and cost-saving advantages as well as other advantages that may be preferred by some staff members.

Use of Preceptors.   Although ideally it might be best for an employee to be supervised by a person who is from the same discipline and who has engaged in or is currently engaged in performing the same tasks, this is not always possible. As managers, social workers sometimes recognize that opportunities for growth of a worker can be limited by the employee receiving all supervision from any one supervisor. The supervisor may lack the knowledge and experience to supervise the worker in activities that are important to that individual's growth. For example, a social worker in an inpatient mental health setting may be interested in learning more about a certain type of group treatment being offered in the hospital. The person who facilitates the group may be a psychologist. In order not to preclude the worker from having this experience and growth opportunity, a manager may assign a portion of the educational supervision to the psychologist. However, supervision of all other professional activities and all administrative and supportive supervision will remain with the social work supervisor. Only a small portion of the task of supervision has been "farmed out" to the psychologist who assumes the role of "preceptor."

Group Supervision by Peers.   There is one supervisory structure that retains the responsibility for supervision within the discipline of the worker but yet allows some supervisory responsibilities to be shared by peers.[15] Supervisors may choose to carry out supervisory activities in a group setting with all or some of their supervisees present. This form of group supervision is an appealing alternative to the manager for a number of reasons. For one thing, many of the learning needs of supervisees are held in common. By addressing them in a group, supervisors can save much of the time and effort that would be required to conduct the same instruction individually for each employee. If several supervisees seem to be at about the same level of professional development and seem to require essentially the same type of educational supervision, group supervision can be an efficient approach to supervision.

Group supervision can also provide the opportunity for employees to learn from each other and from the supervisor in a relatively non-threatening environment. They can share relevant learning experiences, pooling knowledge in a way that provides access to more knowledge than the supervisor alone could provide.

On the negative side, certain supervisory requirements cannot easily be addressed using group supervision. For example, it may not meet legal requirements for child protection cases or court-ordered intervention for other types of client problems. It works far better for educational supervision (as a learning tool) than for supportive or administrative supervision. For example, a worker encountering the stresses of the job can find support through group supervision if others admit to having similar problems. But if others deny having the same difficulties, the worker can be made to feel even more overwhelmed and embarrassed. Similarly, critique of one's work by the supervisor can be more embarrassing if given in front of others than if communicated in one-to-one supervision.

Group supervision is a form of participative management and thus has some of the same advantages and disadvantages. A too-egalitarian approach to supervision can be popular with supervisees, but it can quickly cause problems. The supervisor's advice, admonition, or even directive can begin to be perceived as having no more force than the opinion of other persons in the group and, sometimes, even less than that of an outspoken co-worker. It can become difficult for group members to discern when the supervisor speaks from a position of expertise or of authority (which supervisors continue to possess) and when the supervisor is just offering an observation as a fellow professional.

When group supervision is used, a competition for power and influence may also develop among supervisees. Individuals may seek to "posture" for the position of most knowledgeable or most competent (even to the point of not reporting their own struggles accurately if they might undermine this position). This can threaten supervisors and their role, making it more difficult for them to function, particularly as case consultants. For instance, how can a supervisor tactfully provide a critical evaluation of a supervisee's work when a peer who has claimed the role of expert has just complimented their performance? Or how can supervisors criticize workers' performances that are not satisfactory when the workers' deficiencies were first pointed out by their peers? Will it look like the peer influenced the supervisor's judgment? These and other issues reflect the danger of a kind of role-blurring that can occur if group supervision is not used with extreme caution. For this reason, many managers advocate a combination of group, individual, and other supervisory approaches to capitalize on the advantages inherent in each and to minimize the likelihood of difficulties that can occur when too heavy a reliance on one approach exists.

Interdisciplinary Supervision.   Another form of supervision, interdisciplinary supervision, often makes heavier use of people within other disciplines to provide supervision. It is a supervisory option that has grown in popularity recently because of the formation of interdisciplinary case management teams in many medical and psychiatric work settings. Because of either choice or administrative fiat, now supervision is often provided by an interdisciplinary team consisting of persons from various disciplines. When this situation exists, it is imperative that managers understand the inherent dangers as well as the educational advantages that can exist. For example, there is the potential for professional identity to become confused. A worker may even contribute willingly to this phenomenon, especially if other disciplines on the team are more attractive or possess higher status. Managers need to stress the importance of workers maintaining a professional identity consistent with their educational preparation. They need to make every effort to assure that at least some supervision is provided by persons within their professional discipline (perhaps through outside consultation). They should also assure that, whenever possible, staff members' performances are evaluated by people who understand both the functions and the values and ethics that are unique to their profession.

The social worker assigned to work on a case management team on a medical specialty floor in a large hospital illustrates both the advantages and dangers of interdisciplinary supervision. The Director of Social Services must be extremely skillful in handling the supervision of the social worker who is assigned to, for example, neonatal intensive care, oncology, or eating-disorder units. These assignments offer the kind of growth within a specialized area that is not available within a more generic assignment. Clearly, the physicians who are in charge of such units are more knowledgeable than is the Director of Social Services in their area of specialization. They are logical choices to assume supervisory roles. But how much and at what cost? How does the Director of Social Services avoid a situation where social workers assume the identity of "pediatric care specialist" or some other attractive role that suggests a primary loyalty to the discipline of the physician in charge? How can one assure that when value conflicts occur between medical and social work values (for example, regarding returning a child to an abusive home), the social worker will seek professional consultation and support from the Director of Social Services rather than simply deferring to the physician?

Interdisciplinary supervision is a logical and a desirable alternative to traditional supervisory structures, especially in some work settings, but it also has the potential to weaken or sabotage desirable authority relationships. Annual evaluations and recommendations for promotions or merit raises, for example, are best left to those from the same discipline who understand, appreciate, and share the same values, knowledge, and skills. Staff can lose respect for the supervisor who maintains administrative supervisory authority but who has relinquished most of the functions of supervision to someone in another discipline. Especially when evaluations are unfavorable, there is a tendency for the worker to respond with a kind of "what do they know?" resentment that fails to make use of constructive criticism.

Social workers as managers must weigh the advantages of interdisciplinary supervision with its potential costs. They must remain sensitive to problems in its overuse that can either threaten to undermine supervisory authority or to reduce the potential for worker growth. In the current environment within the helping professions, this means that they must sometimes resist efforts to move toward increased interdisciplinary supervision. Where interdisciplinary supervision is not working, they may need to advocate for change.

Remote Supervision.   Many social workers find themselves in small agencies or in rural areas where there is no possibility of having an on-site supervisor who has the necessary professional credentials. Even in large urban areas, some organizations (most notably medical and psychiatric facilities) have sought to become more cost-efficient by eliminating the jobs of supervisors and re-deploying those who previously held them into direct client services. Staff may have no supervisor per se, at least not for case consultation. This does not mean that decisions must be made unilaterally or that help cannot be obtained. Supervision of professional staff can and sometimes does come through regular or sporadic e-mail conversations with more experienced peers within or outside the organization or through FAX or the telephone. With dependence on technology only likely to increase in the future, this method of acquiring supervision will probably become even more popular. For this "virtual supervision" to be effective, however, it must be thoughtfully implemented. Managers need to provide the necessary time and technological support so that it can happen in an organized way, and to stress its importance for both doing a job well and for continued professional growth.

Attributes of Good Supervision

Whatever supervisory structure or structures a manager employs, it is necessary to keep in mind the importance of promoting employee professional growth. If growth is to occur, the supervision package chosen should reflect certain essential characteristics.

Administrative supervision components should be fair and objective and should be consistent with appropriate personnel standards and practices. If a staff member is a social worker, for example, supervisory procedures should be consistent with the current NASW Standards for Social Work Personnel Practices and/or other local, state, or federal standards that apply. If staff are unionized, the manager must adhere to union supervisory requirements. Not only is this in the best interests of the employee but it also leaves the organization and its staff in a defensible position if employee grievance procedures are later initiated.

Good supervision constantly stresses the need for high-quality and ethical client services. To this end, employees are encouraged to acquire the knowledge and skills to become ever-more competent in their work by attending professional workshops and symposia. Subsequently, they should be assigned tasks that require the use of their newly acquired professional knowledge and skills. Whenever possible, they should be encouraged to exercise professional judgment in decision making and supported in their decisions. They should be recognized and accepted as competent professionals who may, in fact, know more about some areas of practice than do their supervisors.

Good supervision provides both practical assistance and a role model for staff. It also provides a perspective not otherwise available to them. It reminds employees of their responsibility to perform in a way consistent with organizational goals and objectives. Good supervision may also serve as a reminder to employees that they have a responsibility, not only for their own growth, but for the development of knowledge for others who work in the field. It can stress the need for them to base their work on available knowledge and to be active in the regular, ongoing evaluation of their practice effectiveness. If supervision is to be effective in promoting employee growth, it should create a climate for problem-solving in which errors can be freely discussed in a candid manner. Both the supervisee and the person or persons doing the supervising should feel comfortable in giving and taking suggestions. However, it should be emphasized that some decisions cannot be delegated to the supervisee or the supervisory group and that the administrative hierarchy cannot be undermined by whatever supervisory models the manager employs.

Growth through Continuing Education

The background of formal education and experience that workers bring to a human service organization will quickly become obsolete and inadequate for their job responsibilities. Supervision can help to keep them "current," but they also need other learning opportunities.

Learning within organizations is inevitable. Workers learn every day. They learn from co-workers, supervisors, subordinates, clients, clerical staff, and anyone else with whom they have contact. The issue for the manager is: What do they learn, and is what they learn desirable for promoting effective and efficient client services? Sometimes it is, and sometimes it most definitely is not. Informal learning from a co-worker, for example, may suggest a shortcut in record keeping that will result in more time for client service. The saving may have no negative costs or it may result in a disastrous loss of federal reimbursement, if detected. Other well-meaning informal orientation of a new employee by a senior worker may result in a lack of respect for a manager who might otherwise have been respected without the biasing input from the "old hand." If a manager fails to provide for formal learning, other learning will fill the void. But it could just be learning that is undesirable.

Just simply providing learning will not guarantee that it will "take," at least not in the way intended. For example, a training session designed to assure that employees follow appropriate procedures for reimbursement of professional travel expenses can inadvertently suggest ways to use professional travel to conduct personal business. Just what is communicated in programs of formalized learning must be verified and reinforced by the manager, to be certain that it does not produce unintended results.

Addressing Different Needs for Continuing Education

People have a wide variety of learning needs. They range from technical skills to theoretical knowledge to reinforcement of appropriate values. Certain forms of continuing education are appropriate for some learning needs, but less appropriate for others. Three terms—training, education, and staff development—are often used rather freely and even interchangeably to describe the varieties of continuing education methods that exist. Understanding how they differ in purpose, content, and process is very helpful to the manager in identifying what response might be needed by staff for continued growth. Table 6.1 summarizes the distinctive characteristics of each of the three types of continuing education.

Training.   Unlike the other two types of continuing education, *training* is designed to provoke a standardized, "correct" behavior from staff. Like a rule (as discussed in Chapter 4), it is designed to prohibit the exercise of professional discretion. People can be trained to respond in a prescribed way to a predictable and recurring situation. It is possible and desirable to train in those situations where we know in advance that a situation will occur, that there is one acceptable way to respond to it, and that we can be reasonably certain that the way will be effective. Training is appropriate when we know what must be done and wish to make sure that there is no deviation in the way it is done. Training usually involves hands-on practice in performing a task in the approved way. We can and should, for example, train staff to answer the phone in a professional manner, to fill out a form correctly, to enter information into an organization's computer data base, or to comply with requirements for reimbursement from a health insurance organization.

Training is a form of socialization. It helps employees to achieve a basic role competency and to do their work in the acceptable way. It imparts knowledge and provides experience in use of skills that are of immediate value on the job. Thus, it helps employees meet role expectations.

Training can be a very cost-efficient and valuable form of continuing education. With training, workers come on-line quickly and make fewer mistakes. This, in turn, produces less embarrassment for the workers and for the organization and makes staff feel better about their work performance. They are then less likely to engage in absenteeism, complain less, and are less likely to look for other work.

Well-trained workers need less on-site supervision. Once correct methods of responding to situations that can be specified in advance have been learned, staff members can function with more autonomy and feel certain that their handling of a situation is correct. The supervisor, in turn, may be able to devote more time to supervising other workers.

If workers are well-trained, they will provide better services. As behaviors, for which they have been trained, become "second nature," the behaviors become more habitual. This allows them to devote more time and energy to addressing those situations and decisions for which training could not prepare them.

Workers may complain about going to training. But if performed effectively, they almost always appreciate it when it is later put into practice. Unfortunately, in a time of fiscal cutbacks, training sometimes may be viewed as a luxury. It is often one of the first

TABLE 6.1   *Characteristics of Three Types of Continuing Education*

| *Distinguishing Characteristics* | *Type of Activity* | | |
	Training	*Education*	*Staff Development*
Purpose	Socialization (orientation to the organization), standardization of activities to meet a standard	Career advancement through advanced study (within context of the profession)	Acquiring and applying new knowledge (to increase professional competence in service delivery)
Content	Specific "how-to" knowledge (application of policy to procedures)	Theoretical knowledge	Emerging knowledge and insights
Process	Instruction in and exposure to needed knowledge	Providing knowledge that is generalizable	Application of new knowledge to a problem situation

Adapted from Robert W. Weinbach and Karen M. Kuehner, "Trainer or Academician—Who Shall Provide?" *Journal of Continuing Social Work Education,* I, 3, (Summer 1981): 5. Copyright 1981 by the Continuing Education Program, School of Social Welfare, State University of New York at Albany.

activities to be reduced or cut out. This is ironic. At a time when there are reorganizations because of funding cuts or non-replacement or "rifting" of staff, it is more imperative than ever that remaining staff are well-trained.

Education.   In many ways, *education* is designed for learning needs that are almost directly opposite those addressed through training. Education is the communication of a body of general knowledge. It is designed to equip the learner to be able to act competently in some future situation, the specifics of which cannot be clearly envisioned. Education is the only preparation possible for one-time-only, not totally predictable situations. If we knew exactly what the situation would be and what it would require, we could do more than educate—we could train for it.

There is often confusion regarding the respective purpose and meaning of the terms training and education. Social work students and educators are familiar with the confusion generated by their respective meanings and the problems that arise. Faculty perceive themselves as educators, preparing their students by providing them with generalized knowledge designed to assist them in functioning in some future, unspecified practice situation. While social work education may have some training components (most commonly within field agencies and, sometimes, in practice courses where more skill-building takes place), the preponderance of curricula are designed to educate, not to train. There is a compelling logic for this emphasis. We cannot anticipate the precise needs of a client or client group in some future situation or the correct decision or response of a social worker. Furthermore, no two practice situations and no two social work practitioners are identical. The social worker needs to be able to assess the situation, to draw on experience and generalized knowledge acquired through education, and to apply professional discretion in a unique, one-time-only manner. If social workers were trained and not educated, no social worker who attended college before 1980 would have received the formalized learning necessary for working with HIV patients or their families, or for providing services for new categories of the homeless. However, much of the dissatisfaction of social work students seems to arise from concern that they are not getting enough "how-to-do-it" (that is, training) to prepare them for practice. They may enter a program of professional education expecting training which, most faculty would argue, cannot be offered. Just how much training is appropriate within social work curricula remains open to debate, even among educators.

Staff members usually receive additional education by enrolling in short courses, individual academic courses, or in advanced degree programs. If resources are available, released time and even tuition support are much appreciated by staff. In this way, a manager can communicate a belief in the value of continued worker growth.

As staff members acquire more education and particularly if they are awarded advanced degrees, they are likely to expect increased work responsibilities, higher salaries, and continued career advancement.

For an employee, it is demoralizing to invest the time, effort, and expense to go back to school and then return to one's old job with the same responsibilities, perhaps, even with a loss of seniority for time spent in getting an advanced degree. Unless a way can be found to reward employees for their educational achievements, there is a real danger that they may quit their jobs to go elsewhere where they will be "more appreciated."

Staff Development.   The third form of continuing education, *staff development,* can be especially useful to the manager in addressing problem situations or in providing staff with the new or updated learning required to function in changing work environments. Staff development is a kind of hybrid—it contains some elements of both training and education.

What distinguishes staff development is its problem focus. Changing knowledge, changing service needs, and changing standards for their delivery are likely to create practice knowledge gaps and stress among staff. In past years, certain problems have created timely and appropriate topics for staff development. In the early 1980s, it was often burnout or detection of child abuse. In the 1990s it was the use of politically correct language, various topics related to HIV, or managed care and, in the public sector, block grants. More recently it has been a variety of problems related to changes and threats from the conservative George W. Bush administration. Generally, staff development tends to address the needs of practitioners for current knowledge relating to a recently identified (or at least recently spotlighted) problem in the field. It usually employs a short-term intensive format with a fairly narrow focus. State-of-the-art knowledge is presented and discussed along with practical suggestions for addressing the problem. Sometimes, experiential learning is a part of staff development. Overall, it provides the manager with a useful and well-received vehicle for influencing employee growth. Staff members tend to like spending time acquiring new and emerging knowledge and in addressing topics that are widely discussed in both professional and lay circles.

Who Can Provide Continuing Education?

Many different individuals and groups can provide continuing education. Ideally, education is the domain of college or university educators. Training is conducted by staff within the organization, at least within the larger bureaucracies that have staff whose job is continuing education. Staff development is a contested area that is claimed by those possessing various professional affiliations.[16] In recent years, however, these boundaries have become blurred. Schools of social work and other academic units have hired more and more people who are not educators to teach courses as "adjunct faculty." Fiscal necessity and opportunity increasingly have moved academicians into the training and staff development areas. Professional organizations and private, for-profit contractors have seized upon opportunities to contract for training and staff development. The current environment can be a confusing one for social work managers who are unclear as to just what they want in the way of staff development and what they are able to pay in the way of monetary and non-monetary costs. We will explore some of the costs and benefits of available options.

Agency Staff. Certain obvious advantages exist for managers who select in-house providers of continuing education. Agency employees are already on the payroll and usually are committed to the organization; a certain level of loyalty can usually be assumed. They also understand the agency and its unique needs, political constraints, and clientele.

Using in-house staff requires only simple arrangements and agreements, and a minimum of paperwork and red tape. Contracts involving complicated budgeting and time-consuming approvals at several levels are largely unnecessary. However, the extensive use of agency employees and the short-circuiting of multilevel review and approval procedures can be costly. With no written agreements and contracts, monitoring and quality control are difficult.

Too heavy a reliance on one's own employees can also result in a shortage of new ideas or creative approaches to situations. The agency employee may lack familiarity with the theoretical knowledge in a given subject area that is readily available to the academician.

Ironically, the greatest strength of agency employees as providers of continuing education is also their greatest liability. They are clearly identified as agency persons with all the advantages that this entails. But this identification also threatens their credibility and, therefore, the effectiveness of their teaching. Will employees accept their expertise as they would that of an outside "expert" who may hold high academic credentials? Will their employee status make them suspect as continuing education participants? Will trainees seek hidden meaning in what they say or do because they are viewed as agents of the organization? They may bear the dual liability of being perceived as both "prophet without honor" and "spy." Even the most accepted fellow employee may not experience a productive candor from participants. The usefulness of employees as providers of continuing education may be limited to activities where suspicion and doubts about competence and loyalties are least likely to exist.

Generally, when we think of agency staff as potential providers of continuing education, we tend to think of persons employed as trainers or of experienced senior-level staff. But social work managers (particularly those at lower levels of the administrative hierarchy) have another valuable resource at their disposal. As providers of certain types of continuing education—for example, orientation training—an employee's peers may be the option of choice. Peer training is "the use of a more experienced fellow employee to teach specific knowledge and skills to a new employee of the same level and job description."[17] Peers are assigned on a time-limited basis under the direction of a permanent agency training staff member. Several advantages accrue to the use of peer trainers. These include:

1. *Accessibility to staff.* Local peer trainers are more accessible to assist the newly hired worker than are permanent continuing education personnel who or the local supervisor, whose time is consumed by program management and the many needs of other employees.
2. *Individualized attention.* Peer trainers who may have recently experienced the same anxieties and learning needs as the new employee may be able to identify with and relate to their learning difficulties.
3. *Choice of trainer.* From among a variety of persons, the trainee and supervisor can together select the individual who is the best match of personality and teaching/learning styles.
4. *Trust.* New employees may find it easier to trust and to be candid with a peer. They will be less inhibited about asking what they fear may be "dumb" questions of a peer trainer than they might be in questioning the supervisor or a professional trainer in a classroom setting.

Disadvantages of using peer trainers lie primarily in the way in which they can threaten the role and authority of supervision. They should only be employed in a way that it is clear to all concerned that ultimate responsibility for the socialization, job preparation, and performance evaluation of a staff member remains with the manager.

Private Contractors and Larger Continuing Education Programs.   Some large organizations (whether private for profit or associated with universities) make a business of continuing education. The manager who seeks continuing education from private contractors or the larger continuing education programs within universities is buying economic motivation and experience. The organizations want and need the work. Providers generally have many years of experience in offering continuing education and understand what sells and what works. They have developed attractive, copyrighted packages that do not require time for development or major modifications. These packages include such learning supports as workbooks, PowerPoint presentations, videotapes, and other aids that are both well liked by participants and have a record of effectiveness.

Established continuing education programs generally will allow the consumer to specify what is needed, but will take the responsibility for the more specific development and packaging phases. To them, continuing education is a business and subject to the rules of the marketplace. They must deliver on time and satisfactorily. Dependence on future contracts—and the threat of possible legal action—guarantees it.

Agreements with larger social work continuing education programs and private contractors often come with a high price tag. Reimbursement of travel expenses for continuing education staff represents a substantial cost to the purchaser. These programs also must set priorities. They are most interested in those agreements involving the greatest compensation. They actively seek large, long-term contracts that offer large amounts of money and greater job security for their staffs. Managers looking for a single half-day workshop or other low-cost continuing education program may need to either seek local providers or be prepared to wait until the large continuing education organization can find time without jeopardizing other more lucrative commitments.

Other Social Work Academic Programs.   Less established local continuing education programs in social work academic programs may offer continuing education at relatively low cost. Public universities often operate under expectations that their faculty members will provide community services. Social work educators also may need to maintain contact with the practice environment. Inexpensive or even gratis agreements for small continuing education requirements may be possible.

Because continuing education is only a part-time, occasional function of most educators, programs such as one-day workshops or brief training sessions are especially welcomed. The large number of BSW and MSW programs virtually guarantees that there is one in close proximity to any human service organization. Travel and per diem expenses are a relatively low cost item.

Continuing education agreements with social work education programs have a benefit in the form of the aura of the educator. The person delivering the continuing education may have "instant credibility." Academicians are presumed to have knowledge and expertise in their field. Of course, this is not always true. Educators' credibility can be rapidly destroyed by a few comments that indicate that they are out of touch with the real world of professional practice. And, sometimes, educators are simply assumed to be "out of touch," whether this is the case or not.

There are other potential problems in using people less experienced in delivery of continuing education. Certain errors may be made that the larger, experienced program would not make. There is less probability of a smooth, well-implemented product when using social work educators to train. For example, educators may be tempted to use shortcuts to the development of continuing education curricula by trying to adapt content from their existing course materials. This can result in overly theoretical, esoteric presentations that may have little pertinence to the needs of employees. Educators also are accustomed to vigorously guarding principles of academic freedom. They may resent and resist agency efforts to influence the content and/or format of delivery. The manager may have little control over what is actually presented when purchasing continuing education from academicians who are accustomed to exercising a good ideal of autonomy in what and how they teach.

Although the motivation of individual providers is an important variable among all provider groups, it is a special concern in continuing education agreements with people who perceive themselves primarily as academicians. College and university reward systems of tenure, promotion, and merit increases are structured so that some faculty members have less to gain from providing first-rate continuing education activities than others. Identifying those who have the most to gain is an important task. Those who perceive little personal reward for themselves other than a salary supplement are best avoided.

Other College/University Units.   Some of the specialized knowledge and expertise needed within human service organizations is only minimally taught in social work programs. It may be desirable to seek continuing education that is delivered by people who are acknowledged to be "experts" in other areas.

Staff may find it refreshing to be taught by those from another discipline. They may have previously experienced frustration with in-house staff and with social work academicians. The aura of the other discipline can, of course, work against providers if they are perceived as unaware of the unique characteristics of human service delivery systems.

A lack of identification with social work values and ethics also can be a major problem when using providers from other academic disciplines. Before choosing them, a manager should ascertain whether individuals who will deliver continuing education are likely to perceive clients and services in a way consistent with social work values. The best continuing education methods can be of little value when delivered by a provider who, for example, clearly views all single parent families as dysfunctional, or corporal punishment as the right of parents and has little patience with those who believe differently.

Formal Agreements for Continuing Education

Three basic types of agreements are used for the delivery of continuing education services by persons outside the organization. They are: consultation agreements, grants, and contracts. (Of course attendance at conferences and symposia require no formal agreements with professional organizations—just the funds to send staff to them.) Confusion regarding the meaning and implications of the different forms of formal agreements for continuing education can result in problems and a great deal of resentment on the part of those involved. Whether in negotiating with providers of continuing education or in monitoring agreements made, a manager should be careful to avoid using the three terms as if they are somehow interchangeable—they are not.

Consultation Agreements.   A consultation agreement is designed to bring a person or persons into the organization for a limited purpose. These people are hired because of some specific expertise that is needed. Consultants also are hired because they are believed to possess objectivity. This is particularly important when they are hired as "troubleshooters" or to arbitrate in situations of internal conflict. They should have no allegiance to any staff (at any level) and no preconceived biases as to the rightness or wrongness of anyone's position.

In human service organizations, it is sometimes stated that we hire "consultants" to provide regular ongoing services (for example, case supervision) if no one on staff possesses the necessary credentials or expertise. But this is really a misuse of the term. These persons are really just part-time employees. True consultants are involved with an organization on a very time-limited, often problem-focused basis. They might, for example, be brought in to help to revise an organization's personnel benefits, to computerize its client record system, to design a needs assessment for a proposed program, or to help the organization regain its accreditation. Consultants should have knowledge and experience in performing the tasks for which they are hired, attributes that are not available within the organization.

Actual written agreements for consultation can be quite formal (for example, the Veteran's Administration requires extensive paperwork and sometimes even security clearances), but they frequently involve little more than a letter of agreement outlining the general purpose, duties, and compensation involved. Usually, a certain number of hours or days of the consultant's time are purchased. Some of the time may be used in preparing for a consultation visit if that is part of the agreement. The consultant may request documents from the organization to help prepare for the visit or even assign certain tasks to be completed prior to it. Because the consultant is assumed to be the expert, the specific nature of what will be offered during the visit may not be detailed. This is often left to the judgment of the consultant, who should be in the best position to know how to do the job.

It is in the best interests of consultants to keep agreements as vague as possible. That gives them the maximum amount of autonomy. However, a manager who hires a consultant may wish to make the agreement as specific as the consultant will allow in order to be certain that the agency gets exactly what is needed.

Grants.   Grants are really most accurately understood as a sum of money given to individuals or organizations to work in their areas of expertise. Grants are awarded because applicants are believed to possess the necessary credibility, skills, and knowledge about a given subject area to be able to successfully undertake research or continuing education in that area. It is an honor to receive a grant. Frequently, grants are awarded to researchers and academicians to enable them to continue their research agenda or to allow them to pursue some existing area of inquiry on a larger scale. Common sources of grants are federal agencies (for example, National Institute of Mental Health, Department of Education, Bureau of Maternal and Child Health).

Grants afford a relatively large amount of autonomy for the recipient, but grants for continuing education generally allow the recipient less freedom than research grants. University faculty like and actively seek grants because they can provide a significant salary supplement in the form of summer pay as well as other attractive benefits such as budgets for professional travel or purchase of computer hardware and software. As long as faculty demonstrate a reasonable degree of accountability in the expenditure of funds, the grantor will allow them to use discretion in specifically how, for example, they will design and implement a new curriculum or will analyze their research data. Some confusion occurs because federal agencies use the term "training grant" to describe an agreement to develop and to deliver what we would define as training, but also education and staff development. No matter what type of continuing education is purchased through a grant, a fair degree of trust in the provider to develop and deliver a quality product is implied. Social workers who, in their role as manager, are instrumental in offering a grant for continuing education services should be aware that they may have relatively little input or control over the selection of specific content and teaching methods that will be used. A grant, like consultation, assumes that the expertise lies with the recipient and that such decisions are most appropriately left to that person. Grants are more likely to be awarded on a competitive basis than are consultation agreements. Despite the fact that grants frequently involve long written agreements and notarized signatures, they are deliberately vague in some areas where the purchaser defers to the superior knowledge and experience of the grantee.

Contracts.   Because of the freedom implicit in the use of consultation agreements and grants, persons in organizations who are seeking continuing education services often shy away from them. They prefer to use contracts. Contracts simply are more enforceable, holding the provider of continuing education directly responsible for delivering what has been promised in a manner acceptable to the organization. Sometimes, third parties (outside evaluators) are used to guarantee full compliance with the conditions of a contract. Contracts are legally binding; if continuing education is not delivered as specified in the contract, the recipient may not be paid. In contrast, dissatisfaction with services based on a consultation agreement or grant probably will result in a tarnished professional reputation and the provider not receiving future agreements. There is no other penalty.

A contract generally is awarded on a competitive basis—that is, several organizations or individuals usually "bid" for it by submitting a proposal in response to the organization's Request for Proposals (RFP). A "sole source" (no competitive bidding) situation is permitted only if it can be demonstrated that only one organization or individual is qualified to deliver the desired service.

A contract for continuing education services is best understood as being virtually comparable to, for example, a contract a homeowner might sign to have new carpeting installed in the home. Material quality, time of delivery, and quality of work must be that which was agreed upon and must be approved by the homeowner or the homeowner is legally not bound to pay; full or partial payment may be withheld. If all conditions are met, the homeowner is required to pay in full. The contract is designed to protect both parties. They are protected if events unfold in a way that one or the other did not envision or if it is later learned that their perceptions of what the job entailed were not in agreement.

Managers who choose to contract for continuing education, have many protections. They must get what they purchased or they are not obligated to pay for it. The primary protection for providers is that they will be paid promptly if their work is completed and evaluated as satisfactory. Contracts tend to be negotiated and written out in legal jargon and in great detail. Authorized signatures are required. Unlike grants, little is left to the discretion of the provider or the purchaser; at least it should not be.

Unfortunately, even the use of contracts sometimes does not preclude problems if the provider of continuing education does not understand the difference between a contract and a grant or consultation agreement. Professional providers of continuing education in private, for-profit organizations are well aware of the differences. Educators are especially notorious for confusing the three types of agreements. The mind-set of many educators is toward grants or consultation agreements, since those are the agreements that they see most frequently. They may mistakenly believe that any agreement for continuing education services provides for similar autonomy and exercise of professional discretion. When they learn that they are wrong, a strained relationship can occur.

Another frequent source of trouble is the belated realization on the part of educators that a contract usually grants ownership of materials and teaching aids developed under the contract to the purchaser (organization). Professors using treasured course materials developed over the years may be shocked to learn that they no longer own "their" material after being paid for their part in delivery of continuing education. In fact, under agreements contained in most contracts, the educator need not be invited to return to deliver the continuing education a second time. An agency staff member can take notes while sitting in on the professor's instruction and use them to teach subsequent sessions on the same topic.

While contracts with universities for continuing education are generally an organization-to-organization agreement, it would be naive not to understand contracts as an arrangement also made at the human level. Such agreements can vary widely in their desirability for providers of continuing education. Their attitude toward doing the work is likely to be affected by ego needs, financial considerations, career status, and other factors that can either enhance the quality of learning offered or detract from it. For this reason, the manager should, whenever possible, specify the choice of the provider as well as the choice of the organization awarded the contract.

The social worker as manager may, on occasion, have the opportunity to choose from among consultation agreements, grants, and contracts to provide outside instruction for employee professional growth. Because of the limited organizational control that they provide, consultation and grants are used less often than contracts. Overall, contracts provide the best assurance that the organization will receive the kind of quality instruction that is needed. However, until there is greater understanding of the differences among the three types of continuing education, some problems and resentment probably are inevitable when contracts are used. Because of this, managers have a heavy communication responsibility on the front end of any contractual agreement. If agreements for continuing education services are allowed to produce bitterness on the part of providers, it is the potential beneficiaries (staff) who will suffer a loss. They will not receive the quality learning required to enhance their professional growth.

Summary

In this chapter we looked at a second important responsibility of the social worker as manager that is part of the staffing function continued professional growth of staff. We emphasized the importance of an accurate assessment of individual motivation as well as an understanding of how group membership can influence individual behavior. We then concentrated our analysis on two major vehicles for promoting staff growth—supervision and continuing education.

Several of the better-known conceptualizations of individual motivation were presented and discussed. Throughout this chapter, the position was taken that, although individual motivation cannot be created by the manager, it can be sustained or suppressed by a number of factors present in the work situation and how well the manager understands them and responds to them.

Individual motivation was described as emanating primarily from individual needs and pressures for their gratification, but also as heavily influenced by other individuals and groups within the organization. Professional values and their potential to influence worker performance were also examined. Competition was presented as both potentially supportive of desirable behavior but also as a phenomenon that can be destructive of it when it becomes a preoccupation of staff or when it deteriorates into interpersonal conflict.

Group influences on behavior within organizations cannot be understood without recognizing the effects of group cohesiveness. Cohesiveness can support organizational goal achievement if group norms are consistent with organizational goals; it can also present an organized form of resistance to goal achievement if they are not. Ways exist in which the social worker as manager can promote positive group cohesiveness; these were presented and explored. The effect of the informal power structure on individual behavior also was described.

We defined the traditional one-to-one supervisory tasks as that of administrative supervision, educational supervision, supportive supervision, and case consultation. While we did not explore these in detail, we used them to help conceptualize the various ways in which supervision can promote employee growth. Group, interdisciplinary, peer, and remote supervision models also were described and discussed as options available to the manager in enhancing growth through supervision.

In our examination of continuing education, several important distinctions were made. First, we emphasized the important differences in purpose, content, and process that are present in training, education, and staff development. The task of selecting a provider for delivery of continuing education was given thorough consideration. The advantages and disadvantages of the various options were discussed.

Finally, the formal agreement options for acquiring continuing education were examined. Consultation agreements, grants, and contracts were discussed and compared with each other. Common sources of misunderstandings and problems encountered by the manager in their use were noted.

Endnotes

1. Abraham H. Maslow, *Motivation and Personality,* 3rd ed. (New York: Harper & Row, 1987): Abraham H. Maslow, "A Theory of Human Motivation," *Psychological Review,* 50(4), (July 1943): 370–396.

2. Edward E. Lawler III and J. Lloyd Suttle, "A Casual Correlation Test of the Need Hierarchy Concept," *Organizational Behavior and Human Performance,* 7 (1972): 265–587.

3. Douglass T. Hall and Khalil E. Nougaim, "An Examination of Maslow's Need Hierarchy in an Organizational Setting," *Organizational Behavior and Human Performance,* 3 (1968): 12–35.

4. Frederick Herzberg, Bernard Mausner, and Barbara Block Snyderman, *The Motivation to Work* (New York: Wiley, 1959), pp. 3–12 and 126–128; Frederick Herzberg, "One More Time: How Do You Motivate Employees?" *Harvard Business Review,* 46 (January/ February): 53–62.

5. David C. McClelland, *Studies in Motivation* (New York: Appleton-Century-Crofts, 1955).

6. Robert B. Hill, "Integrating Relations," in *Encyclopedia of Social Work,* Vol. 1, (New York: National Association of Social Workers), pp. 951–956.

7. See Musafer Sherif, "Intergroup Relations and Leadership: Introductory Statement," in *Intergroup Relations and Leadership: Approaches and Research in Industrial, Ethnic, Cultural, and Political Areas,* M. Sherif, ed. (New York: Wiley), pp. 3–21.

8. Richard M. Emerson, "Power-Dependence Relationships," *American Sociological Review,* 27 (1962): 31–41.

9. Lewis A. Coser, *The Functions of Social Conflict* (New York: Free Press, 1954): 15–31 and 151–157.

10. See Joseph A. Olmstead, *Working Papers* No. 2. *Organizational Structure and Climate: Implications for Agencies* (Washington, DC: Department of Health, Education and Welfare. Social and Rehabilitative Service, 1973), pp. 95–98.

11. Eileen Gambrill and Theodore Stein, *Supervision: A Decision-Making Approach* (Beverly Hills, CA: Sage, 1983); Ruth Middleman and Gary Rhodes, *Competent Supervision* (Englewood Cliffs, NJ: PrenticeHall, 1985); Carlton Munson, *An Introduction to Clinical Social Work Supervision,* 2nd ed. (New York: The Haworth Press, 1993); Carlton Munson, ed., *Social Work Supervision* (New York: Free Press, 1979); Lawrence Shulman, *Skills of Supervision and Staff Management* (Itasca, IL: F. E. Peacock Publishers, 1982).

12. Alfred Kadushin, *Supervision in Social Work* (New York: Columbia University Press, 1976).

13. Alfred Kadushin, *Consultation in Social Work* (New York: Columbia University Press, 1977).

14. Richard Simpson, "Understanding the Utilization of Research in Social Work and Other Applied Professions," in *Sourcebook on Research Utilization* (New York: Council in Social Work Education, 1979), p. 24.

15. Kadushin, *Supervision in Social Work, op. cit.,* pp. 320–357.

16. Robert Weinbach and Karen Kuehner, "Trainer or Academician—Who Shall Provide?" *Journal of Continuing Social Work Education,* 1(3), (Summer 1981): 4–5.

17. Robert Weinbach and Karen Kuehner, "Improving the Use of Agency Resources through Peer Training," *Social Work,* 32(3), (May/June 1987): 222.

7

Staff Evaluations and Personnel Actions

The hiring and deployment of a diverse staff (Chapter 5) and assessing their motivation and promoting their growth by providing supervision and continuing education (Chapter 6) are some of the more enjoyable tasks that are part of the staffing function of management. Now we turn to some of the staffing functions of management that are among those most dreaded by social work managers. They entail evaluating staff, sometimes finding them lacking, and taking actions to correct deficiencies or even removing them from the organization.

Staff Performance Evaluations

Managers (if they supervise any other individual within the organization) need to know how to evaluate others' work performance. Performing staff evaluations is a task that is frequently mentioned as among those most disliked by social work managers. It is almost universally disliked by those who are evaluated. In this chapter we will examine why social workers often have so much trouble with staff evaluations. We will also see how, if performed correctly, they need not be feared. They can be beneficial to all parties. They also are a necessary prerequisite to the personnel decisions that we will discuss later in this chapter.

Why Evaluations Are Disliked

For an adult the idea of being evaluated can be insulting. It may reawaken all kinds of humiliating feelings associated with the powerlessness of childhood and of student roles. Are we not at a point in life where our competence can just be assumed? Why should we have to be evaluated or to demonstrate our achievements to others? When will we ever stop being evaluated?

We all continue to be evaluated by others, no matter how old we are or how competent we have become. Sometimes, the evaluators are our bosses. Sometimes, they are our peers, for example, when we submit a proposal for a conference presentation or submit a grant proposal to a funding organization. Sometimes our evaluators are our family and friends with whom we interact on a daily basis. Sometimes our evaluators are even deceased! However, we continue to carry around their judgments of our behavior. The point is, evaluation is a fact of life. And as we shall see, evaluation can be very useful!

Much of the mutual dislike of employee evaluations may also result from the attitudes of those doing the evaluations. Sometimes, they act as if evaluations are somehow nothing more than a "necessary evil." This is a bit of a paradox. We appreciate the importance of evaluating many other things. We evaluate the effectiveness of programs and of our individual interventions. We evaluate political climates or community strengths and resources. But when it comes to evaluating the work of a colleague with whom we work, we tend to react with great distaste. The author knows of one supervisor who has postponed evaluation conferences four times for no good reason and has avoided staff in order to defer rescheduling them. Another one does not sleep the night before an evaluation conference. Why do we react so strongly to what should be a normal interchange between people? Perhaps it is because we have been socialized to be non-judgmental. Evaluating another human being seems to be a violation of our professional values.

The dislike of performing staff evaluations necessarily gets communicated to those being evaluated. How? If we don't like evaluating and find the entire task distasteful, there is a tendency to present the evaluation as "not my idea"—it is something imposed upon us by the organization. We might even convey our belief that evaluations are really of little value and that they are best quickly performed and then filed away. Such an attitude contributes to the resentment of evaluations held by those being evaluated. It creates a negative mind-set on the part of both parties. Ultimately the result is likely to be a self-fulfilling prophecy. The evaluation probably will be of little value. The negative experience will then create a negative mind-set for the next evaluation. The vicious circle will continue on indefinitely, if not stopped.

The Value of Evaluations

Evaluation should not be simply a necessary evil. It is consistent with social work knowledge, skills, and values. Performed correctly by persons who recognize its value to all concerned, it can and should be viewed as a valuable opportunity and an essential contribution to both employee growth and organizational goal attainment.

Value to the Person Being Evaluated.   The primary benefit of a performance evaluation for the person being evaluated is feedback. It answers the questions, "How well am I doing?" and "What are my greatest strengths and what weaknesses do I need to address?" But a great amount more can be learned from an evaluation. It also tells a lot about the person doing the evaluation, the supervisor. No evaluation is ever perfect. The flaws in it can provide useful information. For example, it might tell if the evaluator values performance in some areas more than in others, tends to use evaluations to reward or punish, allows personality factors to enter into an evaluation, or values conformity more than initiative. In this way, evaluations can expose the evaluator's values, priorities and biases. These are important to know about, even if they represent the shortcomings of the evaluator as a manager. Based on a knowledge of them, the person who has been evaluated can choose to either make changes to better accommodate them or, at the very least, can know what to expect in the way of future reactions and evaluations.

An evaluation also can provide other benefits (including job security) for the individual being evaluated. An "outstanding" or "exceeds expectations" evaluation (even one that is "inflated" because the evaluator sought to avoid confronting or criticizing a colleague) can be an "insurance policy." It makes it possible to make mistakes or demonstrate a lack of competence in some other way with little fear of being fired or of some other negative personnel action. (With the evaluation inflation that exists in most organizations today, a merely "good" or "meets expectations" evaluation does not offer the same level of security.) Even when the evaluation is not very positive, the person being evaluated should be able to learn from it exactly what must be done to correct deficiencies. If they are subsequently corrected (and work remains satisfactory in other areas), he or she has a good argument for why job requirements have been met when it is time for the next evaluation.

Value to the Evaluator.   Formal evaluations of subordinates also can perform several valuable functions for the evaluator. They provide a periodic vehicle to call staff attention to individual and organizational goals and objectives. As was observed earlier, large human service bureaucracies have a tendency to foster the phenomenon of means–end displacements. Workers can become immersed in keeping paperwork up to date or in compliance with the many rules and procedures that exist. A formal evaluation provides both the manager and the employee with the opportunity to stop, step back, and assess just how well each worker's daily activities contribute to the organization's client service goals and objectives. If a means–end displacement seems to be developing, it can be identified early and steps to eliminate it can be initiated.

Of course, if the manager doing the evaluating has "lost sight of the forest for the trees" and has become preoccupied with a supervisee's performance of tasks that were intended to be a means to an end, an evaluation conference will benefit neither party or the organization. Evaluation in this type of unfortunate situation only tend to reinforce a means–end displacement. The manager bears a heavy responsibility not to lose sight of goals and objectives, even if other staff may have lost sight of them. Evaluation conferences can help to refocus activities and priorities of both the evaluator and of the individual being evaluated.

The person doing the evaluating is required to apply certain approved criteria to judge the work of staff members. By doing this, it is possible to obtain some new and valuable perspectives. For example, in the daily interaction that occurs among employees of an organization, personality traits can sometimes distort the manager's impressions of the abilities and achievements of staff. A personable, confident, outgoing, and articulate staff member may tend to leave a general impression of being knowledgeable and competent. The quiet, withdrawn loner is more likely to elicit doubts about competence. In fact, the contributions of the loner to organizational goal achievement may be comparable to or even greater than those of the more socially adept individual. But this may not be revealed until a formal evaluation forces the manager to apply a yardstick that neither adds nor subtracts points for personality factors that may not be relevant to one's performance on the job. The gregarious individual may, in fact, be using an attractive style as a smoke screen for deficiencies in job performance. The evaluation can serve to point this out, along with the true value of the more socially withdrawn individual. This payoff from the evaluation process will only occur, however, if irrelevant personality factors are not allowed to intrude into the evaluation process where they can distort it. Evaluation time should be one event in the activities of staff when superfluous factors are not allowed a place. If a staff member's personality is a verifiable asset or liability to the delivery of services or to promoting a productive work climate, it has relevance. Otherwise it does not, and it has no place in the evaluation process.

The careful selection or development of a written evaluation instrument will go far toward eliminating the potential for personality bias to occur. Both the business and the social work professional literature contain examples of evaluation forms that can be used as is or adapted for use by the social worker as manager.[1] Specific recommendations for productive use of evaluation conferences are also available.[2] However, in some organizations the manager has little choice but to use certain required instruments and procedures. This can seriously detract from the value of an evaluation because standardized "one size fits all" forms and methods of this type are usually not totally appropriate for the unique requirements of any job.

In large organizations where work roles tend not to overlap—for example, where supervisors do nothing but supervise, only direct service workers see clients, etc.—the evaluation affords the manager (the supervisor) the opportunity to get to know staff members better and to better understand their jobs. Evaluation time may be the only time that a worker receives the undivided attention of a supervisor to focus on that person's performance, career goals, and attitudes toward work. While this is beneficial to those being evaluated, it is especially valuable to the person doing the evaluating. It provides the chance to assess the motivation of staff, to evaluate their potential for promotion, and to compare their career goals with opportunities within the organization. An evaluation also helps the evaluator to predict the likelihood of subordinates fitting into long-range organizational plans or of their seeking employment elsewhere.

For those staff performing well and making valuable contributions to the organization and to its goals and objectives, evaluations provide the manager with a way to reinforce desirable behavior. While staff may sense or even know that they are doing their jobs well, there is something about written and verbal kudos within the context of a periodic evaluation that are especially gratifying for the recipient. This is particularly important in smaller, closer organizations (for example, private practice, satellite clinics) where role differentiation is likely to become somewhat blurred by the necessity for all staff to work closely together, frequently performing the same or comparable tasks. In their role as evaluators, social work managers assume (or should assume) greater credibility than in the informal communication that occurs in the day-to-day work interaction. Very positive formal evaluations based upon pre-determined criteria provide more powerful reinforcement for good work performance than does any general sense of approval that a manager conveys on a daily basis. It also allows the manager to communicate areas where even good staff can improve performance.

On the less pleasant side, evaluations, when performed properly, lay the legal and ethical groundwork for reassignment, denial of merit pay increases, demotion, or even termination of staff who are not performing up to standards or who represent a liability to the organization, its clients, and/or its image within the community. Optimistically, we hope that an evaluation of an employee who is not performing well will provide an impetus for change and improvement. Initially, the manager must proceed on the assumption that staff are capable of improvement, must suggest specific areas where improvement will be required, and must provide support for improvement in the form of supervision and/or continuing education. But there may come a time when it is clear that an employee lacks either the ability or the motivation to improve to the degree necessary and must be dismissed. At that point, written evaluations must be available to provide documentation of the employee's inadequate job performance and that the required warnings and all due process have been in place. Evaluations can be used to provide evidence that the decision to fire an employee is neither arbitrary, capricious, unfair, impulsive, nor in any way unanticipated by all parties involved.

Value to Those Served. It should be obvious that any activity conducted by the manager should have the potential to benefit our prime beneficiaries, clients, either directly or indirectly. Staff evaluations clearly meet this requirement. When managers provide positive reinforcement for good work they increase the likelihood that services to clients will continue to be good or will get even better. Staff know where they stand in relation to their supervisors and the organization. Then, they can operate in an environment of more certainty. They can devote more of their energies to client services and less to worrying about their own job security.

When managers give more critical evaluations to staff, they suggest how their overall performance can be improved. Staff who respond positively to their critiques cannot help but become more effective in their service delivery. Of course, when staff show no improvement and consistently receive poor performance evaluations, clients may also ultimately benefit. The process for terminating them and replacing them with other more competent staff may have been initiated. In this way, performance evaluations help to protect clients from those who are either unqualified or unwilling to provide the help that they need.

Characteristics of a Good Evaluation

What constitutes a good performance evaluation? Like any other management task, a performance evaluation should be performed ethically. The National Association of Social Workers (NASW) in its 1999 Code of Ethics informs us that "Social workers who have responsibility for evaluating the performance of others should fulfill such responsibility in a fair and considerate manner on the basis of clearly stated criteria."[3] This one sentence statement tells us a great deal. It says that above all an evaluation should be both fair and considerate. It does *not* say that it should not be critical or that it is unethical to judge another person's work performance.

Why is fairness so important? Staff evaluations have the potential to seriously affect group morale. While evaluators must maintain the strict confidentiality of an evaluation, in most organizations individuals often choose to discuss all or part of their evaluation with peers. They are especially likely to share those negative communications that they thought were unjustified. A few co-workers may rejoice in a manager's evaluation that is perceived as excessively critical of a peer (if they don't like or respect that person themselves). But a more typical reaction might be "if the manager was unfair to him, she may be the same way with me." The way that evaluations are conducted can enhance the manager's overall reputation for fairness. Or they can do it irreparable harm. What makes an evaluation fair? What is the place of consideration in a good performance evaluation?

Previously Understood Criteria.   It is fair to evaluate an employee based upon criteria that are predetermined by the manager, usually with input from the individual being evaluated. It is unfair to change the rules between evaluations. If, for example, a worker is able to complete a task more quickly than previously anticipated, performance on additional work assignments that are completed by the worker should not be considered for evaluation purposes. That would be unfair. It is quickly perceived as unfair by staff if new standards for evaluation are added that might result in an unfavorable evaluation for individuals who did what was expected of them and did it well.

Evaluation instruments and criteria should be presented and explained to workers when they start working for managers. This is useful for both parties. The workers know the criteria on which the evaluation will be based and can use it for ongoing self-assessment of their work performance. Managers, with the criteria in place, are less likely to make some of the common errors that can occur in staff evaluations, such as evaluating the worker using themselves as a reference point, making a general assessment of the worker first and then subconsciously evaluating all aspects of the worker's performance in a way consistent with that rating, or never giving an "outstanding" rating to a new employee in order to "leave room for improvement."

Avoidance of Comparisons.   It is unfair to evaluate staff using other employees as reference points. While some comparison of staff by a manager is inevitable and even desirable in performing some functions (for example, selecting an employee for promotion), comparison has no place in a performance evaluation of an individual. A statistician will confirm that the use of a normal curve to assign grades to students is, in most cases, unfair. It leaves students less likely to be evaluated based upon their learning or demonstrated knowledge than upon the chance that placed the student in a particular class section. (The student in a "curved" course of 15 students who attends the first session and hears 10 classmates explain to the professor after class that they are taking only one course and would like additional reading assignments had better drop the course fast!) The manager who evaluates using comparisons with other staff creates both a statistical and a managerial error. No group of employees is large enough to produce the normal distribution that might assure a fair evaluation using comparisons. If evaluations are "curved," all employees and their evaluations are vulnerable to the strength or weakness of the group in which they find themselves, and that is unfair.

There is another reason why comparative staff evaluations are a bad idea. They create an undesirable form of competition among staff. This may produce desirable results in the short run, but over time staff will begin to see such a practice as manipulative. It can also be insulting. Adult professionals should not be placed in a position of "sibling rivalry." What matters is how well an individual does a job and contributes to attainment of organizational goals and client services.

One more reason why a manager should avoid comparative evaluation relates to issues of confidentiality. It is impossible for a manager to convince employees that they are being fairly compared with others without revealing too much about other staff members' evaluations. This practice is unethical. It can also discourage the productive and candid discussion of a worker's own performance that should be a part of any good evaluation. A staff member may fear that what is discussed will be shared with others. Evaluations depend on honest communication, and their value is diminished when discussion becomes guarded.

Staff Differentiation. Some evaluations are unfair in a different way. They are equally complimentary of all staff, despite the fact that staff almost always reflect varying levels of competence. Students can easily relate to this inequity. A student who earns an A tends to resent another student who also gets an A but who did C work; that same student also resents the professor who awarded the undeserved A. Workers react similarly when they learn through the grapevine that their "outstanding" evaluations by a supervisor reflect very little if any difference from those received by a peer judged by all to be only marginally competent. Their own ratings communicated very little. They also underwent depreciation in their eyes and those of others if virtually everyone was rated the same. Staff members know that there are differences in the motivation, knowledge, skills, and professional values of their peers. They have a right to expect that a manager's staff evaluations will reflect these differences. If they do not (and staff almost always find out), they will resent the lack of differentiation and morale can be seriously damaged.

A manager can differentiate between staff without resorting to direct comparison of staff with each other. The solution is simple—evaluate all staff employing the predetermined criteria. The differences in staff performance will reveal themselves.

Realistic Expectations for the Individual. The goal of evaluations to be neither too severe nor to be too lenient, (that is, to be fair), can be accomplished only if managers introduce other considerations into the evaluation process. Evaluation must be based upon an assessment of what is a realistic expectation for each worker. Such factors as the worker's stage of career development, professional background, stated career objectives, and previous work experience are logical variables that should be considered. No one can fairly expect the same level of performance (in terms of quality or quantity) from, for example, a new graduate as that expected from a senior, experienced counselor. A certain kind and number of mistakes are expected from the new graduate; the same mistakes might be indicative of apathy or motivational problems for the seasoned professional.

Another factor to consider is the nature of the job itself. The amount of cause–effect knowledge available to help in performing tasks may be considered in evaluating performance. Was the job one in which our professional knowledge base is well developed (for example, nursing home placement)? Or is the level of knowledge so tentative (for example, counseling of sex-offenders) that a high tolerance for a lack of demonstrated success is indicated?

Having assessed what performance standards are reasonable—given knowledge available for use—still another variable must be considered. A fair evaluation should reflect whether or not there is consensus on what is the desirable outcome of an employee's work activities and whether this has been clearly stated. For example, how should an evaluator construe the fact that few of a social worker's clients return for a second treatment interview? Is it indicative of an inability to form treatment relationships or of the successful application of crisis intervention methods? Or is the dissolution of the marriages of three of a social worker's cases an indication that the worker's role as marriage counselor was performed successfully or not? What is a desirable outcome? In evaluating the work of human service professionals, we frequently encounter situations where there is a lack of consensus as to what is successful goal achievement.

Problems in the Work Environment.   Often there were conditions or situations in the work setting that were beyond the control of the individual being evaluated, but yet they impacted on his or her ability to do a job effectively. For example, orientation and training may not have been adequate. Knowledgeable clerical support may not have been available. A supervisor may have been out on extended leave. Co-workers may not have been cooperative and helpful. There may have been technological breakdowns or inadequacies. A noisy workplace or a lack of privacy may have interfered with work completion.

If these or other similar situations existed within the work setting during the period of evaluation, fairness would suggest that the manager should provide an accurate assessment of the level of job performance, but also include something in the evaluation that is a recognition that they might have at least contributed to any shortcomings of the individual being evaluated. For example, the narrative portion of the written evaluation might state that, "Rosalyn is behind in her case recording, a problem that may be at least partially attributable to the fact that she received eight additional cases when another employee resigned suddenly. Rosalyn is aware that this is a problem that must be corrected if she is to continue to receive a "satisfactory" (or higher) rating at her next scheduled evaluation."

Another common situation that should be factored in relates to "inherited problems," problems that may have been either caused by or left over by the previous occupant of the job. They might be, for example, a backlog of paperwork, a poorly functioning subordinate who has never been given an "unsatisfactory" evaluation, or a poor working relationship with staff in other organizations within the organization's task environment. When this situation exists, it would be unfair to evaluate the current job holder as if he or she was responsible for the problem. However, when taking a job, a new employee does assume some responsibility for addressing old problems that are encountered. In situations like this, fairness suggests offering a "grace period," a period of time that common sense would suggest as reasonable for solving the problem. During that grace period, it is fair to evaluate the individual on plans for solving the problem, efforts made toward solving it, and progress that has been made. Following the grace period, if it still exists the individual must assume ownership of the problem and is now responsible for it. Its continued presence would be reason to lower the level of a performance evaluation.

Sometimes a manager knows of extenuating circumstances within the work setting. But, not always. A manager cannot always know everything that goes on that may be impacting work performance. It may be desirable to invite the worker to describe any extenuating circumstances for the manager to consider prior to the evaluation conference.

Many managers in social work now use a method of worker self-evaluation. The evaluation can be a written assessment of work performance along with other factors related to the work setting that the worker thinks the manager should take into consideration. The self evaluation is given to the manager one or more days before the evaluation conference as additional data for conducting the evaluation. Of course, it should be understood in advance that the manager is obligated only to consider the information thus provided. All or part of it may be discounted as incorrect or irrelevant to the worker's performance.

A Mixture of Hard and Soft Criteria.

With an increase in lawsuits and employee grievances, many human service organizations now rely heavily on standardized evaluation instruments that seem designed to promote an image of objectivity and therefore, to protect the organization from potentially costly legal action. But even these instruments (and they vary so widely that the author was unable to include one in this book that could be described as "typical") tend to include criteria that sometimes seem to defy accurate measurement. Invariably, the instruments reflect a mixture of "job performance, personal abilities and personality."[4] Such standard factors as absenteeism, tardiness, initiative, conduct, job knowledge and quality, and timeliness of work often are balanced with much more subjective judgments of qualities such as attitude, cooperativeness, adaptability, use of supervision, and ability to work with peers.

In this age of litigation, there is a tendency to want to evaluate worker performance using only those hard, verifiable criteria that do not leave the manager vulnerable to charges of subjectivity or bias. But an obsession with self-protection does not produce an evaluation that is accurate, useful, or fair. An evaluation that is limited to easily measured criteria tends to be sterile and of little value. For example, it may indicate that a worker is always on time, keeps up-to-date on paperwork, and complies with organizational policies. But it fails to identify the fact that the worker is not growing as a professional, the worker is not very committed to client service or that the worker is not a team player, which are very critical problem areas that should be addressed. Unless an evaluation includes this type of feedback to the worker, steps to remedy the problems are not initiated. Should the manager ultimately conclude that the worker is more a liability than an asset to the organization, the legal and ethical groundwork for termination will not have been laid.

A good evaluation employs some criteria that are easily measured. But, of necessity, it also includes criteria that are "softer" and thus more vulnerable to charges of subjectivity. Some attributes of workers (for example, inability to work well with colleagues, a cynical attitude about clients) are difficult to measure and document, but they are detrimental to the organization and should not be ignored during evaluations. Certain other attributes that are highly desirable (for example, a friendly cooperative approach to co-workers or a good attitude when assigned additional work) should not be ignored at evaluation time either. They should be acknowledged and, whenever possible, rewarded. There are other "soft" criteria (and they vary from organization to organization) that managers may want to build into a staff evaluation. One common one is "value to the organization." It is very difficult to document, but important nevertheless. It is something that a manager feels and senses over time, rather than an assessment based on a simple observation of behavior.

It is not the use of "soft" criteria for measuring staff performance of workers that gets a manager into trouble. It is a lack of articulation of whatever evaluation criteria are to be used or the application of them to some staff but not to others. Social work staff generally recognize the importance of assessments that are based on judgments rather than documentable facts. They recognize that no evaluation criterion is 100 percent objective anyway. They do not object to a package of criteria that contains a mixture of "hard" data and some that are inclined to be softer, so long as they know in advance just what those criteria refer to and are assured that they are applied to others as well. Of course, the use of softer criteria is always less threatening to workers if the manager already has a reputation for fairness and for good assessment skills.

Consideration.   As was mentioned earlier, to be ethical, an evaluation should be both fair and considerate. Fairness suggests that a performance evaluation should reflect the actual level of performance of the individual, no lower and no higher. It is not fair to give a rating lower than deserved. Likewise, an individual who is not meeting job expectations and is hurting the performance of the work unit should not be rated as "meets performance standards" or its equivalent.

We also described how problems in the work environment that are beyond an individual's control should be addressed—mention them but still rate the individual at a level consistent with actual job performance. But what if the problems are more of a personal nature, for example, depression relating to the loss of a partner or something else going on outside the workplace that may have negatively affected work performance during the evaluation period? Wouldn't it be inconsiderate, if not downright cruel, to give someone experiencing such a personal problem a low performance rating, even if it accurately describes the quality or quantity of work performed recently? No. There is a place for consideration in performance evaluation. However, it is not in the level of the evaluation itself. An accurate assessment of recent job performance is needed, both by the evaluator and the person being evaluated. To provide an inflated, inaccurate evaluation, even at a time of personal difficulty, would be a disservice, since the person being evaluated needs to know those areas where work performance has not been up to standard in order to make improvements. It could also prove to be a problem for the evaluator and the organization if it later becomes apparent that, even without personal stressors, work performance does not improve. The presence of the inflated evaluation in the personnel file could make subsequent personal action (reprimands, warnings, termination) more difficult. A manager should also not bring up the personal problem in a performance evaluation. To do so, even in a supportive way, could suggest that it interfered with the evaluator's ability to provide an accurate evaluation, and could potentially cause legal problems at some later date.

So, where *does* consideration enter in? Consideration requires that we treat people respectfully, with politeness, and as we would wish to be treated. A considerate evaluation identifies both strengths (and everyone has some) and weaknesses. It reflects the assumption that an individual (especially one who has functioned better in the past) wants to do better. It tactfully identifies areas of weakness and offers assurances of support in bringing work performance up to an acceptable level. If the individual being evaluated is experiencing a personal crisis of some kind, a slightly longer than usual (but time limited) grace period may be offered to enable him or her to reach that level before any corrective action is initiated.

A considerate evaluation is meant to be constructive. It should never be destructive. If, because of personal crises or some other reason, the individual being evaluated has not been functioning at the acceptable level, more often than not, he or she is aware of it. The evaluation should come as no surprise. However, the evaluator can communicate both verbally and in writing in a way that the evaluation does not exacerbate feelings of frustration, anger, helplessness, rejection or low self-esteem. Even if the evaluator is very displeased with the level of performance and needs to clearly communicate it, a performance evaluation should never contain sarcasm or otherwise ridicule the person being evaluated. Humor (at his or her expense) is not constructive or considerate and has no place in an evaluation.

Conducting Performance Evaluations

Most organizations have written procedures in place for conducting performance evaluations. They must be adhered to by the manager. The procedures and required paperwork tend to vary from organization to organization, but they also have much in common. There are usually two parts to a performance evaluation—a written evaluation and an evaluation conference. A typical written evaluation may consist of a description of the work undertaken during the evaluation period, a form such as a scale containing the evaluation criteria used along with the rating for each of them, and a narrative summary of job performance during the rating period.

Some managers request that the individual being evaluated prepare a draft of one or more parts of the written evaluation. This practice can have a number of advantages for the evaluator. It can be a real time-saver, since he or she does not have to take the time to compile the necessary descriptive data. It also can provide an opportunity to learn about factors that may be interfering with productivity or other problems that may exist in the workplace. Since it requires the person being evaluated to think about and acknowledge strengths and weaknesses, it also can increase the likelihood that the evaluation conference will be more open and productive.

Whether the individual being evaluated prepares a draft of the entire written evaluation or just part of it, the responsibility for it in its final form remains with the evaluator. And, that is the way it should be. Evaluating one's self may produce a hypercritical evaluation or certain deficiencies or important issues may be avoided. Even if the draft was performed conscientiously and honestly, there will invariably be areas where the evaluator has a different perception of performance than the staff member. To simply "sign off" on what was written would be avoiding responsibility and would deprive the staff member of valuable feedback.

It is not unusual for social workers to dread conducting evaluation conferences, especially if they know that the evaluation is not going to be a very favorable one. However, if they have been doing the job of manager all along, there is little to fear. The conference should merely be a confirmation of the messages they have been sending through regular written, verbal, and non-verbal communication. Since the evaluation criteria should have been clarified before the evaluation period began, anything said or anything offered in writing at the evaluation conference should come as no surprise.

While there is no "one best way" to conduct an evaluation conference, there are some methods to increase the likelihood that they will be both fair and considerate. For example, they should be scheduled well in advance and every effort should be made to not re-schedule them. While re-scheduling may not seem like much of a problem to the evaluator, we must remember that an annual or semi-annual performance evaluation is very important to and can be very stressful for the staff member. It is inconsiderate to postpone it after he or she has been anxiously waiting for it to occur.

The evaluator should plan the agenda for the conference and, perhaps, even rehearse what will be said. This reduces the likelihood that anything will be said or done impulsively that will later be regretted or, worse yet, may be the basis for a grievance. Usually, the conference begins pleasantly, perhaps, with some statement by the evaluator expressing appreciation for the contributions of the staff member. A review of the work accomplished may follow. At some point, a draft of the written evaluation is provided and, if it is being seen for the first time, the staff member is given time to read it. Then it is discussed. The evaluator should listen to any explanations given about any deficiencies noted in it, but should avoid getting into an argument over them. The conference may end with a "look ahead," in which the staff member can talk about what goals he or she hopes to attain during the next evaluation period and the evaluator can suggest ways that can be provided (such as training or staff development) to make it easier to attain them. Overall, most evaluation conferences are pleasant, productive meetings in which valuable information is exchanged. Of course, if the evaluation is not a very favorable one, the interchange may be unpleasant, but still useful.

Following the evaluation conference, the evaluator revises the written evaluation where necessary and a second, brief meeting is scheduled for both parties to sign it. Signing one's evaluation does not mean that a staff member necessarily agrees with everything contained in it, only that he or she has read and understands it. If there is still serious disagreement, usually the staff member is allowed to write an addendum to it stating where the areas of disagreement are and explaining why they exist. After both parties have signed it, the written evaluation (including any addenda) is filed in the staff member's personnel file along with a notation of when the evaluation conference took place.

In most human service organizations, managers are required to provide regular written performance evaluations and to conduct evaluation conferences. If they do not provide them, both they and the organization can be in serious trouble. This is especially true in organizations where staff members are unionized. If, for example, a decision is made to terminate a permanent employee and the required annual or semi-annual evaluations were not performed in a timely manner, there may be grounds for a lawsuit. Even if an employee has few legal protections, as is sometimes the case with temporary employees or people hired on "soft" money, regular evaluations are a fair and considerate (that is, ethical) expectation of a manager. While it might be legally possible, for example, to summarily fire an employee in a grant-funded position with no explanation and without ever having conducted a performance evaluation during the years of his or her employment, an ethical manager (and especially a social worker) would never do it.

Promotions

Staff evaluations form the basis for the manager's assessment of staff competence. Along with day-to-day observations, they help to form impressions of, among other things, who

CASE EXAMPLE • *The Cost of Kindness*

Scott was a case supervisor in a large, family service organization offering a variety of counseling services. He came there from a mental health clinic where he had been employed as a psychiatric social worker for six years. He came highly recommended as a replacement for the previous case supervisor who had retired.

Overall, the social workers that Scott "inherited" were a dedicated and competent group. There was, however, one notable exception. Mildred was 57 years old when Scott took the job. In her first supervisory conference with him, Mildred pointedly but pleasantly reminded him that (1) she had grown children older than he and (2) she planned to work eight more years, doing essentially what she had been doing, and then retire. He learned that she had, in fact, been doing very little. She had been hired 27 years earlier along with Scott's predecessor—her former supervisor—and continued to have regular contact with her.

As he learned more about Mildred and got to know her better, Scott's initial irritation at her approach to their first conference subsided. He found himself genuinely liking her. While he intended that she become more productive, he soon concluded that she was probably incapable of doing more. When he assigned several new cases to her, she missed appointments and seemed to become overwhelmed. On those occasions when he needed to use her for work more appropriate to her job level, she generally proved herself to be totally incompetent. The other staff became concerned. They tactfully suggested that Scott just leave her alone and not ask her to do more than she had previously been doing. Her duties had consisted of carrying a few cases that she had carried for many years, doing occasional intake histories, watering the plants in all offices, and keeping the waiting room tidy and uncluttered. She also kept the coffee pot filled.

According to policy, Scott was to conduct regular six-month evaluations of all of his supervisees. He seriously considered rating Mildred as unsatisfactory and confronting her with her shortcomings in her first evaluation conference. He tore up the first written evaluation that he had prepared. He decided that Mildred would be devastated if he rated her objectively, especially since she had always been rated "excellent" by her friend and previous supervisor. He envisioned a hurt, tearful evaluation conference, painful to both parties, and resentment from the rest of the staff for his insensitivity toward her. He couldn't imagine how she could possibly make productive use of a critical evaluation for improvement anyway, given her sensitive nature and her pattern of performance developed over many years. He chose the road of least resistance with a slight effort at compromise—he rated her "excellent" in eight performance categories and "needs improvement" in two. In their conference he quickly explained to her that everyone (even himself) "needs improvement" in the two areas, punctuality and attention to detail. They laughed together about this and, overall, the conference was a pleasant interchange.

Scott was relieved. Her reaction was far better than anticipated; it made him even more fond of her and seemed to confirm that he had chosen the right course of action. He decided not to assign her to any new duties. This would make her happy and would allow him to continue to give her high evaluations on what she did, without grossly distorting reality. After all, she did make great coffee!

For the next two years, Mildred continued to do very little. Her co-workers continued to cover for her and Scott continued to give her very favorable evaluations. Then a new Executive Director was hired. Funding had declined drastically following the loss of a major EAP contract. The Board of Directors gave the new Executive Director a directive. He was to design and implement a reorganization of the organization, "flattening" the organizational

continued

CASE EXAMPLE • *(continued)*

structure by cutting out some mid-level management positions. The Board also denied him permission to replace two caseworkers who had recently resigned.

The Director wasted little time. As part of his response to the Board's instructions, he called his first line supervisors together and explained the situation. He instructed each to develop a plan that would represent no reduction in client services while making full use of remaining staff. Scott considered all possible alternatives. None were ideal and all involved some change that Mildred would see as punitive and that would force her to have more client contact. He finally concluded that the best solution was to assign her full-time to do intake histories, freeing up the other remaining social workers and himself to do more treatment. Predictably, Mildred reacted with incredulity, hurt, and even a little anger. She suggested that she might retire early, a thought that gave Scott no small amount of false hope. But before she could follow through on her threat (which most people doubted would occur anyway), another situation arose.

The reorganization resulted in reassignment and/or a heavier workload for eight other employees in addition to Mildred. Six of them were those most recently hired who were given a full caseload immediately. This was a departure from the usual organization practice of giving new social workers a 3/4 load for their first six months on the job. All six were women. One of the six convinced the others and, eventually, even Mildred, to lend their names to a sex discrimination suit against the organization. The fact that the Executive Director, Scott, and the most other supervisors were male lent even more credence to the complaint.

When he learned just how incompetent Mildred had been for years, the Director grew optimistic. Scott told him that neither he nor his predecessor felt that they could trust her to handle higher-level professional duties and had used her for only routine tasks. The Director asked for documentation. Scott had to respond that he had none. The Director asked to see her six-month employee evaluations; they were, of course, very favorable. The Director was furious, refusing to accept the only explanations that Scott could offer.

The board, not wanting to risk the public reaction to a lawsuit charging sexism in a human service organization, agreed to a substantial financial settlement for participants in the lawsuit. The resignation of Mildred and all but one of the staff involved in the suit left several new vacancies, most of which could not be filled because of new budget deficits. Another painful reorganization had to be implemented.

Discussion Questions

1. How did Scott attempt to justify his decision to give Mildred high evaluations and to assign her little work to do?
2. How did the fact that Scott had continued to rate her highly help to put the agency in legal jeopardy when the reorganization took place?
3. Who else may have been harmed by Scott's actions? How?
4. How could Scott have conducted Mildred's performance evaluations in a way that was both fair and considerate but still reflective of her true level of functioning?
5. Why was Scott likely to receive a poor performance evaluation from his own boss even though Mildred was an "inherited problem"?

is doing the job well, and who may be interested in and capable of assuming greater responsibilities. These impressions, in turn, are what assists the manager in making recommendations or unilateral decisions as to who should be promoted when vacancies occur.

If a current employee is offered a promotion, it generally conveys a message of "job well done!" and the manager's confidence that the individual can adapt to and continue to perform well in a job with different, usually greater responsibilities. But selecting one individual when one or more others may want the job can also be damaging to the self-esteem of those not promoted. Recommending one employee over others (who may be competent, too) for a promotion can leave a manager in what feels like a "no-win" situation. Unless it is handled skillfully and diplomatically, the manager's carefully cultivated reputation for fairness can be jeopardized.

Issues to Be Considered

In determining who is the best person for the job, the manager needs to consider a number of key issues. Some of them are the same issues that we discussed in relation to hiring new employees.

Constraints.   In unionized organizations, managers may not have free rein simply to pick the person they deem to be best for the job. In order to maintain good labor relations, they may need to adhere to union guidelines. Affirmative action restrictions and other legislative and judicial rules and policies may also influence who may be chosen. It is not unusual for social workers as managers to find themselves caught between labor unions with seniority-based requirements on the one hand and federal nondiscrimination requirements on the other. Women and particularly people of color or people with disabilities may possess the least seniority, having been recently hired within many organizations. By union standards, they are not likely to be in line for what would be considered an "early" promotion. Yet efforts to eliminate discrimination (as well as our professional values as social workers) would suggest that, in the interest of achieving diversity, we should promote them. There may be no perfect candidate for a promotion or a perfect solution to the opposing forces that sometimes influence the choice of a candidate for promotion. Social workers as managers must seek a satisfactory solution, not a perfect one, relying at least in part on the knowledge, values, and skills of their profession.

Past Performance.   A recommendation for promotion can be viewed as both a vote of confidence in an individual's potential to function in a higher level job and a reward. The past is a good indicator of the future, but it is far from perfect. We cannot be certain how an employee will perform if promoted, but past and present behaviors and attitudes give us some good hints.

The concept of a reward suggests that people selected for promotion (in the manager's perception) at the very least ought to have been doing a good job in their present positions. While it is conceivable that an employee functioning marginally in a current assignment would rise to new heights if promoted, it is highly unlikely. The idea of "promotion to motivate" rarely works. In addition to the fact that it is unlikely to be successful, it sends the wrong message to other staff, namely do a good job and we will overlook you; do not do a good job, and we may promote you. This same message is conveyed when a highly competent employee is passed over in favor of one less competent because the competent one is viewed as too valuable to the organization to be moved. Some managers have received a less than grateful response when they have paid staff members this kind of "compliment" after denying them a promotion.

Personal Characteristics.   Projections about an individual's ability to function in a higher-level position usually tend to be based upon the person's demonstrated or assumed personal attributes. Certain characteristics such as initiative, intelligence, conceptual abilities, problem-solving skills, interpersonal skills, integrity, communication skills, and commitment to organizational goals tend to be frequently mentioned as indications that an individual is capable of "moving up." These are all important characteristics to possess, but the problem with all of them and most of the others suggested in the literature is that they are desirable attributes for employees at all levels. Besides, how much intelligence, for example, is necessary? We know that it is helpful to be a little brighter than those you supervise. We can also identify persons who are excellent managers but who, nevertheless, seem to lack one or more of the characteristics often suggested as prerequisites for successfully assuming higher-level positions.

One attribute, that is an especially useful assessment tool for the manager, is the desire to perform the functions of manager. (See Chapter 12.) The desire is absolutely essential for individuals seeking promotion to a position that carries more management responsibilities. The question for the social worker as manager charged with choosing or recommending someone for a promotion must be, "Does this person really want the job or just the perks that go with it?" If, in fact, we are not convinced that an individual wants to spend more time managing and would be good at it, he or she might not be a good candidate for promotion.

Needs of the Organization.   As managers, we are committed to placing highest priority on the good of the organization and of the clients who it serves. In respecting these priorities, the person ultimately chosen or recommended sometimes may not be simply the individual who seems to have performed the best in the past or who seems to have the greatest number of desirable personal attributes. Other factors must be considered.

The formal job description of a position may give only a limited hint as to the best person to assume the job. If, for example, it is a case-supervision job that involves overseeing a productive, cooperative, self-motivated group of professionals, one type of supervisor may be appropriate. Another opening, though identical on paper, may require a supervisor who can exert the control necessary to bring to productivity an apathetic or passive-aggressive group who appear to have retired on the job. Especially in the task of selecting a supervisor, the matching of potential supervisory style and attributes with subordinate needs becomes extremely important.

Still Other Issues to Consider.   There is an almost limitless number of other factors that can influence the decision as to who is the best choice for promotion. They include, for example, whether the organization is in a period of relative stability or change, the political visibility of the specific position, the characteristics and success level of the previous occupant, the type of mentoring available to assist the newly promoted employee, and the likely reaction of the candidate's present co-workers who may have sought the promotion themselves. It is virtually impossible to think of everything that should be considered. Sometimes one can benefit from consultation with a peer who might suggest a factor or issue that might otherwise be overlooked.

Promoting from Within versus Hiring from Outside

Should a manager consider only those individuals currently within the work unit (or, perhaps, only those currently employed within the organization) when a higher level vacancy occurs or are persons from outside an alternative? Sometimes policies and, occasionally, even rules (such as the requirement that a position be advertised in the media for a certain number of days) make this decision an easy one for the social worker as manager. But if a policy invites consideration of both alternatives or if no organizational guidance is available, assessment of the costs and benefits of the available choices is indicated.

We will examine a common situation to illustrate the mixed blessings of the alternatives. Consider the selection of a replacement for a case supervisor who has resigned. On first blush, a promotion from within the work unit appears to be the logical option to choose. A pattern of continued looking beyond current staff when opportunities for advancement arise can have a demoralizing effect on staff attitudes. But, if the usual practice is to promote from within, employees not only feel that they have a chance to get ahead but they also feel that their employee status gives them a better opportunity for advancement. What's more, managers considering their own employees for promotion are much more likely to make a knowledgeable decision (they are more likely to know candidates' strengths and weaknesses) than if they were to consider persons outside the unit or outside the organization about whom less is known. Why not tap the management potential of one's own organization?

While a practice of promotion from within has a compelling logic to it and several distinct advantages, a number of cautions regarding its use are in order. Generally, staff members tend to favor the idea of promotion from within and its implicit potential for upward mobility. But among those who seek promotion, we sometimes see resentment about a specific promotion recommendation to promote a co-worker or acquaintance. Jealousies and rivalries can develop within organizations that have a policy of promotion from within. Competition for a position that may become available sometime in the future can be a stimulus for productivity. But it can also promote an attitude that, for example, discourages sharing of essential information with colleagues (potential rivals for a job) or other forms of noncooperation. Staff members may tend to engage in largely self-serving behaviors.

It should also be remembered that a promotion of a competent and proven staff member may weaken the ranks from which that person was drawn. Can an adequate replacement be found within the organization (a double disruption) or hired from outside? Sometimes not.

Arguments for filling higher-level vacancies from outside the unit or the organization relate primarily to how this practice can avoid the problems related to promoting from within, which were discussed. Outside hiring does not directly deplete the work unit.

However, staff may begin to feel career-blocked and leave anyway. In such situations, it may be less personally embarrassing for employees to have someone outside get the job than it is to have a co-worker given a promotion that he or she had sought. While staff may disagree with the principle of filling higher-level vacancies from among those outside the organization, it usually does not produce the same level of bitterness among staff who might have wanted the job.

Open competition for a position among both current employees and outside applicants allows a manager to select from among a larger pool of applicants. However, it puts a heavy burden on managers to demonstrate that the competition is indeed open. They must do so to maintain a reputation for fairness. Despite the existence of such a policy, employees often seem to want to believe that a job was "wired" from the start. So, even open competition, just like promotion from within or promotion from outside can leave some staff angry and resentful. Managers sometimes feel like they just cannot win!

Progressive Discipline

The selection of a current employee for promotion is, overall, a relatively pleasant management task. It allows the manager to reward past performance and to suggest that a staff member is believed to be capable of even greater growth and of assuming more responsibility. Unfortunately, both formal and casual evaluations of staff also reveal that some other individuals are falling short of meeting the expectations of even their present positions. A manager must know how to use a number of actions to address this problem. In most organizations, they follow a sequence of increasing severity that is sometimes referred to as progressive discipline.

If, for whatever reason, employees are not performing satisfactorily, managers need to do whatever possible to communicate to them their deficiencies, provide support for change, and, if improvement does not occur, prepare them for the possibility of termination. If periodic employee evaluations have been performed conscientiously and honestly, they will go a long way toward assisting in all of these activities. But negative evaluations can be somewhat general, especially if the manager is limited by the use of highly structured forms and criteria. The staff member who so chooses can ignore them or fail to hear the messages they convey. Similarly, a staff member may ignore the "friendly reminders" or non-verbal responses of a manager (such as facial expressions or body language) that express dissatisfaction with his or her work performance. When this happens, other forms of communication are required, ones that cannot be so easily ignored.

Verbal Reprimands

The first step in progressive discipline is usually a verbal reprimand. In some organizations, it is referred to as simply "counseling." Whichever term is used, it refers to a meeting to discuss some deficiency in behavior and/or work performance. It entails a direct, one-to-one, private, and confidential communication of employee shortcomings. Depending on organization policy, a first reprimand (and sometimes a second) may be required to be followed up with a dated notation in the employee's record documenting that a verbal reprimand was given. The reprimanded staff member may also be asked to confirm in writing that the verbal reprimand was received.

Social workers as managers have often tended to dread the use of individual verbal reprimands. There is nothing nonjudgmental about a reprimand; it communicates the judgment that another human being has been found to be deficient in some respect. It says that a person needs to change. Because of their distaste for one-to-one reprimands, social work managers sometimes have relied on a substitute that is both inadequate and creates new problems of its own—the group reprimand.

The group reprimand is essentially a contradiction in terms. Unlike an individual reprimand, it is public, not private and confidential. Thus it has the potential to embarrass rather than to protect the offending individual from the gossip and ridicule of peers. It may be easier on the manager than an individual reprimand, but harder on the rest of the work group.

We will use a common example. A supervisor (Sandra) may be having a persistent problem with a worker (Jerry) who spends several hours a day on the phone with family and friends. She chooses to address the problem by means of a group reprimand delivered during a weekly staff meeting. A typical group reprimand in this situation might consist of a stern voice, a scowl, and a statement such as, "Some of you are spending too much time on the telephone handling personal business. This is against organization policy and must stop immediately! You know who you are."

Sandra might feel relieved to have addressed the problem while having avoided an unpleasant direct confrontation with Jerry. She might believe that the problem had been effectively solved. But what is the likely result of the use of such a group reprimand? Those staff members who rarely or never use the phone for personal business will use work time to speculate on just who is the culprit, if they do not already know. They will also likely be angry that they had to listen to Sandra's insulting accusations when they never use the phone for personal business. They will resent the time wasted and will lose some respect for Sandra, who seemed to lack the courage to directly confront their peer.

Some other productive and competent staff members who occasionally use their work phone for necessary personal calls may believe that Sandra was referring to them. They will feel chastised, a little surprised, and shocked at the severity of her reaction. They will probably not make any more personal calls from work even when an emergency personal call is necessary.

Meanwhile, Jerry, the real object of the group reprimand may simply assume that Sandra was not talking about him. Even if he recognizes that he was the target of the reprimand, he will be somewhat reassured to think that he is not the only one using the phone for personal business, and will be unlikely to stop the behavior. There will also be no written record of the group reprimand, either to serve as an ongoing impetus for change for him or to provide Sandra with proof of due process, should he ultimately have to be fired.

Group reprimands can be destructive to both morale and the kind of productive organizational climate that the manager is expected to create. They are not a discharging of managerial responsibility; they are a shirking of it.

Appropriately used, direct, one-to-one verbal reprimands are an unpleasant but absolutely essential part of a social worker's job as manager. They should not be perceived as unfair or insensitive. They represent what is needed by the staff member who receives them; that is, specific, honest communication about where and how to improve in order to avoid future unpleasant consequences. If improvement is insufficient and the staff member must be terminated, reprimands help to expedite the smooth performance of this task.

Written Reprimands

After one or two verbal reprimands (and insufficient improvement), the next reprimand is generally a written one. Copies of the written reprimand are kept, usually in the employee's personnel record, although a manager may elect to use an "under the table" reprimand which, by agreement with the employee, is removed from the record if the deficiency is corrected. A written reprimand is very specific. It spells out in detail what is inadequate about the worker's performance, and it reminds the staff member that this is not the first time that the problem has been noted. It may contain a description of new requirements being imposed in order to address the problem and/or a reference to sources of help (see Figure 7.1). It is an important part of the "paper trail" that must be kept if future personnel action becomes necessary.

Warnings and Contracts

If insufficient improvement occurs following a written reprimand, a staff member is usually given one last chance. It entails another written document that is even more specific and is usually called either a warning or contract, or sometimes even a "final written reprimand." It describes all of the other progressive discipline actions that have previously occurred and all of the continued problems since the last one. It outlines what must be done to avoid dismissal, and where appropriate (as in cases where the problem is required work that was not completed) deadlines are set. The manager makes it clear in the document that this is a final opportunity for the staff member to avoid either suspension without pay or outright dismissal, whichever is specified. The staff member, if he or she wishes to have this final chance, must sign the document agreeing to do what is required exactly as written. The signature is an indication that he or she understands that not doing it will be grounds for the consequences described.

Transfers

For the employee who does not respond to progressive discipline, transfer should be at least considered. But transfers should not be used just to get rid of problem employees by passing them on to others. This is unfair to other managers, who probably already have enough problem employees of their own. It also seems to send the wrong message to one's own staff, especially if problem staff are transferred to another job that may be perceived as more desirable. Used sparingly and appropriately, however, a transfer may represent a good problem solution for the manager. A failure to function in one job (particularly if there are unique situational factors such as personality conflicts that negatively affect performance) may not preclude success in another job.

Transfers may not always be an option in very small organizations or in situations where the employee clearly lacks the credentials for any job other than the current one. If transfers are possible, the potential impact on morale of other employees in both the old

FIGURE 7.1 *Example of a Written Reprimand*

Name of Employee: Mary Doe
Date: 9/5/02

Dear Ms. Doe:

This notice constitutes a written reprimand being issued to you for excessive tardiness and your continuing failure to notify me as required when you are unable to work as scheduled. You were verbally reprimanded for these problems on 6/3/02 and again on 7/1/02. However, reviewing your attendance record since then, I note that you have been absent on six occasions and failed to notify me on four of them (7/8, 7/11, 7/24, and 8/8). You were also absent on 8/19 and 8/26, and I did not receive information concerning your absence until the afternoon, when a co-worker of yours sent me an e-mail stating that you were at home. The messages gave no reason for your absence, and did not indicate if you planned to file for sick leave or file a request for annual leave. Furthermore, since 7/1/02 you have been late for work on nine additional days.

Beginning immediately, in the event you are unable to report for work because of illness, you must call and speak to either me or my administrative assistant by 10:00 AM. You must also provide a physician's statement with a brief description of your illness when you report back to work. Emergency situations will be handled on a case-by-case basis. Annual leave must be requested and approved at least five working days in advance. Failure to adhere to these requirements will constitute insubordination and a refusal to accept a reasonable and proper request from an authorized supervisor.

In an effort to assist you, I am suggesting that you contact our Employee Assistance Program (EAP) at Family Service, 201 Elm Street. They may be able to provide counseling to help you meet job requirements. You may call to make an appointment at 555-1234. All visits should be scheduled on your personal time during weekends or evenings.

We must work as a productive, cooperative team and adhere to acceptable standards and practices if we are to serve our clients effectively. Your past absences and tardiness have made the work of your co-workers more difficult. Any further deviation from your normal work schedule may result in further disciplinary action, including dismissal. Please let me know if you have any questions about the contents of this notice.

Received by:

Mary Doe   *9/5/02*

Employee Signature   Date
(Signature denotes only that this document has been received and read)

Sally Smith   *9/5/02*

Supervisor Signature   Date

---

and new work groups should be carefully evaluated. When decisions to transfer staff members are made, it should be made clear to those transferred that the transfers should be viewed as a second chance and not an indication that staff have been absolved of responsibility for their previous level of functioning. Their performance evaluations remain a part of their personnel records.

Termination of Staff

There are many different reasons why staff members leave their jobs. They may voluntarily resign to take a better position or for personal reasons. Sometimes, they leave by "mutual agreement" because, after a trial period, it has become obvious that their knowledge and skills do not match up well with the needs of the organization. Employees also retire or have to leave because of a reduction in force (RIF) necessitated by financial emergencies and/or reorganization that has caused their jobs to be eliminated. In the latter case, their leaving the organization may be only temporary as they generally are given priority to be rehired when an opening occurs, if they are still available for employment. While the loss of workers in any of these ways may be harmful to the organization and can cause serious disruption in service delivery and in the effective functioning of the work group, loss of workers in these ways is almost inevitable in human service organizations from time to time. It is a difficult but predictable problem to be confronted.

There is another type of termination that is technically voluntary, but that is sometimes used to dismiss an employee who is either not doing the job or is chronically absent from work—job abandonment. Depending on the rules or policies of an organization, it may be possible to dismiss an employee who simply fails to report to work for a certain number of consecutive days without either calling in sick or requesting administrative leave using the correct procedures. If so, this can be a relatively "painless" way to remove the individual from employment. It requires only a written notice of the action (abandonment of position), a listing of the dates during which the employee was absent and a reminder that they have been charged the appropriate number of days of unauthorized leave. The organization's rule or policy is generally cited. The employee is generally sent the notice of abandonment by registered mail and given a date (a reasonable time period such as one week) to provide an acceptable written explanation of his or her absence. Unless one is received, the "voluntary" termination is effective on that date.

Involuntary Terminations.   Termination of a worker who does not want to leave often creates special problems for the social worker as manager. As social workers, we seek to help people, not be instrumental in making their lives more difficult. But firing employees that are a liability to the organization and its clients is a task that must be accomplished. Even such an unpleasant part of the manager's job can be made easier if we understand some of the issues involved and know how to do the job properly.

There are generally two reasons for the involuntary dismissal of an employee—termination because of misconduct or termination because of unsatisfactory work performance. Each is handled quite differently by the manager.

Termination for misconduct (sometimes referred to as "gross misconduct") usually requires no prior warning. It may not require the payment of severance pay. Personnel standards may require a period of suspension, either with or without pay. If so, investigation and opportunities to contest charges or appeal decisions may have to take place before an employee can be actually fired. However, termination for misconduct may allow an employee to be fired "on the spot" for some behavior that has occurred on the job that is clearly forbidden in writing such as conviction of a felony, theft of organization property, sexual involvement with a client, violence or threats of violence, or simply refusing to do one's job as directed. When it is allowed, immediate termination for gross misconduct is not a matter of discretion or judgment for the manager; if termination did not occur, the manager would be in trouble for not doing what is required by the policy manual. Employees fired "on the spot" generally are gone in a matter of minutes; the manager thus does not have to face them again or deal with their disruptive influence on the work environment for another two weeks or more. Of course, if the decision to fire is appealed or legal action is brought, an adversarial relationship may go on for months or even years.

Termination because of unsatisfactory work performance is often especially difficult for the social worker as manager. It follows a period of effort to correct the worker's deficiencies that may entail a series of low staff performance evaluations, oral and written reprimands, and one or more warnings. During this time the individual should have been told repeatedly what was required to bring work performance up to standard and that termination would occur if that standard was not met.

Even if all of the required measures to ensure due process have been used properly and "just cause" has been established, there still remains the possibility that the decision to terminate an employee for unsatisfactory performance may be viewed as unfair and discriminatory. Before termination proceedings begin, several final, general questions should be asked by the manager:

- Will anyone (including other staff who work with the individual) be surprised by the decision to fire the individual? The manager should not be the only one who noticed that work was substandard.
- What similar situations have existed within the organization in the past, and were other employees treated any differently? Has anyone else not been fired for performance that was consistently as bad or even worse? If the manager has been documenting examples of poor work performance, was similar documentation kept on other workers whose work was not up to standard? Will the worker appear to have been "singled out"?
- Is there anything in the employee's record to contradict the conclusion that the worker cannot do the job? Letters of commendation, "employee of the month" awards, or even a small merit raise in the last year or two may make it difficult, if not impossible, to fire the worker at the present time.

A manager should avoid a battle that cannot be won. To try to fire an employee and then learn that it cannot be done can result in embarrassment and loss of respect for the manager. If it appears that an employee might be successful in fighting termination now, it might be better to wait, carefully documenting work performance, and avoid any action that might preclude or delay future termination. A word of caution is in order though. Managers cannot always wait until they are on totally firm ground. In their professional judgment, the continued employment of a worker may be so detrimental to the functioning of the organization and its clients that it may be necessary to go ahead and terminate the worker even though a battle is likely to ensue. With the current proclivity of people to file grievances and to seek legal restitution, any manager can expect some lawsuits. One who proudly states that "no one has ever sued me" probably has never taken a necessary risk. Lawsuits and threats of lawsuits are a fact of life for today's managers. They cannot afford to be intimidated and immobilized every time a staff member or client threatens to sue. Sometimes, we have to "take our chances" and let people go ahead and sue when the good of the organization or our clients' welfare is at stake. That is why individual professionals and human service organizations carry malpractice insurance and employ legal consultants.

Termination Interviews

Once the decision is made to fire an employee either because of gross misconduct or continued unsatisfactory work performance, a private meeting should be scheduled. A witness (usually a personnel officer or higher level administrator) should also be present. If there is no sense of urgency, as in the case with employees terminated for unsatisfactory work performance, termination interviews usually are scheduled at the end of the day or even on Friday afternoon. Then the employee will not have to face co-workers afterward and can go home to supportive family or friends. Of course, if the reason for termination is gross misconduct and the manager wants the employee out of the office immediately and does not mind making an example of the fired staff member, such a consideration may be unnecessary.

There are right ways and wrong ways to conduct termination interviews.[5] The manager should make it clear from the outset that termination is the interview's focus and that the decision is not reversible. Usually, a letter of dismissal has been previously prepared. It is given to the employee. In announcing the decision to terminate an individual, the manager should use direct and clear statements. For example, "Shelby, I have concluded that you will not be employed here after the seventh of August" or (if termination is for misconduct) "Chet, you are fired," or "Suzette, I've concluded that your work has not met our standard" would be appropriate. A more vague statement like, "Suzette, I think you might be happier working in another organization" is not appropriate. The reason given should not come as a surprise, but the worker may wish to dispute the manager's assessment or demand to know why the decision was made at the present time. If so, it is best to listen politely, but to avoid an argument by reiterating that the decision is final and by not becoming defensive.

Future employment advice would probably go unappreciated in the emotion of the moment and might only make the worker more angry. Supportive comments that are intended to be kind statements may be resented by the terminated employee. Some comments might even provide the ammunition for a lawsuit. For example, statements to employees terminated for unsatisfactory work performance such as, "I recognize that it must have been difficult to try to learn so much new at your age" or "I'm sure that being the only African American didn't make your job any easier" should never be made. They are almost certain to land the manager and the organization in court in the middle of a discrimination suit. It is best to make no reference whatsoever to any demographic characteristics of the worker. Even if the worker brings up demographic characteristics, the manager should be careful not to even hint that they may have been related in any way to their job performance or to the termination decision.

Any benefits available to the worker (termination pay, payment for unused vacation days, continued medical coverage, etc.) should be outlined, even if the employee appears to be too preoccupied with the impact of the termination decision to be listening. If nothing else, the manager's description of remaining benefits may help to underline the reality of the decision, helping it to "sink in" for the worker. The information can be repeated later by the manager or a specialist in the personnel office. When necessary information has been communicated, the interview should end. A termination interview should not be allowed to go on once the necessary business has been transacted and the worker is sufficiently emotionally settled to leave the manager's office. After the terminated employee has left, a confidential memo should be written and hand-delivered (if possible) the same day to confirm that the termination interview took place. A copy should be placed in the personnel file.

If there is ever a time for the social worker as manager to be businesslike, it is in a termination interview. Any soul-searching and emotional struggle should have occurred earlier, before the decision to terminate the employee was made. The interview should be conducted with sensitivity, but also with the legal interests of the organization in mind. If the manager has followed all appropriate courses of action and has made a decision that is in the best interest of the organization and the clients it serves, the manager can take comfort in the fact that, while terminating the employment of the worker may have been difficult, the *decision* to terminate was the correct one.

Dealing with Terminated Employees

Having completed the termination interview, the manager may experience a great sense of relief. An unpleasant job has been completed. But the most unpleasant part of the experience may still lie ahead. An employee who has been employed for some length of time and is fired for unsatisfactory work performance is likely to remain on the job for a while. Generally, under organizational policy, employees terminated for reasons other than gross misconduct are given at least two weeks notice at the time of the termination interview, sometimes 30 days. Sometimes workers have vacation time saved up and choose to use it rather than return to work. But organizational policy may allow them to opt to come to work and to be paid for accrued vacation time.

The manager may wish to avoid the terminated employee. The feeling may be mutual. But for managers, this would be irresponsible. First, a follow-up interview may be required. If employees were highly emotional and upset during the termination interview, they may have failed to ask questions about the termination or may have failed to hear or comprehend all of what was said. The opportunity for a follow-up interview should be provided while, again, making it clear that the decision to terminate is not negotiable.

Even if there is no particular need for or interest in a follow-up interview, contact with terminated employees should not be avoided. Bitter, openly hostile employees may need to be confronted and dealt with for the good of the organization. Even an employee who was calm and seemed resigned to the termination decision at the time of the termination interview may harbor a great amount of repressed anger or may be depressed. The manager should monitor terminated employees' emotions and behavior to assure that responses to termination decisions are within normal limits. If response seems extreme and shows no sign of dissipating, it might be necessary to try to refer the terminated employee for counseling, but not to attempt to provide it! As with other management tasks, the social worker's knowledge of human behavior can be invaluable in making these kind of assessments.

The continued presence of terminated workers can be uncomfortable for other employees, the workers themselves and for the manager. Managers who have made the decision to fire workers are likely to bear the brunt of anger from them and from any other employees who might disagree with their decisions. Even co-workers who know staff have been fired and agree with the decision to fire them are likely to have problems in knowing how to relate to fired workers and what to say to them.

Occasionally, terminated employees may work hard (perhaps harder than in the past) up until their last day on the job. Perhaps, they want to prove that the decision to fire them was incorrect, or maybe they continue to hold out the false hope that managers will change their minds. Others just go about their jobs as usual and keep a low profile. Still others seem more intent on venting their anger and resentment and stirring up as much trouble as they can. The latter group often presents special problems to the manager. Often, the attitude of a terminated worker may reflect an attitude like "If I don't do what you ask, what are you going to do about it—fire me?!" It is not unusual or particularly surprising that a terminated worker may become very apathetic, "passive-aggressive," cynical, or even obstructive of organizational goal achievement.

It might be better for the organization if a bitter, fired worker would just stay home. But this may not be possible if the organization has a rule that terminated employees must be on the job in order to be paid.

Exit Interviews

An exit interview (usually conducted on an employee's last day on the job) customarily is offered to all employees (except for those fired for misconduct) who are leaving the organization. For those who are leaving voluntarily (for example, those who are retiring), it affords a pleasant opportunity to reflect back on years of employment and to review the contributions of the individual to organizational goal attainment. The interview generally entails a congenial exchange of compliments between the manager and the departing employee and some occasional constructive suggestions for change that the departing employee might previously have been reluctant to make.

For the employee who has abandoned a job or who has been involuntarily terminated for unsatisfactory work performance, the offer of an exit interview may be refused. The manager should offer one, but should not "force it." But if the employee consents to one, it may be beneficial to all parties. The combination of anger and embarrassment felt by a fired worker doesn't always go away on its own before the last day of employment. It can be carried over to a subsequent job or into the community and have a negative effect on the public image of an organization. Bitterness about having been fired from a job sometimes can be partially "defused" by the use of an exit interview.

An exit interview has other potential benefits as well. Fired employees have opportunities to ventilate anger and frustration or, if they choose, to try to end a relationship with the manager on a better footing than may have existed at the time of the termination interview. Managers can use the occasion of an exit interview to improve interpersonal relations with terminated workers by identifying some of the worker's achievements (and everyone has some) and reassuring them that, at least to some degree, a mismatch between worker attributes and organizational needs may have contributed to the necessity for terminating employment.

For a terminated employee, an exit interview is a kind of postmortem in which both parties examine what went wrong. Some of what the fired worker may say is likely to be a rationalization or an effort to blame others for poor performance. When this occurs, the manager should listen, but not provide validation for everything that is said. But other explanations may contain elements of truth and can provide the manager with insights that might lead to changes that will prevent problems for some future employee.

The offer of an exit interview is a courtesy. If the offer is accepted, it can be a valuable contribution to future organizational functioning. It can provide insight into organizational morale and turnover problems.[6] Even if a departing employee chooses to make it an unpleasant occasion, the manager should regard it as an opportunity to acquire useful feedback.

Summary

In this chapter we have examined some important tasks of managers that are frequently among their least favorite. We looked at why staff evaluations often are unpleasant for both the manager and the subordinate and why they need not be so. We outlined how they provide numerous benefits to all concerned.

We emphasized fairness and consideration in conducting staff evaluations. We warned that evaluations that rely too heavily on only easily measured evaluation criteria tend to be of limited value. Some of the most important attributes of valuable workers are difficult to measure. Some use of softer criteria are inevitable and desirable in promoting fairness.

Staff evaluations, if performed well, facilitate good personnel actions that affect the careers of current employees. We focused on a number of personnel actions in which the manager is likely to become involved. We examined the pros and cons of three policies that may apply when a vacancy in a higher level job occurs—promotion from within, hiring from outside the unit or organization, and open competition. It was emphasized that all three may result in staff dissatisfaction and morale problems unless the manager successfully communicates that the process of selection was handled fairly and in the best interest of the organization and its clients.

Employees who are not performing up to the requirements of their jobs require a series of actions designed to give them every opportunity to correct deficiencies. The usual sequence of events known as progressive discipline was described.

If employees do not respond to progressive discipline, it may be necessary to fire them. Some staff must be terminated for misconduct—termination may be immediate. Decisions to involuntarily terminate an employee for job abandonment or for unsatisfactory work performance require documentation over time. We stressed that the termination interview is a time for special caution, as the terminated employee may be seeking ways to either get the manager to reverse the decision or to gather ammunition for a lawsuit. Finally, we suggested how another planned discussion with employees about to leave an organization, the exit interview, can be valuable to staff, the manager, and the organization.

Endnotes

1. Walter Christian and Gerald Hannah, *Effective Management in the Human Services* (Englewood Cliffs, NJ: Prentice-Hall, 1983), pp. 213–241; Eileen Gambrill and Theodore Stein, *Supervision: A Decision-Making Approach* (Beverly Hills, CA,: Sage, 1983), pp. 39–106.

2. Alfred Kadushin, *Supervision in Social Work,* 1st ed. (New York: Columbia University Press, 1976), pp. 286–313.

3. National Association of Social Workers, *Code of Ethics.* (NASW Press: Alexandria, VA, 1999), paragraph 3.03.

4. Theo Haimann and Raymond Hilgert, *Supervision: Concepts and Practices of Management,* 4th ed. (Cincinnati, OH: South-Western Publishing, 1987), p. 276.

5. J. Jensen, "Letting Go: The Difficult Art of Firing," *The Grantsmanship Center News* 9 (1981): 38–42.

6. A. Sherwood, "Exit Interviews: Don't Just Say Goodbye," *Personnel Journal,* 62 (1983): 744–750.

8

Organizing Work Activities

In the previous three chapters, we examined a wide variety of issues relating to the hiring, assessment, evaluation, and progressive discipline of staff—all part of what we have described somewhat loosely as the staffing function of managers. We now turn to the third major function of managers, organizing.

In all human service organizations, but especially in larger ones, it is necessary to organize staff activities in order to integrate them and to promote unity of function. In this chapter we will address three major questions related to organization which must be answered by managers in all human service organizations:

- What is the general way that the organization is structured for service delivery?
- How are staff and their activities divided into units of a manageable size?
- How are authority and tasks distributed within the organization's units?

As any student of basic systems theory will recall, organization is an inherent characteristic of any system. No viable system can exist without it. It falls to the manager to select from among available ways to structure and to group the activities of staff. The manager must ensure coordination of the efforts of individuals and of work groups. Organizing entails the delineation of roles and ways that staff are to interact, as well as the maintenance of an overall plan where individual and group roles mesh to facilitate attainment of objectives.

Basic Ways of Organizing

Human service organizations tend to reflect one of three general organizing patterns. The pattern is selected by the individuals in high-level administrative positions who are frequently responding to the wishes of the board of directors and the mission of the organization that has been legitimized by its task environment. The basic way in which the organization is organized for delivery of services tends to influence the activities of all staff, no matter where they are located in the organization's hierarchy.

The Production Line Organization

One way that organizations can be organized for delivery of services is as a production line. This organizing pattern, promoted by early management theorists, involves a sequence of individuals performing their own rather specialized tasks. It also has been referred to as "long-linked" or "sequential processing."[1] On first blush, this method of organizing would seem to be suited for only manufacturing facilities such as automobile plants. It is easy to picture an assembly line where workers perform repetitive tasks, each making a contribution to the construction of the vehicle that emerges at the end of the line. Creative task completion or the use of professional judgment would definitely not be valued; it would actually disrupt the flow of activities. The increased use of robotics in such organizations underlines the fact that the standardization of activities, not human creativity or judgment, is desirable in organizations that rely on the assembly line as their primary pattern of organization.

While there are professional values and ethical constraints that would seem to argue against the widespread use of the assembly line approach to setting up an organization for delivery of human services, this method is not as foreign to social work practice as we might initially believe. For example, eligibility for economic services has often been characterized by strict adherence to a kind of sequential processing of clients. Similarly, a common method of organizing within some mental health facilities has involved a rather rigid sequence of demographic information collection by a receptionist, social history taken by a social worker, psychological testing by the psychologist, medical examination (if medication may be needed) by a psychiatrist, staffing and development of a treatment plan by the treatment team, and (finally) assignment to a clinician for treatment. In this variation on the assembly line, a patient is clearly "processed" through several stages until assigned to a therapist who then undertakes a course of individualized therapy.

No organization that is set up entirely like a production line would be suitable to human service delivery. We cannot standardize the treatment of people—individuals, families, groups, or communities. Neither can we hope to nor would we wish to totally standardize the activities of staff who try to help people with their problems. An automobile manufacturer knows what the final, standardized product should look like and what it should be able to do. We could never have agreement as to how the desirable output of our production line (our clients) should look or act. Our clients (whose self-determination rights would have to be respected), staff, and the task environment could probably never agree on, for example, the best outcome for all marital counseling.

Even if we could agree on desirable outcomes of services, technology in the helping professions is far from an exact science. We lack the cause–effect knowledge required to guarantee that a treatment goal will be achieved if certain activities occur.

Production lines probably are suitable for only selected activities within human service organizations—those where there is goal consensus and more cause–effect knowledge than is typical within most human service organizations. When they can be used appropriately, they have one major advantage—efficiency. Critics of managed care within the health care industry have sometimes charged that it promotes a production line approach to medical and psychiatric treatment. Perhaps, so. Since the primary goal of managed care is reduction in health care costs, a general method for organizing services that resembles a production line would only seem logical.

The Linkage Organization

Some human service organizations appear to be organized in such a way that their primary function is that of a mediator or broker. The activities of people within the organization and staff job descriptions make it clear that the organization's mission is to provide primarily one service—bringing people and services together. In the business world, a savings and loan association or credit union is a linkage organization. It functions as a mediator between those who wish to invest their savings and those who need to borrow money. A stock brokerage firm functions similarly by making it possible for a woman in Spokane to sell 100 shares of General Motors to a man in Tampa whom she has never met and would likely never meet. The business of these organizations is linking people who have something to offer with others who need or want it.

Do human service agencies ever organize their activities around bringing people and services together? Certainly. Adoption agencies offer a service of bringing together those who want a child with a child who needs a home. Traveler's assistance divisions of some national family counseling organizations offer some crisis intervention services but function primarily as mediators between clients and other human service organizations. Any social agency that serves as a mediator or has referral as its principal function may appear to be organized in a way similar to that of a credit union or stock brokerage firm. While social work values require individualized, personalized, and sensitive service to clients, timely and appropriate referrals are important to client well-being. Consequently, activities of staff may center around collecting and maintaining current data about community resources, networking with intake personnel in other agencies, and even development of contractual arrangements to assure that individuals and services are brought together.

As case management has gained in popularity in recent years, some organizations, or at least some of their programs, have been pressured to move away from costly individualized services to people with problems. They have concentrated more on the coordination of services that are offered by other organizations. Thus they have begun to function in a way that is more characteristic of linkage organizations.

Especially within medical facilities, social work professionals have vigorously fought the transition from the delivery of traditional case services to a case management model of service delivery. They have argued that professional social work practice is much more than just case management. They have contended that case management does not require the knowledge and skills of a professionally educated social worker. Others, taking the opposite position, have argued that linking clients with needed services has always been an important part of the job of the professional social worker—who is better prepared to offer this valuable service? Despite the fact that many social workers opposed having their jobs redefined as "merely" case managers, some organizations (primarily hospitals) have reorganized to form case management interdisciplinary teams. In some settings where this has happened, social workers now find themselves called case managers, not social workers. They work on teams alongside other case managers trained in other disciplines (for example, registered nurses) who have identical job descriptions and who (in theory) perform the same functions. In fact, because of their professional preparation, social workers on the teams are much better prepared to offer case management services than those professionals from other disciplines. Not surprisingly, the task of linking clients to other organizations within the community, in order for them to receive services, falls heavily onto social workers.

It does not appear that a case management emphasis on social work services will disappear any time soon. On the contrary, it is likely to become more widespread. As it does, more and more organizations are likely to be organized primarily as linkage organizations.

The Custom Service Organization

Despite increased emphasis on case management, many human service organizations continue to provide specialized services to clients. While they may make referrals to other organizations for unusual client needs, professional staff generally are expected to design and implement individualized treatment plans for clients that are designed to address their problems. In these settings, called custom service organizations, the prevailing philosophy is that services cannot be standardized; they must be individualized to the uniqueness of the client or the client group and to the nature of the problem. Neither input (the client or client group) nor output (the goal of intervention) is ever the same. Neither are the other variables in the equation (professional staff and intervention methods). Individualized treatment is what makes many social work services so expensive.

Despite the fact that client services must be individualized, many other activities of staff need not be idiosyncratic. Organizing structures still can be used to coordinate staff activities and can help to create a climate of reasonable certainty in which staff can function. This is frequently accomplished by the use of job descriptions. Job descriptions are used to suggest the general tasks and duties of the individuals and how they are supposed to relate to each other in the course of their job performance. However, in custom service organizations they generally stop short of saying specifically what services an individual is to offer clients or even exactly what the nature of the individual's interaction is to be with peers. Those decisions are left to professional discretion.

If we were to examine the mission statements of a large number of human service organizations, a large percentage of them would seem to suggest that the organization relies on custom services to clients. That should not be surprising. As we discussed in Chapter 4, a mission statement, among other things, reflects a philosophy with which the various components of the organization's task environment cannot help but agree. Thus, we would expect most human service organizations to have mission statements that would seem to promise individualized treatment or services. We would hardly expect them to have mission statements that suggest a production line philosophy when it comes to client services. However, since custom treatment is so expensive and because organizations cannot operate "in the red" for very long, in reality organizations that rely exclusively on custom services to clients are becoming increasingly rare. Virtually all organizations, even those who serve only affluent clients who can pay for their own treatment, use standardized services to some degree. Of course, they do not advertise it!

In all organizations, even in those that have not yet been significantly influenced by cost containment methods such as managed care, managers have a responsibility to cut costs of services wherever possible. They are expected to identify those activities where standardization is both possible and desirable (to promote efficiency). They also must organize the activities of staff into manageable units that operate efficiently, the focus of our next discussion. Simply put, managers are expected to help organizations to function more like production lines while not compromising their public image as custom service organizations.

The Departmentation Menu

The selection of the basic way in which a human service organization is organized to deliver services is made in relation to its mission when the organization first comes into existence. Sometimes, new developments such as the advent of managed care or a case management approach to services necessitate a shift to one of the two other general ways for an organization to be organized. Even when this occurs, only the highest levels of management may be directly involved in the decision. Often the choice from among a production line, linkage, or custom service organization model may be a *fait accompli,* given the nature of clients to be served, their problems, and the types of services that are appropriate for meeting client needs. As we have indicated, even when, for example, needs for efficiency and the potential to standardize services to some degree result in an organization that starts to look more and more like a production line (as in some elements of the public sector), it is still likely to be claimed that custom services are offered.

The general model for delivering services that seems to be most prevalent provides only the most general guidelines for organizing staff activities. Within all human service organizations, but especially in larger ones, the manager must somehow subdivide the many activities of staff in a logical way. It is impossible to be aware of, much less influence, the activities of staff unless some way is found to reduce organizational activities into subunits that are sufficiently small to be managed by individuals. This is the organizational activity generally referred to as *departmentation*. It refers to the grouping of people and their activities along some basic pattern or model in order that their activities can be adequately supervised coordinated, and managed.

Koontz, O'Donnell, and Weihrich,[2] in their classic text on business management, suggest many different ways that a manager can choose to handle the task of departmentation. On first blush, their methods of departmentation would seem to be very profit- and product-oriented (rather than service-oriented). They appear to be of little relevance for human service organizations. We will look at some of them, translate rather liberally so that they relate more directly to social work (see Figure 8.1) and add a few that are more unique to human service organizations.

Simple Numbers

One method of departmentation involves simply grouping those who perform the same duties under a single manager (a supervisor in most human service organizations). If there are too many of these individuals for one supervisor to manage effectively, two or more

FIGURE 8.1   *The Departmentation Menu—Ways to Reduce an Organization into Units*

1. Simple numbers—Units consist of equal numbers of staff, all having similar knowledge and skills and all performing the same functions or serving similar clients.
2. Time worked—Units consist of staff from different professional disciplines who have in common the time of day (shift) that they work.
3. Discipline—In an organization containing several different professional types, units consist of staff who are grouped together solely because they are members of the same professional discipline.
4. Enterprise—Units consist of all persons engaged in the same primary enterprise activity, regardless of discipline. Service to clients generally is just one of these enterprises.
5. Territory served—Units consist of all staff who serve the same geographical territory.
6. Service offered—Distinctly different types of services are offered and units consist of staff who offer the same type of specialized service to clients with various problems.
7. Client problem—Different units specialize in offering services to clients who share a single diagnostic category or who share a common problem.
8. Interdisciplinary teams—In an organization serving those with different types of client problems, units consist of staff from *different* professional backgrounds who offer a variety of services.
9. Marketing channels—Units consist of staff who all offer services (often information) within similar types of settings or through similar means.

parallel, equal-sized units can be created. The equal numbers principle might be applied even further by assigning an equal number of work units to each staff member within the unit or units. For example, all secretaries might each do the secretarial work of six professional staff members or all professional staff members might carry the same number of active cases.

The biggest drawback to the simple-numbers method of departmentation may be its lack of recognition of the individual capacities of staff. People are not interchangeable parts with the same knowledge, skills, and capacities. To treat them as such is to not take full advantage of a staff member's uniqueness. Within social agencies, for example, a professional staff member may have a special aptitude for working with adolescents; another may not relate well to young people, but may develop a productive rapport with older clients. A counseling agency that features departmentation by simple numbers might not allow sufficient opportunity for specialization or for the use of special competencies. But combined with another method of departmentation that we will examine a little later (service), it has been used successfully in human service organizations; for example, public child welfare and mental health facilities.

As the only method of organizing, the simple-numbers model rarely works well. It may have been more functional in Frederick Taylor's day or in an earlier agrarian society when the number of persons required to pick a crop was more important for organizing than the individual attributes of the people doing the work. Historically and even today it is the departmentation method employed most by the military. Standard characteristics (rather than individual identity) of service personnel is emphasized. Units are viewed as "so many troops" rather than a collection of individuals. But the utility of departmentation by simple numbers for today's social agencies is somewhat limited. Perhaps some word processing pools may still be suited to this single method of departmentation, although full use of individual abilities may even argue against its use for clerical staff. Departmentation by simple numbers is mentioned in this text primarily because it is seen in combination with other departmentation methods within some social agencies. Social workers as managers must be able to recognize and consider it, even if they generally reject it in favor of some other method of departmentation.

Time Worked

For those organizations that must or should operate during evening and/or weekend hours, departmentation by time may be used. While shift work is more commonly seen in manufacturing plants as a means to more efficient use of machinery and to increase productivity, it is not unknown in social agencies. Medical and psychiatric facilities and many other human service organizations cannot limit client services to the 9-to-5, Monday-through-Friday model. Shift work among social work staff is relatively rare, but not unheard of. While social workers are more likely to be part of an on-call roster than part of a night or weekend shift, other professionals such as nurses and aides have come to expect shift work. Some prefer it for a variety of reasons, including higher pay, compatibility with a partner's work schedule, or because the demands of student or parent roles can be more easily met when days are free.

Although social work managers do not generally use time departmentation for organization of social work staff into units, they may find themselves with authority over a variety of other staff who might be grouped according to their work hours. Many private counseling organizations tend to have clearly identified day staffs and evening staffs. Clients of a Traveler's Aid type of agency are very likely to require professional services during evenings and weekends; it may be logical to schedule paid staff and/or volunteers in such a way that two or more distinct work groups (shifts) are employed.

Time departmentation has the obvious advantage of increased availability of client services. It also has several potential disadvantages for the social worker as manager. Hiring and keeping competent staff on the "night shift" may be difficult because of the different nature of the work (often more "downtime," more emergencies) and how it often is perceived by others. Despite the fact that the important business of client service occurs at any time that staff and clients interact, there persists the idea that the "real" business of the organization gets transacted during the day when higher-level administrators and higher-status staff are more likely to be present. Night-shift work can be viewed as less important and, therefore, less attractive to professionals.

Probably the greatest disadvantage of time departmentation for the manager relates to its potential to fragment agency functioning and to interfere with integration of the organization (as a system). Valuable communication between shifts can be difficult, especially if work hours are not structured so that there is some overlap. Generally, anything that the manager can do to promote interaction among staff who work different shifts helps to minimize this problem. Staff who know, respect, and like those who work the other shift are likely to facilitate their work by telling them what they need to know about what occurs while they are off-duty. A "that's their problem" attitude or other dysfunctional attitudes (such as "leave it for the next shift") are less likely to exist if the manager has regularly communicated a message that emphasizes the existence of one team. One way of doing this is through the encouragement of social events where staff get to know each other. Occasions during which the valuable contributions of both shifts are recognized also help to minimize the likelihood of nonproductive fragmentation of the organization.

Discipline

In some organizations where several different professional disciplines are employed, it makes sense to create units that consist of all people from the same discipline. For example, in a large community mental health center, there might be one or more units of just social workers, one or more units of nurses, and so forth. If preprofessionals or paraprofessionals are employed, they would be assigned to units with professionals from their own disciplines. Departmentation by discipline is a time-honored tradition within many human service organizations. It promotes professional identification and assures that professionals are supervised by and work most closely with people who should be able to understand their work and who share their knowledge, values and skills. Of course, a weakness of this way of organizing staff into units is that it may deprive them of regular interaction with staff from other disciplines who might have a different perspective on situations and from whom they might learn.

Enterprise

Departmentation within for-profit corporations often group employees by enterprise, that is, according to their major activity—for example, production, sales, and finance. To group people by enterprise function is to recognize (especially in larger organizations) that there is room for and value in a certain type of specialization and that it may be an advantage to form work groups of people who share a specialization. It can focus people's activities in that area where they perform best, ideally the same area where they have both preparation and interest. Employees need not be good at everything that falls under the description of their profession or trade, but they are expected to be competent in their area of specialization.

As demands for financial accountability have increased, the differences between for-profit businesses and nonprofit organizations have tended to blur. Human service organizations have had to pay more attention to efficiency issues, and businesses have become more aware of the relationship between human factors and profit. Some observers have suggested that not-for-profit organizations are really businesses in which profits are simply put back into the organization in the form of salaries. The increase in proprietary human service organizations (for example, many long-term care facilities) and the growth in the private practice of social work also suggest that some variation of departmentation along the line of the usual business enterprises may be appropriate for organizing within many human service agencies as well.

What are the human service organization counterparts of, for example, production, sales, and finance? Production would logically translate into service delivery or direct practice with clients at different systems levels (individuals, families, groups, communities, etc.). Sales might equate with the public relations enterprise that is so essential to organizational success within a task environment that is naturally inclined to be unfriendly. It might also involve outreach to potential clients and the building of linkages and networks to other organizations and individuals outside the organization who represent potential sources of referral. Financing requires no translation in today's service environment. Every organization can use people who are specialists in grant writing, fundraising, and financial resource allocation. It might include developing and monitoring budgets.

Departmentation by enterprise function may have particular utility for the higher-level manager as an overall method of reducing organizational activities into three or more major units. The units can then be managed by a mid-level manager within each enterprise. It may also be useful for mid-level managers themselves, such as supervisors in situations where the activities of staff tend to be specialized and fall into a small number of distinguishable "enterprises" (for example, evaluation treatment, or referral).

A major advantage to enterprise function departmentation lies in its potential to create esprit de corps among staff within each enterprise. People who may have widely varying academic backgrounds but who share similar interests—"kindred spirits"—work together toward achievement of similar and/or shared goals. A feeling of camaraderie is likely to result, although the manager should also be alert to the possibility of nonproductive conflict when specialists (who sometimes tend to be "prima donnas") must interact with each other on a daily basis.

A possible difficulty with enterprise departmentation can also occur if inter-enterprise rivalry is allowed to get out of hand. Human service programs inevitably require the cooperation and mutual support of the various enterprises in order to succeed. If people become too territorial or too obsessed with their own unit's success, organizational goal attainment can be jeopardized. For example, finance personnel within human service organizations may be aware that their performance is evaluated by the amount of grant or contract money that they bring in. Unless they remain sensitive to the wishes and needs of other staff and clients, they can end up pursuing dollars to offer programs that are outside of staff interests and areas of competence or, even more importantly, do not result in services that clients need or want. The pursuit of grant or contract money can become a near obsession for the finance specialist. A dollar is a dollar in its effect on a funding specialist's semi-annual evaluation. A grant or contract received for any purpose also has the potential to make others look good and, of course, to pay the bills. So, high-level managers are unlikely to object too vigorously if the funding specialist's focus becomes a little misdirected. But the subtle and long-range costs of overzealous grant activity can be great, particularly if staff morale is jeopardized because agency direction appears to be missing. The tail should never be allowed to wag the dog; that is, services require dollars but dollars should not be the only consideration in deciding what services will be offered. Unfortunately, in recent hard times for human service agencies, the quest for needed funding has led some organizations to venture into areas of service that are inappropriate for their mission.

The manager who selects enterprise function as a method of departmentation will need to remain alert to dangers that include means–end displacements and the development of excessively narrow orientations on the part of staff. The sensitive manager will be able to strike a balance in which staff are conscious of both their specialized function and their place in the overall functioning of the organization. Occasional reminders about staff interdependence and about the superordinate goals of the organization (that all managers must address) may be useful for the manager who organizes using enterprise functions.

Territory Served

Departmentation by territory sometimes is employed in human service organizations where similar activities take place over a wide geographical area. Territory departmentation is a way of deciding whom each staff member will serve and whom they will not serve. Particularly in large organizations it may be logical to subdivide the organization by territory in order to reduce it into manageable subunits and to reduce the likelihood of staff heading off both literally and figuratively in all directions. For example, a large public assistance caseload might be divided up based on the place of residence of clients served. Caseworker X would serve all clients in one 10-square block area, but Caseworker Y would serve clients who live in the adjoining geographical area. Adjustments to boundaries might be made from time to time so that the number of clients likely to be served would be comparable—the territory with the greater client population density sometimes might be smaller than another territory where relatively few residents receive public assistance.

In a similar way, the satellite clinics of a community mental health center might divide up client service by the place of residence of potential clients. If they live one place, they are served by one clinic; if they live one block over, they may have to be seen at another clinic. (The respective territories are sometimes referred to as "catchment areas" in the mental health field.)

Definite advantages accrue to the manager who chooses to use territory departmentation. Questions relative to the issue of "whose job is it?" are less likely to occur than if other methods of organizing are used. Identity with a community and clear-cut responsibilities can be promoted quite easily.

When professionals focus their activities on services to people residing in a relatively small geographical area, they are also likely to become very familiar with that area. For social workers serving a territory, there is increased potential to understand a community's problems and to get to know, understand, and build relationships with its leaders and other key people. The problems of the individual client are also put into better perspective when they are viewed in the context of problems of other persons, families, and groups that live within an area, community resources, or the politics that impact on client social functioning. Overall, concentrated attention and familiarity with an area offer many advantages to the manager and to staff who are likely to benefit from feeling that they are able to really know all that they require to do their job.

A primary advantage of territory departmentation for the manager *can* be efficiency. If territories can be kept small, less time and money are spent in travel and less effort is devoted to making contacts, to becoming acquainted with community resources, and so forth. However, dividing activities by territory can cause problems of inefficient use of staff. No matter how much planning goes into departmentation, workload is rarely ever in balance for a long period of time. Inevitably, some territories will provide an overload while, simultaneously, staff serving other territories will seem to not have enough to do.

Some territories, based on the nature of the community, its location, its clientele, or other factors, will inevitably be labeled less desirable than others. Someone must be assigned to work there, however. This can lead to morale problems and to charges of favoritism on the part of the manager who makes the work assignments. Skillful managers will find ways to help staff understand that all territories have their benefits and their liabilities. They may also try to compensate those staff who receive the unpopular assignments. However, the compensation itself may cause resentment by other staff members who feel that they work in unpleasant conditions too and should also be compensated. While the services that are offered may be comparable, the conditions, in which the services are offered, are rarely comparable. Managers can quickly find themselves feeling as if they cannot win no matter how they try to adjust for these differences.

Another problem of territory departmentation relates to the enforcement of geographical boundaries. In the purest of applications, no exceptions are made. This can lead to situations that, at best, appear absurd. They can also be downright contrary to the best interests of clients and their service. Charges of rigidity will inevitably be made. For example, if Ms. Smith lives in the 800 block of a street and her sister, Ms. Jones, lives across the street in the 900 block, they may be served by two different social workers. The workers may both make separate home visits to the two clients, perhaps even on the same day. If either client decides to move a relatively short distance, she may have to be reassigned to yet another (third) social worker. Continuity of services may be disrupted.

A social worker in the role of manager will need to respond to the appeals of clients and staff to make exceptions when territory departmentation is used. In effect, territory lines should be applied as policies rather than rules. Territorial boundaries can be stretched to reduce the number of absurdities, hardship, and inefficiencies that they impose. But where do managers ultimately draw the line and say no? Eventually, someone will always conclude bitterly that the manager could have been a little more flexible.

The placement of boundaries can be problematic in itself. Social workers know that communities do not always conform to streets, subdivisions, or other boundaries that appear on maps. Their boundaries are in a constant state of flux. If one of the advantages of territory departmentation, namely knowledge of the community, is to be enjoyed, territories should be formed in such a way that communities are not split up. This may not be possible. Even if a community can be fairly easily defined, it may not be practical to form a territory that has similar boundaries because the community may be too large or too small to be used as a territory for departmentation purposes.

If managers select departmentation by territory as a primary way of performing their task of organizing, they should know that the benefit of clarity of work responsibilities will have a cost. Specifically, they can expect to be the target of staff dissatisfaction over perceived inequities. Unless they are willing to risk the virtual dissolution of territory boundaries, they will almost inevitably be perceived as rigid, both by staff and by clients. A manager must be able to live with more than the usual amount of criticism and challenges to decisions regarding exceptions to policies.

Territory departmentation also leaves little room for workers who deliver services to become specialists in one or more types of intervention. One's territory *is* one's specialty. Staff must be prepared to offer a wide range of services to a widely divergent group of clients with varying problems. The need to be all things to all people can be a definite disadvantage of this type of departmentation. Even if people from several different disciplines serve a geographical area (as is the case with hospice or home health services) few people can do everything well, even within their own professional discipline.

Service Offered

Departmentation by service (in the profit sector referred to as "product") should be familiar to the social worker in that it is based on a belief in the benefits of specialization by treatment method. Because of the wide diversity of help offered to clients by social workers, we have usually tended to use subcategories to describe the major types of services offered. Early in the history of our profession we observed that social workers tended to specialize in this way. Social work education tended to mirror this natural tendency by providing the opportunity for students to concentrate their studies in order to prepare for specialized practice. A popular way of doing this in the 1960s and early 1970s was to require students to select among three primary services: casework, group work, and community organization. While it has always been acknowledged that social work practice requires knowledge and skills in all three areas of activity, a service concentration has always been granted legitimacy in social work.

As with other types of departmentation that we have discussed and that we will discuss, the advantages and disadvantages of service departmentation are really two sides of the same coin. If, for example, a manager in a family agency chooses to divide services into referral, individual treatment, group services, and family counseling, the manager will have the reasonable expectation that staff will become very knowledgeable about and skilled in what they do. For example, people who do nothing but group treatment should get very good at it. Or, people who do nothing but make referrals should get to know the helping resources in the community very well; they should have formed valuable networks with their counterparts in other social agencies. It seems logical to conclude that having responsibility for a narrow sphere of activity (a type of service) will result in greater mastery of the knowledge and skills needed to offer that service effectively.

The narrowness of an employee's tasks, of course, is also the greatest disadvantage of service departmentation. When there is virtually no overlap between one person's job and that of another, there is likely to be a reduced knowledge of and interest in the activities of others. Desirable sharing of information and a team spirit that includes people in different areas of specialization can be inhibited.

Services to clients may suffer too. Social workers often attempt to help those with multiple problems requiring many different types of assistance. It has been found, for example, that clients in the public sector may need both economic assistance and less tangible forms of help such as family or employment counseling. Departmentation that does not recognize this may not provide the coordinated service package that the client requires.

The manager who is considering organizing using only—or primarily—service departmentation should first determine that a high degree of specialization is both possible and desirable. For example, while it might be possible for a social worker in a counseling agency to do nothing but group treatment while a colleague offers only one-to-one counseling, this might not be best for either staff, client, or the organization. For staff members, a lack of diversity in their workday can become tedious. They also may begin to lose touch with the knowledge and skills of other specialties. This could become an obstacle to current job functioning while also limiting job mobility.

Clients in an organization whose staff are organized by services offered have the benefits of having the services of a "specialist," but they would have the usual drawbacks as well. If they require more than one type of service, they would need to see more than one treatment specialist, requiring them to form more than one therapeutic relationship. The issue of primary responsibility for their treatment could also be problematic.

Departmentation by service offered might also result in an inefficient use of staff within the organization. For example, there might be a waiting list of clients requiring the specialized services of the group treatment worker while the family treatment specialist might be experiencing a lull in referrals for services or vice versa.

Client Problems

An alternative to organizing that is based upon services performed is based on a typology of client problems. How might clients be classified in order to use this organizing approach? Social work staff in a family counseling agency might be grouped into units based upon the primary diagnosis or problem of clients. One unit might consist of all social workers who specialize in treatment of substance abuse; another unit might consist of all social workers who deal with problems of child abuse and neglect, and so forth. It is assumed that, overall, clients in the same diagnostic category or with similar problems will share many of the same service needs, needs that are different from those in other categories.

The advantages of departmentation by client problem can be great. It can provide the benefits of specialization to clients while allowing them to avoid the necessity of having to relate to two or more helping professionals. Of course, like all the other forms of departmentation that we have described, it is not universally appropriate. We know, for example, that the problem of family violence often is accompanied by substance abuse, parent-child problems, marital difficulties, and many other problems that could just as well serve as the basis for categorizing a client using this method of organizing staff. We know that a client's presenting complaint or problem (the basis for assignment of a case under departmentation by clients served) often turns out not to be the primary problem at all. Because of the complexity of human behavior, we cannot always say which problem is primary or that one is the cause while another is only a symptom. Many human social problems are not easily classified using a primary diagnosis.

In the real world, departmentation by client problem often does not work. Professionals who offer services may find that the ideal of a narrow range of services for each of a limited number of categories of client problems cannot be achieved. If professionals are to serve the diverse needs of clients, they must be knowledgeable and skilled in many areas, becoming far more "generic" in their practice than they might have anticipated or chosen.

Interdisciplinary Teams

Several times in earlier discussions we have referred to the growing number of organizations that now are using interdisciplinary teams. As we noted, they are replacing units grouped by discipline in many medical and psychiatric settings. Within this method of departmentation, there are two variations. In the one variation, staff from different disciplines contribute primarily the knowledge and skills unique to their discipline. They maintain their own professional identities, have different job responsibilities, are paid commensurate with the usual expectations for their own professions, and so forth. However, they work together with other disciplines as a team, sharing clients or patients. This model of departmentation (sometimes called the interprofessional model) has been in place in many mental health settings and other organizations for years and has seemed to work quite well.

The newer, more controversial type of interdisciplinary team is the one that is organized in the way that was described earlier in this chapter when we discussed the growth of case management teams within hospitals. In it, staff from different professional disciplines are "all equals." It is still quite experimental—only time will tell if it can be an effective method to group staff. However, based on problems that the author has observed, we might predict that it will inevitably lead to work distribution inequities and morale problems among team members, if not problems in delivery of services to clients.

Either variation of the interdisciplinary team model has the inherent advantage of exposing staff to the knowledge and skills of other disciplines on a regular basis, although the former much more than the latter. Interdisciplinary learning and (conceivably) understanding can be enhanced. However, interdisciplinary teams can also weaken professional identification of staff and lines of supervision can be blurred. Among other problems, there is the issue of just who (logically) should be a staff member's supervisor.

Marketing Channels

Social marketing is a rapidly developing field of study. A service, not unlike a product, needs to be publicized and needs to be "sold" to potential consumers. There may be several different "markets" in which this can be accomplished. They are referred to as *marketing channels*.

Some potential clients gain access to a service in one way; others are more comfortable using other methods and channels. What is an acceptable way to receive needed help for one client may not be acceptable (for any number of reasons) for others. For example, we might consider the various channels used to "market" AIDS education. A variety of market channels might be used. A social work manager might decide to organize staff activities around these channels. Staff might be assigned to work primarily in one of them.

What different marketing channels might be used? The public school system, the media, presentations to community groups, and counseling of in-patient hospital populations could all be different channels used to accomplish the same objective. However, the methods used would vary greatly based upon political factors, characteristics of those who are the target of efforts to educate, and other factors. A specialist in working within one market channel would get to know and understand a particular "market" and thus would likely get very good at doing the job. There might be real advantages to this form of departmentation, especially since a certain level of trust and acceptance would be required to be able to get through to those who are most at risk.

In those organizations where services can be offered in several different arenas, marketing-channel departmentation can work well. Where education is the service itself (designed to prevent a problem), it may be an especially appropriate way to organize into work groups. It offers the advantage of creating staff groupings of people who face the same problems and use the same strategies. They can share their insights and ideas and offer support to each other.

The major disadvantage of marketing departmentation for organizing is its limited applicability to human services organizations. In manufacturing, it is easy to visualize marketing a product with acceptable success, using many different market channels. A wrench, for example, is sold in hardware stores, department stores, auto parts stores, as well as in many other outlets. But for many human services, there may be a very limited number of outlets deemed to be acceptable. Although we have broadened our thinking a little in recent years (for example, psychiatric services are now offered in the community, on the job, and in other settings besides hospitals, which were the primary outlets before the Community Mental Health Act of 1963[3]), many services offered by social workers and other health professionals would not seem appropriate for multiple outlets. For reasons of efficiency, professional ethics, and (all too often) inflexibility, we are still reluctant to offer many services anywhere but within the physical confines of an office, usually grouped with similar enterprises. While public assistance or public adoption services may be regularly offered in shopping malls, through the churches, or in any one of several other innovative ways that have been tried successfully on an experimental basis, these market channels may just seem "unprofessional" or inappropriate to many members of the general public and to some of us. Turf issues and the influence of a hostile task environment are likely to continue to constrain the marketing channels available for many of our services. Consequently, only some managers in some settings will find marketing-channel departmentation to be a viable alternative for organizing, at least in the near future.

Combining Two or More Methods of Departmentation

It is not at all unusual for a single organization to have two or even several different ways of organizing its staff into work groups. There is nothing wrong with this. In fact, since all of the methods for departmentation that we have discussed seem to work better in some situations than in others, we should expect to see this occur. For example, an extended care facility may have an administrator who chooses to organize all staff by enterprise, say, patient services, public relations, support services, finance, personnel, records, and so forth. In turn, the manager in charge of each enterprise might group staff into several units based upon (depending on the enterprise) some other method. Patient services might be subdivided by discipline, service offered, client served, interdisciplinary team, and so forth. Public relations might choose to use marketing channels. The manager of support services might find that simple numbers works best or, perhaps, time worked. If the organization is especially large, additional subunits could be used. They need not use the same method of departmentation. Of course, there is a danger in too much departmentation. Especially when many different methods are used within the same organization, confusion can result. Organization thus can produce chaos!

When managers group people into small units they make them more manageable for those charged with overseeing their work. However, as we noted in our description of several of the available forms of departmentation above, the organization can also become fragmented, and undesirable conflict between units can occur. To avoid these negative consequences of departmentation it may be necessary for managers to use regular reminders of common goals and objectives and to create activities that cross unit barriers and thus promote teamwork.

Delegation as a Way of Organizing

Managers cannot perform every task that technically falls under the functions of planning, staffing, organizing, controlling and leading. Nor should they try. To do so would only result in the problem of "micro-managing." Even in small human service organizations, managers cannot perform or even directly oversee all activities, collect all necessary data for decision making, or make all management decisions. The option, of course, is to delegate.

Organizing entails helping staff members make the best possible use of their time. It also makes sure that the manager's own time is used efficiently. This means doing things and making those decisions that are the specific responsibility of the manager. No one else can handle them. Other tasks and other decisions can be handled by subordinates. Delegation should be considered.

Key Terminology

One goal of delegation is to maximize the manager's influence while enhancing the quality of the activities within an organization. Delegation empowers staff to do things, sometimes even things that are not technically part of their job. While everyone would agree that delegation is a necessary and desirable part of the manager's organizing function, there is far less consensus as to what can or should be delegated and how much delegation is desirable.

There are a few general principles of management that can be used to sort out some of the confusion that surrounds the topic of delegation. An understanding of certain key terminology is critical. When we delegate as managers, we are giving to a subordinate something that would otherwise be associated with the expectations held for our position. If others do not take it on, it would fall to us.

What is it that managers can delegate? What can they not delegate? For one thing they can delegate a *task,* assuming that it is reasonably commensurate with a subordinate's job description. Since most job descriptions have a statement like "and other duties as assigned," that means that a manager *can* delegate many tasks to subordinates. The task can be one time only, such as calling managers of other agencies to arrange an emergency meeting, or ongoing, such as recording and transcribing the minutes of staff meetings, serving as a mentor to a new staff person, or providing supervision to a group of volunteers.

Managers also can and must delegate *authority.* A delegated task requires the possession of enough authority to complete it. It is unfair to expect someone to perform a task if they have not been given the necessary authority to perform it. Authority allows a person, who is delegated a task, to "fill-in" for the manager, to have and to exercise the authority that rightly belongs to the manager. It lets that person act for the manager by having the same rights and privileges (in a limited sphere) as the manager.

Suppose a manager delegates the task of planning a meeting to a subordinate. To get the job done, the subordinate will need to know and others will need to know that a certain amount of authority has been delegated along with the task. Otherwise, it will not get done correctly. For example, the person granted authority will need to be able to call or e-mail other managers to ask them about their schedules, to schedule a meeting room, to order refreshments, and so forth. Under ordinary conditions, the subordinate would not have the authority to do any of these. However, with the authority granted by the manager, the subordinate is acting for the manager—no one else should object to the subordinate's reasonable requests. Without that authority, no cooperation from others could be expected. Of course, the authority delegated would be limited to that required to complete the specific delegated task. The subordinate would not, for example, be delegated the authority to see a co-worker's personnel record.

What about responsibility for delegated tasks? Much of the confusion surrounding delegation centers around the issue of whether or not managers can delegate *responsibility.* This is the issue of who ultimately can be held accountable for the performance or non-performance of a delegated task. When managers assign all or part of a task to other staff members that they would otherwise perform themselves, and if the satisfactory performance of that task is a reasonable expectation for staff members given their job description, managers should be able to hold staff responsible for the performance of the task. If the task is reasonable (given the job description of the staff member), not too large (given the staff member's other responsibilities), and if the staff member is given the necessary authority to carry it out, the manager is justified in expecting satisfactory performance of the task. If these criteria are not met or some other aspect of poor delegation on the part of the manager exists, fairness suggests that it is unreasonable for the manager to expect the task to be satisfactorily performed. Appropriate delegation of a task results in a legitimate expectation on the part of the manager that the staff member will meet a standard; inappropriate delegation would seem to relieve the staff member (at least partially) of full responsibility for satisfactory or unsatisfactory task completion.

Under conditions of appropriate delegation of tasks, managers can legitimately hold subordinates responsible to them for their completion, but the question of ultimate responsibility for delegated tasks is another matter. If a task is not completed or is completed poorly, the manager may still be held responsible for the problems created. Why? First, the task was one that was originally within the manager's job description—delegation does not rid the manager of responsibility for its completion as far as the manager's superior is concerned. Second, a manager can be held responsible for all management judgments and decisions. If the decision to delegate or the choice of a person to whom the task was delegated turned out to be bad and the task was not satisfactorily completed, the manager can be faulted. In the broadest sense, a manager can delegate a task, but not the ultimate responsibility for its completion. In some ways delegation brings more responsibility to the manager, not less. A manager is held responsible for the task completion *and* for the decision to delegate.

Types of Authority

Within human service organizations, there are three different types of authority that can exist. We shall discuss how they differ, the major advantages and disadvantages of each, and how they can assist the manager in performing the functions of manager.

Line Management Authority.   *Line management* authority involves no delegation; it exists without any relinquishment of authority by the manager or any tampering with what is already in place. It is the authority to make certain decisions and to engage in certain activities that exist because of one's job position and its relation to other job positions. Literally, line management authority exists because of the line (or box) occupied by one's job on an organizational chart relative to the position of the jobs of others on the chart. It comes with the job.

Line management authority provides supervisors with all the legitimacy they need to influence some aspect of the work of supervisees. It is what dictates the respective roles of every employee in relation to every other employee. The formal organizational chart displays the authority legitimized by the organization—who has the authority to make certain decisions, to tell others what to do and how to do it, and what not to do.

Social workers as managers who rely solely on line management authority as a primary method of organizing activities are on safe ground in some respects. They are exercising authority that was granted by "the organization." One cannot successfully challenge the authority of a manager who relies heavily on line management authority. But total reliance on line management authority deprives managers of the benefits of delegation. Managers who cannot or will not delegate usually end up trying to do too much themselves and spreading themselves too thin. They also deprive subordinates of the opportunity to grow and to prepare for assumption of more responsibility and autonomy.

Another major problem with total reliance on line management authority is it does not take full advantage of the special knowledge and skills of those who occupy subordinate positions. People often are capable of doing more than their job description suggests. Sometimes they, not the manager, are best suited to do certain jobs or make certain decisions. As the author has repeatedly emphasized, all individuals have strengths and weaknesses. Unless delegation is used, managers can find themselves constrained by the organizational chart. They may not be able to use the best person for a job or to bring the best expertise to bear on a decision. Of course, too much delegation of authority can create a different set of problems.

Staff Authority.   One form of authority that a manager can choose to delegate is *staff authority*. It entails the creation of a particular kind of relationship between manager and staff members that is different from what line management authority would suggest as appropriate. The granting of staff authority creates a relationship between a staff member and a manager that can best be described as advisory.[4]

People, who have been assigned staff authority, frequently perform certain tasks and collect certain information with the goal of giving advice to the manager. A social work manager might, for example, delegate staff authority to a subordinate to explore options for the location of a new satellite office and then recommend to the manager where it should be located. Another manager might delegate staff authority to a subordinate to contact other similar organizations to see how they are addressing some problem related to managed care and to then recommend how the manager should address the problem. Advice or recommendations are supposed to be the end product of the subordinate's research and investigation. At the point that advice is given, the delegated task is completed.

It is both natural and expected that the person granted staff authority will form opinions and will try to "sell" the manager on the recommended decision or course of action. But because staff authority is meant to be only advisory, it does not carry with it any guarantee that the manager will do more than just listen to whatever advice is given. The manager can ignore it or go along with it. If the manager takes the advice of a subordinate and makes the decision that was recommended, there is no obligation to give the subordinate any credit for it if the decision turns out to be a good one (though many managers choose to do it). However, if the decision turns out to be a bad one, the manager cannot pass the blame for it onto the staff member who recommended it. After all, the decision was always the manager's to make. If a bad decision was made, probably the manager either (1) granted staff authority to the wrong person; (2) did not give clear directions or provide enough assistance to the staff member to do the job well; or (3) failed to adequately consider other information that was not available to the staff member when the decision was made. In any case, responsibility for the bad decision still rests with the manager.

Staff authority is most frequently seen in large organizations, particularly in bureaucracies. It is used frequently in the military and in government circles. Leaders may surround themselves with individuals granted staff authority who do much of the groundwork that makes it possible for them to make wide-ranging decisions. Such individuals are often called staff—for example, a general's "staff officer." They give advice or recommendations and do not expect to get credit or take blame for decisions, or to be involved in implementing them.

The advantages of the use of staff authority are obvious. A person assigned to research a topic and to give advice can greatly facilitate the decision making of the manager. The disadvantages of using staff authority relate to what can happen if it is used excessively or unwisely. If used too frequently with the same subordinates, line management authority can be weakened. By definition, staff authority is a relaxing of the usual lines of authority. If it becomes a regular occurrence, lines of supervision can become undermined.

CASE EXAMPLE • *A Problem in Use of Staff Authority*

Katherine was the Chief of Social Services in an outpatient psychiatric clinic. As the end of the fiscal year approached, she learned that there were excess staff development funds available that could not be carried over into the next year. She shared this information with the social work staff and encouraged them to consider attending any workshops that might be coming up. She subsequently approved funding for four staff members to attend workshops that seemed relevant to their work responsibilities.

Katherine was pleased that one of her supervisors, Gilbert, had requested funding to enroll in a workshop on a new and controversial approach to working with hostile clients. When she approved his request, she called him in to talk about the workshop. She asked Gilbert to pick up extra copies of any written materials and to take notes. She asked him to provide her with a written summary of what he thought about the new treatment and to suggest a plan for how it might be used within the clinic. Gilbert was happy to comply with her requests. He began researching the literature on the new treatment even before he attended the workshop.

In her first meeting with Gilbert, Katherine was careful to use words like advise, investigate, and research. In her mind, she felt that she had made it very clear that she was delegating staff authority to him. Unfortunately, because of his enthusiasm about attending the workshop and the fact that Katherine had assigned this task to him, Gilbert did not really listen very carefully to Katherine's instructions and explanation of what she was asking him to do.

Immediately after attending the workshop, Gilbert requested a meeting with Katherine to "let you know how we will be using" the new treatment. Katherine rearranged her schedule to see Gilbert as soon as possible, fearful that a miscommunication had occurred. Her fears were confirmed.

Gilbert came to the meeting with his written report in hand. It was immediately apparent that he assumed that the implementation of his recommendations for use of the new treatment was a *fait accompli.* Even worse, he expected to supervise the implementation of his recommendations throughout all units.

Katherine quickly knew that a misunderstanding had taken place. She thanked him for his report and complimented him on its promptness. She explained that she had intended that his special responsibilities would end with the submission of his report and recommendations. But she explained to him that she retained the authority to determine if any or all of the recommendations would be implemented and, if so, by whom.

Gilbert was both disappointed and angry. Katherine admitted to some responsibility for the misunderstanding by not reminding him of the fact that he had been given only staff authority. It did little good. He threw the report on her desk and left.

As she read more about the new treatment Katherine became convinced that it probably would not be effective with the type of clients served by the clinic. She decided not to implement any of the recommendations in Gilbert's report. While her decision was a necessary and correct one, it gave Gilbert additional cause for resentment and confirmed his impression that she had just been "playing a power game" with him. Her relationship with him remained strained until he finally took another job several months later.

Discussion Questions

1. What else could Katherine have done to insure that Gilbert understood just what she was asking him to do?
2. What kind of authority did Gilbert think he was given? Why might he have come to that conclusion?

CASE EXAMPLE • *(continued)*

3. Why does it appear that Gilbert was not a good choice for delegation of staff authority?
4. Should Katherine have done anything to attempt to improve her relationship with Gilbert after the misunderstanding occurred?
5. What could Katherine do to make sure that future misunderstandings about delegation of authority do not occur among her staff?

Staff authority can also create accountability problems in other ways. If staff are granted staff authority on a regular basis, they can begin to perceive themselves as primarily thinkers, a breed distinct from the doers. They can start to lose touch with those who must perform the primary work of the organization (that is, those who deliver services to clients). Before long, their advice can become impractical or unrealistic.

Staff authority can also have a deleterious effect on the morale of those granted it because it is so limited. It can be frustrating to be asked repeatedly to research a topic and to make recommendations only to have the recommendations not followed by the manager. Even if advice is regularly taken, frustration can still occur. It is not terribly gratifying (especially for those with a high need for self-actualization) to have one's authority end with giving advice. Many of us need to "see through" a task and to be involved in implementing a decision that we recommended. Also, there is the problem of who gets the credit for a good decision that was possible only because of the work of a staff member. Persons assigned staff authority may find it demoralizing to see the manager praised for following their advice.

Some people like working with only staff authority. They enjoy researching and recommending to others, but they do not want to have final decision making authority. They enjoy making others look good and receive their gratification from appreciative managers who recognize the importance of letting them know how much their work is appreciated. These are the individuals who should be granted staff authority by managers when delegation is desirable. Others, especially those who become easily frustrated by its limitations, should not.

Functional Authority. The other type of authority that can be delegated, *functional authority,* involves greater delegation than does staff authority. Staff members who receive functional authority are given much authority, but on a time-limited basis, than that which they would otherwise possess. Authority is granted to do much more than just gather information or advise others; one who has functional authority can make decisions and implement them.

The term functional authority as we will use it is drawn from the literature of the business sector. There it is defined as "the right which is delegated to an individual or a department to control specified processes, practices, policies or other matters relating to activities undertaken by personnel in other departments."[5] Let us see what that would mean within human service organizations.

Usually functional authority is granted in order to bring the best possible expertise to bear on a problem or task. For example, let us suppose that two new social workers have been hired as child-protection workers in a public agency. The head of child-protection services for the agency normally would assign the task of their orientation to the person who is their line supervisor; this would be totally consistent with line management authority. But the manager recognizes that the supervisor, recently hired from outside the state, is probably not the best person to handle one aspect of their orientation, those state laws that impact on the job of child protection. The manager *could* tell the supervisor to consult with the unit's legal counsel (a lawyer) to get advice on how to orient the new workers. But this would be a cumbersome and inefficient way to get the job done. The manager might decide instead to grant functional authority to the legal consultant to develop and implement a component of the training that focuses on legal aspects of the job. Or, the manager might prefer to use another, more experienced supervisor who is more knowledgeable of and experienced in application of state laws to handle this part of the new workers' training. In either case, the manager would inform the new workers' supervisor of the decision to grant functional authority for part of the training to someone else. The supervisor might be invited to attend the training too. The person given functional authority (legal counsel or other supervisor) would take full responsibility for the workers' activities during the legal orientation. For example, they might be required to participate in specific learning exercises, might be told when to take a break, would be tested on their newly acquired knowledge, and so forth. Both before and after their legal training, the responsibility for their other orientation would lie with their line supervisor.

Our example of the use of functional authority illustrates both the major advantages and the potential disadvantages of the use of functional authority by managers. Functional authority is logical. It probably would not make sense for the supervisor to first learn about state laws from the legal counsel in order to then turn around and teach the two new workers. Why not simply let the lawyer or another knowledgeable supervisor both develop and deliver the training in the first place? If the line supervisor were to attend too, all three could learn at once. The trainer would be very knowledgeable—the new workers could ask and receive accurate answers to any questions that they might ask. As long as the line supervisor would not be threatened by this arrangement and the granting of functional authority to someone else for part of the orientation were just a one-time thing, the temporary suspension of line management authority should not be a problem.

Disadvantages of functional authority relate primarily to using it in the wrong situations or using it too often. If used in situations where line supervisors are insecure and easily threatened or if used too frequently, it can weaken the capacity of the line supervisor to manage. If, for example, all or most modules of the new workers' orientation were to be delegated out to "experts," the supervisor might lose credibility with the new workers. Or, if the manager regularly removed them from the line authority of their supervisor, they might begin to question whether their supervisor really has the necessary expertise to supervise them.

In many social agencies, functional authority is unavoidable. It is both efficient and well liked by professionals. It is logical because people (especially professionals) tend to have special areas of interest and expertise. Why not take advantage of their knowledge by letting them have time-limited authority over others who lack that knowledge and can learn from them? Too heavy a reliance on line management authority and strict adherence to the formal organizational chart can get in the way of tapping available staff resources.

Professional staff like functional authority for several reasons. It allows a worker to see a task through from start to finish (unlike staff authority) and to get credit for any successes that occur. It also tends to put less emphasis on the formal organizational hierarchy that many professionals find unnatural, demeaning, and an obstacle to the formation of collegial relationships. Unlike adherence to formal lines of authority, functional authority says, in effect, "We have to have leaders and followers, but we can all learn from each other now and then," an attitude that is very consistent with social work values.

Functional authority seems to work well for many social work managers. It allows them to delegate some tasks to people who they can depend upon to do a good job, thereby giving themselves more time to focus on other things. It allows others to have experience in decision making and other tasks of managers and thus prepares them for assuming increasing management responsibilities. Functional authority also is philosophically compatible with the many variations of participative management (such as TQM) that are being adapted for use within human service settings.

Desirable Characteristics for Delegation

Delegation of authority is essential both to good social work management and to employee growth. Social work practice in any setting is more than just a technical skill. It requires thought, judgment, and the application of knowledge to situations that are likely to be unique. A practitioner can only acquire competence in exercising judgment if managers are comfortable with delegation and are willing to trust people other than themselves to evaluate situations and to take necessary action.

There is a management principle that relates directly to delegation. It states that, for efficiency, tasks should be performed by those at the lowest level capable of performing them, usually those who are paid the least. This is a principle that is difficult to implement for many social workers as managers. It requires them to delegate some tasks to others that they enjoy performing themselves. They know that they should delegate more to others, but they sometimes do not want to do it. For example, as professionals, social workers need and like to remain close to practice. Sometimes, this leads higher-level managers to insist on continuing to see clients for treatment or to offer other forms of direct intervention. These tasks could be offered by subordinates, thus leaving managers more time to focus on management-related tasks.

To delegate either staff or functional authority to others, managers have to be able to trust them to do a job satisfactorily. They must be open to others' ideas and methods of performing tasks that may be different from their own. Delegation requires letting go of tight control and being content with broadly overseeing activities.

When functional authority is used, delegation may require managers to allow others to make mistakes that they might not have made. Managers (and parents!) find it very difficult to see that things are going wrong or to recognize that they will go wrong without jumping in to "rescue" a subordinate. But when we use functional authority we must be able to use restraint, recognizing that most errors are not irreversible. Overriding a staff member's functional authority in order to avoid a mistake may avoid trouble in the short run. However, such a practice can be very costly in terms of erosion of staff confidence and morale. It also makes staff less willing to assume functional authority in the future. Besides, taking back authority that has been delegated does not allow staff members to learn from their mistakes, something that we all need to learn to do.

Managers who delegate authority must be skillful communicators. Careful delineation of the type of authority being delegated and its limits must be communicated to both the subordinate and to all others involved. "Superior and subordinate alike must know whether they are working in a staff or line capacity. Lack of clarity on this point often causes friction."[6] The same principle applies to functional authority. Workers who thought their role was purely advisory (staff) may become resentful when asked to make and to implement a decision. They thought their work was over when they made recommendations. Conversely, workers who perceived that they had functional authority may become angry and feel insulted when told that their role was to be only advisory. They may have looked forward to deciding on and implementing a course of action or to assuming responsibilities that they normally lack. The time for a manager to explain clearly the type of authority delegated and its limits is before the task begins. Special skill and tact are also necessary to avoid offending others in the administrative hierarchy who might be inclined to feel that their authority is somehow being usurped or that the person to whom authority is delegated is regarded as "special" by the manager.

How Much Organizing Is Desirable?

Organizing is an important part of managing; a well-coordinated system does not occur by chance. It should be remembered, however, that organizing is designed to promote the achievement of goals and objectives; it should not become an obstacle to their achievement. As is true of the other managerial functions that we discuss in this book, it is possible to have too much of a good thing. An "over-organized" organization or work unit is just as dysfunctional as a chaotic one that lacks organization. The ideal organization is only as organized as it needs to be, and no more. It allows staff to be creative and autonomous while promoting the integration of individual activities.

The decision regarding how tightly organized an organization should be is a difficult one. We must rely heavily on a few general principles, and on common sense and our knowledge of human behavior. In general, large, multipurpose bureaucracies reflect a need for more organizing on the part of the manager. Departmentation is absolutely essential. Smaller organizations usually can tolerate some blurring of roles, functions, and lines of authority. They may require fewer organizing activities on the part of the manager.

The capacity of staff to tolerate and to accept the need for structure also influences the degree of organization that is optimal. Generally, paraprofessionals, preprofessionals, and clerical staff expect and appreciate the degree of certainty in their jobs that accompanies a tightly organized work environment. Professional staff are more likely to value professional autonomy and may be more resistive to many of the organizing efforts of the manager. As we have indicated, however, such organizing activities as the delegation of functional authority provide an acceptable mix of autonomy and structure for professionals.

The personality of managers themselves help to determine the amount of structure that is optimal for a work setting. The style of a manager and the manager's approaches to the various tasks of management should be a logical extension of the manager's personality. Easy-going managers will become uncomfortable and may be unsuccessful if they attempt to create a tightly organized work environment. Conversely, managers with a need to maintain tight control will not function well if they attempt a more "hands off" approach to organizing. While managers, like all human beings, are capable of growth and change, a total turnaround in style is probably not possible or would at least be very difficult for most of us. This is something to consider before taking a job as manager in a human service organization. Problems occur in those settings where the needs of the organization do not match the needs of a manager.

Summary

In this chapter we examined some of the concepts and issues that relate to the management function of organizing. There are three basic ways that managers in human service organizations are set up for the delivery of services. We examined the characteristics of each with special references to how recent emphasis on managed care may be producing changes.

Even relatively small organizations generally group their staff into small units to increase management efficiency. We looked at how departmentation by simple numbers, time worked, discipline, enterprise function, territory served, service offered, clients served, interdisciplinary team, and market channels all have been tried in human service organizations with varying degrees of success. Often, large organizations use two or more different methods to create units of manageable size.

The relationship between power and authority was explored as a preface to our analysis of the three different types of authority that exists within organizations. It was noted that line management authority exists based solely upon the position in the organizational hierarchy occupied by the manager. As a manager, a social worker can also choose to delegate to others a task and the authority to accomplish it. But the responsibility for the task's successful completion remains with the manager who delegated it. Staff authority and functional authority were presented as two delegation options that have both advantages and disadvantages. Both were proposed as potentially useful if they meet the needs of both management and staff and if their expectations and limits are communicated clearly.

We discussed those personal characteristics that can either facilitate or make delegation difficult for the manager. Finally, we identified factors that help to determine how little or how much organization is desirable. The next chapter will return to some of these same variables as we look at how much control is optimal in an organization or its units.

Endnotes

1. James D. Thompson, *Organizations in Action* (New York: McGraw-Hill, 1967), p. 40.

2. Harold Koontz, Cyril O'Donnell, and Heinz Weihrich, *Essentials of Management,* 4th ed. (New York: McGraw-Hill, 1986), pp. 180–201.

3. Bruce S. Jannson, "Federal Social Legislation Since 1961," in *Encyclopedia of Social Work,* Vol. 1 (18th ed., 1987), p. 594.

4. Koontz, O'Donnell, and Weihrich, *Essentials of Management, op. cit.,* pp. 226–233.

5. Ibid., pp. 209–215.

6. Grover Starling, *Managing the Public Sector,* 4th ed. (Belmont, CA: Wadsworth, 1993), p. 303.

9

Controlling Staff Behavior

It may seem a little redundant to devote one of the later chapters of this book to the management function of control. After all, haven't all of the management functions that we have discussed to this point contained elements of control? Yes, they have. Such activities as planning, staffing, and organizing are designed to help the social worker as manager to influence, shape, constrain, and direct the activities of staff in such a way that they will contribute to the attainment of group and organizational objectives.

Indeed, there is some blurring of boundaries between the management function of control and other management functions. While this may present the student of management or the authors of textbooks with occasional conceptual problems, it really is reflective of life as it exists for social workers as managers. They often are performing two or more management functions simultaneously with little time to worry about what their activities should be labeled or where the boundaries of their functions should be drawn. In fact, the same activity sometimes can be construed as performing more than one important management function. For example, the activity of employee evaluation is a part of staffing as we noted in Chapter 7 but (as we shall see) it can be used to control staff behavior. Similarly, the use of a policy or rule performs both planning and control functions, training is used to promote staff growth as well as to control staff behavior, and so forth.

The Elements of Control

When we use the word *control,* we tend to think of limits. This is not a bad place to start in order to understand what we mean by the management function of control. The activities of children, adolescents, and even adult professionals occasionally require limits and constraints to assure that their activities are safe, appropriate, and productive. The manager, whether in the job of first-line supervisor or at a higher administrative level, has a broader perspective than do subordinates. Managers often are in better positions than those who work under their supervision to know when staff behaviors threaten the welfare of the organization or when they are contributing to the attainment of objectives and when they are not. Consequently, it falls to managers to exercise control over the activities of others to assure that what they do is desirable and productive for the organization and for its clients.

Bernard Neugeboren described control as evolving from "the need to integrate individual and organizational goals."[1] His description of the mechanisms of control available to the human service manager differs little from the control menus described in the business literature. In fact, it is also a comprehensive list of control methods available to managers within most any other social system (for example, families or communities).

Controlling involves both the assessment of staff performance and the setting up of vehicles to amend behavior that is not contributing to attainment of objectives. It involves a three-step process: (1) establishing standards, (2) measuring performance against these standards, and (3) correcting variations from standards and plans.[2] The first step, establishing standards, may be less necessary if planning (Chapter 4) has been performed well. Planning sets most of the standards that are needed within organizations. (Certain staff behaviors, those that could not have been anticipated, may require the introduction of some additional standards as part of control.) But good planning creates most of the "yardsticks" (for example, missions, budgets, and so forth) necessary to evaluate staff behavior and to make necessary corrections in it.

Not surprisingly, controlling is another one of those management functions that many social workers often do not relish. It requires the assumption of a kind of "parent" role in relation to one's professional colleagues, a relationship that seems both unnatural and demeaning. Control often is unpleasant for both managers and those who they must control. It can lead to resentment and strained interpersonal relationships. But controlling is an absolutely essential part of the job of the manager; it is critical for the good of the organization and for effective and efficient service to our prime beneficiary, the client.

Many of the words associated with the function of controlling help to explain some of the resentment that employees often feel toward it and toward managers who are just doing their jobs. The vocabulary of controlling includes words and phrases like *curbing, restraining, indoctrinating, regulating, checking up on, holding to a standard,* or *verifying.* All of these activities are almost universally resented, especially by mature professionals who jealously guard their autonomy and their right to exercise professional discretion. Controlling can seem to be infringement on autonomy. In fact, that is exactly what it is designed to do.

One of the most difficult tasks faced by the manager is finding ways to control staff behavior in a way that neither humiliates staff nor builds unhealthy and counterproductive resentment toward the manager. To accomplish this, managers (once again) can choose from a menu of different methods. They are sometimes interchangeable—more than one might do the job. Other times, one and only one is clearly indicated. They may have very different effects on the morale of individual staff and of work groups. Sensitive managers who know their staff are able to develop a positive, dynamic package of controls. They can accomplish the task of controlling while not seriously jeopardizing morale and manager–staff relationships.

In some organizations, control methods are almost universally resented by staff. This should not have to be the case. Controls that are chosen and implemented with tact and sensitivity tend not to be resented and, are sometimes even appreciated by staff. They actually can enhance staff morale and staff–manager relationships. This is most likely to occur when controls are perceived as no more limiting of autonomy than necessary. It is perceived that they are present because of organizational and client interests (and not because of the psychological needs of the manager for exerting his or her power). Controls (like plans) also can offer a sense of certainty and security that allows employees to know that what they are doing is acceptable to the organization. This allows them to devote more time and energies to client services.

Managers, who can institute controls on staff behavior in ways that are perceived as a necessary and helpful addition to the work environment, will find that they contribute to positive manager-staff relationships. Obviously, some controls are more likely to contribute to this desirable state than others. Some, by their very nature, have a greater potential for resentment. As we look at the options within the control menu that is available to managers, we will also look at the strengths and weaknesses of each. We will see how each can affect the work climate within a human service organization.

The Basis for Control

Managers can (and are expected to) control many of the activities of others within organizations because they possess the authority to do it. When a manager is hired to occupy a certain position on an organizational chart, the organization grants the manager the power to control some of the work related activities of certain other individuals who appear in subordinate positions on that chart. This is the line authority that was described in Chapter 8. It is easily identified in the formal organizational charts that are often distributed at orientation sessions for new employees. The charts contain boxes to represent people or groups of people and solid or dotted lines to denote the various types of authority relationships (Chapter 8) that exist.

Line authority is power that has been legitimized by the organization. However, it is only one source of power that influences the activities, attitudes, and even the beliefs of others within organizations. Some people acquire power because of special skills or knowledge. For example, a computer "guru" who develops a reputation for solving technological problems of other staff can become quite powerful and can thus get others to do things they might not otherwise choose to do. Experience and the knowledge of the history of an organization also can be sources of power. Association (kinship or close friendship) with others who hold legitimate authority can result in power. Some people are bullies—they acquire power by intimidating others. Others, because of other personality traits or simply that hard to define characteristic known as charisma seem to be able to get others to comply with their wishes. These other sources of power are what determines the place of individuals in the informal organization that invariably exists within organizations.

We first mentioned the informal organization back in Chapter 3 when we described some of the shortcomings of the classical management theories. The failure to acknowledge the presence of an informal organization can lead to an incomplete understanding of organizational behavior. The informal organization does not appear on a chart somewhere, but it is just as powerful (and, sometimes, more powerful) an influence on people's behavior than the formal organization.

Understanding of the informal organization may begin at orientation. It rarely occurs in a methodical or planned way. A perceptive new employee may pick up on the subtle communications of "older hands" who seem to imply that the organizational chart "is not always the way things work," or the revelation that no one really takes a high-ranking administrator's requests very seriously begin to complete the picture of how the informal organization operates. Learning about the informal organization continues as time goes on and never really ends.

In many human service organizations, a very senior secretary or business manager may be quite powerful in the informal organization because of knowledge, experience, and the confidence of other powerful people. In the military, new recruits quickly learn that it is the company first sergeant, not the junior officer or company commander, who is the real power with which to be reckoned and to be accommodated. This is generally true despite the officer's higher rank and superior place on the formal organizational chart.

Current theory suggests that the presence of an informal organization can be a valuable vehicle of support for such tasks as communication of needed information or providing support for control of staff behaviors. The message to the manager should probably be to acknowledge its existence, understand it as much as is possible, and use it when appropriate. Sensitive managers who identify the real locus of power in an organization can use these key people as allies to reinforce their own focus on the attainment of organizational goals. Their potential to influence the behavior of other employees cuts both ways, of course. If the manager is unsuccessful at achieving their cooperation and support, key persons in the informal organization can sabotage organizational efforts to control others. Even employees who are strongly motivated to do good work may not feel that they are able to risk the ire of a powerful individual in the informal organization who does not value effective performance and communicates the suggestion that they had better not become a "curve breaker" by doing more or doing it better than other staff.

The Control Menu

The control menu consists of a very diverse collection of influences that a manager can bring to bear to control employee behavior (see Figure 9.1). Some—for example, performance review or punishment—are manager-directed and manager-implemented activities. Others, such as idealism or professional values, are equally powerful influences but seem to "exist" in some degree, at least in part, because of the long-term attitudes and behaviors of the manager. They can be nurtured by the manager, but not created. They can be used on occasion to assist in performing the function of control as a need arises. As we have done with other "menus" in this book, we will view the control menu as a "mixed bag" of control vehicles available to the manager for consideration in situations where control is indicated.

Plans

A plan, by its very nature, is designed to constrain and to control. The reader will recall from Chapter 4 that one of the objectives of planning is to not allow events and behaviors to simply happen naturally or at the whim of the actors involved. Plans make it possible to shape behavior in some predetermined direction. They also set standards for staff. They

FIGURE 9.1 *The Control Menu*

1. Plans—structures that have been put in place to shape future events within an organization; formal guides for action designed to constrain by defining what is acceptable and unacceptable staff behavior.

2. Training—planned socialization designed to standardize staff behavior through a mixture of didactic instruction and structured experiences.

3. Staff performance evaluations—regular, periodic, and structured feedback vehicles designed to offer positive reinforcement for desirable behavior and to discourage undesirable behavior.

4. Information—planned sharing of knowledge designed to help staff to understand (and thus avoid) what constitutes undesirable behavior.

5. Advice—ostensibly non-directive suggestions from a superior to a subordinate that are designed to change behavior in a relatively uninsulting manner.

6. Directives—orders or overt instructions expressed verbally or in writing that are designed to communicate clearly and unequivocally what a subordinate is to do, say, etc.

7. Negative sanctions—punishments or penalties imposed when an intolerable staff behavior occurs that was previously forbidden.

8. Loyalties—staff allegiance to some group or organization that may result in desirable behavior or exceptional dedication.

9. Staff idealism—commitments based upon certain strongly held personal belief systems (e.g., altruism) that may result in desirable behavior or exceptional dedication.

10. Professional values and ethics—beliefs and ethical principles that are consistent with those of one's profession. They generally are acquired or reinforced through a process of socialization that takes place as part of one's professional education.

11. Natural consequences—the phenomenon by which certain organizational behaviors tend to modify themselves over time through no efforts of the manager.

12. Manager's example—the phenomenon through which staff behavior is modified as a result of observing and attempting to emulate the behavior of the manager.

reflect a hoped-for outcome and, as such, they serve as a yardstick by which the manager can evaluate performance of staff and to intervene if necessary to change their behavior. Plans, therefore, are a prerequisite to most other kinds of control. One cannot evaluate behavior without some reference point by which to evaluate it. Plans provide that reference point. When managers plan, they are attempting to control. They are also laying the groundwork for all other controlling activities.

Plans are very powerful control vehicles. For example, "the budget of an organization can be regarded as primarily a planning and control system."[3] One of its two main functions has been described as "to provide a monitor for the financial activities throughout the year."[4] A budget thus has the potential to support or to disallow the various activities of staff. If an activity is regarded as desirable and appropriate, that activity is granted legitimacy by provisions made for it within the budget. The budget can also provide the rationale for managers to disallow certain activities, usually those that involve some monetary cost. They can merely point out that the activity has not been granted legitimacy as evidenced by the fact that there is no money for it in the budget.

Another type of control that we talked about in Chapter 4 when we discussed planning is what we will refer to collectively as "formal guides for action." They include a variety of constraining vehicles that define what is acceptable and what is not acceptable behavior among staff. Examples are rules, policies, strategies, and procedures. In Chapter 4 we discussed them as methods to shape future events. Here we are concerned primarily with their potential to control the present activities of staff.

Formal guides for action are a useful reference for all employees. They take most of the guesswork and the risk out of decision making for both managers and their subordinates. They help managers to know when a staff behavior is unacceptable and needs to be stopped. They also keep managers from mistakenly trying to control behaviors that they may personally dislike but that are, for example, not in violation of agency policy. Staff, in turn, are reminded of what is acceptable and unacceptable behavior, thus helping them to decide whether or not to engage in certain behaviors.

Formal guides for action are impersonal and designed for use by any individual who occupies a given position within the organization. Consequently, they are less likely to be resented than are some other types of control that are perceived as aimed specifically at a given individual. They are also always available for staff to "check out" whether a behavior is acceptable or not. The manager who developed them can be on vacation, on sick leave, or even no longer with the organization. It does not matter; a manager's influence and preferences continue to control staff behavior as long as the guide remains in effect. This is a mixed blessing. Whether the manager who created them is present or not, staff cannot ignore formal guides by pretending that they do not know what behavior is acceptable. On the other hand, formal guides, once in place, can sometimes produce decisions and behaviors that are less than optimal. They can control behaviors in circumstances that the manager might not have envisioned. Unless the manager is present to override them, an employee who complies with them will be beyond reproach, but their behaviors may still not be in the best interests of the organization. Of course, as we indicated in Chapter 4, some guides are inherently more flexible than others. For example, because policies encourage the use of discretion and rules do not, managers who are concerned with the danger of overly rigid compliance with formal guides during their absence may wish to rely more on policies for control and less on rules.

As with other types of controls, use of formal guides for action within a work environment characterized by trust and mutual respect between manager and staff can greatly facilitate the work of all involved. They can increase certainty for managers by expanding their potential to control, even when not physically present. Staff, in turn, can operate with the reasonable assurance that, if they are in compliance with formal guides, they will be "OK," and their decisions and activities should not be criticized. Formal guides also protect subordinates from the use of arbitrary or capricious criteria for evaluation of their performance by the manager. However, the very same formal guides used in a climate of distrust and a lack of mutual respect can become weapons to wage war between managers and staff. Managers can use them as unnecessary reminders of their greater power or to stifle the initiative and creativity of a staff member. In turn, staff members can blindly and rigidly comply with formal guides in situations where they know that they were not meant to apply in order to highlight a manager's "rigidity" or otherwise embarrass the manager in some other passive-aggressive manner.

Formal guides can either promote goal attainment and a healthy work environment or they can sabotage it. The key to their successful or unsuccessful application, as in so much of management, lies in the nature of the relationship that exists between the manager and subordinates. Once again we see that management and other areas of social work practice are far more similar than dissimilar. A positive working relationship is critical both to successful social work intervention with clients and to effective management.

Training

We last discussed training in Chapter 6 as one way to support employee growth. But training is also a very effective control vehicle available to the manager. While in some situations it is desirable for the manager to promote initiative and creative solutions on the part of staff, other situations suggest the need for standardization through training. For example, there are certain right and wrong ways (legally and professionally) for a child-protection worker to handle a report of suspected child abuse or to complete a form for third-party reimbursement for services. Creativity and initiative are not desirable. On the contrary, managers need to assure that workers are sufficiently socialized so that there is little room for discretion in those situations where discretion simply cannot be tolerated. They want to convert and standardize staff to think and to act in a way that is regarded as correct. "Indoctrination" is required. Staff are expected to possess the same values, to operate on the same premises and priorities, and to absorb these to the point where they are, for all intents and purposes, their own.

Training makes people look and act more alike. In some work situations this is desirable, if not absolutely necessary. Particularly when direct supervision is not always possible, training is useful. Like formal guides for action, it allows a manager's controls to be exercised even when the manager cannot be physically present. If an employee has internalized the correct sequence for performing a task, for example, there is every reason to assume that the task will be performed in the correct sequence. What is more, the employee who is well trained will probably not even be consciously aware of the manager's control and will, therefore, not resent it. Because the behavior is so well internalized, it will just seem natural, correct, and an extension of one's own work habits and style. For example, it is training that makes it possible for social workers to obey protocol while making home visits even though they do not take their supervisors along with them. Workers are made to feel more free and able to function autonomously when they are well trained. A manager uses training to standardize employees so that they can work with less supervision. Training actually can allow staff to feel less controlled. It provides "alternatives to the exercise of authority or advice as a means of control over the subordinate's decision."[5]

Training is an expensive (in terms of dollars and time) method of planning and control, but it is one that is usually appreciated by employees. Confident, well-trained employees have a tendency to feel better about their job and are more likely to be positively predisposed toward the manager who provides the training. What's more, as we suggested in Chapter 6, the cost of not training is often much greater for both the employee and the organization (in errors and embarrassment) than is the cost of training.

Staff Performance Evaluations

Staff performance evaluations can exert a considerable amount of control over the behavior of employees. As was suggested in Chapter 7, review of recent work tells staff and their supervisors how they compare with expectations that have been established for them. If certain types of very precise plans are in use within an organization (for example, management by objectives), performance review provides managers with an even clearer reading of when work has been satisfactory and when it has not. Review of work suggests where changes in employees' work performance are indicated and where additional control over their performance needs to be added. For example, it may suggest what type of training an employee requires or which activities need to be more carefully supervised. A performance evaluation may also suggest that inadequate performance was not the fault of the individual evaluated. For example, the identification of poor decisions may suggest that inadequate information was available or that the employee was inadequately prepared for decision making responsibilities.

The promise (or, perhaps, threat) of future performance reviews also exerts a considerable amount of control over employee behaviors. Staff members, knowing that there will be a regular, periodic day of accounting, are less likely to engage in behaviors that they will not be able to justify or that will leave them vulnerable to poor evaluations. All of us (including those of us who are classroom teachers) tend (to a greater or lesser degree) to carry our evaluation forms in the back of our minds. Their presence and the inevitability of their application are likely to curb those behaviors that we know are likely to result in critical reviews.

While the threat of staff performance evaluations can be a useful and constructive control on employee behavior, an obsession with them can be counterproductive. Employees preoccupied with getting good performance evaluations will tend to "play" to the evaluation instrument too much. A means–end displacement can occur. It can, for example, result in behaviors such as shirking tasks that are not in one's job description (since they will not result in "credit"). Or, staff might refuse to use certain effective intervention methods with clients (for example, confrontation) that might result in client complaints that could affect their job performance evaluations.

Sensitive managers are aware of the dangers that exist when the promise of staff evaluations becomes a specter to be feared or the driving force behind doing a good job. They use performance evaluations as a method of control, but they do it in such a way that they are perceived by staff as useful aids to job performance. They function as gentle reminders, not as clubs poised over employees' heads. If performance evaluations seem to be becoming an obsession for staff that overly or inappropriately controls their behavior, a manager needs to try to bring them back into perspective.

Information

Often staff engage in certain undesirable behaviors simply because they lack knowledge or are misinformed. A manager sometimes can extinguish undesirable behaviors by disseminating information either in writing or face-to-face. Information can be considered a type of plan (Chapter 4) since it sometimes is designed to keep a behavior from occurring or re-occurring. It also might be thought of as a special form of staff development (Chapter 6) that uses education to change a specific negative behavior. It is also a type of control. We have included it in our discussion of the latter since it relates most directly to eliminating undesirable behavior that is likely to already be occurring, at least to some degree.

What kind of undesirable behaviors can information control? Cultural insensitivity is a good example. Staff may not show proper respect to a co-worker from a different cultural or ethnic background because of a lack of awareness or what a particular behavior means to that individual. For example, staff may unwittingly regularly insult an older Korean co-worker by handing items to him with their left hand (use of two hands, with the right hand supported by the left, would be more respectful). Or they may, with good intentions, praise the individual achievements of a co-worker from another Asian country where only group achievement is highly valued, thereby causing her to become embarrassed and uncomfortable.

Staff may also engage in behavior that may border on the unethical or unprofessional, because they never "quite thought of it that way." Even illegal behavior sometimes occurs because people have not been sensitized to it or are operating on the basis of misinformation. For example, we might assume that, with all of the recent media attention given to the problem of sexual harassment in the workplace, everyone now knows what it is and what it is not. However, even many well-educated people hold erroneous beliefs about it. For example, some people still believe that it is only unwanted physical contact or that it is all behavior that can be considered sexist. (Both beliefs are wrong!) Even some managers themselves may still believe (erroneously) that they and their organization cannot become part of a sexual harassment lawsuit if it is reported to them and they choose to do nothing about it. Definitions of sexual harassment are still evolving based upon recent court decisions. Managers need to know the most current interpretations and convey them as information to staff as changes occur.

Certain behaviors such as sexual harassment clearly should not occur. Managers should do everything that they can to prevent them. But merely forbidding unacceptable behaviors without providing needed information may not be sufficient to preclude their occurrence. Besides, fairness also suggests that staff are entitled to know exactly which behaviors are acceptable and which ones are not, if they do not already know. The manager has a responsibility to provide needed information if staff are expected to behave responsibly.

Sometimes, despite the efforts of the manager to provide all needed information, severe negative behaviors occur anyway within organizations. When they do, they must be dealt with promptly and firmly, often through negative sanctions (see below) and, in extreme cases, by termination for misconduct (see Chapter 7).

Advice

We all are quite generous with our advice. Usually gratuitously, we pass on the benefits of our life experiences to others. Between peers or persons of comparable power, advice is available to be heeded, ignored, or even never heard. But when a person with more power and/or authority than another person gives advice, it should be received as more than just advice or a recommendation. It may be a vehicle of control.

The advice of a parent may be only advice, or it may be a tactful, non-humiliating attempt at telling a child what to do. Advice to a 3-year-old is usually synonymous with a directive; it is expected to control behavior. Advice to a teenager is likely to carry less expectation of compliance or of heeding the advice.

Advice may be purely "for your information" in one aspect of a relationship yet may carry the intent of control in another. A professor who suggests that a student apply for a job she heard about expects the student to follow up on the information or not, based purely on the student's interest. A "thank you" is about all that the professor expects. But when the same professor suggests that a student include some content in a term paper, she has every expectation that the content will be in the student's paper. The student who ignores the information may discover that the "advice" really was much more than just advice.

Relationships between managers and their subordinates are clearly not equal. Consequently, advice offered to a subordinate has much more expectation of and potential for control than advice passed between and among peers. It is done with the intention of shaping and controlling the behavior of the staff member. Because the great majority of advice given by managers is designed to affect the behavior of subordinates, staff sometimes assume that all of a manager's advice is a thinly veiled directive. This can cause problems. If social workers intend to step out of their manager's roles long enough to simply offer advice, peer-to-peer, without wishing to influence their staff members' decisions or behavior in any way, they had better make their intentions very clear. If not, subordinates may respond to what is perceived to be directives when none were intended.

Because advice can be communicated in a way that controls while not calling attention to an existing power differential, it is a favorite vehicle of control among professionals. Managers enjoy being able to set necessary limits on the behavior of staff while not having to do it in a way that "puts down" the knowledge and professional competence of a colleague who happens to occupy a lower position on the organizational chart. In turn, subordinates enjoy the face-saving offered by advice. They are not likely to feel as controlled or harassed as when some other forms of control are used. They appreciate not having to be reminded of the power differential. Unlike, for example, directives (which we shall discuss next), staff members can at least partially delude themselves into believing that "it's just advice." Of course, knowledgeable subordinates know that advice, given the source, is usually meant to control. They know better than to ignore it.

Directives

Sometimes, for one reason or another, staff control through the use of advice and information just does not work. Some individuals never quite get the message. Some managers never become competent at the subtleties of their use and feel more comfortable saying exactly what they mean. Sometimes there is no time for subtlety since the cost of miscommunication would be too great. Other times, a situation may suggest the need for a reminder of the power differential that staff may have forgotten.

Directives take the form of orders, overt instructions, or other specific demands. They may be aimed at individuals and/or groups and may be used to exert control over a variety of behaviors. They are an especially good choice from the control menu when a conflict situation exists, and it has become apparent that consensus cannot be achieved. If, for example, two factions seem unable to work out a compromise over the sharing of space or equipment, the manager may have to resort to directives. This is a responsibility that the manager cannot shirk. An organization cannot afford the expense of prolonged debate over an issue of relatively low importance to client service, particularly when it becomes apparent that winning the debate is rapidly becoming a higher priority for staff than resolution of the conflict. Someone (the manager) must terminate debate and initiate action. Of course, this can only occur in situations where the manager has the authority to issue a directive.

Not surprisingly, directives are some of the least popular methods of control among those used by social workers in their roles as managers. Social workers are socialized to be non-directive with their clients; they have little experience in telling others what they must do. Subordinates, in turn, often find directives humiliating. However, though they are often reluctant to admit it, most staff are usually relieved when a directive writes *finis* to an interminable debate among staff.

Directives generally are viewed as a reminder of the manager's authority that staff prefer not to see. To most of us, directives reawaken feelings of powerlessness and the figurative slap on the wrist that we thought we left behind when we left our home of origin, turned 18, graduated, or achieved some other rite of maturity. We naively thought that no one would ever again be able to tell us what to do. Of course, few people ever get to this point in even one sphere of their lives. None of us ever gets to this point in all of life's spheres. However, no one ever enjoys being reminded of a power differential.

Social workers as managers often dislike using directives for control because, on the surface, they seem inappropriate for use between or among helping professionals. We believe that professionals and other dedicated helpers should be able to communicate in ways that are respectful, not parental. Directives may seem anti-egalitarian and a bit in conflict with our professional values relating to equal worth among human beings. Shouldn't advice and a smile be enough to control dedicated people of good will? Perhaps, but as we suggested above, there are many situations when they are not sufficient. Directives are required.

If used where necessary and appropriate, directives are very efficient methods of control. They can save a considerable amount of time by not requiring staff to guess just what it is that managers want. Miscommunication can be virtually eliminated. Managers in the business world have long been accustomed to using directives to control. Corporate managers who regularly use them do not seem to exhibit that self-consciousness and apologetic demeanor sometimes seen among social work managers. Perhaps, as social workers, we are overly concerned with questioning our motivation for using directives. We may spend too much time asking ourselves if we select directives for control because they control well or because we get some sense of gratification (a "power trip") out of using them. Just maybe, the good feeling that sometimes accompanies the use of directives occurs because they seem to work so well!

Most mature professionals and other human service staff recognize the need for directives on occasion. They may even appreciate them as a refreshing change from the approaches of some social work managers whom they regard as overly concerned with possibly insulting or offending subordinates. Employees expect to be told what to do by the boss now and then. The judicious use of directives often is perceived as an indication of strength on the part of a manager, of a willingness to take control and to assume the responsibilities of the job. There also are many employees who "just want to be told what to do," especially in situations where there is little time for tact and subtlety. However, this is not meant to imply that there is no room for tact in the use of directives. A skillful manager will state a directive in a way that makes the message clear but that does not remind the recipient of a power differential any more than absolutely necessary. Among other things, directives given in private or on a one-to-one basis are usually less likely to be resented than those given in the presence of others.

Obviously, if a social worker as manager relies on directives almost exclusively or in situations where other control vehicles would be preferable, there is likely to be a problem. Morale can be undermined along with initiative of staff. Confidence in and respect for the manager is likely to erode if managers are perceived as enjoying the use of directives just a little too much. But autocratic managers who relish the use of directives are relatively rare in social work. A more common problem is managers who do not make sufficient use of this valuable method of control.

Negative Sanctions

Managers sometimes need to employ sanctions to avoid or punish certain behaviors that are intolerable. They are used less frequently as methods of control within organizations than the other methods that we have discussed up to this point. There are good reasons for this. For one thing, people in human service organizations generally are quite well-behaved. The behavior of professionals usually is adequately controlled by other methods of control, for example, performance evaluations and professional values and ethics. Besides, managers are supposed to spend most of their time being supportive, not punishing or imposing negative sanctions. We focus most of our attention on appealing to an individual's sources of motivation (needs) and building on strengths, not calling attention to and punishing shortcomings. Both as social workers and as managers, our professional values imply a firm belief in the superiority of the carrot over the stick.

Negative sanctions, while used relatively rarely, are a legitimate control tool that should be in the repertoire of the manager. While they have very limited use, they can be very effective. A sanction spells out both what an employee is forbidden to do and the negative consequences of doing it. The consequences are usually quite drastic. For example, if a manager determines that an organization's programs might be seriously jeopardized by the release of the report of an internal evaluation or audit to the press, the manager might inform all employees that no portion of the report is to be shared with anyone outside the organization. The penalty for violation (the sanction) would also be clearly stated (for example, immediate dismissal). The threat would not be an idle one; if a violation were proven (following all due process), the offending employee would be fired. There generally would be no effort to hide from other staff the reason why the employee was fired. The action would be an example to others, reminding them that sanctions are not idle threats—they will be imposed.

Negative sanctions are effective. People will avoid behaviors when they understand that a substantial punishment will be enacted, especially if they see it enacted on another. But sanctions are of very limited use in promoting positive behaviors or desirable activities. They can also have a very damaging effect on morale and on relationships between staff and managers if they are perceived as excessively severe. Consequently, sanctions should be used very sparingly and only to prevent and address intolerable behaviors.

Loyalties

Loyalties cannot be easily created by the manager. But they can be promoted and fostered when desirable. They can be powerful vehicles for control. Loyalties, in some form or other, are always present within work situations. Appropriately focused, they contribute to organizational goal attainment. They can also present major obstacles to goal attainment if they are misplaced.

Ideally, employees possess loyalties to the organization, and they share and endorse its mission, goals, and objectives. Use of training and indoctrination can go a long way toward creating this desirable state. Other loyalties can exist too. They may be toward peers and subordinates, toward one or more superiors, and, of course, toward one's self. Self-interest is always a major controlling force for staff. The manager may as well acknowledge this truth. A staff member's loyalties toward other persons within the organization can be either positive or negative. Depending on whether or not the objects of their loyalty are competent, dedicated employees themselves, they can promote either desirable or undesirable behavior.

Organizational loyalties are almost always desirable. When employees feel good about where they work and are proud of an organization's services, the manager is indeed fortunate. Organizational loyalties can serve as powerful inducements to do what is necessary for the good of the organization and for the clients it serves. An employee who is loyal to the organization, for example, might agree to postpone a vacation in order to complete a task such as the timely submission of a grant proposal. Employees are less likely to complain or to insist on extra compensation for doing what is in the best interest of the organization. Similarly loyalty to an organization will prevent employees from certain behaviors (for example, ridiculing the organization in public) that might be harmful to it.

Managers should foster the growth of organizational loyalties, but they may also find it useful to appeal to loyalties that already exist. When managers appeal to organizational loyalties, they are saying, in effect, "I'm not asking for me, but for the organization." Genuine, occasional appeals of this sort can elicit desirable behavior among employees who are loyal to the organization. They can result in employees doing something that the manager has no legitimate right to require them to do. Of course, if appeals to organizational loyalties are used too frequently or when no real emergency exists, they can quickly lose their capacity to exert control. Once a manager is perceived as using appeals to organizational loyalty as a means to manipulate or to exploit staff, resentment will occur. Even appropriate appeals then may meet with resistance. Managers should be careful in the use of organizational loyalties, using them sparingly in only those situations where other more traditional methods of control would not work. They clearly are not suitable for regular, day-to-day control of behavior.

Staff possess organizational loyalty in various degrees. Sensitive managers learn to identify those employees for whom organizational loyalties represent a powerful source of control, those who are influenced somewhat by them, and those for whom they represent little or no source of leverage. Loyalties also should not be regarded as simply a static characteristic of individual staff. They tend to ebb and flow based on employees' current attitudes toward their jobs.

Organizational loyalties can be nurtured by the manager so that they are available when needed. This is best done by regular reminders of organizational goals and frequent positive communication to staff about the organization during times when no special requests are being made. Staff are most likely to develop good feelings about their association with the organization during those routine but rewarding times when its representatives (managers) are asking no special favors of them except that they do their job as outlined in their job descriptions.

Staff Idealism

Idealism is another vehicle for control that cannot be created easily by the manager. Like organizational loyalty, idealism tends to exist in people in various degrees. Many people who enter the helping professions possess a strong sense of altruism, perhaps in the form of a felt need to help others. For example, among some people, the Judeo-Christian ethic, with its emphasis on helping one's fellow human being, provides individuals with an extra sense of purpose and enhances their dedication to their work. Idealism is certainly appropriate and desirable in fields such as social work. It can be an important source of motivation that, for example, makes it possible for individuals to perform needed services and tasks where conditions are less than favorable and tangible rewards are few. Idealism can also assist the helping professional to see potential for change in situations where other, less idealistic individuals would have given up hope or even would have refused to get involved in the first place.

The manager can and should work to create an organizational climate where individuals' personal ideals can serve as motivators. It generally is in the best interests of all concerned, especially of clients. Ideals should never be ridiculed or allowed to be ridiculed by others. As we suggested in our discussion of organizational loyalties, appeals to an individual's ideals, if employed judiciously, may be used by the manager to elicit behavior that is consistent with organizational goal attainment. Of course, frequent appeals to an employee's ideals can also be quickly perceived as manipulative behavior on the part of the manager. Like loyalties, such appeals are best reserved for occasional use.

Professional Values and Ethics

Professional values are acquired through a process of education and socialization. But they can help to control much of staff behavior on the job and, to a greater or lesser degree, even off the job. For example, espousal of professional values regarding the primacy of client needs may keep a social worker in the office until 8 PM to deal with an emergency despite the fact that workday technically ends at 5 PM. Professional values, as we have suggested throughout this book, also govern our behavior as managers. Most of the time they are supportive of good management practice. Now and then, however, professional values seem (at least on the surface) to run counter to what we as managers must do.

Professional values, because of their capacity to control other employees' behavior, can be a mixed blessing for the manager seeking to promote organizational goal attainment. Usually professional values are consistent with and supportive of the goals of human service organizations. A manager can appeal to them on occasion to promote desired behavior and to constrain undesirable behavior. A good manager should help to promote organizational goals that are consistent with professional values. But sometimes this ideal state is not possible. For example, human service organizations sometimes must function as businesses. They sometimes cannot afford to offer services that are inefficient or those that threaten the support of the task environment for the organization. Consequently, staff members occasionally find that their professional values are in conflict with organizational goals. Lower-level staff spend less time in management activities and more in direct client service. Therefore, they can afford to concern themselves a little less with such matters as organization funding or community relations and find it relatively easy to stand behind their professional values in the face of organization demands. The point for the manager is this: professional values consistent with the organization's objectives help to facilitate control. But conflict between professional values and the organization's goals, policies, or procedures provides a rationale for employees to resist control. A certain amount of tension between professional values and an organization's objectives is inevitable and also healthy. Professional values help to hold the organization accountable. Fortunately, tension usually remains at a healthy and tolerable level in most human service organizations.

Professional ethics (like values) are acquired as part of socialization to a profession. They (and reminders about them) offer a wide range of control over staff behaviors. The 1996 NASW Code of Ethics (revised in 1999)[6] specifies what is considered ethical and unethical professional conduct in relating to clients (for example, issues of confidentiality and record keeping). But it also describes, for example, how a social worker is supposed to relate to colleagues (respectfully) and one's professional obligation to report a colleague's impairment, incompetence, or unethical behavior. Other issues such as conflict of interest, record keeping and commitment to one's employer are also addressed.

If staff behaviors were to be in total compliance with the NASW Code of Ethics at all times, there might be little need for other forms of control! Very few, if any, current or potential problems are not addressed. For example, item 4.04 states that "social workers should not participate in, condone, or be associated with dishonesty, fraud, or deception."[7] This should eliminate such problematic behaviors as falsification of case records, fraudulent travel reimbursement requests, or even dishonest presentation of a staff member's work in supervisory conferences or annual performance reviews. However, a manager cannot assume that professional ethics (or values) alone will eliminate such problems. Monitoring is required and other control methods may be needed.

Natural Consequences

Sometimes managers control staff by letting time and certain predictable events influence their behavior. A manager may make the conscious decision to do nothing because, based upon certain insights or experience, an undesirable attitude or behavior either dissipates on its own or is extinguished by consequences that it produces in the work setting. Teachers may elect not to confront a student about disruptive classroom behavior (at least for a while) because they have observed that if students do not get the desired attention, they stop being disruptive or other students generally will step in to exercise social pressures for conformity. Similarly, a manager in a human service organization may conclude that it is inadvisable to deal with the angry and frustrated outbursts of a new child protection worker because, based on past experience, the outbursts are likely to stop as the worker gets more comfortable on the job and learns how to cope. Or, a manager may choose not to confront a worker about wearing clothing that is slightly "unprofessional" because, based on past experience, most staff usually "tune in" to what others are wearing after they realize that they stand out.

In many problem situations (but not all), one choice a manager has is to do nothing. A conscious decision not to act at the present time because, based on the manager's experience and judgment, a problem is (1) not a severe one and (2) very likely to go away naturally, can be an appropriate management behavior. The manager, if pressed, could justify this inaction based upon a sound rationale. Control by natural consequences entails a careful weighing of alternatives and the conclusion that doing nothing (at least for the time being) is the best course of action. It should not be confused with the unfortunate tendency of some managers to try to ignore a sticky problem that they are not comfortable in addressing or the tendency of others to fail to take indicated action with the hope that a problem might go away.

Of course, the decision to control by natural consequences is appropriate in only a limited number of problem situations. Even some problems that might go away on their own cannot be allowed to exist for a minute longer. Control by natural consequences is not an option. For example, an allegation of sexual harassment (see discussion of "Information" above) cannot be ignored, even though in some situations we might have reason to believe that the behavior would be extinguished by peer pressure (or an angry victim) over time. The law, and thus the good of the organization, demand that it be dealt with by some other means of control.

Control by natural consequences often is used when the manager believes that other methods of control might be premature or are unnecessary. It assumes that there is good predictive knowledge available to be reasonably certain that the problem will not get worse or cause any major difficulties if it continues for a while, and that it will go away on its own if no action is taken. Unless these conditions are present, another control that offers an immediate problem solution, like a directive, may be required.

The Manager's Example

The final control vehicle on our menu is one that we seldom think of as a method for controlling, yet it exerts great influence over the behavior of staff. It can be a source of either support for or resistance to desirable employee behavior.

The *example* set by the manager can affect the behavior of all employees who seek the manager's good will, who wish to emulate the manager, and/or who simply wish to advance within the organization. It is less likely to be seen as manipulative on the part of the manager than either appeals to organizational loyalty, to idealism, or to professional values and ethics. The thoughts, actions, attitudes, and values that the manager reflects are generally perceived to be norms for the group, the standard to be met. If managers are well respected, their behavior is an especially powerful positive influence on others. For example, highly respected managers who sometimes put aside their own personal best interests for the good of their organizations and their clients will influence others to do the same.

If managers interact at all with staff, even if they are just seen occasionally by them, they will set an example that will affect subordinate behavior. The issue is not whether they will control by example but *how* their example will influence behavior. Will their examples have a positive influence on organizational behavior? Or will their attitudes and behaviors convey the message that short of doing one's best is an acceptable level of performance. Managers who attempt to communicate the message of "do as I say, not as I do?" rarely succeed in controlling staff behavior. Even other methods of control that are used (for example, formal guides, advice and information, or directives) will be less successful if managers convey a belief in a double standard. Staff may reluctantly allow themselves to be constrained. But they will resent it and will likely engage in other undesirable, nonproductive behavior when the occasion arises.

In a sense, the manager is always on stage. In the role of manager, the social worker is watched for clues as to how to act, think, and what attitudes are appropriate. When another staff member engages in a particular behavior, there is less danger that many others will try to emulate it. But when a manager (particularly a higher-level one) does something, a large number of staff are likely to notice and to assume that it represents an example for others to follow. It is a good idea to remember this at social functions and other times after work hours as well as on the job.

Staff are more likely to participate in a behavior that they know is not acceptable when they can use a manager's example to rationalize it. For example, lower-level staff members are more likely to call in sick to catch up on their holiday shopping when they see the manager do it. If managers want to support some staff behaviors and constrain others, they are most likely to be successful if their own behavior reflects the desired standards. They may possess the authority to live by different standards, but their poor example will cause resentment and will weaken their overall capacity to control.

The Ideal Control Package

The package of controls that managers select to perform their controlling function will change naturally with conditions, with the changing needs of personnel, and with changes in personnel themselves. Selecting a control package is a rather imprecise science. There is no formula available that can tell us, for example, just what percentage of our controlling should be handled using directives, what percentage by formal guides, etc. One thing is certain. If managers find themselves relying very heavily on only one or two control methods from the menu, they should become concerned. The widely diverse control needs of the human service organization and of those employed within it suggest that a varied package is almost always ideal.

Certain broad guidelines are available to help us in development of an effective and efficient control package.[8] They characterize a good package, one that will control as much as is necessary, while not stifling staff initiative.

It Is Comfortable

Perhaps most importantly, the control package selected should "feel right" to managers. It should not leave them and others with the feeling that they are playing a role or are using methods that are somehow out of character. Whereas managers may need to use every one of the controls on the menu at some point, in most situations more than one could be selected to do the job. Managers should use most frequently those that fit their personality and style of management. For example, those who are most comfortable giving advice or information to control and do it effectively should use this method far more often than directives. Of course, when only directives will do the job, they must be able to use them, too. Conversely, a manager with a more authoritarian personality may rarely use advice and information to control and may rely heavily on directives.

The real emphasis in selection of controls should be on the quality of interaction between controller and controllee that is sought. As much as possible, the interaction should be natural and comfortable for both. For example, neither participant in the interaction between a relatively young supervisor and a senior subordinate may feel comfortable with the frequent use of directives. Yet directives may be a much more natural way to control if the same supervisor is very senior to a subordinate.

It Is De-personalized

The package selected should be perceived as necessary for the good of the organization. No matter what controls are selected, it should not appear to others that they are designed to "get" someone or to reward someone, but rather to maintain a standard of services that is in the best interest of all. At the same time, a problem behavior that is unique to one individual should not result in unnecessary controls on others. For example, if there has been a pattern of past problems, the manager may require that the correspondence of one individual must be screened by a supervisor before it is allowed to be sent out. It would be an unnecessary imposition on other staff to apply this requirement to anyone else who does not require it.

It Has the Potential to Improve Conditions

A good package of controls is not there just to monitor the activities of others. It is there to shape them in a way more consistent with organizational goals. Unless staff members perceive controls as a prelude to change, they are not likely to look favorably on them. If, however, they see them as resulting in improved working conditions and, ultimately, in better client services, they will tolerate them much more easily.

Two questions that should be asked about a control package are: (1) Will it point out shortcomings? and; (2) Will awareness of them result in corrective action? It is unfair to burden staff with control packages that do not promise to improve conditions after they have been identified.

It Is Efficient

A control package should be relatively inexpensive to administer and to maintain. Specifically, it should result in a net overall saving for the organization. Some controls can cost more than they save in time and resources. For example, daily staff meetings to review policies and procedures can increase control and reduce problem behaviors, but can they be justified in terms of time taken away from client services or other valuable activities?

Some overly rigid control packages control well but at a heavy cost to morale. For example, a manager might maintain tight control over staff activities by not allowing compensatory time for evening work or by denying the request of an employee who commutes 60 miles to work to move to a four-day, 10-hour per day work week. But the objective of creating a work environment where organizational loyalty is high might be jeopardized in the process. The vigorous use of some controls actually undermines the effectiveness of others. The net gain (in control) may be zero or even a minus.

It Is Enforceable

A control package must have good potential for success. If it contains elements such as rules or directives that clearly are unenforceable, all efforts of the manager to control behavior can start to be taken less seriously.

Not every behavior that the manager would like to control or even all behaviors that are potentially harmful to the organization can be controlled. It is better to not even try to control them, just acknowledging their inevitable presence, than to attempt to control them, only to fail. For example, all managers might like to control or, better yet, eliminate staff ridicule or mimicking of their bosses behind their backs. But to circulate a memorandum to staff stating either "staff will not engage in ridicule of their supervisors" or "staff may not discuss their supervisors with co-workers" would be worse than just a waste of time. These directives cannot be enforced and would only leave the manager subject to more ridicule and additional loss of respect.

It Focuses on Critical Control Needs

Some undesirable behaviors can be controlled, but controlling them is not worth the effort—there are more important negative behaviors that need to be controlled. Some poorly managed organizations seem to emphasize control of relatively minor behaviors (minutiae) while larger problem behaviors that threaten organizational goal attainment go unchecked. For example, a manager can devote great amounts of time to policing the use of telephones by staff, pouring over printouts of long distance calls for hours to see who made them and if they constitute official business. Meanwhile, while focusing on a few occasional short personal calls that represent no real threat to anyone, the manager may

CASE EXAMPLE • *A Problem of Inefficient Control*

Mario was the director of an extended-care facility. He prided himself on running a tightly controlled, fiscally sound organization that consistently ended each year in the black. He was regarded as a rising star within his parent organization, a publicly owned corporation.

Mario had originally disliked the control responsibilities that went with the job. But he had come to appreciate the value of strict control over staff behavior. He took special care to monitor and approve the expenditure of funds. He was unaware that his careful fiscal scrutiny was beginning to cause resentment among several of his employees. A few of the professional staff felt insulted by what they saw as Mario's lack of trust of their behavior. But Mario became aware that he had a problem only following the implementation of his infamous "pen rule."

For several months, Mario had observed what he believed to be unnecessarily high bills for office supplies. He was especially concerned over the great number of pens that staff members were using. It seemed as though every time he looked, a staff member was grabbing another handful of pens. He noticed that several invariably had a pen or two in their pocket when they left work. They took new pens when they reported to work the next morning. He began to wonder whether the organization was not supplying writing supplies for staff, their children, and half the community.

Mario first brought up the pen issue in a staff meeting. He commented on the rising cost of pens and other supplies. He asked staff to please help conserve the number of pens used. A month later, having noticed little improvement, he shared his observation that staff seemed to be leaving with pens in pockets (hadn't he done the same thing absentmindedly himself!) but rarely bringing them back to work. He wondered aloud if any staff members ever bought school supplies (his effort at a humorous way to address the problem). Several

staff members obviously were not amused. (Mario was not known for his sense of humor.)

Two more months passed. Meanwhile, the amount of pens being consumed continued to increase. Unbeknownst to Mario, what was being referred to as his "pen obsession" was becoming a source of amusement and ridicule among staff. One social worker even began slipping pens into Mario's coat pocket before he left work for the day. The occasional amusement provided by the pen issue was short-lived, however. Mario's next effort at control made everyone furious.

Mario decided that staff were challenging his authority by ignoring his requests. He was concerned over the continued financial loss to the organization, but he was more concerned over his feelings of powerlessness to do anything about it. He announced and immediately implemented rules and procedures that (in his mind) were certain to solve the pen problem once and for all. The pens were placed in a locked cabinet. A single key was issued to his administrative assistant who was told to make up a roster of secretarial staff who would be in charge of the pen cabinet. The secretary in charge of the cabinet was to sign the key out and sign it back in.

Each staff member was to be issued three new pens. No exceptions were to be made. Following the initial issue, staff members would not be able to receive a new pen unless they turned in an old one to the secretary in charge of the pen cabinet. The secretary was to test the pen to assure that it was no longer usable. If it was, it would be given back to the staff member and no new pen would be issued. If it did not work, a new one would be issued.

What had been a generally cooperative, congenial work environment quickly deteriorated. Professional staff found Mario's pen solution to be totally demeaning and unacceptable. The secretaries assigned to the pen cabinet and his administrative assistant hated their new assignments. They felt that they had better things to do. (They were right.) They were

CASE EXAMPLE • *(continued)*

regularly taken away from their usual duties in order to get a new pen for a staff member. Relationships between secretarial and professional staffs became more strained. Respect for Mario was obviously at a new low. Other new cost-saving controls that he implemented that might ordinarily have been accepted without comment produced ridicule and resentment on the part of staff. They began to resist other rules and policies that had previously gone unchallenged. Finally, most of the staff signed a petition criticizing Mario's controlling and humiliating management style and threatening to resign unless changes were made. They mailed it to the parent corporation.

Mario received a copy of the petition from his boss along with a request that he address the problem immediately. When he received the letter, Mario finally recognized the problems that his concern over pen costs had caused. His options were to continue to try to function as a manager in a hostile work environment, resign, or lose a little face and admit his mistake. He chose the last option. In a staff meeting he acknowledged that his concern with controlling costs had, perhaps, gotten a little out of hand. He cited the pen problem as an example. The pen cabinet would be immediately unlocked and available for whomever needed a pen.

While a few staff members initially gloated over the fact that he had been forced to back down, Mario was surprised to see that many more staff members seemed to have a new respect for him. After a while, the pen issue became an inside joke, and he was able to use it on occasion in staff meetings to relieve tension that had become high. When Mario ultimately left the organization for a higher-level job in the corporation, he was given an appreciative farewell dinner by staff. Among his gifts was (what else?) an expensive pen.

Discussion Questions

1. What issues should Mario have considered before he implemented his pen rule?
2. Why did Mario's pen rule probably result in a net financial loss to his organization?
3. What other costs did it produce?
4. When he finally recognized that his pen rule had been a mistake, did Mario handle the problem well? Why or why not?
5. Should Mario have simply pretended that he did not notice the large number of pens that were being taken? Why or why not?

fail to observe a much more dangerous staff behavior (for example, the unethical denial of services and referral of clients to a friend in private practice) that may jeopardize the reputation of the entire organization.

What is a critical problem suggesting the need for controls? A lack of attention to clients, their rights, and their need for services is critical and is the legitimate focus of a control package. So is behavior that is illegal, unethical, or grossly unprofessional. These problems and the staff behaviors that contribute to them cannot be ignored. Managers clearly do not have the time to control all staff behaviors that are undesirable. They must maintain a set of priorities that suggests which behaviors should be controlled and which should not. Remembering that the client is the prime beneficiary of a human service organization will go a long way toward helping the manager identify and maintain an appropriate control package that focuses on critical behaviors.

Building flexibility into a control package to accommodate changing conditions will also help to avoid controlling negative behaviors that are relatively trivial. Many undesirable behaviors are not all that bad in certain situations; they are more problematic in others. A flexible control package may allow certain behaviors to be overlooked in some situations and addressed at other times when they represent more of a threat.

Finally, some behavior problems, which are referred to as "corruption" in the literature,[9] would simply cost more to control than they are costing the organization by their existence. They are probably best "not seen" by the manager. Once acknowledged, they must be controlled or, if not, they may appear to be encouraged by the manager—not a desirable practice. Unless the problem is one that threatens goal attainment, it may be best not to call attention to it.

The Optimum Amount of Control

The role of manager carries with it the responsibility and the authority to constrain and to control the activities of others. Managers must insure that staff behavior is adequately controlled. However, as we all know, controlling is sometimes quite pleasurable and gratifying. We can easily lose sight of why managers are supposed to control as we get caught up in the gratification that comes with controlling. As we have repeatedly suggested throughout this chapter, the need for control should come from organizational needs (and, of course, the needs of clients) and not solely from the needs of the manager. Control should be viewed as a means to an end, never an end in itself. The potential for a means–end displacement is great. We can easily become obsessed with the process of controlling while losing sight of its purposes.

Complete control cannot be achieved. But a major benefit of control for both the manager and other employees is the reduction of uncertainty within the work environment. Too much uncertainty about what to do or how one will be perceived and evaluated can create anxiety in staff, sometimes to the point of immobilizing them. But a moderate level of uncertainty is both inevitable and desirable. It can be achieved if controls are used appropriately and well.

Excessive control can stifle initiative of staff. The overzealous creation of uniformity and standardization by a manager can quickly communicate to staff that conformity is always desirable. Such a message can cheat the organization of the special and unique talents and expertise of its members. In addition, an overly controlling, heavy-handed approach to management can also promote a type of passive-aggressive response on the part of staff that is not healthy for the organization. Staff members will begin to avoid decision making, passing such matters on to management with an attitude of "You want to control everything, then you make the decision." The expertise of staff (to make their own decisions) goes underutilized.

Summary

In this chapter the management function of controlling was presented as closely linked with and sometimes overlapping with other managerial functions, primarily planning. We discussed controlling as the setting of limits and the establishment of standards, the measuring of performance against these standards, and doing whatever is necessary to correct deficiencies. Controlling involves those actions taken by the social worker as manager to influence the behavior of others so that it is more consistent with organizational goals and objectives. While social workers frequently dread the function of controlling, if done tactfully and well it can provide benefits to both management and other staff; primarily in the form of increased certainty within the work environment.

The various methods for controlling were presented as a menu available to the manager. Control vehicles on the menu included plans, formal guides for action, training, performance review, advice, information, directives, sanctions, loyalties, idealism, professional values and ethics, natural consequences, and example. The advantages and disadvantages of each were discussed.

It was emphasized that, whatever package of controls a manager selects, it must remain dynamic and flexible. The package, no matter what its specific composition, should be comfortable for staff involved, should be perceived as de-personalized, have the potential to improve conditions, should be efficient, enforceable, and should focus on those areas where control is critical. The dangers of over-control were especially noted. We discussed how too much control on the part of the manager can stifle staff initiative and can result in a situation where individual expertise will not be fully utilized.

Endnotes

1. Bernard Neugeboren, *Organization, Policy and Practice in the Human Services* (New York: Longman. 1985), p. 130.

2. Harold Koontz, Cyril O'Donnell, and Heinz Weihrich, *Essentials of Management,* 4th ed. (New York: McGraw-Hill, 1986), p. 448.

3. Walter Christian and Gerald Hannah, *Effective Management in Human Services* (Englewood Cliffs, NJ: Prentice-Hall, 1983), p. 136.

4. Rex Skidmore, *Social Work Administration* (Englewood Cliffs, NJ: Prentice-Hall, 1983), p. 72.

5. Herbert Simon, *Administrative Behavior* (New York: Macmillan, 1957), p. 16.

6. National Association of Social Workers, *Code of Ethics,* 1999. Alexandria, VA.

7. Ibid., p. 18.

8. Koontz, O'Donnell, and Weihrich, *op. cit.,* pp. 459–463.

9 Amatai Etzioni, *Capital Corruption: The New Attack on American Democracy* (San Diego: Harcourt Brace Jovanovich, 1984), pp. 76–80.

10

Leading

Leadership entails the manager's conscious efforts to influence other people within the organization to engage willingly in those behaviors that contribute to the attainment of organizational goals. We probably could build a legitimate argument for the position that all management is leadership. In fact, our discussion of the role of the social worker as manager in earlier chapters has frequently spilled over into the function of leadership. Managers exert leadership (or they should) when they plan, staff, organize, and control. However, since leadership is so critical to successful management, it is worthy of individual focus.

We all would agree that good leadership is desirable and that poor leadership or the absence of leadership is undesirable within human service organizations. We probably can give examples of leadership that we have observed that have been good or bad. But when we are asked to specify why leadership was good or bad, or why we perceive one individual to be an effective leader and why another person is viewed as ineffective in a leadership role, we may struggle a little. The difficulty of defining leadership is one that has perplexed theorists over the past half century. Researchers and academicians have devoted entire careers to the pursuit of a better understanding of leadership. We will begin by summarizing some of the past and current thinking on the subject.

The Elements of Leadership

A large portion of leadership relates to the concept of influence. Leadership is a little less direct and obvious than, for example, planning or controlling in the ways that it influences staff behavior (some would say it is less oppressive). But it is no less powerful in shaping what people do within organizations. In fact, it could be argued, managers will be successful in their efforts to perform the other functions of management only if they are first perceived as effective leaders. People want to follow the directives and the example of good leaders. They may ignore or may circumvent the management efforts of ineffective leaders.

Leadership seeks to influence and to shape behaviors of staff so that they are supportive (rather than obstructive) of organizational goal attainment. Specifically, in human service organizations, managers hope to lead in such a way that they will influence the behavior of others to maximize their contributions to efficient and effective client services.

Leadership employs a combination of personal characteristics (of the manager), knowledge, and skills in attempting to influence the behavior of others. In this sense, it is closely related to the concept of motivation (see Chapter 6). While we have discussed motivation as a part of staffing, it could just as logically have been considered a component of good leadership.

Ideally, we would like to have our fellow employees willingly do what is in the best interests of the organization and of the clients who it serves. With good leadership, this can occur. But those tasks that, by their very nature, are regarded as unpleasant or that are perceived as in conflict with the self-interest of staff may require especially adept leadership. For example, special leadership may be required to elicit any kind of employee enthusiasm for performing cumbersome record keeping, which is required for federal reimbursement in large public welfare agencies and which may leave less time for meeting other, more enjoyable job expectations. Yet some managers are able to lead in such a way that employees spend very little time complaining and approach this task in a relatively "upbeat" fashion. Somehow these managers' requests are viewed as reasonable and credible and their motives are not suspect. Clearly, trust is a component of effective leadership. This should come as no surprise to us; we identified it as an important element for success in performing all of the functions of the manager.

Leadership Tasks

The actual tasks of leadership (like the other management functions that we have discussed) tend to vary dependent on the position in the organization that a manager occupies. For example, we expect higher-level administrators to lead through such diverse activities as implementing the policies set by the Board, formulating standards for the delivery of professional services, representing the organization to the media, fund raising, "schmoozing" with politicians and community leaders, and guaranteeing the long-range survival of the organization. In contrast, mid-level managers such as supervisors are more likely to lead by assuring that staff do not become so immersed in their work that they lose sight of organizational goals of service, or they may show leadership by allocating resources in ways that promote professional growth and that support lower level staff in their job performance. For them, leadership also may entail such activities as resolving interpersonal conflicts, advocating for better fringe benefits for staff, or promoting pleasant working relationships by scheduling "attitude adjustment" social occasions. Activities of leadership at any level are designed to exert a positive influence over the daily performance of others. But the tasks of leadership tend to vary, depending on the manager's position in the organization.

Theories of Leadership

Both research and leadership theory (as reflected in the literature) have reflected a number of schools of thought over the years. Each has had its vocal advocates and each continues to contribute to our current understanding of leadership.

Trait Theories

Some of the earliest studies of leadership in the United States were based on the assumption that good leadership is synonymous with the possession of certain traits. Research was based in part on studies of persons generally believed to have exhibited good leadership. Attempts were made to identify those "common denominators" possessed by them. One theorist[1] compiled a long list of traits that included such widely diverse attributes as social characteristics, intelligence, and even physical appearance. Another list developed by a different researcher contained such traits as ability to supervise, intelligence, initiative, self-assurance, and individualized approaches to work.[2] Many such lists were constructed. Ability to communicate was mentioned in many of them, as were credibility and vision. All of the lists appeared logical. Unfortunately, they rarely agreed with each other. A few traits (flexibility, initiative, self-confidence, and intelligence) appeared in virtually every list in some related form. Yet this observation was not, in itself, much of a contribution to our understanding of leadership. True, these traits probably are associated with good leadership, but they are also traits common to good followers, good friends, and even to preferred pets! They are assets that increase the likelihood of success in most any arena or at any level in life. Besides, some people who lack one or more of these traits have nevertheless demonstrated themselves to be good leaders. Others have failed as leaders despite the presence of all four of them.

Trait theories of leadership had other problems. They seemed to suggest in a rather undemocratic way that some people are born with the characteristics that are required to become leaders, and some decidedly are not. This is not a view that sits well with social workers, who believe that individuals can change and grow. It also does not hold out much hope for leadership training or education. Instead, selecting a leader would entail simply finding a person who had the requisite traits, rather than working with current staff to acquire the knowledge and skills needed.

Still another shortcoming of the trait theories of leadership relates to the problem of measurement. Most personality characteristics are not easily measured. Researchers have labored for most of the past century to measure intelligence in ways that do not reflect cultural, ethnic, racial, gender, age, or other types of bias. The other traits believed to be common to good leaders have received even less attention. Standardized instruments designed to measure them are probably even less reliable (consistent) and valid than those used to measure intelligence.

Often a thin line separates a desirable leadership trait from a closely related but undesirable one. Often the undesirable trait is really just too much of the desirable one. Efforts at measurement may miss this fine distinction. For example, can we say with certainty that a standardized instrument that claims to measure initiative is really valid, that is, it measures what it claims to measure? Or is it possible that what might appear to be initiative is really an undesirable lack of caution or impetuousness? Similarly, while we may agree that self-confidence is desirable for managers performing leadership functions, arrogance is not. But can we say with certainty that what we are measuring is the former and not the latter? Can we even be certain that a potential leader has not successfully feigned self-confidence? Can we say with certainty that what we are measuring is flexibility and not an unwillingness or inability to enforce needed controls? We know that too much flexibility can be undesirable—but just how much is too much? Measurements of personality characteristics exist, but they are simply not refined to the point where it is possible to use them to make good decisions about the leadership potential of human beings.

Those researchers who advocated the trait theories of leadership contributed to our understanding of leadership. But the traits that they identified are not enough to guarantee good leadership behavior—they just help to explain why some people struggle as leaders and others have an easier time of it. They also may go a long way toward explaining why some managers struggle to promote loyalty both to themselves and to the goals that they are attempting to achieve while other managers find that loyalties occur more naturally.

Behavioral Theories

During the 1950s and 1960s, the behavioral theories of leadership were developed. They were based on the assumption that if one could identify exactly how strong leaders act differently from weak leaders, then we would know what is good leadership behavior. Then others could be taught to behave in a way more consistent with good leadership through training and education.

A major advantage of the behavioral theories of leadership (over the trait theories) is the relative ease with which behavior can be measured (compared to personality characteristics). Unlike traits, behaviors can be seen, recorded, and verified. Current staff can be taught to practice desirable leadership behaviors. Leader replacement can be accomplished by retraining rather than by seeking people with certain characteristics.

Advocates of the behavioral approaches to leadership shared a problem with trait theory researchers, however. They had difficulty in achieving any real consensus about which behaviors are reflective of good leadership and which are not. Early research sought to classify leadership behavior based upon how leaders used the authority granted to them. For example, some leaders tended to be democratic, others authoritarian, and still others seemed to exert little direct influence over subordinates. None of the three types were found to be consistently effective leadership styles or consistently ineffective ones. One type (the autocratic) seemed to be best for productivity in short-term situations, but it seemed to be more injurious to group morale over longer periods of time than was a more democratic style.[3]

Conceptual Models of Leadership

The Managerial Grid

Behavioral approaches to the study of leadership have resulted in a focus on leadership style that has persisted into the 1990s. *The Managerial Grid,* developed in the 1950s and refined in later years by Blake and Mouton[4] was a commonly used framework for examining the different styles of leadership that exist. A later version is called the *Leadership Grid©* and was authored by Blake and McCanse.[5] The authors suggest that leadership style can be plotted along a grid based on behaviors. The points on the grid that represent one's leadership style are based on (1) the degree to which the individual exhibits concern for production and; (2) the degree to which the individual exhibits concern for people.

Individuals can receive a "score" of between 1 and 9 for either behavior. Thus, a manager may be characterized as a 2,6 or a 7,4 and so forth.

Blake and McCanse have identified the characteristics of leaders who fall at some of the most common positions on the grid and assigned labels and descriptions to their leadership styles. For example, 9,1 managers, referred to as having an "authority-compliance" style (those who are autocratic), are concerned primarily with tasks, and much less with people's needs. They control and direct their subordinates with little concern for their personal needs. At the opposite extreme, a 1,9 manager, referred to as having a "country club management" style, offers a very friendly, people-oriented environment, but provides very little emphasis on production. A 9,9 leadership style, described as "team management," places heavy emphasis on both, whereas a 5,5 style, described as "middle of the road," puts a balanced but moderate emphasis on both production and the creation of a supportive work environment.

The Leadership Grid© is useful for identifying the leadership style of a given manager and what that manager offers. It does not suggest how managers can develop a particular style or how an ineffective style can be improved. It also does not seem to assert that any one style of leadership is best overall, although the description of a 9,9 style certainly sounds the most like what modern management theorists advocate. However, descriptions of the other styles also are quite positive—each may be the most appropriate to get the job done in a given situation. Even a 1,1 manager, a leadership style referred to as "impoverished management" may, in very rare situations, be suited to the needs of an organization. For example, it might be appropriate with a staff of "self-starters" who know exactly what needs to be done and just do it. Managers with a 1,1 style offer very little concern for production and very little concern for people. They are active as managers, but just barely.

There is another very useful way in which the Leadership Grid© can be employed. It can be very effective as a way for managers to learn how they are perceived by subordinates. It can sometimes be a real revelation to learn that our own perception of our management style differs markedly from the way subordinates view our approach to management. We may also be surprised to observe the difference in the way that two or more subordinates perceive our style as a manager. This can provide valuable feedback and, in some cases, impetus for needed change. Few of us really have an accurate perception of how we "come across." The Leadership Grid©, plotted by ourselves (how we perceive our style) and by subordinates (how they perceive our style), can produce some interesting and productive insights.

Theory X and Theory Y

Douglas McGregor's Theory X and Theory Y[6] is one of the better known explanations of organizational behavior. In many management textbooks, it is discussed along with Herzberg's or Maslow's theories (Chapter 6) of individual motivation. It is discussed here instead because it seems to be a better indicator of why leaders (managers) treat staff as they do than as an explanation for individual staff behavior.

McGregor proposed that there are two rather diametrically opposed views (theories) of human nature and people's attitudes toward work. Theory X holds that people have an inherent dislike for work and must be threatened and controlled in order to make them be productive. They want security in the form of financial rewards, but dislike responsibility. If a manager adheres to this theory and acts accordingly, staff will eventually lack ambition, act irresponsibly, resist change and prefer to be led rather than to lead. Even if Theory X is not accurate, the manager and the organization (especially if it is highly bureaucratized) will make staff act as if it is—a kind of self-fulfilling prophecy.

How would managers who believe in Theory X act? They would be inclined to use tangible rewards and punishment (or threat of it) to get others to do what needs to be done. They would assume that their authority is resented and would adopt a "we/they" attitude, employing coercion when it might not be needed. They would institute an oppressive, controlling collection of rules and procedures designed to enforce compliance. They would regularly "check up" on subordinates, expecting (perhaps hoping) to catch them in a moment of idleness or following a mistake.

Theory Y, in contrast, assumes that people are willing to work and to accept responsibility. They want to control their own behavior and are capable of creative solutions to problems. Work is a natural activity for them. If committed to a goal, they will willingly do what is required to achieve it without the need for threats of punishment or special rewards. They will seek the authority necessary to do what needs to be done. Most human beings would be perceived as having an underutilized potential for growth, imagination, and creativity; that is, they are motivated by a need for self-actualization (see Chapter 6).

Not surprisingly, managers who possess a Theory Y orientation toward people exert a style of leadership designed to capitalize on what they believe to be true of their subordinates. They act in a way that communicates trust and a belief in their good intentions. They treat staff as valued, responsible team members. They promote staff "ownership" of their work. They assume that subordinates want to work toward organization goal attainment. They would work actively to set up and maintain a work environment that enhances growth and creativity and would use no more restrictive controls than are absolutely necessary.

Of course, purely Theory X and Theory Y approaches to leadership are extremes on a continuum. They rarely, if ever, exist. A purely Theory Y orientation might border on the "Pollyanna." It would produce a leadership style that might be too permissive. It would almost certainly lead to problems and abuses. A purely Theory X orientation would produce a leadership style that would be so repressive and "heavy-handed" that it would almost certainly lead to a breakdown in group morale. The attitudes of most managers (and their related management styles) fall somewhere in between these two extreme orientations.

As social workers, most of us probably tend to be more Theory Y than Theory X in our assumptions about human beings. But as realists we must also acknowledge that it is not unusual to encounter people who look more like Theory X stereotypes. We also become more Theory X or more Theory Y as a result of our life experiences. For example, some social work managers seem to enter large bureaucracies with Theory Y beliefs about people. However, after observing the behaviors (laziness, irresponsibility, resistance to change, and so forth) of some staff, they may become more Theory X in their beliefs about people. (Perhaps, as suggested earlier, it is the bureaucracy that promotes behavior that fits the Theory X stereotype; perhaps only people who fit the stereotype can survive in bureaucracies for very long.) Changes in orientation can occur in the opposite direction too. Sometimes, managers with Theory X orientations are pleasantly surprised to find that their staff is hard-working, eager for responsibility, creative, and so forth. They then change their attitudes about people and become more Theory Y.

McGregor's contribution to our understanding of leadership lies in the insight that, frequently, how we act as leaders is based largely on our perceptions of people and their preferences regarding work. If we as managers allow our assumptions (lying anywhere along the continuum) to dictate our leadership behaviors without bothering to form an accurate assessment of our subordinates are and what motivates them, we are destined to have problems. Leading, like other areas of management and other areas of social work practice, is a people skill. It requires a knowledge of human behavior and the capacity to recognize individual employee differences. It also requires us as managers to be flexible enough to adapt our leadership style to the needs of individuals and of situations.

Contingency Theories

There is another whole "school" of leadership that says, in effect, good leadership depends on the needs of the situation. The trait approaches to leadership fell short of providing a comprehensive understanding of what makes a good leader. Leadership also is not simply synonymous with acting in certain ways. Contingency theories of motivation evolved from the observed shortcomings of the other two leadership theories and are an extension of them.

Ralph Stogdill conducted leadership studies over several decades. In many ways his conclusions about leadership paralleled the changing attitudes about leadership that occurred from the time that he first studied leadership until his later work. As we noted earlier, Stogdill began as an advocate of the trait theories in the 1940s.[7] He later focused more on behaviors, identifying two behaviors, consideration and structure, as essential to good leadership.[8] These two behaviors are very similar to the two axes on the Blake and Mouton managerial grid, concern for people and concern for production. Consideration can be understood as, for example, acting friendly and warm to subordinates and being open to suggestions. Structure relates to a regular emphasis on budgets, deadlines, and objectives. It is often difficult for the social worker as manager to find the appropriate balance between consideration and structure. Subordinates love consideration, but one's superiors may view it with suspicion or perceive it as being too "nice" or allowing too much freedom for the requirements of a situation. Conversely, use of structure is well liked by one's superiors, but it can be viewed unnecessarily controlling by subordinates. Can a manager really offer both simultaneously, or are the two behaviors really in conflict with each other?

Eventually, in his later work, Stogdill found a way to resolve the theoretical dilemma of how managers can offer the optimal amounts of both consideration and structure. He concluded that the best mix of the two (that is, good leadership) depends on situational factors. Sometimes more structure is needed; sometimes more consideration. This line of thinking, the *contingency approach,* takes the position that a person is not inherently a good or a bad leader, or a capable or an incompetent one. Good or bad leadership depends on the leadership qualities of an individual and how well they match the kind of leadership that is needed. Characteristics or behaviors that meet the leadership needs of one situation may not be right for another. There are no characteristics or behaviors that guarantee that one will be a good leader in any situation. However, there are some (for example, an inability to provide either consideration or structure) that will almost invariably produce failure as a leader.

Generally, nations, communities, and organizations have selected leaders who they believe possess those leadership qualities that are needed at the time. Yet the same qualities may have made them ill-suited as leaders at another time and place. For example, Winston Churchill, Margaret Thatcher, Golda Meir, Nelson Mandela, Adolf Hitler, Mahatma Gandhi, Ayatollah Khomieni, Saddam Hussein, Mullah Omar—all of these people (despite our personal judgments of them) fit the leadership needs of their respective nations at the time.

In twentieth-century U.S. history, Franklin D. Roosevelt had the leadership qualities necessary to restore the confidence of a nation reeling from the Great Depression. John F. Kennedy's relatively young, vigorous, and idealistic leadership was what was desired and needed following the more paternal style of the Eisenhower years. Gerald Ford's leadership with its emphasis on integrity and openness was what was needed in the years after Watergate, despite the fact that in other times Ford might have been viewed as an ineffective leader. A nation disillusioned with inflation and cynicism welcomed the leadership style of Ronald Reagan and re-elected him by an overwhelming margin in 1984. Reagan's characteristic optimism, his belief in traditional values, and his conservative appeals to those who had come to resent high taxes, social programs, and minority advances made him a natural leader for the 1980s. Only late in his second term of office did the "Teflon" begin to wear thin as his laid-back approach to management and misplaced trust of subordinates became increasingly problematic. Reagan's approaches to leadership were no different in 1988 than they were in 1980. But conditions had changed and they were no longer what was needed and wanted. George H. W. Bush's early popularity was largely attributable to his more "hands-on" management style, a welcomed change from the Reagan administrations. His failure to be re-elected in 1992 and Bill Clinton's continued popularity in 1996 tell us what were perceived to be the leadership qualities that were needed in those years. Following Clinton's embarrassing personal problems, the voting public (or at least almost 50 percent of them) elected George W. Bush in what may have been a wish to return to the values and policies of the conservative Reagan–Bush years of the 1980s.

Contingency theories of management emphasize that leadership traits and behaviors are more or less desirable, depending on the situation. There are certain situations in which consideration by leaders is more important to organizational functioning than structure; sometimes, it is the other way around. For example, when strangers must work together and when time deadlines or other emergency situations exist, it is probably structure that is needed most from the leader. In related research in a social agency, York[9] found that, in times of rapid change, concern for production may be a more valued leadership characteristic than concern for people.

Fred Fiedler, the theoretician most frequently associated with the contingency theories of leadership, sees a leader's capacity to influence subordinates as largely a matter of fit among the leader's style and personality, the characteristics of the work group, and the needs of the work situation.[10] Fiedler observed that the attitudes and needs of individual managers tend to change little; leaders do not adapt well to changing situations. He concluded that it is probably more efficient for organizations to create managerial positions to fit the leadership characteristics of existing personnel than to try to change people through training to fit the needs of existing positions. As managers, a good portion of our management style may be a "given." But while our style may be reasonably "fixed," there are skills that can be learned (for example, delegation, grant writing, constructing budgets, and so forth).

Other Variables in the Leadership Equation

While management style is an important part of the complex equation that is leadership within organizations, we also must remember that there are many other pieces. A manager's superior (or, in the case of a chief executive, the Board of Directors) also possesses a "style" and definite expectations that must be understood and addressed. The organization itself, primarily through its mission, goals and objectives, also suggests what is expected of a leader. Even one's peers, other managers at the same organizational level, also cannot be ignored. A manager cannot afford to lead in a way that is too out-of-step with how peers are handling the function of leadership. When this happens, morale problems may occur. Staff may conclude that "they have it better than we have it."

Subordinates are another very important part of the leadership equation that is often overlooked. Their own styles and expectations as followers can have a great effect on a manager's ability to lead. Successful leaders have good followers; unsuccessful ones do not.

If social workers as managers are to lead successfully, they must be able to identify the elements of good followership and to promote it among staff. Generally those same traits and behaviors that make good followers are the same ones that make good leaders. In the same way that leadership skills can be developed, followership skills can also be developed.

There are many different ways in which one can follow. Each can be more or less suited to the style and demands of the leader. For example, many social workers in public human service organizations have experienced only authoritarian leadership styles. They have learned from experience that good followership entailed primarily doing what their superior told them to do, doing it promptly, doing it without questioning or thinking, and so forth. But when they encounter a new leader who advocates a participatory management approach, the old definition of good followership no longer applies. In fact, their old good followership behaviors will be dysfunctional both for them and for the new leader. A whole new set of expectations (for what constitutes good followership) must be learned and old expectations and behaviors must be unlearned.

Fortunately, there are some characteristics and behaviors that need not change when a different approach to leadership is implemented. Some of what constitutes good followership is pretty universal. (We will recall that there is even limited agreement on what are desirable leadership traits and behaviors in most any situation.) There is limited consensus as to what characteristics seem to contribute to (but do not guarantee) good followership in all working relationships. For example, a good follower is dependable, is a good team player, possesses needed technical knowledge, uses sound judgment, makes rational decisions, keeps leaders informed of developments, knows when to ask for assistance from the leader, and, not surprisingly, understands and supports organizational missions and goals. Good followers must be able to manage themselves; but they also need to know how to manage their job and to manage their boss.

For the good follower, self-management involves the ability to handle relationships with clients and co-workers and the ability to take responsibility for one's own feelings, decisions and behaviors. It involves maintaining a confident, positive attitude toward one's work and a belief in the goals and objectives of the organization.

Job management involves the skillful organization and management of time, duties, and workload. It entails knowing how to find and access needed knowledge for doing one's job. It also entails skill in problem solving and making the relatively routine situations that go with the job so that the follower need not be overly dependent on the leader.

Boss management requires followers to be able to accurately read and assess both the boss's strengths and weaknesses and their own as well as those of other members of the work group. A good follower will find ways to complement the boss's functioning and to thereby improve the functioning of the entire work unit. Boss management is closely related to a concept called "managing up" that has been formulated by Austin. He notes that managing up not only helps the boss but also the follower. If the boss does a better job, the subordinate's job is made easier and both look good.[11]

Followers generally lack the authority that their bosses possess (unless it is delegated to them). But they influence how well their bosses are able to perform their jobs. They influence both what gets done and how well it gets done through their followership. Generally, leadership style influences what constitutes good followership. But influence can flow in the other direction too. The followership style of subordinates sometimes can influence the leadership style of their boss. For example, an inexperienced and overly dependent group of followers can elicit certain leader behaviors such as verifying compliance with rules, giving detailed instructions, or allowing very little autonomy in decision making. The leader may not fall naturally into this type of management style but may view it as necessary, given the style of followership that exists. Similarly, a leader who naturally tends to be very controlling may loosen up a little as followers demonstrate that they can assume more responsibility, have no problems in abiding by rules, or otherwise convince their boss that they function just fine on their own most of the time.

Good followers can exert positive influences on the work environment and on organization goal attainment because they contribute a valuable perspective that managers may lack. Followers are often in closer touch with client services in a human service agency than are leaders. From their perspective, they may be able to identify problems when they can still be easily addressed. This can save the leader from having to address more severe problems later. They can shape the work environment by providing advice and information to their bosses, helping them to stay in touch with "life in the trenches."

Creating the Right Organizational Climate

We are all familiar with the term climate as it relates to cities or other geographical entities. The term is also used in describing organizations or their subunits. It refers to the feeling that one gets while working somewhere. Like the weather, that feeling can be warm and hospitable; it can also be cold and hostile. Of course, like the weather, it can be too warm, almost stifling.

Ideally, the climate of an organization should be pleasant and supportive of good work, People want to be a part of the organization or the unit. Usually it takes a while to get an accurate reading of organizational climate; but, sometimes one can spend five minutes in a work setting and accurately sense it.

Effective leaders recognize that productivity and performance are influenced by the climate of an organization, that is, the overall environment in which people do their jobs. They strive to create a work environment that is as favorable as it can be, given the nature of the work that must be done and the needs of those doing the work. They understand that even undesirable tasks do not seem as bad in a favorable organizational climate; even a task that should be enjoyable can be unpleasant in an unfavorable one. We will examine some of the characteristics that generally are found within favorable organizational climates.

Teamwork

When they perform leadership functions, managers function much like athletic coaches or captains. They endeavor to make both leaders and followers (and we all are both on occasion) feel as if they all are members of a team, working together to attain common goals. Leaders help others to see that all benefit. If they work cooperatively toward these goals, it is more likely that they will be attained through team play.

Healthy and successful organizations are those in which all participants have a sense of "team" and appreciate the value of teamwork. Managers sometimes devote staff development time to sessions that teach about teamwork and contain various team building exercises designed to demonstrate that some tasks can only be accomplished by teamwork. Such exercises can make a point. However, they are not a substitute for actual work-related tasks that demonstrate the value of teamwork and provide practice in working as a team. Teamwork can be felt in the way that staff approach various situations. Members work cooperatively and for the common good. A lack of team work similarly can be sensed within other organizations. What are the differences in the way people act? Figure 10.1 gives some examples of how the presence or absence of a sense of teamwork can produce different responses to the same situations.

Mutual Respect and Confidence

A work climate conducive to productivity reflects mutual respect and confidence. There is an absence of any unnecessary reminders of the power differential that exists. Leaders are charged with certain responsibilities and with making certain decisions from a perspective somewhat different from subordinates. But this does not mean that they are more intelligent, more knowledgeable about everything, or that only their perception of a situation is the correct one. They may be no more experienced, creative, or better-informed about an issue than those who they supervise. They simply occupy a different position, do a different job, and make decisions with access to different information. Failure to remember this can seriously damage morale.

FIGURE 10.1 *Different Responses to the Same Situations: Organizational Climates with Teamwork (T) and Those without (NT)*

1. People see things going wrong.
   - (T) "Let's deal with it now. It may only get worse."
   - (NT) "Forget about it. It hasn't affected me yet."
2. There is a job to be done.
   - (T) "How can we get it done?"
   - (NT) "Whose job is it anyway?"
3. A co-worker receives recognition.
   - (T) "Congratulations! This makes us all look good!"
   - (NT) "Let me tell you why it is no big deal."
4. A suggestion for improvement is made.
   - (T) "Let's consider it. They may be right."
   - (NT) "What will the boss want?"
5. Someone offers help with a problem.
   - (T) "Thanks. Maybe I can return the favor someday."
   - (NT) "Its not your problem. Why do you want to help me?"
6. A mistake is made.
   - (T) "What can we all learn from this?"
   - (NT) "Who did it and what will happen to them?"
7. A personal conflict occurs.
   - (T) "Can we get together and talk this out? This is doing nobody any good."
   - (NT) "I don't get mad; I get even."
8. A suggestion is made.
   - (T) "Thanks. I'll certainly consider it."
   - (NT) "Mind your own business. I don't tell you how to do your job."
9. A job is performed well.
   - (T) "I'm proud to have been a part of it."
   - (NT) "Who will get the credit?"
10. A job is performed poorly.
    - (T) "We have to share the responsibility and keep it from happening again."
    - (NT) "Who is to blame for this?"

Managers usually are more similar to those who work under them than they are dissimilar. It is easy to forget this in one's role as manager and to make erroneous assumptions about the motivation, capacities, and knowledge of people who occupy a lower place on an organizational chart. Individuals treated as inferiors frequently respond as inferiors. There is no reason why managers, in performing their leadership functions, need to treat others in a condescending manner when their inferior status is limited to only one rather narrow sphere of life—their place on the organizational chart. Subtle and less-than-subtle reminders of the relative status of subordinates are only appropriate in matters that relate to this sphere. Even then, such reminders should be used only as a last resort. They usually are appropriate only when other efforts to influence, those that convey mutual respect, have failed. Reminders of subordinate status can quickly injure the mutual respect that is critical to maintaining a healthy work climate.

Mutual confidence is closely related to mutual respect. It evolves in those work settings where the leader and other staff have had experience working together successfully. To achieve it, leaders need to develop a "track record" for competence and skilled leadership under pressure. In turn, subordinates need to show that they too can "deliver" under stress. Confidence also involves feelings of integrity and trustworthiness on the part of all parties involved. There must be a shared understanding that both leaders and their subordinates will be judged fairly. We discussed the need for this perception among staff in Chapter 7. But perceptions of fairness (or lack of it) run in both directions. Managers are also sensitive to how their own performance is evaluated by their subordinates. They may receive regularly scheduled and written evaluations by subordinates (a practice that is growing in popularity). Or their "evaluations" may consist of overheard comments made by staff within the organization or staff comments made in the community that are reported back to them.

Managers should not be fair to subordinates only because they wish to be treated fairly in turn. In organizations, as in other spheres of life, fairness often begets fairness. If we are fair to others, they are generally fair to us. However, as some managers have learned, treating staff fairly is no guarantee that they will respond in kind. Some people seem to resent managers and are unfairly critical of them no matter how they are treated. (Perhaps, they just resent the power differential that exists.) Others seem to perceive fairness on the part of a manager as a sign of weakness or that they have been successful in intimidating the manager. For example, they may perceive a second chance following a costly error as an indication that a manager is unwilling or unable to punish unacceptable behaviors. It often is difficult to be fair to staff when one knows that they are not being fair in return. But it must be done anyway. The real reasons managers treat others fairly is because (1) it is the right thing to do; (2) they need to develop a reputation for fairness to be able to manage effectively; and (3) it sets a good example for others.

Understanding of Respective Roles

A climate of mutual fairness requires an understanding of the respective roles of all parties. Do subordinates really understand the responsibilities of the leader? If not, they may evaluate the leader's performance unfairly based on mistaken notions of what they think the leader should be doing and how the leader should be doing it. Leaders need to dispel the mystery that often surrounds the role of managers. While they may have different perspectives on some things and go about their jobs a little differently than subordinates, much of what people do is (or should be) directed at achieving the same objectives. It helps to remind others of this sometimes.

Understanding, like fairness works both ways in those organizations where leaders have created and nurtured a good organizational climate. Managers should remain in touch with their staff. A leader should understand what a subordinate does and, perhaps more importantly, know how it feels to do it. While we would not argue that social workers as managers should always have previously occupied lower-ranking positions in the hierarchy, it helps to have this experience. If they have not had it, it is essential that they get close enough to the jobs of their subordinates to have a real understanding of the rewards and difficulties that go with their jobs. Even those managers who have come up

CASE EXAMPLE • *A Missed Leadership Opportunity*

Amber was a supervisor in a large daycare center that employed several social workers. One of the social workers that she supervised, Jerome, was accused of sexually abusing a 4-year-old girl who was a client at the center. His accuser, the child's parent, demanded an investigation. The local child-protection unit of the Department of Social Services thoroughly investigated the complaint, concluded that there was no indication that abuse had occurred, and closed the case for lack of evidence. No criminal charges were filed. Jerome, who had been suspended from work until he was cleared of charges, was reinstated. The director of the agency called him in and expressed her delight that Jerome, who was regarded as an excellent worker, had been found innocent. She asserted her complete confidence in him. Jerome returned to his job and again demonstrated the competence and dedication that had been reflected in his previous work.

A year later, Jerome's former wife sued for custody of their 3-year-old daughter. In a deposition, she charged that Jerome had "inappropriately fondled" the child during a recent visit and that she suspected that he had been sexually abusing her in the past. She also initiated criminal charges against him that were reported in a Saturday edition of the local newspaper. A member of the board of directors, who knew about the previous charge, called the director at 7 AM on Saturday.

The director immediately called Amber and demanded that she meet with Jerome at 9 o'clock Monday morning to learn more about the situation. Despite the fact that the newspaper notice gave few details and did not mention Jerome's place of employment, the director was fearful of a telephone call from a parent and wanted to have all available information to be able to respond to inquiries.

Amber was very anxious as she anticipated her meeting with Jerome. The meeting did not go well. Jerome unequivocally denied any wrongdoing. He had a ready explanation

for his former wife's charges. His wife's sister had recently been involved in a custody battle and had gained custody of her children after threatening to charge her husband with sexual abuse. He explained that his former wife, who had threatened to "get" him anyway, was simply trying a tactic that had worked well for her sister.

Amber felt herself getting annoyed with Jerome's seeming lack of concern about the charges. She didn't seem to be able to get him to understand the potential harm that the allegations might cause the center. He remarked that he felt that Amber was "making a big deal over nothing." He demanded, "So, what do you expect me to do?" Amber replied, "Perhaps you should consider resigning. If the director asks for your resignation, I certainly cannot support you." Jerome left and slammed the door. Later, the director expressed satisfaction with the way that Amber had handled the matter.

Jerome tendered his resignation. But before he left, he gave the other staff his explanation of his wife's charges and also told them that Amber had requested his resignation. Three other professional staff members came to see Amber to request that she ask Jerome to reconsider. She stated simply that the decision was his and that the matter was closed.

On his last day on the job, Jerome came in for his exit interview. He told Amber that he had generally been pleased with his job at the center and with her as his supervisor. But he felt he had not been treated fairly when his wife's charges were made public. In his opinion, Amber should have supported him since "people are considered innocent until proven guilty."

By this time, Amber was no longer angry with Jerome. She told him that she personally believed that he was innocent, as did the director and other staff. But as a manager, she had to consider the best interests of the center, which, she feared, could be destroyed by charges of sexual abuse. Amber spoke

CASE EXAMPLE • *(continued)*

honestly and sincerely, but Jerome was not impressed. He left with a look of disgust, shaking his head. Amber was satisfied that the whole messy business was over. It was not.

Within the next three weeks, the other two men on the staff resigned. In their exit interviews, they told Amber that the job just was "not worth the risk." They knew that, as males, they were particularly vulnerable to reputation-destroying charges of child abuse. But prior to Jerome's problems, they had believed that, if charged, the administration would come to their defense and support. They no longer believed this. They stated that they could not work for a leader who would not serve as their advocate when needed.

The departure of the three men and the general animosity of the remaining staff made Amber's job very difficult. She hired two new social workers (both female; no males applied) but both the two new employees quickly adopted the attitude toward Amber that the

others exhibited. She suspected that they had been "oriented" by Megan, the staff member who had been most openly hostile to her.

Amber held a special meeting of her staff to discuss morale problems. She stated that she felt that she owed them an explanation for her actions. She told them that, while she could not reveal the specifics of their conversations, she believed that Jerome's resignation was best for the center. Besides, she emphasized, she had not asked for his resignation; it had been his decision. Megan sarcastically replied, "Obviously, Jerome remembered your conversation a little differently."

The meeting accomplished little. If anything, the staff were even more angry. When three additional months passed and she began to feel even more isolated from the group, Amber left to take another job. The staff clearly no longer trusted her and she felt that her ability to be an effective supervisor had been irreparably damaged.

Discussion Questions

1. Was Amber's suggestion that Jerome resign appropriate? Why or why not?
2. What were Amber's ethical obligations to Jerome, to her agency, and to the agency's clients? Why was this an ethical conflict for her?
3. What other conflicts did Amber face as a manager?
4. Were the other staff justified in reacting to Amber's handling of the situation the way they did? Why or why not?
5. What might have been a better way for Amber to handle her meeting with Jerome?

through the ranks often have a tendency to forget what their old jobs were like and to lose sight of the pressures that govern day-to-day activities. As leaders, managers should strive to stay in touch. This may entail getting out of one's office and just stopping and talking to staff about their jobs from time to time. This is what has come to be referred to as "managing by wandering around."

Staff members need to know that, despite assuming a job with major management responsibilities, their boss can still empathize with their concerns. Unfortunately, assumption of the role of manager often creates a distance between manager and subordinates that the manager neither sought nor anticipated. This phenomenon probably results in part from the assumptions of staff that managers are not interested in the work of their subordinates and in part from a natural tendency of managers to become emersed in their management functions. They forget what it was like before they became managers. For example, a manager who is praised by the Board of Directors for the recent development of a new program is likely to continue to propose more new programs. The manager may have difficulty understanding why lower-level staff are less euphoric about heading off in still more new directions, especially if no new staff are to be hired. But if the manager has not lost touch with the needs and priorities of staff, their attitudes will be more predictable and understandable. Ways can be found to reduce the resistance to any new programs that must be developed. Should the manager decide not to implement the proposed program because it is clearly not in the best interests of or within the interest area of staff, it would be wise to let them know of the decision and why it was made. It is always a good idea to let people see that one remains sensitive to their needs.

Advocacy

In an organization with a healthy organizational climate, leaders sometimes serve as advocates for staff, even risking their own position of favor with higher-ups to battle for the rights and well-being of their subordinates. It is very easy for managers to slip quickly into a comfortable stance that entails courting the favor of superiors while showing little regard for the special interests of subordinates. The evaluations of subordinates generally represent little more than feedback to them. However, their careers are generally dependent on evaluations by superiors. Rewards in the form of praise, promotion, and salary increases are given for compliance with the wishes of superiors, not for doing battle with them in an advocacy role.

It is easy to rationalize that, since the good will of a board of directors or a chief executive officer is generally desirable for all persons in an organization, avoidance of conflict with one's bosses is in everyone's best interests. So why, risk antagonizing them? Besides, the best interests of the manager are synonymous with the best interests of subordinates, right? Not always. Managers who do not occasionally take a stand to advocate for staff interests are reneging on the responsibilities of a leader. They will eventually pay a price in the form of a loss of respect and confidence. Respect will only begin to be restored when they start advocating for staff interests in situations where they have nothing personally to gain and may even be inviting the temporary disfavor of their superiors.

Social workers who assume management responsibilities are still social workers. They still have an obligation to be an advocate for change that will benefit clients and the society as a whole. Because many managers are employed in bureaucracies, they are sometimes stereotyped as conservative and as attempting to maintain the status quo. However, research has demonstrated that this perception is no longer valid, if it ever was. It was found that higher-level "administrators devote more time to advocacy and are more politically active than other social workers."[12]

While involved in advocacy within the organization and within it's task environment, managers also need to help others to fulfill their professional obligations as advocates for change. Being a good role model may not be enough. Specific actions should be taken. Managers may need to write advocacy expectations into staff job descriptions and develop policies to protect staff who advocate for change. It also may help to provide continuing education on advocacy to staff to teach them which procedures are most effective and what legal protections are available.

Maximum Autonomy

Another characteristic of a human service organization with a healthy climate is the presence of autonomy at all levels. Because professional staff and other personnel frequently possess widely diverse knowledge and skills, considerable autonomy is both possible and desirable. The leader should seek to create an environment that fosters independence.

An optimal level of autonomy is one in which persons are constrained in the use of their professional judgment no more than is absolutely necessary. The goal is to promote, not to stifle, creative thinking and decision making. Leaders need to sort out carefully those activities where creativity is not desirable and to set up appropriate planning vehicles (Chapter 4) and controls (Chapter 9). But in those activities where creativity can and should be employed, support for it should be offered. Staff need to feel free to act without always consulting others first. As long as a decision or behavior is within policies and guidelines, they need to be able to assume that they will be supported, even if things go wrong.

Good Communication

The type and purpose of communication within an organization is a major factor in shaping its climate. Communication occurs in two forms. In its more desirable form, it consists of information directly related to and supportive of the organization's mission. For example, it may consist of policy information, advice on how to do a job, and feedback about progress toward desired ends. There are many different vehicles for desirable communication. For example, it can be received by notices on bulletin boards, memos, newsletters, staff meetings, phone, or electronic mail.

A second form of communication that exists within organizations does not relate directly to the organization's mission. It consists of emotional reactions to what is occurring within the organization and the ways that they are shared with others. This type of communication is not desirable; it often has a negative effect on group and individual morale.

Formal Communication Breakdowns.   As a leader, the manager's task is to promote the flow of good, useful, supportive communication while limiting the flow of communication that is destructive of morale and that sidetracks individual and group energies that could be put to more constructive use. This would seem to be a goal that is easily attainable. But why do efforts to promote positive communication so often fail? Sometimes it is the fault of managers who initiate communication—messages are not well thought out or articulated. Why? Managers may assume that the receiver will understand the jargon that they use or they may assume that the receiver will want to understand. They may assume that staff members will regularly read the bulletin board for clarification of their message (they do not). Managers may mistakenly believe that a receiver will read or hear the entire message before concluding what the essence of the communication is, or they may even assume that communication is unnecessary because "everyone already knows."

Communication of even well-articulated messages can break down and cause problems. Anyone who has ever played the childhood game where participants whisper a message from one person to another around a circle will recall that the message received back from the initiator rarely bears much resemblance to the one given. This occurs without any malevolence or self-interest on the part of those doing the communicating. Within organizations, this "line loss" may be unintentional and a function of the number of times a message is transferred. Or it may result from an intentional selective emphasis, addition, or omission designed to modify the message to reflect what the person relaying it wanted it to say.

The presence of a power differential also can hinder good communication from managers to subordinates. Even a well-stated message can be misconstrued because of who initiated it and the sender's assumed intent. For example, a manager may intend to make a suggestion and may make one, but the suggestion may be perceived as an order. For example, the request to be a little more careful about copy costs may be incorrectly perceived as a warning that a time of austerity (and possible staff reduction) is imminent. Panic may result.

The fact that a power differential exists between a manager and subordinates can also lead to the manager being cut off from needed information. Managers have power and the authority needed to use it. They can take information and use it to harm those less powerful. Staff may wonder how information will be used by the manager. Will admission of a mistake or a request for help be construed as useful communication or will it be viewed as evidence of incompetence that will be brought up at evaluation time? If the latter is believed to be the case, needed communication with the manager may not occur.

How much and how accurately subordinates communicate with a leader is largely dependent on the leader's past reactions to subordinates' communication. If subordinates reported bad news, was it responded to with anger or defensiveness? Was the messenger "beheaded," or was the messenger thanked for providing the needed information? Did communication about a problem that another worker was having result in extra work for the messenger? Were confidences kept as requested, or did the manager reveal the source of information resulting in alienation of the messenger from peers? (The author once registered dissatisfaction with a supervisor about a secretary's breach of confidentiality. The communication was made with all assurances of anonymity. The next day, the secretary accosted the author with the statement, "I hear you don't like the way I do my job!") Such responses are destructive of trust for the manager and will almost certainly result in future elimination of or distortion of communication. The communicator is likely to say, "I learned my lesson—next time I'll keep it to myself." This only contributes to an ever-growing cycle of distrust between managers and others within the organization.

Promoting Good Communication.   When formal channels are found to be untrustworthy, informal channels of communication will inevitably develop to fill the void. Managers then usually have little control over what is transferred. It can become a dangerous combination of half-truths, rumors, and even information that is simply wrong. Worst of all, the manager may not even know what information is being sent along informal channels.

What can a manager do to enhance good formal communication and reduce the likelihood of dangerous informal communication? Once again, we come back to that critical element for a healthy organizational climate and for effective management—trust. Both trust and distrust come from past experience. Trust that promotes productive and accurate formal communication must be built over time. Managers must learn to trust the information received from those both above and below them on the organizational chart. They must also communicate the importance of trust to others. A manager who displays little trust will eventually receive little trust in return. Suspicion, hostility, and resentment promote an in-kind response.

In a healthy work climate, trust fosters desirable formal communication and even desirable informal communication in both directions. (The latter supplements and reinforces the former.) Good leaders freely share needed information regularly and honestly. They tell subordinates what they need to know to do their jobs. They also communicate a belief that errors and problems will occur, but it is always best if those who must and will eventually know about them (themselves) find out as soon as possible. Managers who first learn about problems from superiors or a hostile public have reason to be irate with subordinates who failed to inform them. Those who are warned about problems can at least be prepared to defend themselves and others. They are not caught off-guard.

Staff should understand that there are rewards, not punishment, for good, accurate communication, regardless of the message. Only failure to communicate needed information is intolerable. The attitude of a "Theory Y manager" toward communication is that it is a necessary and a desirable vehicle that derives from the demands and expectations of a job. It is used to support the work of other staff and of managers themselves. This is a positive attitude based on the assumption that human beings value their work, want to perform well, and will use communication to help them achieve organizational objectives. This attitude results in the use of communication for the mutual benefit of all staff in doing their jobs.

Unfortunately, communication is also used by managers with more of a Theory X orientation. They have learned that communication (or lack of it) can be a powerful vehicle for control and manipulation of staff. It can also be used to remind staff of their subordinate position. Withholding of information can concentrate power (knowledge *is* power) in the hands of the manager. Propaganda and misinformation can be used to change people. A manager can "leak" a possible future change to get a staff reaction before making a final decision or otherwise use communication in a way that is demeaning and manipulative.

A particularly destructive form of communication by some managers involves the use of numerous confidants. Believing that staff can be easily manipulated, managers have been known to confide in several different staff members, implying to them all that they alone are special and uniquely worthy of trust. They may criticize and even ridicule other staff. In the short run, this behavior can co-opt staff members who may be impressed and pleased with their "special" status. But before long, they begin to notice that they are not the only participants in the game. They conclude (correctly) that if their leaders are critical of others to them, they are probably also critical of them to others. They feel manipulated and perceive that their intelligence has been insulted. They become resentful, and trust is eroded.

The prescription for the manager should be obvious. Avoid communicating information about problems of staff performance to anyone other than the individuals themselves. If others must be consulted, it should be the manager's peers, or better yet, one's own supervisor. Never communicate to subordinates that they are any more "special" than any other person and avoid any overtures on the part of staff members to form a relationship that sets them apart from their peers. The temptation to use communication as power is tempting, but it should be avoided.

Feedback to Managers

One type of communication essential to a healthy work climate is upward feedback, which tells managers, among other things, how well they have done their jobs. In their role as managers and functioning as leaders, social workers can easily slip into a pattern of weighing more heavily the feedback received from those who present a more positive, flattering picture of their leadership than information from those who are more critical. It is definitely more pleasant to receive (and to give) favorable feedback than unfavorable feedback, but both types of communication are essential.

There is a tendency on the part of some managers to surround themselves with people who think like they do. Naturally, such people tend to admire them and their work. The admiration may be genuine or it may be the flattery of a sycophant who hopes to profit by meeting the need of the manager for flattery. However, a person who thinks and/ or states that a manager is the most brilliant and skillful individual whom they have ever had the pleasure of knowing is really not a very useful source of information. Consciously or unconsciously, such people are likely to screen and shield the manager from needed criticism. They may also tend to impugn the motives of others who try to offer well-intended, unsolicited criticism.

If managers are receiving many more compliments than critical questions, this could mean that they are doing a good job. Or, it could mean that their subordinates are not doing theirs. However, if managers find themselves listening primarily to those who think that they "hung the moon" and are distancing themselves even further from those who occasionally take the time and risk disfavor to be critical, they should view this as a warning. Perhaps their need for compliments has become more important than the need for valid feedback. Social workers as managers need to know what they have done well so that they can do it again, but they also need to know when they make mistakes (and we all make them) so that they can avoid repeating them. They must make a constant effort to keep open all lines of communication, not just the ones that bring the feedback that they like to hear.

One trend that we briefly mentioned earlier that emerged in the 1990s may be making it more and more difficult for managers to avoid feedback from their critics. While, historically, evaluation has been a one-way process with managers evaluating their staff in a "top-down" model (Chapter 7), an increasing number of organizations are now requiring that staff provide (usually anonymously) evaluations of their boss. The evaluations or a summary of them generally are sent directly to their boss's superiors and then shared with the managers as part of their own performance evaluations. In the case of the very top level managers, evaluations by staff may go directly to them or may even be submitted to some other individual or group such as the organization's board. This trend has one distinct benefit. The managers at least get to know what all of their subordinates really think of them as managers—not just what a few might risk saying directly. The managers can respond by making adjustments in their approach to management or choose to ignore the feedback (perhaps at some risk to their own career).

It is hard to argue with the notion of two-way evaluation and feedback. It only seems fair that those who are being evaluated should have the opportunity to evaluate their boss's performance as managers. Two-way evaluation also would seem to have the potential to increase accountable behavior by managers who know that evaluation by subordinates will occur. However, like many trends that should promote positive change, new problems may be created. A manager, fearing a negative evaluation by staff, may not do a job that should be done (e.g., reprimanding staff, denying a subordinate a merit pay increase, or giving a subordinate a justifiably low staff evaluation) because the manager believes that staff may retaliate when it is time for him or her to be evaluated. As two-way evaluations become more commonplace, will managers be derelict in their responsibilities? Will they take the self-serving road and attempt to manipulate and "play to" the wishes of staff in order to court high evaluations by them? Will a "quid pro quo" agreement become common whereby staff evaluations will become even more inflated than they currently are in exchange for good evaluations of managers' performance by their staff? We can only hope that people will continue to do what is in the best interest of the organization and its clients and will not succumb to these temptations.

Summary

Leadership was described as the manager's conscious efforts to influence other persons within the organization to engage willingly in those behaviors that contribute to the attainment of organizational goals. We acknowledged that leadership overlaps with the other management functions and that, for many people, leadership and management are virtually synonymous.

Chapter 10 examined efforts to understand what makes some people good leaders while others are less successful in their leadership efforts. The contributions and shortcomings of the trait, behavioral, and contingency theories of leadership were summarized. Leadership style was discussed, but it was emphasized that it is only one variable in what might constitute good leadership in a given work situation.

It was suggested that, in any situation, good leadership requires the creation and maintenance of an organizational climate that is conducive to goal attainment. The elements of that climate were proposed. They include teamwork, mutual respect and confidence, understanding of respective roles, advocacy, maximum autonomy, good communication, and valid feedback to managers.

Endnotes

1. Ralph Stogdill, "Personal Factors Associated with Leadership," *Journal of Psychology,* 25 (1948): 35–71.

2. E. E. Ghiselli, "Managerial Talent," *American Psychologist,* XVI (1963): 632–641.

3. Fremont Kast and James Rosenzweig, *Organization and Management: A Systems Approach,* 2nd ed. (New York: McGraw-Hill, 1974), p. 349.

4. Robert Blake, and Jane Mouton, *The Managerial Grid III: The Key to Leadership Excellence* (Houston, TX: Gulf Publishing Co., 1985).

5. Robert R. Blake, and Anne Adams McCanse, *Leadership Dilemmas—Grid Solutions* (Houston, TX: Gulf Publishing Company, 1991).

6. Douglas McGregor, *The Human Side of Enterprise* (New York: McGraw-Hill, 1960).

7. Stogdill, "Personal Factors," *op. cit.*

8. Ralph Stogdill, *Handbook of Leadership: A Survey of Theory and Research* (New York: Free Press, 1974).

9. Reginald York, "Can Change Be Effectively Managed?" *Administration in Social Work,* 1(2), (Summary 1977): 196.

10. Fred Fiedler, *A Theory of Leadership Effectiveness* (New York: McGraw-Hill, 1967).

11. Michael Austin, "Managing Up: Relationship Building Between Middle Management and Top Management." Presentation at the National Association of Social Workers Annual Conference. New Orleans, September 12, 1987.

12. Mark Ezell, "Administrators as Advocates," *Administration in Social Work,* 15 (1991): 15.

Part **III**

Completing the Management Picture

The five management functions that we described in the previous chapters represent most of what management involves for a social worker. However, there are a few more tasks that are so important that they deserve special attention. These are described in Chapter 11. They help to present a more complete picture of the job of manager. Chapter 12 further enriches that picture with special emphasis on the intrapersonal and interpersonal stresses usually associated with the role of manager. It draws upon material in earlier chapters to help the reader decide whether increased management responsibilities should be sought. Of course, whether a promotion is offered and accepted or not, every social worker will continue to spend a greater or lesser part of the day as a manager. Therefore, some final suggestions for developing and recognizing one's management style are offered, along with some practical ideas for fostering a personal identification as a manager.

11

Other Important Management Tasks

Within human service organizations, there are some tasks that have historically involved only those at the highest management levels of the organization. Tasks such as financial management, implementation of technological changes, or evaluation of program effectiveness were viewed as the work of the executive director or someone else bearing a similar title. However, over time we have come to realize that many of these tasks are better performed with involvement from managers at many different levels. At the very least, other managers need to be aware of what they entail and how they can provide necessary support for those responsible for their completion.

Financial Management

In the traditional sense, financial management refers to developing budgets and monitoring expenditures to ensure that the organization lives within its means. It may also entail shifting of funds whenever possible as it becomes apparent that more money is needed in one area and less in another. Historically, good financial managers were people who stayed within budget and who shopped wisely for such things as supplies, facilities or consultation. Their financial dealings were open and ethical, without any hint of favoritism or that they in any way personally profited from them through kick-backs or other benefits.

Good, ethical management of money is still an important element of good management. However, in recent years, because of increased competition for funding and other developments (for example, managed care, block grants, and privatization of services), managers have had to spend much more time acquiring funding than spending it. An increasingly large percentage of their time has been occupied with fund-raising.

Historically, the funding for human services has come from some combination of (1) government appropriations, (2) allocations from the private sector (federated agencies like United Way and private foundations), (3) fees (collected directly from clients or through third party payments), (4) grants and contracts, and (5) contributions from individuals or the corporate sector. In recent years, writing grant proposals, negotiating contracts, and finding creative ways to obtain money from individuals or corporations to implement new, needed programs or to continue to operate existing ones have taken on ever-increasing importance for managers.

In seeking funding from grants or contracts, it is no longer unusual for staff at many levels to contribute to a proposal. Often, the specialized expertise required to produce a credible document with high potential to be funded lies not with the executive director but with lower level staff, who may not perceive themselves as managers. Sometimes those with the needed expertise are even volunteers or students. The author knows of one manager who, noting the recent influx of Mexican workers into the community, concluded that local state agency personnel might be willing to purchase translation services in order to better work with Mexican families. She sought and received funding for such a program, but with significant input from several Spanish speaking social work students who were former Peace Corps volunteers. By using the students to help to design a needed and culturally sensitive program, she greatly improved its funding prospects.

The need to find new sources of funding in a highly competitive environment has also brought other changes for managers. They have had to learn to "think outside the box." That has meant using some pretty unconventional approaches to individuals and corporations that a decade or so ago might have been considered inappropriate or even unprofessional. For example, an agency director mailed out thousands of letters to people about to receive their 2001 federal tax refund reminding them of their unexpected good fortune and suggesting that a good use of ten percent of the money (a reminder of "tithing" for those belonging to certain religious denominations) would be a contribution to her agency which was seeking to address the problem of child abuse. The request was highly successful, especially among those seeking election to public office in November. Apparently they viewed a $60 tax-deductible contribution as an inexpensive way to gain the good will of a large number of staff and agency supporters who would see the list of contributors when it was published in the agency's newsletter. At the time that the contributions were rolling in, the same manager asked a mid-level manager who was a self-avowed "NASCAR fanatic" to use her personal contacts to see if a certain stock car racing team would be interested in becoming an agency sponsor. Positive publicity for the racing team—increased funding for the agency!

In the twenty-first century, successful financial managers will continue to be those social workers who are creative, recognizing and seizing opportunities as they present themselves. They will also use the expertise and diversity that their staff provides to gain an advantage over those other managers who continue to rely on traditional funding sources.

No matter how creative a manager is in seeking funding, unforeseen problems and just the cyclical nature of our economy will periodically produce funding shortfalls. When this inevitably occurs, financial management entails performing the usual management functions, but doing it even better. The margin for error is reduced. Efficiency becomes critical; waste of limited resources cannot be permitted.

What are some specific ways in which economic austerity may affect the five general functions of the manager? For example, *planning* may entail the development of new policies regarding professional travel or the construction of several "contingency budgets" reflecting economic improvement, level funding or further loss of funding. *Staffing* may entail dealing with a hiring freeze, re-assigning staff, or relying more heavily on paraprofessionals or volunteers. The structure and nature of supervision may have to be changed as staff diminishes. Elimination of less competent staff may have to be accomplished as quickly as possible, if they can be replaced, or delayed if they cannot. If staff positions are lost, *organizing* may entail the development of a flatter formal organization structure or the use of more delegation of staff or functional authority to those capable of assuming it. *Controlling* may require more use of directives and less use of advice or information to communicate needed information as a kind of "bunker mentality" may prevail. *Leading* may require more structure for those staff asked to perform tasks new to them. Yet they will also need increased consideration as they will inevitably make some mistakes. Managers may have to develop a more autocratic approach to decision making since certain decisions affecting organizational survival will have to be made and they are in the best position to make them. At the same time, trust in the leader must be maintained—a difficult balancing act.

Time Management

Successful managers are able to manage their time well and to increase the likelihood that others will do the same. They are able to be supportive of staff and to be available when needed, but at the same time they are able to isolate themselves when they have work to be done that cannot be delegated to others. While the "open door policy" sounds good, no successful manager can always be available to answer a question or just to chat. Most situations can and should wait until a time convenient for the manager. There are many time management tools available to the manager and time management workshops remain popular. The suggestions and techniques offered by them (too many to be repeated here) range from the useful to the impractical. However, they all emphasize the importance of a system that conserves the time of the manager and reduces the amount of time spent in fruitless activities.

Time management is especially important for human service managers since they so often must operate under time pressures. Not unlike their business counterparts, they find themselves facing nearly impossible deadlines. For example, senior administrators within bureaucracies may impose deadlines for procedural changes that leave little time to prepare and to learn new methods of performing tasks. A public relations crisis may require that policies and procedures designed to prevent an unfortunate incident from reoccurring must be developed and implemented almost immediately. Or, little warning may precede the submission deadline for a grant proposal that, if funded, can assure the financial survival of the organization or the continued employment of current staff. The manager who must plan, staff, organize, control, and lead work group activities so objectives are not just met but met by a certain impending time or date must provide a specialized form of management. As in times of austerity, good management practices and a reputation for fairness will go a long way toward successful management under time pressures.

While some adaptation in the manager's approaches to all the functions of management may be indicated, leadership deserves special focus. The kind of leadership needed by the work group operating under time pressures may be quite different from that which is otherwise effective. Specifically, an authoritarian, even dictatorial style of leadership may be preferable and is more likely to be tolerated when staff members are working against time. A "tell me what to do and I'll do it" attitude is likely to exist. Of course, acceptance of and even support for this type of leadership is dependent on staff acceptance of the importance of successful meeting of deadlines, of the completion of the task itself and of its potential rewards. A work group that, for example, really does not want the work that would result from the awarding of a grant or contract cannot be expected to respond well to authoritarian leadership by the manager seeking to meet the deadline for its submission. There must be a common, desired goal. Authoritarian leadership is also more readily tolerated and even sought when the manager is successful in communicating why discussion, debate, and staff input into decision making are a luxury that cannot be afforded. If staff believe that time constraints are the reason for authoritarian leadership, it will likely be tolerated more readily than if they believe that they are simply perceived as having little knowledge and insight to contribute.

Confidence in the manager's ability to help the group succeed in meeting the time deadline is critical. Reasonable people will work toward a desired goal if they perceive a high likelihood of success. They will not, however, if they seriously doubt that the manager has the leadership abilities or the other required attributes to "pull it off." Past successes in meeting time deadlines and in producing quality results will help to ensure confidence in the manager's leadership. As during many other times, trust is critical to successful management under conditions of time pressure. Especially important are trust in the motives of the manager in committing resources to the task and trust that work expectations for individual staff will not be excessive.

Change Management

The nature of social work practice and those people who we serve guarantee that some level of change is almost always in the works. Some changes within organizations are greater than others. Any change can represent a severe threat to service delivery if not prepared for and implemented well by the manager.

Many different areas of change tend to affect the work environment in human service organizations. Changes in technology (for example, methods of psychiatric treatment, approaches to rehabilitation of those in correctional facilities, community versus institution-based work with certain client populations) can require rapid and comprehensive change within organizations. The identification of new client groups (for example, HIV patients and their families, battered husbands, the homeless, or abused siblings) can lead to the creation of new structures and programs. Both rapid organizational growth and dramatic cutbacks in provision of some services created the need for changes within human service organizations during the 1990s.

In recent years, most changes have not resulted from enlightened concern for improved service delivery. Funding cutbacks, threatened and curtailed programs, and conservative attacks on many fronts have compounded the need for change within organizations and accelerated it. Changes have occurred in services, structure, role, and personnel. Bewildered clients and staff have required the help of social workers to try to sort through changes resulting from growth in practice knowledge, administrative necessity, and/or governmental dictates and to assess their ultimate impact on services.[1]

Change and its implementation occupy a large percentage of managers' time. Managers require the theoretical preparation related to organizational change that Granvold has proposed; for example, "a comprehensive knowledge of organizational theory, administration, management and supervision."[2] Much of the discussion in earlier chapters of this text should be of help to managers who must deal with organizational change. Certain other specific insights, drawn from studies of organizations, seem particularly useful for managers seeking to implement change successfully.

During times of change, it is important to maintain organizational continuity and to preserve the integrity of the organization as a system. This would seem to be especially critical for work in the human services. A manufacturing plant can close down to retool for the next year's model; a service delivery system cannot stop service delivery to prepare for change. Change must be absorbed while services continue to be delivered. The basic character of the organization, and both its public and its internal identity, cannot be altered to the point where critical relationships and linkages to other organizations and systems are jeopardized.

Times of change may shake the staff's usually solid commitment to the organization and its goals. As one observer noted, "It is at this juncture that conflict between the worker and the organization become most clearly manifest."[3] The relationship between superiors and subordinates may undergo unusual stress during times of change, and managers are natural targets for resentment and frustration that cannot easily be directed at the more esoteric "organization." Managers can anticipate this reaction, try to understand it, and put it into perspective. It helps to remember that managers constitute a "buffer zone which contains heretical confrontations between the individual and the social organizations."[4]

Managers need to communicate both stability and certainty[5] at the same time that they are working to implement change. Staff and clients must be helped to recognize that the mission, objectives, and essential characteristics of the organization, in most instances, will remain largely unchanged. If chaos and trauma are to be avoided, the manager must also assure that change is incremental and that it will be implemented in tolerable amounts.

The change strategies of the manager are more likely to succeed if the complete cycle of change is accomplished, that is, unfreezing, change, and refreezing.[6] This theory suggests that each step is a prerequisite to the next. Failure to achieve the ultimate change objective, where new behaviors or attitudes finally become comfortable and natural, is usually explained by inadequate attention to earlier stages, particularly to the first stage, unfreezing. In the unfreezing stage, the individual who is being asked to change (staff member for our purposes) must become sufficiently uncomfortable with the old way of doing things to want to change. Unfreezing by the manager can be brought about through any combination of presentation of data, appeals to professional values and ethics, logic, bargaining, or even threats. Of course, the specific strategy or combination of strategies used will be a function of the personality and style of the manager and of the worker. It also is a function of the time available for change, the scope and nature of the change desired, and the amount of flexibility inherent in the requirement for change. The second step, the change itself, will occur only after unfreezing has occurred.

The final stage of change (refreezing) can occur only if the manager provides adequate reinforcement of learning. The methods employed to accomplish this must be individualized to both manager and staff. They can take the form of a variety of rewards, compliments, and encouragement. Whenever possible, staff members should be encouraged to adopt a response to change based upon their own preferences. It can be selected from among possible alternatives. In the ideal world, when refreezing takes place the new way of doing things will become so comfortable that it is no longer even identifiable as someone else's idea, suggestion, or directive. The new way will appear to be only logical and natural to the worker. If this ideal can be achieved, resistance to the change will dissipate.

Some changes occur largely as a response to problems identified by the manager. This happens naturally for social workers as managers because of the perspective on the organization that they possess.[7] Quite often, changes result from administrative pressures, fiscal expediency, or some other force not related to problems or needs identified by the manager. Managers may face differing levels of resistance and even outright hostility to changes that are not of their own doing. The decision to use participative management approaches to change implementation, adversarial approaches that assume that resistance will occur, or any other approach between these two extremes must be made based upon an accurate assessment of personnel. Specifically, managers must assess the staff's capacity, readiness, and motivation to change. Of course, they must also use self-awareness in selecting an approach that is within the range of their management style and their personality.

Managers sometimes attempt to use participative management methods when the nature of the change or the time constraints required for its implementation do not allow for flexibility. Real participation in decision making is appreciated; obvious efforts to co-opt staff are not. Real input, when appropriate, can result in a more cooperative approach to change on the part of staff. However, most reasonable professionals also understand that some changes, particularly those that evolve from state or federal mandate or from fiscal necessity, may leave little or no room for negotiation or creative input at the local level.

Support for staff is both needed and welcomed during times of change. However, different individuals may seek different forms of support from managers. For example, close monitoring of staff behavior may be welcomed by one individual but resented by another. Some individuals may require frequent reassurance that they are meeting expectations while others may prefer to receive initial orientation and then be left alone while only occasionally "touching base" with the manager.

Resistance to Change

Almost any change will be resisted to some degree by at least some staff members. Any time that change is being discussed, there are both driving forces (for change) and resisting forces (against change). There is tension created between these opposing forces. It is what prevents change from occurring easily. Change will occur only if either driving forces for change can be increased so as to overwhelm restraining forces, or if restraining forces are reduced. These are the two options available to the manager. The first, increasing driving forces, is the far less desirable method. Why? Because increasing driving forces often only tends to increase resistance—people "dig in their heels" and resist the change more strongly. Then the driving forces for change must be increased again, the resistance will increase further, and so forth. A vicious cycle and, frequently, a power struggle will result.[8]

The preferable approach to implementing change is to identify the resisting forces that exist. Then the manager can select some of the more promising ones (those that can be most easily addressed) as targets. The literature suggests many reasons why staff might resist change.[9] The reasons overlap slightly, but taken individually or as a group, they represent formidable obstacles for the manager seeking to implement change. They include:

1. *Changes can appear to violate professional values.* Professionals can be expected to (and should) resist a change if they perceive it as a violation of client rights or professional ethics. (Managers should probably question their own position regarding the change if workers' concerns are found to have validity.)

2. *Inertia.* The laws of physics suggest that, unless challenged, we tend not to change. To do anything differently requires a conscious effort. For example, people, when not assigned seats, will sit almost always in the same place in classrooms or meetings. We drive the same route to work, even though other, equally good routes are available. Routines are comfortable and conserve energy; we resist change that might upset these routines.

3. *Change produces uncertainty.* People may know from experience that they can succeed in the old way of doing things; but there is no such assurance after change. Successful and competent staff are sometimes those most likely to resist changes that threaten to remove them from the favorable known and into the unknown. Less competent staff may be less resistive because they have less to lose from the journey into the unknown.

4. *Misunderstanding of the change.* Rumors can spread quickly and exaggerations often occur before changes are fully understood. Sometimes one or two possible but very unlikely effects of a proposed change are widely discussed as if they were a virtual certainty, creating resistance among even the most level-headed of staff. A "worst case scenario" is a frequent occurrence in staff discussions about a proposed change.

5. *Fear of loss.* Changes may result in obsolescence of many types. Feared loss of job is the most dramatic source of resistance, particularly among staff with little seniority. But loss of prestige (or fear of losing it) as the rules are changed can cause senior employees, currently valued for their knowledge and skills, to resist changes as vigorously as if their jobs were threatened.

6. *Antagonism toward the personnel proposing the change.* Even changes that would benefit staff are sometimes resisted because of a combination of distrust and dislike based upon previous interaction with the proposer. The person who proposes a change can pre-doom it to resistance, especially if staff does not trust the person.

7. *Lack of confidence in the manager.* A staff member may like the change and the proposer of change but resist change because of a lack of confidence in the manager's ability to implement it successfully. Does the manager have a history of

"waffling" or of being unable to function under pressure when problems arise? If so, why waste the necessary effort to engage in the change? (This source of resistance was discussed earlier as a potential problem of the manager when time pressures are present.)

8. *Lack of participation.* Occasionally staff members may believe that they should have been involved in planning for change because of certain expertise or insights. Resentment at noninvolvement can result in resistance to change that might otherwise have been supported. Staff members may be seeking to save face among peers who may question, if the idea has merit, why weren't they involved in suggesting it?

9. *Failure to see the need.* A staff member may be genuinely unconvinced as to why the change represents a preferable alternative to present approaches. Old methods or procedures may have brought little criticism, so why change? Inability to perceive the need for different behaviors can be a major source of resistance.

10. *Timing.* Some changes, normally acceptable, may be resisted in time of overwork, interpersonal conflict, or when they just seem to come too soon after other changes. The tolerance for change of individuals (as well as organizations) has its limits.

11. *Social relationships.* A staff member may resist change if it threatens existing social structures, of great importance to some individuals in organizations (Chapter 6). For example, if a proposed change would make it impossible for a staff member to eat lunch with a friend or walk to the parking lot with a co-worker, great resistance to a perfectly rational change may occur.

12. *Change can upset power balances.* Factions and cliques inevitably exist within organizations. Some very dismayed managers have observed that nearly everyone may resist a good change suggestion if individuals on both sides believe that the other side may stand to benefit more than their group.

13. *Informal organizational pressure.* In order to maintain friendships, staff members may resist a change that they might otherwise support. Disapproval of the manager is probably preferable to peer ostracism or other sanctions for most staff.

14. *Belief that change equals criticism.* If not tactfully presented, change may be perceived as a message that staff have not been doing a good job. It may be seen as an effort to correct some deficiency in an individual's job performance.

15. *Resistance to change is a personality characteristic.* Some staff members are just negative and pessimistic by nature. They have taken on the role of resident foot-dragger and will resist any change because they think it is expected of them.

16. *Resistance to change has its own rewards.* Poor workers have found that by organizing change resistance they can (a) make new friends among co-workers of varying competencies and (b) divert attention away from their work performance.

Many of the sources of resistance to change have one thing in common—they result from an individual's recognition or belief that change may depreciate one's value, particularly the value of experience. Ironically, those individuals upon whom a supervisor usually has depended in the past may become leaders in resistance unless they can be convinced that their skills and knowledge will continue to be valued in the future. Those who have been marginal in their work performance may be less likely to resist change—what do they have to lose? It is true that change is somewhat of an equalizer among staff members. All must start new and prove themselves competent again.

It may be some consolation for the manager to remember that a massive, undifferentiated resistance to change rarely occurs in any but its earliest stages.[10] Because of factions that exist within work groups, staff are rarely unanimous in their reaction to anything. After a while there almost always will exist advocates for nearly any change, as well as opponents of it.

Implementing Change

Problems relating to change, including resistance, can be avoided or at least lessened through a proactive approach. The difficulties inherent in the task of change implementation can be greatly reduced if the manager has been successful in creating and in maintaining a managerial climate conducive to change. Managers can regularly suggest that change is both natural and desirable within human service organizations. They can assert their belief that change cannot be avoided, given the nature of social work services and the changing service needs of members of our society. Presented this way, it is less likely to be perceived as criticism of past staff performance when it occurs. This message should be communicated at the time that a staff member is hired and reinforced regularly thereafter.

Strategies for Presentation.   The literature is helpful in suggesting a variety of strategies for successful presentation of change. It stresses the importance of maintaining a managerial climate supportive of change.

Both the preparation for and the implementation of change are ongoing processes for the manager. In discussing the role of the supervisor, Kadushin[11] suggests those conditions under which successful change is most likely to occur. For example, change is best accomplished if staff participate from the start in planning the change, if they are informed early of the nature of the planned change, if the change is introduced slowly (preferably with some initial trial effort), and if expectations are made clear and understandable. Staff will be less resistant to change if the change is consistent with perceived organization norms and objectives, if there is some assurance that the change will have the predicted effects, if managers communicate strong conviction in the desirability of the change, if there is some appreciation of and empathy with the difficulties that change will create for staff, and if provisions are made to reduce the costs of it for staff.

Tact is imperative in all areas of interpersonal management behavior, but especially in presentation of change. Change should be presented in such a way that it does not suggest a criticism of staff. Ideally, change should be presented as a process that has been designed by intelligent and dedicated professionals. Managers need to explain the need for change and its most likely ramifications in an honest, straightforward manner. If possible, the limits of threat to job security and possible loss of status should be discussed. Assurances of training and support should be given, but only if they can be offered. If new role expectations are to result, specific criteria for job performance must be developed in such a way that accusations of arbitrariness and favoritism can be avoided.[12] Changes can be viewed by staff as an opportunity to reward or to punish; it must be clear that a manager has no intention of engaging in either behavior.

When changes must be made in service delivery, it is also desirable to review with staff what the profession has learned about clients and their likely reactions to change. This will help to reinforce the perception that the needs of clients remain the highest priority. Staff should be reminded that many clients, particularly those served by many governmental organizations, may be operating at the security-need level. Clients live with almost daily threats to their health and mental health care, food stamps, Social Security, and so forth. The media are forever reporting on efforts of legislators to cut out or curtail unpopular entitlement programs. Clients may perceive any change as a first step in some master plan for withdrawal of assistance and/or services. Feelings of clients may surface in the form of distrust or anger with the slightest provocation if the change appears to represent a threat to their security.[13] Managers may need to help staff to anticipate, to understand, and to handle these reactions so that they will not become just an additional source of frustration and of conflict for staff during the time of transition.

Generally, impending changes should be discussed freely with staff, as soon as they are perceived as very likely to occur (see contingency planning—Chapter 4). Staff should not be allowed to become embarrassed by learning of changes from media or from clients. Information regarding changes should not be withheld or used by managers to manipulate behavior. A manager with a reputation for open, equal-access presentation of change plans is more likely to be trusted when changes occur than one who "plays it close to the vest." A manager's credibility is important if effective communication about the change is to occur. What is said must be heard accurately, without second-guessing or reading between the lines by staff. The motives and sincerity of the manager should be unquestioned. A manager with a policy and a reputation for fair treatment of people during change will be trusted the next time that changes occur.

Social workers as managers should not attempt to delegate the responsibility for explaining about changes or for working with staff to help them adjust to the changes. It also is not enough simply to announce changes and then wait for them to occur. When changes are announced, staff may listen politely but they may not feel comfortable in asking about areas of their concern. They will not have had the time and opportunity to talk to others about the changes or to think through how their job might be affected.

Managerial Doubts about Changes.   What if managers themselves are doubtful regarding the merits of the change? Kadushin suggests that "responsibility of acting in defense of organization policy can be a source of considerable dissatisfaction."[14] Defending any organization policy to staff can be difficult; if the manager does not agree with it, the job can be made worse. As we have discussed in other contexts, attempts at duplicity by managers are useless and ill-advised. Staff members, who have worked any length of time with a manager, should know that manager well. They would certainly know if the manager were trying to promote a change that is totally out of character for the manager. When managers have their own doubts about the advisability of a change that must be implemented, a certain amount of healthy skepticism in presenting the change to staff is not harmful; it is just honest. Skepticism communicates doubt about the value of a change but withholds judgment pending time and an honest effort. It says, "As you might imagine, I have some questions about the change myself, but I will give it a 100 percent effort and evaluate its viability at some later date. I expect you to do the same."

Skepticism, if displayed occasionally by managers, can be healthy and natural. The same cannot be said for cynicism. It is never appropriate. Cynicism would tend to ridicule a required change, exaggerate its shortcomings, and downplay its virtues. It would suggest that the manager hopes the change will prove to be a failure. It would say, in effect:

I think the change is ridiculous, don't think it will work, and hope it does not. It is probably in your best interest to agree with me. I will not work hard toward its achievement and really wish that you would join me in sabotaging it, or at least in hoping that my prediction will be fulfilled.

Skepticism is normal among thinking, concerned professionals. If held within check, it provides the potential for a valid assessment of change. Cynicism is never helpful during times of change. It pre-dooms the best of ideas and innovations by helping to reinforce negativism and resistance by staff. It can help to create a self-fulfilling prophecy.

Support for Staff during Change.   Support for staff during times of change is also important, and several questions must be addressed. What types of support are needed and by whom? Are tooling-up and training-time allowances for staff adequate and reasonable? How can mistakes, unavoidable whenever new learning is occurring, be handled with consideration? How can mistakes be used to increase their learning potential, rather than as occasions to punish staff? How can staff evaluations be conducted fairly so as to reflect an understanding of the difficulty of first-time efforts? This last question is especially important. Immediately following a time of change, it may be more fair to evaluate staff based on the effort that they made to implement change rather than on the success of the change itself. The latter may be something that was not within their control.

As changes are being implemented, managers need to maintain an optimistic stance toward change and should communicate a belief that most changes ultimately have positive results. Fearful, anxious discussions with staff regarding problems related to change can be harmful to morale. During times of change, the manager can and should be a role model for other staff, maintaining an attitude that change is essential for growth and ever-improving services to clients.

The existence of a sense of humor regarding change also is essential. In our society, changes within human service organizations sometimes occur so rapidly that all of us will feel overwhelmed at times. Sound insights regarding change, tempered with a sense of humor, will help the manager to promote an organizational climate where change is viewed as both tolerable and challenging.[15]

Technology Management

There was a time in the twentieth century when we took for granted the statement that the invention of the automobile did more to change life than any other invention in history. (Prior to that, it was gunpowder.) Now there is almost universal agreement that the computer has that distinction.

The successful integration of information technology into human service organizations depends heavily on the knowledge and sensitivity of managers. Depending on how they choose to present and use it, it can be either a bonanza or an impediment to achievement of organizational goals. Generally, it is somewhere in between.

At this point, we are only beginning to see some of the dramatic changes that information technology is making in the workplace. Managers now regularly use electronic mail to communicate with staff at distant geographical locations or just down the hall.

They download a vast amount of information to assist them in performing daily tasks such as receiving RFPs (request for grant proposals) or learning about related programs in other organizations. Many tasks that previously required face-to-face contact, or at least a phone call, now are easily performed anonymously by computer. Even "virtual meetings" are becoming common. For example, managers serve on advisory boards for other organizations in which all meetings are conducted by computer with members never leaving their offices. This can be a real time-saver for a manager. The "down side" to it may be a loss of valuable networking as well as other problems that can result when one lacks access to nonverbal communication.

Almost every task within an organization has been or soon will be computer-assisted. Computers are being used in human service organizations for such widely diverse tasks as word processing, desktop publishing, tracking of parents for enforcement of child support, quality control of food stamp distribution, computer-assisted continuing education, and client intake and diagnostic work.[16] It can safely be predicted that the opportunity and the pressure to further computerize service delivery will be great for human service managers in future years. Computerization is no longer a choice. As human service organizations become more and more competitive, managers who resist information technology advances are likely to be left behind. Those who use it creatively will be at a distinct advantage.

Problems Associated with the Introduction of Technology

Computerization or introduction of other new information technology within human service organizations offers great potential for improvement in services to clients. But, unless it is approached in a planned and thoughtful way, it can bring more problems than benefits. We will examine a few of the more common problems associated with the introduction of new technology into human service organizations and then suggest ways to avoid them, or at least to minimize their negative impact.

Resistance and Confusion.   Some managers have been fortunate enough to introduce technology in stages and over a period of many years. However, a more typical scenario involves a decision to move into the computer age almost overnight. Computerization may be precipitated by the acquisition of a grant or contract that suddenly makes it possible to purchase information technology or as a response to the heavy-handed influence of one powerful individual (such as a board member or new executive) with a technological bias. It is not unusual for organizations to move quickly from an organizational climate of near universal skepticism about and rejection of technology to one in which there are strong pressures on all to "go high-tech" and implicit threats for any who resist.

Adventitious computerization may lead to a situation where staff simply cannot keep pace with the technology, even if they wish to change. They may become both confused and demoralized when a job that previously was manageable suddenly becomes incredibly complicated, at least in the beginning.

Managers often have to "seize the moment" when the opportunity to acquire technology occurs. But there is no requirement that it all be used instantaneously. It should be gradually introduced into work flow at a pace that does not disrupt ongoing activities or overwhelm the capacity of staff to learn and adapt to it. Managers need to thoughtfully consider its potential uses, choosing to adopt some and to reject others that would be too costly, at least initially, for the work climate of the organization or for delivery of client services. Unfortunately pressures from others (and the temptation to demonstrate that one is "state of the art") often preclude these common sense approaches to computerization. It takes a secure manager to move cautiously amidst pressure to institute dramatic technological changes once the opportunity to do so is present.

Challenges to the Informal Organization

As was discussed earlier, the informal organization can perform valuable functions within an organization. One's place in the informal organization is normally quite stable. It is based on such factors as seniority, interpersonal relationships, political expertise, and knowledge. For example, one may gain a place of status within the informal organization by building a reputation for "having the answers," knowing how to perform an important task especially well, how to circumvent the system, or by being able to provide the historical perspective to an individual or on a problem. Generally, upward or downward mobility within the informal organization is slow if not altogether nonexistent.

The introduction of technology can cause rapid, upsetting changes to the informal organization. When a human service organization computerizes, some individuals are catapulted to positions of high value and status. They generally are those who are already computer literate and who enjoy the thought of combining their avocation with their job. They not only know how to use newer technology—they also know how to speak the language. Their comfort with the jargon makes them the envy of those who are struggling just to learn basic skills. They are clearly "one up" on their less fluent co-workers. They can choose to become invaluable team members giving unselfishly of their time and expertise. Or, if so inclined, they may prefer to build a power base by helping those who pay deference to them and denying assistance to those who do not.

Those who may be catapulted to the top of the informal organization when technology is introduced or upgraded are likely to be individuals who are relatively new to the human service organization. They are likely to be younger, recent graduates of academic programs, those who normally would have to wait a long while before obtaining power. They will not have earned their positions through interpersonal and political skill or by demonstrating that they are skilled providers of services to clients. They simply have mastered a technical skill that others find baffling. Meanwhile, the "old hand" worker who earned a position of status over a period of years on the job may suddenly be devalued in the eyes of the work group. Knowledge and skills that previously were admired suddenly may be perceived as obsolete to others. For example, client intake diagnostic skills and insights developed over many years suddenly may be less important than the technical skill needed to use this month's "expert computer software" package that can generate a psychiatric diagnosis from data entered into a computer by a client. In a computerized organization, basic competence can easily become synonymous with using the latest computer software packages or in accessing needed information from the Internet.

The informal organization is likely to undergo rapid change when information technology is introduced or upgraded. But, the formal organization is also likely to experience stress. Supervisors are likely to find themselves needing to seek the technical expertise of subordinates. Some who are already insecure in their role may find this threatening. Staff who already have a reputation for challenging the authority of superiors and denigrating their competence to others may relish the opportunity to flaunt their superior knowledge and skills. In a healthy organizational climate, managers and staff may be able to laugh and to learn together during a time of technological change. In an unhealthy one, resentment and uncertainty are likely to increase and power struggles and interpersonal tension are likely to become exacerbated.

Communication Problems and Isolation.   Logically, information technology should produce better communication, and better communication should result in better decision making. At least that is the way it is supposed to work. But, better access to vehicles for information transfer may or may not produce better communication. At least initially, organizations may be characterized by increased human isolation, a condition that is hardly conducive to better communication.

Computerization is most likely to have occurred first among clerical staff who began to use computers for word processing. When professionals and other staff moved into the computer age, secretaries temporarily became valuable consultants and moved up within the informal power structure. But soon most professional staff learn to perform tasks like word processing, data entry and analysis, and intra-organization communication for themselves. Clerical staff find themselves with little to do and either have time to waste or are reassigned to keep them busy. Professional staff have little need to interact with them. Also, professional staff do not need to interact with each other as much. While, previously, even those who did not like each other much had to negotiate and cooperate to get their work done, interaction for this purpose is no longer required.

The need for face-to-face communication among staff may be greatly reduced in other ways or may even disappear with the increased use of information technology. Office doors may be closed an increased percentage of the time to minimize distractions. There may be little informal networking or support offered within such a work environment.

Need for Proactive Management Methods

A certain amount of discomfort and unfamiliarity with new ways of doing one's job can be productive and motivating. But not if it reaches the point where it demoralizes and overwhelms staff. During times of technological change a supportive, understanding approach to management can go a long way toward promoting a comfortable transition. It will be even more successful if the manager has anticipated potential problems in areas such as the informal power structure and staff communication and taken steps to prevent them before the transition begins. As with most other areas of management, it is far better to be proactive than to sit by waiting to respond to problems.

Proactive managers have a planned approach to technological change. They have thought through and have begun to implement a change package to minimize possible negative effects long before the first (or new) hardware is unpacked. The package is designed with a knowledge of human behavior and of organizational theory. It recognizes that people are and will continue to remain the most important asset of human service organizations.

Based upon what we know about the needs of human beings within organizations and our experiences with the impact of information technology, there are a number of ways in which managers can ease the transition of an organization into a technology-assisted service delivery. If the manager has done a good job of presenting the inevitability of change within human service organizations, professionals and other staff within those organizations should not become overwhelmed by the introduction of new information technology. Still, some resistance is likely to occur. To reduce it as much as possible and to attempt to avoid other problems the social worker as manager might consider the following:

- *Provide assurances about continuity.* When technological change occurs, it is widely discussed and appears to threaten virtually all of the activities of an organization. But it rarely is as pervasive of organizational activities as it might appear when it is first presented. Of course, the manager will want to describe areas where changes will occur. But it can help to put it in perspective by also reminding staff of areas that are *not* affected (and there will be many). If possible, staff may need to be assured, for example, that client services will not be disrupted, that work units will not be reorganized, or that staff layoffs are not being considered. If it entails the use of expert systems for client diagnostic work, staff should be reminded that they will be used merely as aids to decision making and will not replace professional expertise and judgment.
- *Compensate for individual losses.* The manager, anticipating the loss of status within the informal power structure for some staff, should be creative in finding new roles to maintain their status among co-workers. As much as possible, their input should be sought in order to learn of their preferences as to how this can be accomplished, either by reassignment, continuing education, or some other method.
- *Use functional authority.* Certain individuals will inevitably possess the skills and expertise needed to assist in implementing technological advances. Since they are likely to be some of the most junior employees within the organization, some way must be found to tap into their technical expertise while not undermining line position authority or unnecessarily threatening the formal power structure. Functional authority can be useful in preserving it while still taking advantage of the expertise within the organization.
- *Replace lost face-to-face communication.* The manager should try to substitute for the human communication that is no longer necessary for information transfer. There may be a need for more staff meetings, preferably informal ones focused on sharing with others the "trial and error" in learning how to use new technology. Required staff presentations and "cross-teaching" are especially effective for this purpose. Promoting more after-hour social gatherings can also help to fill the communication void and help staff to promote interpersonal interaction.
- *Do not flaunt information technology.* Especially when technology is new, there is a tendency to want to show it off. But there is a good reason for not yielding to this temptation. Staff, many of whom would never choose to use it if given an option,

should not have new equipment shoved in their faces. It should not be the first thing they see when they arrive for work and the last when they leave. It should be placed in the most functional place, not the most prominent. Initially, it should be used for only those tasks where it is virtually certain to be appreciated as a timesaver or a worksaver. Later, when skeptics become more convinced of its value, experimentation with tasks that are questionable as to their contributions to efficiency can be undertaken. Generally, staff should be discouraged from using technology in ways that represent no real improvement over direct human communication.

• *Technology should have low client visibility too.* The manager cannot expect clients to be impressed or pleased by the fact that an organization is introducing or upgrading its technology. On the contrary, awareness of its presence is likely to produce fears of increased impersonality or questions about how the organization could afford such luxuries. Prominently placed reminders can be especially threatening to therapeutic helping relationships. The desk between helper and client is enough of a barrier; the presence of a state-of-the-art personal computer between them can serve as yet another reminder of status differential.

• *Use parallel expert and human systems.* In the pressure to employ the latest technology within a human service organization, the manager should try to maintain a balance between technological expertise and human expertise. Today's expert systems exist because human helping professionals were available to provide the practice knowledge to program into them. The manager, concerned about future client services, should continue to foster the growth of and reward thinking, innovative "people professionals" who may or may not be highly computer literate. It is they who will be depended upon to provide the expertise for the next generation of expert systems.

Management of Staff Turnover

Staff turnover is characteristic of almost all organizations. However, in the human services it can be especially problematic for managers. In some of the less popular areas such as child protection or public welfare, there appears to be a virtual "revolving door" as staff often come and leave in less than a year.

Social workers and other helping professionals rarely take a first job (or a subsequent one) with the idea that they will spend their entire careers with the organization. In fact, one of the features of a profession like social work is that one can easily move about from one organization to another or from one field of practice to another. It is possible to sample various settings and specializations (without stigma) until finding a "good fit." In fact, that is what most social workers do, at least early in their careers. Of course, helping professionals may also move from job to job because they are seeking to better their situations. Salaries generally are relatively low and the offer of a few thousand dollars per year more somewhere else can make a move appear quite attractive.

Staff turnover causes many problems for organizations and for the clients that they serve. In the public sector, it can take six weeks or more to advertise for, interview, and train new staff members to the point that they reach full productivity. This causes an economic drain on an organization's resources. Not only is bringing new staff "on line" costly in terms of the demands made on other staff during this time, but very little or no revenue is generated (in the form of reimbursement for services) during the time that a position is vacant or a new employee is being trained. Even when new staff first assume a full workload, mistakes and judgment errors are likely to occur. These can be detrimental to client services and costly in many ways to the organization (for example, in morale, supervisory time, or dollars).

What can social workers as managers do to help to retain good, productive staff members? The first step is to identify what it is that makes staff want to seek a job elsewhere. While there are many reasons why turnover occurs, three of the most common ones in the human services are: (1) burnout, (2) lack of professional stimulation, and (3) lack of opportunity for advancement. As was suggested earlier, there is a common fourth reason, a lack of a good "match" between staff members and the job, for example, they may decide that they do not like working with adolescents. If this is the case, there is not much that can (or should) be done to try to retain these individuals.

Burnout

Burnout has been defined as "a state of physical, emotional, and mental exhaustion resulting from involvement with people in emotionally demanding situations."[17] The problem of burnout received much attention in the 1980s. It was the focus of many staff development workshops. Burnout is an occupational hazard that produces changes in both attitudes and behavior. For example, staff who are identified as "burned out" while working in a field like child protection might exhibit cynicism and less humanitarian concern for their clients. They might "go through the motions" of doing their jobs, but might lose patience with colleagues and clients, or might blame the organization or even clients themselves for their inability to make an impact on a social problem. A staff member working in hospice services might exhibit some of the same behaviors, but might be more likely to report feeling emotionally drained and having "no more to give."

The concept of burnout was probably over-used for a while. Many employees who were just unwilling or unable to do their jobs tried to use burnout as an excuse for their performance. But how could they have been "burned out" when they had never really caught fire?

Despite the inappropriate use of the concept in some instances, burnout (or the potential for it) is a very real problem in some human service work. What can a manager do to prevent it, and thus to reduce the risk that a good employee might feel the need to take a job elsewhere? Depending on the situational variables that may produce burnout, a wide variety of strategies have been proposed. Providing additional supervision (especially supportive supervision, see Chapter 6) would seem a good place to start. Support groups and counseling from employee assistance programs (if available) might also help. If possible, the manager might consider re-structuring jobs, perhaps, by re-writing job descriptions to increase the amount of interaction with peers, since many workers experiencing burnout complain of loneliness and isolation. Even job rotation (Chapter 6) might be considered.

A proactive approach to the problem of burnout is essential. After it has been identified, it may be too late for the manager to do anything that might keep a staff member from leaving.

CASE EXAMPLE • *Recognizing and Responding to the Need for Change*

Nathan was the director of a well-established private out-patient psychiatric clinic. His most senior clinician was Elvira. She was well-respected in the community as a family therapist. When Nathan conducted periodic client satisfaction surveys, Elvira's former clients were always highly complimentary of her and of the help that she had given their families.

Because of her consistently high-quality work, Nathan had little trouble filling out Elvira's annual performance evaluation when the time came around again. As he had for the previous five years, he evaluated her work as "outstanding" in every respect. He noted in his narrative comments that she was a role model and mentor for the more junior family therapists on the staff. He invited her to meet with him to discuss her evaluation. He was not prepared for her response.

After the first few minutes, it was obvious that the meeting was not the usual exchange of pleasantries this time. When Nathan complimented her on her good work, Elvira did not seem particularly pleased by the compliments. Even the news that she would be getting a substantial pay raise did not seem to create any enthusiasm. Nathan wondered if she might be having some personal problems. He asked her if everything was all right. She looked at him for a moment and then replied, "I think I'm just burned out! I've gotten to the point where I just dread seeing another family come in with the same old problems. I think I just need to do something totally different."

Nathan was reassuring. He told her that everyone feels that way from time to time, even himself, and that she'd probably feel better about it in the morning. She replied that she did not think so, that she had felt this way for some time. In fact she had an idea and she wanted to know if he would support her in a plan that she had made. She wanted to attend a staff development workshop on relaxation therapy for older people at her own expense and using vacation time. But then she wanted to start two groups for older clients to practice what she had learned. If the groups went well, she might want to spend about half of her work week leading other groups for older people, but still continue to do family therapy half-time.

Nathan was amused at first as Elvira described her plans, then he got a little annoyed. He told Elvira that she was a very valuable member of the staff—the best family therapist that he knew. And she had been rewarded well for her work. While he appreciated the fact that she thought she might want to try something new, he needed her to keep on doing what she did so well, family therapy. That was where she was valuable to the organization. He promised to give her idea more consideration (since it had caught him by surprise) and they would discuss it again next year if she still felt the same way. "But," he concluded, "by then I feel sure you will think it was not a good idea. You are a great family therapist. You would never be happy doing anything else." He said that he wished he could meet with her longer but the half hour was up and he had another appointment scheduled. Elvira left, looking angry, but said nothing else. He later overheard her complaining to a co-worker that she was "sick of this whole place," but he assumed she was just having a bad day.

One year later, Nathan again met with Elvira to discuss her most recent written performance evaluation. As in the past, he was highly complimentary. He never brought up her idea of developing greater proficiency in working with older clients and was relieved that she did not bring it up again. Despite the fact that she had mentioned it to him on four separate occasions during the previous year, he assumed that she had now forgotten all about it. After a lull in their discussion she asked, "Are we finished?" "Sure," he answered, "what else is there to add? You're still

CASE EXAMPLE • *(continued)*

the best family therapist we have and I hope you know how much I appreciate your good work!" She did not reply.

Two weeks later, Elvira asked to see Nathan. She asked him if he would be willing to write a letter of reference for her. She had applied for a position as a group therapist at a nearby nursing home. Nathan agreed, but blurted out, "Why would you want to do that?" Then he spent the next hour listening to Elvira for the first time. He understood that she had lost interest in her work as a family therapist, that it did not provide enough opportunity for her growth. She had entered social work because of the wide variety of work experiences that it offered, yet she had done nothing but family therapy for fifteen years. She was ready for a change.

Nathan remembered what she had said a year earlier. He apologized for not listening better and asked her to reconsider leaving the agency. She replied that she had already decided to take the new job if it was offered to her. Fortunately for Nathan, it was not.

Elvira told Nathan that she did not get the job. He immediately asked her to come into his office to discuss a plan he had been working on, just in case she did not leave the agency. He spent the next hour with her and one hour a week for the next month discussing ways to

make her job more interesting. He offered that, if she would continue as a family therapist half-time for six months he would send her to the next available staff development workshop on relaxation therapy. She could run relaxation therapy groups with older clients as soon as she could get them organized. She told him that she also wanted to learn more about play therapy with young children from another staff member who was considered an expert in the area. He arranged for Elvira to sit in on play therapy sessions that the other staff member was conducting. She could stop doing family therapy altogether after six months if an AAMFT certified supervisor could be hired by then.

Elvira never became a very skilled relaxation therapist but her clients commented on her enthusiasm and interest. She quickly saw enough of play therapy to understand that it was beneficial for children, but doing it was not something that she enjoyed. After a while she began taking on more family therapy cases again, but also began seeing several adolescents individually who were addicted to alcohol. She maintained her two relaxation therapy groups of older adults until she left to take a job in another state where here daughter and grandchildren lived.

Discussion Questions

1. What mistakes did Nathan make when he conducted his first performance evaluation conference with Elvira?
2. Why did Nathan resist allowing Elvira to make changes in her work? Was he justified in doing so?
3. Why did Nathan "just not get it" even after the second performance evaluation conference with Elvira?
4. What were the costs and benefits to the organization of supporting Elvira's plans?
5. In the future, should Nathan insist that all staff members be required to learn new methods of intervention or otherwise seek to "grow" professionally? Why or why not?

Lack of Stimulation

While burnout represents a kind of emotional overload, a lack of professional stimulation can also cause a good employee to look elsewhere for work. This can occur when the organization is relatively static and staff members are asked to do their jobs in much the same way, year after year. For example, primary job responsibilities in some private psychiatric treatment facilities (performing intake histories) or in some adoption agencies (conducting home studies) may not be very professionally stimulating after a while. Even a good job can become boring once one has mastered it and can now do what is required without much thought.

What can the manager do with very capable people who have become bored with doing the same thing over and over in a relatively static organization? To recapture their earlier enthusiasm for their work, some form of continuing education may be required. Staff should be encouraged to grow and to seek new and different types of activities. A reward system that values new behaviors (for example, a senior staff person who begins to write for publication or to present papers at conferences) will communicate to others that new approaches to one's job and the incorporation of new ideas are important. Professional growth and the obligation to share knowledge with others should be portrayed as career-long activities.

Occasionally, job changes within the organization should be considered if staff are agreeable. For example, senior professionals might be reassigned to other duties that require them to offer new types of services or to offer services to different types of clients than those who they normally serve (job rotation—Chapter 6). On the surface, it would not seem to make sense to move competent employees to new jobs where mistakes are likely to be made. But, sometimes staff with less experience in a given practice method or with a particular client group can be "revitalized" by new experiences. Clients may even benefit from their newly found enthusiasm.

An organization may appear to be static on the outside—solid, well established, accepted by the community, and doing what it does best. But it does not have to be undynamic within. The manager who makes a practice of rewarding innovation and staff growth and who is constantly seeking to bring new challenges to people within the organization can help to fight lack of professional stimulation and thus can reduce the likelihood of losing good staff.

Lack of Opportunity for Advancement

Even in very dynamic human service organizations, another problem can be harmful to staff morale—professional staff may soon find that they have no potential for upward mobility. In many professions, people can look forward to an ever better future as their career progresses, for example, increased earnings, responsibility, status, and other benefits. An attorney, for example, might start out as a law clerk after graduation or as a junior member of a law firm. But over the next 30, 40, or even 50 years, the attorney's job is likely to get better and better. As senior law partners, such individuals may reach their peak in earnings and status when they are in their sixties and seventies and they may also have the luxury of setting their own hours and selecting the most interesting cases. Physicians generally have similar career patterns. These two professions are referred to as "late ceiling" occupations. They possess a kind of built-in source of motivation—the belief that even better times are coming.

Not surprisingly, there are also "early ceiling" occupations. Some examples are professional athletes, fashion models, or other types of work where youth, appearance, or physical strength are important to success. Unfortunately (and for other reasons), social work and some of the other helping professions also qualify as early ceiling. People in early ceiling occupations tend to get to the top early in their career. Some, like professional athletes or fashion models, subsequently experience a rapid decline in their status and income. Social workers and other professionals usually do not experience a decline after an early peak, but they may experience only minimal improvement in their situation or even a holding action after a point that occurs relatively early in their career.

It is not unusual for social workers to reach a relatively high level (supervisor, mid-level manager) fairly soon after they complete their professional education. Especially in small organizations, they may perceive that they have little upward mobility left unless their boss leaves or they leave the organization. Neither possibility is desirable for the organization. In some settings, it is difficult for the manager to be able to offer much hope for upward mobility for relatively young professional staff who believe that they have already "peaked out."

Retaining Early Ceiling Professionals

Particularly in small organizations or in larger ones that hire only a few people within a given professional discipline, efforts must be made to retain early ceiling professionals. Unless this is accomplished successfully, managers may find themselves frequently hiring and developing new staff, only to have them leave as soon as they become really competent at performing their jobs.

Providing Opportunities for Self-Actualization. Faced with the motivation problems of good professional staff in an early ceiling occupation, managers might consider ways to allow professional staff to spend more of their days doing challenging, stimulating work. This can be done through a type of job redesigning. For example, managers might try to hire paraprofessionals or even use volunteers to take over some of the more routine, repetitive tasks that normally fall to professionals. Perhaps professional staff could be relieved of intake history taking. Or, they could be given extra secretarial support or computer software for meeting recording responsibilities. Job redesigning that can free staff from tedious tasks and allow them to devote more time to the esoteric or the one-time-only, higher-level tasks might appeal to needs for self-actualization.

Non-monetary factors can increase the likelihood of retention of people within early ceiling professions. Sue Henry concluded that efforts to further professional enrichment, contribution to the profession, and the exercise of professional autonomy are appreciated by social workers and may be related to the decision to stay in jobs where upward mobility is limited. She argued for the value of a participative management structure to "spread retention incentive measures through a system."[18]

Raising the Ceiling.   As we noted in Chapter 6, salary is not regarded as a motivator for most people. But employees who perceive that they have little opportunity to improve themselves financially if they stay in their current job can feel compelled to leave for employment elsewhere to meet changing financial responsibilities. For example, increasing health care costs for parents or impending tuition expenses for children can cause some professionals to seek a more high-paying job elsewhere even if they really enjoy their current work. If the employee is one that the organization cannot afford to lose, this is to be avoided. But how? A partial solution may exist in what has been called a "dual career ladder."[19] It is a little unconventional. It has high potential for resentment by some employees because it runs counter to traditional personnel practices. Thus, a dual career ladder requires the development of support at all levels of an organization.

A dual career ladder entails raising the ceiling for early ceiling occupations. It involves the setting aside of usual salary scales and offers potentially high monetary rewards for persons who lack an opportunity for promotion or who may even prefer not to move up within the organizational hierarchy.

We can best illustrate how a dual career ladder works through comparison with a salary scale that is more typical in many human service organizations. Figure 11.1 is a traditional single career ladder. Figure 11.2 is a dual career ladder for the same organization. Note that in the single career ladder the opportunity to earn more money is available

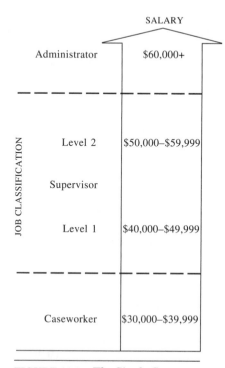

FIGURE 11.1   *The Single Career Ladder*

only to those who are able and willing to move to the next higher level in the organizational hierarchy—for example, from caseworker to supervisor or from supervisor to administrator. Employees facing a situation with no opening above them have "topped out" in terms of salary and can only hope for an across-the-board cost-of-living increase or that an opening above them will occur. (Thus, they may engage in frequent inquiries into the happiness or even the health of their superiors.)

When a single career ladder (such as the one in Figure 11.1) is in place, skilled caseworkers who really are not interested in supervision (even if openings were to occur) remain in their jobs at a price. Such individuals must sacrifice the opportunity to make considerably more money. They will also probably have to deal with innuendoes and beliefs of other employees who may start to question their competence because they are "still just caseworkers." These costs may eventually pressure them to leave the organization in order to find higher paying caseworker jobs or to take any promotions that become available. Even if they stay and take promotions to supervisor, the caseworker ranks will have been deprived of good workers. What's more, they will then be in jobs where their lack of interest and desire to manage may doom them to failure. Success in one job is no guarantee of success in another, especially when people do not really want the job in the first place.

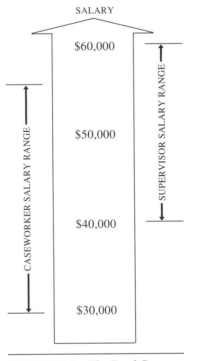

FIGURE 11.2   *The Dual Career Ladder*

Let us see why a dual career ladder might be preferable for early ceiling professions. The dual career ladder, if the manager can successfully implement it, has the potential to raise the ceiling for an employee in an early ceiling occupation without taking individuals out of a job that they do well. Note that the dual career ladder rewards employees who are exceptionally good at their job and who either wish to stay there or have nowhere else to go. It suggests, in a way consistent with current thought, that a supervisor is not necessarily worth more or even as much to an organization than a "foot soldier" who is very competent. Caseworkers and supervisors perform different tasks, but their jobs are not inherently hierarchical in nature. Why force caseworkers to "move up" to supervisors or supervisors to move even higher in the organizational hierarchy just so they can receive more tangible rewards?

An obvious and frequent objection to the dual career ladder arises from the traditional belief that an employee can only supervise another if the supervisor is clearly superior in all respects. Specifically, it seems "unnatural" and dangerous for a supervisee to make more money than one's "superior" or, for that matter, to have as much status or prestige within the organization. These beliefs and attitudes quickly can condemn a dual career ladder to failure. This is why it is critical to successful implementation that employees at all levels are sold on it as a concept.

If successfully implemented, a dual career ladder can provide at least a tangible reward for good work in the form of higher pay for the early ceiling employee. It probably will not motivate an employee to be more productive or to do better work. But it may provide enough compensation for staff who cannot or do not want to move up in the organization to keep them from quitting in order to seek jobs with higher ceilings in other organizations. Besides, as we know, within most societies other sought after rewards (for example, respect, deference, status) often tend to follow when people are well-paid for their work.

Program Evaluation

We would be remiss if we did not also include one more related management activity that occupies a sizeable portion of social workers' time and energies. It entails collecting vast amounts of data relative to planned or existing programs. Program evaluation (and the related activity of monitoring) are systematic, objective activities designed to test whether programs that may sound very good in theory really are needed and really work.

Many good books on the topic of program evaluation[20] have been written recently. They describe the correct ways to collect data, to interpret it, and to draw conclusions about programs. What we will present here is only a brief overview of this important task of the manager.

Program evaluations take many forms and have many different purposes. They are conducted when programs are in the planning stages or when the need for an existing program in its present form has been questioned (needs assessments), when a program is underway and we wish to assess how well it has been implemented (formative/process evaluations), and when a program is nearing completion or has been completed (out come/impact evaluations). In addition, there are several different specialized forms of evaluation that focus on a particular aspect of a program, for example, time and motion studies, administrative audits, social accounting, or program structure evaluations.

Evaluations may be internally driven (managers choose to conduct them for regular feedforward and feedback) or externally driven, for example, they may be required by funding organizations and are conducted by outside evaluators. Data are often collected using a variety of methods including administering of standardized instruments, community forums, telephone surveys, focus groups, mailed surveys, and direct observations. Data sources include former, present and potential clients, staff, "key informants," and even the friends and enemies of a program.

Managers have several responsibilities related to monitoring and evaluation. First, they need to assure that program missions, goals and (especially) objectives (Chapter 4) are articulated in such a way that it is possible to evaluate a program. Second, they should attempt to create a work environment in which collecting and analyzing program data is viewed as a normal part of day-to-day activities and is regarded as a valuable activity. Third, they should learn how to design and conduct appropriate program evaluations or, at the very least, to know what constitutes an evaluation that is feasible, useful, fair and accurate. Finally, they should be aware of the ways in which evaluations can be misused and should make every effort to assure that they are used ethically.

Program Evaluation and Management Ethics

The issue of ethics in evaluations deserves special mention. While monitoring and evaluation often are designed to improve programs and services, they sometimes are used for other purposes as well. That takes us into ethical "gray areas." Managers may use an evaluation to protect the organization or to deflect negative publicity. For example, learning that some problem within a program is likely to be exposed to the public, a manager may decide to quickly initiate an evaluation so that when the problem hits the papers or the 7 PM news it can be stated that "we have already begun an extensive evaluation of the program in order to make necessary changes." This can help to buffer criticism from a hostile task environment. Is this an unethical use of an evaluation? The answer is not a clear-cut one. It would depend in part on whether the results of the evaluation are actually used to make program improvements or simply to respond to criticism in a defensive manner.

A second common use of evaluations is to justify the additional funding necessary for the continuation of a program. An evaluation (a positive one) might be necessary for the survival of a program, to save staff jobs, or to avoid having to terminate client services. If the evaluation is a fair, honest one, there may be no violation of ethics involved. However, if the evaluation is deliberately biased in order to produce a favorable report, this is not ethical. An evaluation can be biased by managers in a number of ways, for example, through careful selection of who will provide data, by restricting what research design can be used, or by influencing how data are interpreted. It is unethical and but also unwise for a manager to deliberately distort the results of an evaluation for purely self-serving reasons. After all, if a program is really not all that effective, perhaps it should be discontinued. The money to support it might better benefit those in need of help in some other way.

There are still other questionable reasons why monitoring and evaluation sometimes are conducted. The real purpose of an evaluation may be to justify a decision already made about a program (for example, that it should be discontinued) or to justify firing one or more individuals working in the program. Is the use of evaluation to pursue these kinds of hidden agenda ethical? It may be, if the evaluation is fair and objective and designed to confirm (or fail to confirm) impressions already held. If the manager keeps an open mind and is willing to re-consider decisions based on the findings, there is probably no problem with doing this. After all, research often tests a hypothesis regarding what we expect to find, and sometimes we find just the opposite. However, if the evaluation were to be "stacked" so as to produce the desired findings, that would be considered unethical. Such a practice also may be unnecessary. For example, for personnel decisions, there are other ways to justify management decisions (such as annual performance evaluations and progressive discipline—see Chapter 7) that do not risk hurting the credibility of future evaluation activities.

Other ethical issues in monitoring and evaluation relate to the handling and dissemination of findings. Good evaluation requires candor on the part of those providing information. Clients and staff may be critical of a program or of personnel within it. What they reveal may leave them vulnerable to retribution if their identities become known. The manager has an ethical responsibility to assure that they are protected, usually by insuring that promises of confidentiality or anonymity are kept.

The writing of a report of a program evaluation must also be handled ethically. The report should be honest and complete. Unethical managers have been known to write them in a misleading way with some data highlighted for presentation and other data deliberately omitted.

The question of who will have access to the results of an evaluation also has ethical implications. Some people might seek access to it so that they can use it for some purpose other than that intended. Data may be taken out of context or misrepresented in some other way. A manager may need to carefully screen who is allowed to see the report of an evaluation in order to, for example, protect vulnerable clients from "victim blaming" or other practices that might be harmful to them.

The ethical issues involved in the management tasks of monitoring and evaluation are not easily resolved. There is likely to be conflict between a manager's need to be ethical and, for example, good financial management. When fund-raising is so critical to an organization, it is difficult (some would say masochistic), to always insist on an honest, objective evaluation. Suppose, for example, that a federally funded program that generates a large part of the organization's annual budget is being evaluated. The manager knows that the program has not yet produced many results, but it has promise. A totally objective evaluation is likely to conclude that continued funding cannot be justified. Should the manager attempt to hide the program's shortcomings and ask other staff to help in the cover-up? Could doing this be justified based on the manager's belief that the program will eventually prove to be worthwhile? Or, would it simply constitute unethical behavior? It would be hard to know what to do in this situation, even if one is trying to do the ethical thing. Perhaps, the most ethical approach to this dilemma would be to encourage a totally honest assessment of the program (even if it means putting the program in jeopardy), but also to collect additional data to attempt to convince others of the program's potential.

Some behaviors, for example, falsifying client files in order to make a program appear more effective, are simply unethical. They are both self-serving and in violation of the NASW Code of Ethics. Thus, there is no ethical issue involved. An ethical issue or dilemma, by definition, entails a situation in which a course of action is not clearly ethical or unethical. Some of the ethical issues relating to evaluation that we have described are among the most difficult. Even the most ethical managers sometimes have to balance their idealism with a dose of reality or pragmatism. Sometimes the solution leaves one feeling "a little uneasy." This can make the job of manager very stressful.

Summary

In this chapter we have examined some management activities that overlap somewhat with the five major management functions discussed in earlier chapters, but that do not fit cleanly within any one of them. Nevertheless, they are important management activities, ones that are occupying an increasing amount of a manager's time and efforts as the role of manager undergoes constant metamorphosis. We identified financial management, time management, change management, technology management, management of staff turnover, and monitoring and program evaluation as tasks that are gaining in importance for managers at all levels.

Of course, there are still other tasks that we have not discussed in detail that, while not gaining in importance, continue to occupy a fair amount of the manager's time. For example, hosting and attending social functions (some of which we would rather skip), chairing and participating in staff meetings, dealing with the media, or helping to arbitrate disagreements among staff are also important tasks that cannot be ignored. Depending on one's perspective, they may be regarded as either rewarding activities or simply jobs that must be done. In the final chapter of this book we will see how one's attitude toward these and the other tasks that we have described can be important determinants in whether or not he or she should seek a job with more management responsibilities.

Endnotes

1. Robert W. Weinbach, "Implementing Change: Insights and Strategies for the Supervisor," *Social Work,* 29 (1984): 282–286.

2. Donald K. Granvold, "Training Social Work Supervisors to Meet Organizational and Worker Objectives," *Journal of Education for Social Work,* 14 (1978): 44.

3. Alfred Kadushin, *Supervision in Social Work* (New York: Columbia University Press, 1976), p. 68.

4. Dwight Harshbarger, "The Individual and the Social Order: Notes on the Management of Heresy and Deviance in Complex Organizations," *Human Relations,* 26 (2) (1973): 264.

5. James D. Thompson, *Organizations in Action* (New York: McGraw-Hill, 1967), pp. 148–149.

6. Kurt Lewin, *Field Theory in Social Science* (New York: Harper & Row, 1951).

7. Harleigh B. Trecker, *Social Work Administration* (New York: Association Press, 1971), pp. 172–173.

8. Fremont E. Kast and James E. Rosenzweig, *Organization and Management: A Systems Approach* (New York: McGraw-Hill, 1974), pp. 590–591.

9. Steven Kerr and Elaine B. Kerr, "Why Your Employees Resist Perfectly Rational Changes," *Hospital Financial Management,* 26 (January 1972): 4–6; Bernard Neugeboren, *Organization, Policy and Practice in the*

Human Services (New York: Longman, 1985), pp. 182–188.

10. Herman Resnick, "Tasks in Changing the Organization from Within (COFW)," *Administration in Social Work,* 2 (1978): 36–37.

11. Kadushin, *Supervision in Social Work, op. cit.,* p. 70.

12. Edward Lowenstein et al., "The Management of Organizational Change: Some Findings and Suggestions," *Public Welfare,* 31 (1) (Winter 1973): 56–57.

13. Arthur Pierson, "Social Work Techniques with the Poor," *Social Casework,* 51 (8) (October 1970): 481–485.

14. Kadushin, *Supervision in Social Work, op. cit.,* p. 69.

15. The preceding discussion of "Change" is from *Social Work.* Copyright 1984, National Association of Social Workers, Inc. Portions of this article have appeared in *Social Work,* 29 (3), (March 1984), pp. 282–286.

16. Leon Ginsberg, "Data Processing and Social Work Management," Paul Keyes and Leon Ginsberg, eds., *New Management in the Human Services* (Silver Spring, MD: NASW, 1988): 53–64.

17. Johnson, M. and Stone, G. "Social Workers and Burnout: A Psychological Description," *Journal of Social Science Research,* 10 (1), (1987): 67.

18. Sue Henry, "Non-Salary Retention Incentives for Social Workers in Public Mental Health," *Administration in Social Work,* 14 (3), (1990): 1–15.

19. See Joseph A. Raeline, "Two-Track Plans for One-Track Careers," *Personnel Journal,* 66 (1), (January 1987): 96–101.

20. See, e.g., Royse, D. et al. *Program Evaluation: An Introduction,* 3rd. ed. (Belmont, CA: Brooks/Cole, 2001), or Unrau, Y., Gabor, P., and Grinnell, R., Jr. *Evaluation in the Human Services* (Itasca, IL: F. E. Peacock, 2001), or Ginsberg, L. *Social Work Evaluation* (Boston, MA: Allyn & Bacon, 2001).

12

Becoming an Effective Manager

We began our introduction to the study of management by making the point that everyone is a manager, that is, everyone performs management functions at least some portion of every work day. Some do more of it, and some less. We have taken a good look at some of the factors that make performing these functions more or less difficult. At this point, the reader should have at least a good general understanding of what social work management is all about and should have begun to develop some ideas about which management tasks seem appealing and which do not.

Not surprisingly, there is much more to the role of manager than just performing certain functions and tasks. Like any role, there are certain interpersonal expectations. Some of these are pleasurable; others can be stressful. Some people handle the potentially stressful ones in stride; other people find them to be so unpleasant that they make the job of manager almost unbearable. In this final chapter, we will further "flesh out" what it is like to be a social work manager and explore what it is like to move into a job with more management responsibilities.

Common Sources of Stress

In their roles as managers, all social workers necessarily experience a certain amount of stress that "goes with the territory." Even direct practitioners who devote relatively little of their day to the functions of management (as opposed to, for example, executive directors who are engaged in management functions most of every day) experience the stresses of management from time to time. These stressors are closely related; when they exist simultaneously they can have a compounding effect that sometimes can be overwhelming.

Criticism and Conflict

When social workers move into positions where much of their days are occupied with performing management functions it is not as easy to assume the comfortable position of "we" (the practitioner) and "they" (the administrator) that is available to people who have very few management responsibilities. When they assume more management responsibilities, social workers are reminded that, in their role, they are part of the establishment that they may have complained about so often. As managers, they will be the target for some of the resentment generally reserved for those higher up in the administration. Both staff and clients are likely to vent their frustrations on the manager, particularly within highly bureaucratized organizations where managers often symbolize "the organization" and the constraints it places on them.

A mid-level manager (such as a supervisor) can easily feel caught in the middle of conflicts that inevitably occur between lower-level staff and upper-level administrators. This can leave managers in a state of conflicting loyalties (to peers? to the organization?). The role of manager forces one to assume a new perspective and to think and to act like "management."

Loss of Client Contact

Many social workers enter the profession because they seek the gratification that comes from working directly with individual clients and client groups. The functions of management can be time-consuming and can curtail or even make it impossible to continue to work with clients. Managers may have to spend sizable portions of their day in completing paperwork or in seeing only other professionals. They may miss the direct client contact and the satisfaction of knowing that they were able to help clients solve problems. Their only contact with clients may be when they must try to resolve client complaints about services. There is also another related frustration for managers. Because of their knowledge of budgets and personnel matters, managers are aware of the limited resources available to assist both staff and clients—they wish that they could be more helpful, but they cannot.

Responsibility for Decision Making

Many people resent the fact that others (their bosses) make decisions that affect their jobs and their lives. They think that they would like to be able to make those decisions for themselves and others. But decision making can be stressful. Sometimes it is far less stressful to let others make decisions than to have the responsibility for those decisions.

Managers make many decisions each day. They may have a boss to take on the ultimate responsibility for the consequences of some of their decisions. But many of the decisions that managers make are their responsibility and theirs alone. Some of them (for example, those relating to personnel actions) have major impact on the lives and careers of people, a realization that can be stressful. Often making the correct decision (for example, deciding to fire a subordinate) creates additional interpersonal conflict with other staff members.

Frequently, managers feel like they are in a "no-win" situation—whatever decision they make will be criticized. For example, during the terrorist attacks on the United States on September 11, 2001, some agency administrators who closed their agencies and sent their employees home were criticized for "overreacting" and inconveniencing others. Other managers who decided not to close were criticized for being "insensitive." In a more common scenario, a manager may be told that she has a pool of money (say, 4 percent of the current year's salary budget) that she can divide up any way that she likes as pay raises

for her staff for the next year. She wants to be fair, and to be perceived that way by staff. She could give everyone a 4 percent pay raise. But that would mean some staff (the higher paid ones) would get larger raises than others. Also, those staff who had performed the best over the past year would be rewarded the same as those who did not do nearly as well. So what would be the manager's option? She could assign pay raises based on merit, using recent annual staff performance evaluations. Some staff might get more because they had a good year; others would get less because of their weaker performance. But if she did this, she would be evaluating staff by comparing them with other staff, a practice (Chapter 7) that we warned against. Besides, while those receiving high merit raises would undoubtedly appreciate her fairness, would all those receiving low ones see her decision as fair? Not likely! Any decisions about staff pay raises are likely to be regarded as unfair by at least some staff. Unfortunately, managers find themselves in many other decision making situations where they feel like, no matter what they decide, the decision will displease some one.

Unwanted Power

Much of what managers find distasteful about their decision making responsibilities relates to attitudes about power. While some people undoubtedly enjoy being able to get others to do what they might otherwise not choose to do, many people in the helping professions would prefer not to be in positions where they are expected to exert their power over others. This may be especially true among many social workers since they rarely select their profession because they seek power. As part of their education they have been taught to help to empower others rather than to use the power they have over clients to impose their own values or wishes on them. Gender may also affect attitudes toward power. One researcher[1] concluded that one reason why so few female social workers have historically sought higher-level management positions is that they may have been socialized to believe that power is undesirable. It is probably safe to say that many social work managers are uncomfortable with the power that goes with the job of manager but feel compelled to use it anyway in the interest of good management practice.

Social workers as managers often experience stress related to power for a very different reason. Despite the authority that goes with their jobs, they often feel that most of what goes on within organizations is really beyond their control. Despite their efforts to manage the behavior of their staff, people will often do as they please. The author heard one manager describe his job as "like being the caretaker in a cemetery. You have a lot of people under you but nobody listens!" This is a fairly common complaint among managers, especially in those organizations where staff acquire permanent employee status or tenure following a brief period of evaluation. Managers may sometimes feel powerless to influence their behavior. They may listen politely, but that is no guarantee that they will do what is requested.

Limited Social Relationships

Another problem often experienced by managers can best be summed up in one word—isolation. As managers, social workers may feel that they have no close friends on the job. Inevitably, they must reconcile their need to work in a cordial and mutually supportive environment with their need as managers to be perceived as fair, objective, and trustworthy people. As a co-worker, both informal interaction and socialization (fraternization) done during working hours and outside of them are natural, pleasurable, and generally innocuous behaviors. In the role of manager, however, the issue of how much to be personally involved with staff is a difficult one. Intimate personal relationships between managers and those that, for example, they supervise and evaluate are universally labeled as unethical. But is all socializing with staff to be discouraged? Can a manager be both a friend to a staff member and an effective manager? There are no simple answers.

As we have discussed throughout this book, most all of a manager's functions are facilitated if that manager is perceived as fair and worthy of trust. Friendships with staff that go beyond job requirements have the potential to lead to staff members questioning whether the manager has these characteristics. On the other hand, aloofness and deliberate efforts to keep a social distance from staff can also erode feelings of trust in the manager. People who do not know us very well are likely to perceive us as untrustworthy and unpredictable. This is not a perception that is conducive to good management. So, what is the appropriate mix of friendship and distance between manager and staff? The answer is, as in most management issues, it depends. Some managers are able to maintain close personal relationships with staff, yet their objectivity when it comes to, for example, staff evaluations remains unquestioned. For other managers, even a little socialization can produce a threat to their image. As social workers, we know that the different capacities of people involved in any human interaction affect its meaning to them and how it is perceived by others. Socialization between managers and other staff is no different.

The manager seeking to establish the ideal balance in regard to socializing with staff—one that promotes a staff perception of objectivity and trust—must give serious thought to three questions and their most likely answers:

- To what degree can I be involved in friendship relationships with staff without it compromising my ability to be objective?
- To what degree can the other person (each person must be considered individually) be involved in a friendship relationship with me without that person relating differently (inappropriately) in some way to me in my role as manager? Is he or she capable of maintaining professional boundaries?
- To what degree will others' perception of my objectivity and trustworthiness be affected because of my friendship relationship with a staff member, regardless of how well the two of us are able to handle it?

The Manager.   The first question can be addressed primarily through self-analysis. Managers must determine whether they can make necessary role shifts (from friend to boss and back to friend again) when required. For example, can they have dinner at the home of a staff member on Sunday night and objectively evaluate or, if necessary, reprimand that same person on Monday? Few of us could do this without compromising our ability to be objective and to manage effectively. But most of us could attend a staff party on the weekend and still evaluate staff objectively on Monday. Others could not even do this. Because they have enough insight to recognize this, they choose to have no outside-the-office contact with staff. They know that socializing would be likely to limit their ability to manage. So, they deliberately avoid any outside friendships with those with whom they work. Any of these behaviors can be appropriate, based on managers' knowledge of themselves and their capacities.

The Other Individual.   Even if a manager is perfectly capable of making necessary role switches, the other individual involved may not be, or may attempt to use a friendship to manipulate the manager's behavior. Some staff will easily recognize the different roles that must be played and will make the shift accordingly. Others may intentionally (or even inadvertently) let the roles blur a little. They may attempt to use a friendship or a shared social occasion to their advantage, either by applying pressure to the manager ("I thought we were friends!") or by implying to other staff that a "special" relationship exists. Any socialization or implication of a personal friendship by the manager thus would be a mistake. Letting down of barriers would only provide an opportunity for exploitation and for manipulation.

Other Staff.   A manager may be able to "switch hats" with ease, comfortably being both a friend and a boss to a staff member. The staff member also may recognize the need for strict role differentiation and may be able to accomplish it. In fact, a social relationship with one or more staff members may be totally dependent from and in no way impinge on manager–staff relationships. But other staff may not perceive this to be the case. Their perception may be reason enough to avoid the friendship. After all, what is perceived to be true might as well be true in terms of its consequences.

Many reasons exist why other staff members might perceive that a friendship with a subordinate is a problem, even when the two parties involved have completely worked through their respective relationships. There is a natural tendency of staff to assume that managers have favorites and give preferential treatment. Unfortunately, they are often correct. Speculation on who is the favorite (office gossip) is interesting grist for dull days. Those who are not receiving good evaluations or are being passed over for promotion may have a special need to rationalize to themselves and to others why they are not receiving more positive feedback. ("Maybe I should start seeing the boss socially. I might get better evaluations!")

Even the staff member/friend can suffer when these perceptions exist among staff. Rewards and kudos that are earned legitimately and objectively awarded by the manager may be discounted by other staff members, especially those who are jealous and/or not happy with their own rewards. They may be looking for excuses to criticize the manager anyway. ("I guess we know why he got the promotion, don't we!")

Other staff may seek to form different relationships with a co-worker who is perceived to be a friend of the boss. Some staff members may become inordinately friendly, hoping to benefit by association. Others may resent and shun their co-worker. Good honest communication and collegial working relationships can thus be damaged or can be prevented from developing.

Striking a Balance.   Before breaking down the natural barriers that exist between managers and their subordinates, social workers must be certain that they, the other individual, and all other staff members can tolerate a less "businesslike" relationship. Can they maintain or establish closer relationships without damaging their reputation for objectivity and trust, so essential for good management practice? If not, socialization much beyond attendance at mandatory social functions is probably a dangerous practice. But then so can refusal to socialize, which appears to be a pompous reminder of a status differential!

When it comes to socialization, managers must be sensitive to the needs of the work environment but also to the rights of individuals. Many managers believe that staff would work more effectively if they got together socially now and then. They may either host or sponsor a holiday party or other such occasion. However, it should be made clear to staff that socializing after work hours with co-workers is voluntary for all employees and not a requirement of the job. A "command" social performance can produce more bad feelings than good ones about one's job. It can be viewed as an unwarranted intrusion on one's own time.

Managers who are too encouraging of even good, wholesome social relationships among staff or who allow other staff to put pressure on subordinates to socialize can make everyone's job more difficult. Many people just want to do their jobs and be left out of the socializing that goes on in an office. After work hours, they may prefer to enjoy themselves alone, or with family, friends, or neighbors and leave their jobs (including the other people who work there) at the office. The manager should respect that choice and protect such individuals from pressure to socialize either with the manager (how can they refuse?) or with other co-workers. As long as they are doing their jobs, it is their right to accept or to reject social overtures on or off the job and to not be resented, penalized, criticized, or ridiculed for their decision. Workers are paid to do a job for a certain number of hours per week. Emergencies may occur that occasionally will justify the manager requesting a little more time from them. But the manager, the organization, or co-workers have no legitimate claim on employees' relaxation or recreation time.

It is hard to know just how much socializing (both on and off the job) is desirable for the health of an organization. It depends in large part on the personalities of the individuals involved. Some people think they work better with people if they know them well. But, it is knowledge of others' work persona, not of their private lives, that facilitates productive interaction.

Besides, sometimes seeing the "other side" of a co-worker can harm one's ability to work with that individual. Workers need to know and understand the management style of managers and the work style of co-workers, and managers need to know the work style of their subordinates. We should rarely be surprised by others' behaviors or attitudes on the job. But a more personal knowledge of each other is not necessary. Especially between management and staff, such a relationship can be dangerous. For the manager in any work situation, there is a socialization threshold that, if crossed, can hinder the manager's capacity to manage. Finding where that threshold is (and it changes over time) and not crossing it requires a knowledge of one's self and of the work persona of others.

Is a Management Career Right for Me?

Sooner or later, virtually every social worker will have the opportunity to move into a position that requires that a sizable portion of the day will be spent in management activities. Frequently, the issue of whether or not to "move into management" occurs when one is offered a position of administrative supervisor. The occasion can be the beginning of a rewarding career with ever-increasing management responsibilities. Or, it can be the beginning of a period of frustration and unhappiness. A cautious, informed approach to the offer of a promotion into a management position (including consultation with those already in similar positions) is needed.[2] Unfortunately, that often is not what occurs.

Not every social worker needs to become a full-time manager. The human services require good managers but they also need competent clinicians who want to spend only the minimum amount of time necessary performing management functions. Only a relatively small percentage of social work jobs require that the social worker be a full-time manager or even spend most of the day performing management tasks.

Some people simply do not have good potential as managers. They may lack one or more of the traits that we usually associate with good leaders (Chapter 10). They may possess certain other personality traits or characteristics that would be problematic if they were to assume more management responsibilities. They may know it. If not, others probably do, and an offer of a management job may never occur.

Among those who have been identified as having the desirable characteristics for more management responsibility, most will get an offer of a promotion into management. But they may simply not want the job. They are aware of what management entails, and they prefer to let someone else do it. The decision not to take the offer of a management position is easy for them. But for many other potential managers, the question, "Is management really for me?" is a difficult one.

Errors in Decision Making

Some social workers have impulsively said "no, thank you" to the opportunity because they could think only of the negative aspects of management. Perhaps, they had worked for a cynical or "burned-out" boss and had adopted the boss' attitudes about management. Or, they may have held the erroneous belief that management is not really part of social work practice. For whatever reasons, they hastily turned down the opportunity for more management responsibilities and then later regretted their decision, wishing that they had more carefully explored what the job offer entailed.

A more frequent error involves the tendency to impulsively accept the offer of a management position. Some new managers have approached their new jobs with totally unrealistic expectations. They have subsequently been miserable and finally they have to quit, disillusioned and determined to never repeat their mistake. A few may be able to move back into a direct treatment position, even getting their old jobs back. They are the fortunate ones. Others, bearing the real or imagined stigma of failure, have felt the need to leave the organization where they once had been happy and productive employees.

The Lure of a Management Job. The recognition that one is being considered for a promotion can be very flattering. It is, after all, a validation of competence. It represents both an appreciation of past achievements and of others' belief in one's ability to assume even greater responsibilities. It suggests that an individual not only has done a job well, but also is capable of assuming responsibility for the work of others. Who would not like to receive that kind of message?

In a competitive, success-oriented society, saying "yes" to a promotion offer can be ever so attractive. A move into a position with greater management responsibilities is viewed by many people as "making it." Becoming a manager is something that the majority of workers in our society aspire to achieve. Unfortunately, the reasons why they covet the job often have little to do with the job itself.

There are many reasons why one might impulsively say "yes" to the offer of a promotion into a job with more management responsibilities. A higher salary and a more prestigious job title have obvious appeal. Despite the increased use of dual career ladders (Chapter 11) in some human service organizations, in most organizations tangible and intangible rewards still go most often to those who move up the organizational hierarchy. A move into a management position may be the best way, if not the only way, to make more money. Awareness of this fact can be a compelling reason to accept a move into management, even among those who seriously doubt whether it is what they really want. Scurfield surveyed social work administrators. He observed that, "a substantial number of current administrators would choose to be clinicians if promotional and financial opportunities in clinical practice were equivalent to those in administration."[3] Social workers may take promotions into jobs with more management responsibilities simply because they know that career advancement may occur only if they move into such positions.

There are other enticing rewards associated with moving into management. They may include such "perks" as a reserved parking place, professional travel, the latest computer, better secretarial support, or a larger and more attractive office that may even have one or more windows! A manager generally is granted more autonomy in such areas as work scheduling, making long distance phone calls, or choosing whether to perform a task oneself or to delegate it to another. The prospect of increased autonomy can be appealing especially for a social worker who has felt oppressed and inhibited by rules and policies or constrained by a supervisor who seems to have a need to control more than is necessary. The possibility of being out from under the many restrictions that often apply only to "lower-ranking" staff can be appealing. Then there is the prospect of a more prestigious manager's title as part of one's signature block on correspondence. People also tend to treat managers with a little more respect and deference. Who would not like more of those?

There are other seductive interpersonal attractions associated with a promotion into management. In imagining what it would be like to become a manager, one is likely to envision how it would feel to tell family, friends, and other well-wishers about a promotion or, perhaps, to see the look on the face of a rival when the news is announced.

Even the opportunity just to have what others may want can be an important impetus for saying "yes." Saying "no" is especially difficult if the list of applicants is long or if some very good workers also want the job. The logic goes like this: "They all want it, so it must be something good. I can have it, so I had better take it."

The desire to prevent others from getting positions with greater management responsibilities can cloud people's judgment. They can leave little room for honest assessments of whether these positions are what individuals really want. Some management jobs undoubtedly have been accepted just to keep a rival or feared co-worker from getting a job. Other times, it is clear that one individual may be the only inside candidate for a job that carries more management responsibilities. Other staff, fearing change and the unknown, may implore "one of their own" to take the job. The candidate may end up taking the job primarily as a favor to others.

The fear of the long-term career consequences of not saying "yes" also has been known to produce a hasty affirmative response. We have all heard stories of workers (usually in the business world) who declined a promotion into a higher-level management position. Later, when they were ready to move into management, another offer never came. In most human service organizations, such a fear is largely unfounded. Refusal of a promotion is unlikely to be interpreted as suggesting that one will never have an interest in any kind of management position. Opportunities to move into positions with greater management responsibility usually occur more than once over the course of a social worker's career, especially if one is free to leave the organization where currently employed. Nevertheless, the specter of missing an only chance (even though it may have little basis in reality) may contribute to making a decision that later is regretted.

A more realistic fear of saying "no" relates to what others might think. There is likely to be concern as to how co-workers, professional colleagues outside the organization or family, friends, and neighbors interpret a lack of upward mobility. Will they speculate that the social worker is really only marginally competent and incapable of going much farther? When the offer of a promotion is turned down, it often is impossible to let others know that the offer was made and declined. Telling others about it would be a disservice to the person who ultimately takes the job. And, new managers have enough problems without others knowing that they were not the first choice for a job.

Convincing one's self that "no, thank you" is the correct response is especially difficult. If a promotion into a position with increased management responsibilities is declined, it is impossible to know for certain whether or not one really could have done the job well. If people do not try, how will they ever really know? There are likely to be other doubts too. For example, we may wonder if it really is easier to criticize others for their management practices than to be a good manager. Avoidance of self-doubt can be a powerful impetus to impulsively say "yes" when the offer of a promotion comes along. Of course, the presence of self-doubt is also the reason why some potentially good managers say "no" to the offer of a promotion.

The Rude Awakening.

If social workers accept the offer of a promotion into a job with greater management responsibilities based solely on one or more of the reasons that we just discussed, they will quickly learn something. A "yes" answer is almost certain to result in disillusionment and regret. The benefits and "perks" that initially were so appealing lose their value rather quickly. They just do not seem very important after a little while. For example, telling others about one's promotion can be very enjoyable, but soon everyone who cares already knows. That attractive private office with the window and the better grade of carpet soon becomes simply "the office." It will have good or bad associations depending on what one thinks about the job itself. The reserved parking place soon is just taken for granted. It can even cause aggravation and necessitate unwanted conflicts with visitors and other staff who may choose to park in it.

Professional travel to conferences and meetings in pleasant locations look like wonderful fringe benefits to those who do not get the opportunity to go places at company expense. But they quickly can lose appeal when managers have to make many trips, some

CASE EXAMPLE • *Wanting to Be a Manager, or Wanting to Manage?*

Marina had been preparing for a career in management before she ever took her first social work job. She had selected a concentration of studies in administration. But when she finished her social work education she was forced to take the only social work job that was available at the time in the town where her partner worked. She became a dedicated and competent caseworker in a family preservation unit at the local Department of Social Services (DSS). She really liked what she was doing. But she regularly told her friends that she would "grab" the first job with more management responsibilities (and higher pay) that came along. Her career goal was to become the director of a human service organization before she was 35 (in ten years).

Marina worked as a caseworker for three years. Then her supervisor suffered a severe stroke. Marina was made acting supervisor until he could return but, in fact, she did very little management. Most tasks were "put on hold" until the supervisor could return to work. After a few more months, he suffered a second, much more severe stroke and took a disability retirement. Marina and a co-worker, Jongsook, both immediately applied for his job. Based upon her high staff performance evaluations and the fact that there had been no complaints about her work as acting supervisor, Marina was offered the job. She was delighted, and accepted without hesitation. She had been afraid that Jongsook would get the job and felt that there was no way that she could continue in her old job with Jongsook as her supervisor—they had never gotten along well.

The following weekend was one of the happiest of Marina's life. She called her parents to tell them about her promotion. They told her how proud they were of her. She went to the agency and took the measurements of her new office and planned how she would decorate it. While there, she filled out the form to have new calling cards made with her new job title and checked the dates of the annual supervisor's meeting to be sure that she would be able to attend. Then she left and went shopping for a new car, since the raise that she was about to receive would now make it possible for her to make payments. On Saturday night she treated her partner to dinner at a restaurant that she had always wanted to try but could not afford.

For about a month Marina continued to be thrilled with the idea of being a supervisor. Then things seemed to change. Former co-workers started to avoid her now that she was their boss. On several occasions she heard them laughing and left her office to join in the fun. The laughing stopped. She was not asked to join their bowling team as she had been in previous years. She did not feel like she could ask why and decided that, although she missed being on the team, it probably was not a good idea to continue to socialize with subordinates in the same way as she had when she had been their co-worker.

Marina knew that she should become more friendly with the other supervisors but she did not feel that they really wanted to be friendly. They seemed to not accept her since she was much younger than they were. She saw them only rarely, usually at some special called meeting at 5 PM to address some problem that had come up. She began to resent these intrusions on what she regarded as her free time. Being new to the job, she got behind on paperwork and also had to use most of her Saturdays to catch up. She hated the paperwork and felt as though two-thirds of it was unnecessary.

To her surprise, Marina really missed her work with clients. She felt that she had let some of them down when she later learned that problems had occurred for them. She also had not realized just how much gratification she had received from her "successes." She asked her boss about the possibility of carrying a small caseload but was told that it was not possible, given her management duties and the fact that she was already behind on her

CASE EXAMPLE • *(continued)*

paperwork. Besides, the boss confided to her, the family preservation program was probably going to be discontinued soon. She would be given another supervisor's job, but she should begin contingency planning to determine which of her current staff could be assigned to other duties and which would have to be fired.

Marina began to have trouble sleeping as she wrestled with the idea of which of her friends might have to lose their jobs. She concluded that she had wanted the power to reward friends, not to cause them harm. She began calling in sick and got further behind on her paperwork. She longed to be back in her old job, but knew that was not possible. Even if it were, she believed that "admitting failure" as a supervisor would be too humiliating.

Marina was fortunate. Her partner was transferred to the corporate office in a large city before the family preservation unit was abolished. She was able to resign her job and move without losing face. She continued to stay in touch with her old co-workers. She was able to get good reference letters that described how effective she had been as a caseworker. She quickly found a job in her new home as a counselor in a family agency.

Discussion Questions

1. What opportunities did Marina fail to take advantage of that might have prevented her from making a career mistake?
2. What questions should Marina have asked herself that might have convinced her to decline the offer of the supervisor's job?
3. What were the "wrong reasons" why Marina took the supervisory job when it was offered?
4. What aspects of the job of supervisor contributed to her unhappiness?
5. Why would it have been difficult for Marina to go back to her old job or to another one that held fewer management responsibilities?

of which they would rather not make. Professional travel can become a fatiguing responsibility that takes managers away from the job more than they would like, leaving them behind in their work. Many senior managers find themselves seeking ways to avoid professional travel by sending others to represent them whenever possible.

The increased autonomy that goes with most higher-level management positions is not a luxury; it is a necessity. It simply allows managers to be able to perform the many, varied tasks that are required in the way and in the sequence that works best for them. The title that goes with being a manager is useful only on those rare occasions when it is desirable to "pull rank" or to remind others of one's greater authority. But it also can be a barrier between a manager and other staff. It can interfere with needed communication. A manager may miss the honest critique that used to be offered gratuitously by former peers, who now seem more concerned with practicing ingratiation than with saying what they really think.

The pleasure of having kept a disliked co-worker or other fellow professional from getting the job does not last long either. Soon the other individual's career aspirations really do not matter much. After a week or two, what really matters is the job.

Even a raise in pay may not result in any net gain. Increased income taxes and additional expenses generally accompany a promotion. A lower-level staff member can make a $1 contribution for flowers for a hospitalized co-worker. The manager is expected to make a larger contribution. When others' donations do not cover the cost of the flowers, guess who makes up the difference? There also may be an expectation that managers give holiday gifts to staff or host social events. Either can be expensive. A new "manager's wardrobe" may have to be purchased when one is promoted. Perhaps even the ten-year-old car that was just fine before will be deemed inadequate for transporting those influential people with whom managers must frequently socialize.

Soon, most of those reasons why taking a position with greater management responsibilities that seemed so attractive have been depreciated. They are no longer important. What matters is the new job and its expectations.

Changes to Expect

As we have discussed throughout this book, many of the responsibilities of the manager are pleasurable and very consistent with the needs of most social workers. For example, increased influence over organization policies and services can be gratifying, especially for the social worker who may have felt powerless to initiate needed changes. "Troubleshooting" in order to address unique problems can be a more challenging and intellectually stimulating way to spend the day than performing repetitive tasks. But other management activities such as conducting staff evaluation conferences, overseeing the daily work of others, making budget cuts, or firing or putting staff on probation are not enjoyable. The need to give specific direction to subordinates can be especially difficult for social workers who are far more comfortable using non-directive approaches in working with others.[4]

As one takes on more management responsibilities, changes in one's work day occur. Managers are expected to be involved in overseeing what others are doing. As suggested in the discussion of delegation in Chapter 8, more management responsibility often leaves managers accountable for not only their own actions, but also for those of others. Managers learn what it is like to become a scapegoat for what is often the fault of others or for situations beyond anyone's control.

Difficult decisions must be made; they cannot simply be turned over to a superior. The nature of problems and decisions to be made by managers tend to be of the one-time only variety. There are fewer routine decisions that are a response to predictable and recurring situations.

Politicking and diplomacy are important skills for the manager. Especially in the public sector (where the task environment may be especially hostile), a human service organization should be recognized for what it is, a political arena.[5] The internal environment of an organization also requires managerial diplomacy. The job of manager may require a considerable amount of "asking or persuading others to do things, involving the manager in face-to-face verbal communication of limited duration."[6]

Higher-level managers are highly visible. Their behavior on business and even social occasions is often noticed and discussed by others. Some amount of criticism or even ridicule is likely to occur. Virtually everyone makes fun of the boss now and then. Managers must expect it and try not to take it personally. Staff at the lowest organizational levels are evaluated by superiors. But higher-level managers are evaluated by superiors and their subordinates. This is something to seriously consider before accepting a job with greater management responsibilities if one is especially sensitive to criticism.

Jobs that carry heavy management responsibilities are not for everyone. Refusing the offer of a management position may be the correct decision, if it is based on the recognition that one does not enjoy managing. But a bad decision to take on greater management responsibilities based on the wrong reasons may have permanent negative consequences for the individual, for the organization, and, most importantly, for the clients we seek to help.

A Guide for Decision Making

The statements in Figure 12.1 are a summary of our discussion of the role of the social worker as manager. They also can be used as a stimulus for a social worker to explore personal career goals with friends, family, and, especially, their bosses—people who already know what the job of manager entails. There are many attributes that are desirable for one who is contemplating a management career. For example, initiative, problem-solving skills, trustworthiness, intelligence, and a commitment to the goals of the organization are virtual prerequisites to success as a manager. However, the most important characteristic is the desire to do the job of manager. It is what often separates good managers from managers who are bitter and frustrated with their jobs.

While even the most happy and successful manager would not be expected to agree with all twenty-five statements in Figure 12.1. However, if a social worker disagrees with a large percentage of them (perhaps, over ten?) this should serve as a warning signal that a career shift into a position with more management responsibilities might not be such a good idea, at least at the present time.

Taking the Job

When, after careful consideration of just what management entails, social workers decide to "go for it," they most frequently move into positions created long before their arrival. Few social workers assume their management responsibilities within a brand-new organization. They take over from other people whose past management styles, personalities, and behaviors have left "acts to follow." Inevitably, the influence of managers' predecessors continue to be felt for a period of time after they have moved on to other responsibilities. Depending on how their predecessors were perceived by staff, new managers face certain predictable difficulties that will impact on their ability to perform the functions of management.

Following the Popular Manager

In assuming management responsibilities previously performed by another individual who was highly liked and respected, a new manager faces an uphill battle. Comparisons, usually negative ones, are inevitable, at least in the beginning. Even if the previous manager had a few faults, they are likely to be forgotten or glossed over by a loyal staff. The

FIGURE 12.1 *Do I Want More Management Responsibilities?*

Directions: Place a check mark alongside each statement with which you agree.

1. I would welcome additional management responsibilities, even if they did not result in a pay increase.
2. I would rather have more management responsibilities than the title, privileges, or other "perks" that might go with a management job
3. I want more management responsibilities for myself, not because of others' wishes or ambitions.
4. I view more management responsibilities as consistent with my long-range career goals.
5. I would not mind having less direct contact with clients.
6. I recognize the importance of paperwork.
7. I enjoy overseeing the work of others.
8. I can delegate responsibility when the situation requires it.
9. I do not mind assuming the ultimate responsibility for others' actions.
10. I can handle saying "no" to others' requests when the situation requires it.
11. I believe that I can be objective in evaluating the contributions and achievements of others.
12. I am comfortable with being directive and authoritarian with others when the situation requires it.
13. I recognize that the good of the organization or of its clients collectively sometimes must take priority over individual client needs and requests.
14. I have relationships outside the workplace that can meet my social needs.
15. I can live with being the object of criticism or ridicule by subordinates.
16. I have no personal secrets that might be detrimental to the image of the organization if they were to become public knowledge.
17. I can implement decisions with which I may personally disagree.
18. I would rather lead than follow.
19. I would enjoy having increased interaction with higher level managers.
20. Words like "uncertainty" and "challenge" sound exciting to me.
21. I would be willing to risk offending my superiors in order to advocate for others.
22. I would enjoy the increased social obligations that go with assuming a higher position in the organization.
23. I would enjoy becoming more "political."
24. My past experiences in performing management functions have been enjoyable.
25. I am willing to commit the time required to become a good manager.

How many check marks did you make?
    Twenty or more?—Go for it!
    Ten–nineteen?—Better give it careful consideration.
    Less than ten?—You'd probably be pretty unhappy.

Rebecca Myth,[7] or the tendency to idealize a former leader and to regard the new one with suspicion and resentment, is a common problem. When the new manager makes mistakes, which most certainly will happen while functioning in a new role, staff may express feelings of disgust and longing for the return of the new manager's predecessor. If the previous manager is still employed within the organization, the problem can be exacerbated. Staff members may hope for and even scheme to get the old manager to return.

The difficulties inherent in succeeding a popular manager often dissipate with time. But they may not. Especially if differences in management style are very obvious, problems can get worse rather than better. If staff attitudes do not improve after a reasonable period of time, it may be necessary to address the problem directly. Negative comparisons, old loyalties, and unrealistic antagonism toward the new manager can be unpleasant for the manager. But, more importantly, they can interfere with organizational goal attainment. Staff may need to be reminded as clearly and directly as possible that the manager is indeed a different person with a different style and a different way of doing things. However, they will have to adjust to these realities. This point may have to be made repeatedly. If staff expect to be treated as individuals by the manager (and this is a reasonable expectation), they will also need to treat the manager as a unique individual. They should be told this. However, the previous manager should not be disparaged in any way; this would only increase staff resentment.

As we discussed in the previous chapter, a social worker's management style should not be a carefully kept secret. It should be communicated regularly to staff members, thus making it possible for staff to predict with reasonable certainty what their boss will do, think, say, and so forth. It is, therefore, not enough for new managers simply to state that they are different from their popular predecessors. Examples of their management behaviors and philosophies should be stated and practiced. As their differences from their predecessors become known and (it is hoped) appreciated, fewer comparisons will be made. Managers, like any other professionals, have a right to be judged on their own performance without reference to others. This is a principle that is consistent with social work practice values. When presented as such, it is usually well received and accepted by staff.

Following the Unpopular Manager

The social worker who succeeds another manager who was generally disliked and resented would seem to be fortunate. Assuming that most staff are dedicated and competent and that the cause of resentment was primarily the predecessor's shortcomings, the new manager cannot help but look good. Indeed, a "honeymoon period" is likely to occur. Flattery will abound. Compliments on the new manager's approach to the job (usually accompanied by comparisons with the previous manager's approaches) are likely to be common. Compliments can be very nice to hear, can be quite seductive, and can give the new manager a false sense of security. But the honeymoon period may not last for long.

When the new manager makes the first mistake or just makes an unpopular decision, a tolerant attitude may prevail. Staff may remind themselves and each other that "it used to be much worse." But as the new manager continues to make demands and occasionally to offend (an inevitable part of the job of managing), harsh judgment may follow and resentment may quickly build. Another kind of comparison will occur. Similarities between the old and new managers will be pointed out along with expressions of disappointment. Some similarities inevitably will exist, in part because the previous manager performed some tasks according to sound management principles. However, inaccurate and unfair generalizations may begin to occur as the new manager is erroneously perceived by staff as "really no different" from the old manager. Staff may become quickly disillusioned with and turn against the new manager. If their tendency was to blame the previous manager for problems on the job, they may easily fall back into their old pattern in their relationship with the new manager.

Addressing the potential problems inherent in succeeding an unpopular manager involves a process very similar to that used in situations where managers must succeed other managers who were popular. In both instances, comparison and an inability of staff to recognize and to respond to differences are the enemies. As we discussed earlier, they must be confronted and neutralized. When following an unpopular manager, it may be necessary to remind staff that the new manager is different, but not totally different, from the previous occupant of the job. Defense of the predecessor's practices (those that were good) should be open and frequent, and complaints, criticism, and, especially, ridicule of the former manager's work should be discouraged. It is tempting and easy to listen to "war stories" about the previous manager's blunders. Derogation of their work can seem like a shortcut to acceptance by staff. But this is a bad practice that will eventually cost a new manager more than it will gain. Not only is such behavior unprofessional, but it also sets a poor example for staff by saying that it is okay to disparage other members of the team. Besides, neither the new manager nor other staff members are in a position to fully understand the reasons behind the previous manager's decisions and behaviors.

A Proactive Approach to Management Succession.   No matter how the new manager's predecessor was regarded, comparisons are likely to cause problems. Can they be totally avoided? Probably not. But they can be greatly diminished if the new manager takes a proactive approach to management succession. A new manager needs to acknowledge and even to emphasize differences from the previous occupant of the job, preferably before comparisons can begin. A first staff meeting is an excellent occasion to send the loud and clear message that a new era has begun. In words and actions that exemplify the new manager's individualistic approach to the job, it is a good idea to communicate the following message:

> My predecessor made some valuable contributions to this organization. I also plan to do what I can to help us achieve our objectives. But, I want you to know that I am a different person. Sometimes I will act like your old boss and sometimes I will act quite differently. What I do I will do because, I believe, it is the best way to get the job done. Whenever possible, I will try to let you know why we are doing things the way we are. I want you to know and understand my approach to my work, my "style." And you have a right to know what I expect from you. Ask questions if I do not always make my expectations clear. Let me assure you that I will respect (and evaluate) each of you as an individual. I expect you to do the same for me.

Such a strong statement is likely to get the attention of staff. It is also likely to add to the anxiety over a change in managers that probably already exists. If the manager sees that this is occurring, the emphasis on difference should be tempered with assurances (if they can be made) that staff members who do a good, competent job have nothing to fear from the change.

Of course, the proactive communication that a new manager is both similar to and different from the previous manager should be more than simply a verbal one. Actions should reinforce the message. If there is not an immediate opportunity to do this, the manager may wish to deliberately create one. Some clear-cut differences in expectations or behavior that everyone notices will suffice. They need not be differences of any great importance, only obvious ones. For example, did the previous manager remind a member of the support staff whenever it was time to make another pot of coffee? The new manager might simply go and make more coffee occasionally—a gesture that costs little in time or effort but is often appreciated. What if the previous manager sometimes made coffee when the pot was empty? The new manager might deliberately set up a roster of support staff to perform the coffee making job. Support staff may be initially resentful, but they soon will just accept it as part of their "other duties as assigned." The new manager can find some other (new) way to show consideration for support staff. Meanwhile, the manager will have reinforced the verbal message that differences in management style can be expected.

Differences in management style can either be an impediment to or an asset to successful management. As social workers, we are taught to value diversity and to use it productively. The manager who proactively helps staff to recognize differences is more likely to experience the differences as an asset, the desirable phenomenon. When managers remind staff of how they approach the role of manager differently from their predecessors, staff members are given the opportunity to gain insight into their unique philosophy and style of management. These insights can then be used productively to achieve organizational goals.

Relating to Former Co-Workers

The social worker who assumes a new role as manager is not always new to the work environment and to continuing staff. In fact, a more likely situation in human service organizations involves promotion from within the work group. In the new role, a manager may have administrative authority over those who previously occupied the same or a comparable position on the formal organizational chart. The new manager's former peers suddenly are subordinates. This situation can produce special problems. They can interfere with the manager's abilities to effectively do the job of manager.

People tend to establish levels of formality and familiarity that are appropriate for the respective roles that they occupy. For example, close friendships, intense rivalries, good-natured ridicule, and sharing of office gossip are not unusual among peers in a work environment. As long as they exist by mutual consent and do not interfere with the productivity of those involved, this interaction between peers can be harmless and can make the job a little more enjoyable.

When a person assumes greater management responsibility and becomes the boss of former peers, previous relationships must change. As one assumes new responsibilities and spends more time as a manager, new patterns of relating to others will have to be developed. It is often difficult for the social worker as manager to make this transition. It can also be difficult for the former peers who are now subordinates. The isolation that we discussed earlier in this chapter may be especially felt during the time of transition.

Depending on the situation and the people involved, changes in relationships may need to be slight or they may need to be more dramatic. The secret for the manager is to make only necessary changes. In making whatever changes are required, it is helpful if managers communicate clearly to staff that it is the needs of the organization and not their own intra-personal needs that require the changes. Managers do not want staff to conclude that they are now "too good for their old friends" or otherwise are impressed with themselves and their new status. However, reality dictates that managers probably cannot remain "one of the gang," and efforts to do so can result in staff resentment.

Sensitive staff members generally recognize the need for establishing new relationships when one of their peers becomes their boss. While some might occasionally use old friendships to try to manipulate the manager or to seek special favors, most former peers know better than to try to exploit the situation. This is a time of experimentation for all parties involved as staff and the manager re-negotiate their relationships with each other. Behavior will change in many ways. For example, staff probably will not complain about "the administration" as freely around the manager as they previously did. In turn, some topics (such as the work of other staff) that the manager previously discussed with co-workers are no longer suitable for even casual discussion between the staff members and their new boss.

Some initial overreaction to the assumption of new roles is likely to occur on the part of both the manager and former peers. New managers often use reminders of their change in status (for example, titles, formal correspondence, and so forth) when none is needed. Staff may create a greater social distance from their new boss than is necessary. These responses can be useful. They serve to underline the reality that managers and those over whom they have authority are not and cannot be peers. Reassurances of mutual respect and continued friendships (but on a different level) usually come a little later as relationships gradually become redefined.

Bitterness between some staff members and the new manager over the loss of a "special" friendship can usually be expected. If a staff member sought the manager's job but did not get it, bitterness may be even more intense. Even if a former close friend remains a confidant for a while as a manager assumes new responsibilities, the same relationship probably will not continue. The power differential that will exist will almost certainly cause it to change. It is just as well. It is not good for group morale to have one subordinate who has greater access to or who appears to be treated in a special way by the manager. Certain boundaries are useful.

Inevitably, a former peer and close friend will be critical of the manager's style or behavior. He or she will disagree about a decision or the way that the manager performs some aspect of the job. The critical response to the manager may result at least in part from bitterness over changes in the friendship relationship. But the criticism and disagreement, if expressed openly and logically, may also be an indication that the difficult interpersonal transition has been accomplished. The manager is now open to the second guessing and critique by all staff that comes with the job of manager. Managers usually can assume the latter. They can objectively evaluate the criticism of the other individual, and encourage additional feedback. They should resist the temptation to dismiss the criticism as bitterness turning instead to those other staff members who are all too ready with praise.

Managers who possess the values, knowledge, and skills of the social worker should be adequately prepared to handle the interpersonal problems that can occur when they find themselves with administrative authority over those who were previously their peers. They should be able to assess and to understand the motivation behind staff reactions and behaviors as well as their own. But this still does not guarantee that the transition will be an easy one.

Developing a Management Style

Whether we ultimately decide to seek a position with increased management responsibilities or remain in one with more direct client contact, all of us develop a certain approach to the role of manager. It (what is referred to as our "management style") is likely to resemble that of others, particularly managers whom we have known and admired. But it also will be distinctive. We are who we are and we respond to situations in certain ways because of a complex interaction of life experience, psychological, cultural and biological factors, and the impact of other social systems with which we must interact. We have developed our own distinctive personalities. They affect how we live, love, play, and so forth. Similarly, our distinctive management styles affect the way that we approach different management tasks.

Our management styles are likely to be (and should be) extensions of our personalities. Thus our approach to the tasks of management likely will bear a close resemblance to our approach to the other tasks of life. But how we perform management functions and tasks also is based on the specific needs of a situation, what others have taught us about management and what we have found to work. Thus, our management styles usually reflect comfortable compromises between our perceptions of the requirements of a situation and the way to address them that seems to be both logical and natural (that is, consistent with our personalities).

There is some good advice that is essential for good social work practice (and for a happy life). It is—"know thyself." For managers, this translates to "know your management style, let others know it, but do not be afraid to grow." How can we identify our management style? Several theorists have attempted to identify management "types" that occur in organizations. We alluded to one of these in Chapter 10 when we discussed Theory X and Theory Y. There are numerous others. One, Champagne and Hogan's "Personal Style Inventory,"[8] is especially useful for understanding our management styles. A hint of our managerial style also can be gleaned in response to certain questions that we might ask ourselves based upon our discussions of the five management functions (Figure 12.2).

Our personality and its reflection in our management style rest somewhere along a continuum between untrusting and controlling on one extreme and trusting and permissive on the other. Kotin and Sharaf use the terms "tight" and "loose" to describe these two extreme types.[9] They noted that tight administrators use formal reminders of their status differential, clear-cut delegation of authority and responsibility, reliance on rules and traditions, adherence to the hierarchical chain of command, and formal communication through regular meetings, memos, reports, and forms. On the opposite end of the continuum, loose administrators use primarily informal reminders of status differential, rarely fall back on rules and traditions to influence, bypass the chain of command when desirable, prefer informal communication methods, and show a capacity to tolerate some of the

FIGURE 12.2   *Understanding My Management Style*

1. Which of the classical management theories do I think makes the most sense for me? How comfortable am I with participative management approaches that allow others to share in decision making?

2. Would I prefer to use planning methods such as rules that allow for little discretion in staff decision making or would I rather use those such as policies that offer more staff autonomy and encourage the use of professional discretion? How important is contingency planning for me?

3. Am I comfortable with a variety of types of staff and their unique contributions as well as the potential problems that they bring? Do I prefer general job descriptions or carefully defined ones? How important do I think it is to "professionalize" a human service organization?

4. What are my attitudes about the relative importance of supervision and continuing education for employee growth? Do I see the professional career development of staff as more the responsibility of managers or of individuals themselves? Would I rather work with locals or cosmopolitans?

5. What is my attitude toward staff performance evaluations and personnel actions? Do I think that they are more useful for helping individual staff to improve their performance or for protecting the organization and its clients?

6. Can I accept and appreciate staff who approach their jobs differently from the way that I approach mine, or do I work to shape staff into people who are more like me?

7. How comfortable am I with group cohesiveness among subordinates and the presence of an informal organization? What is my attitude about conflict within the organization? What do I see as the most important purpose of communication, and what methods do I prefer?

8. How comfortable am I with delegating tasks and authority to others? If I were to delegate, would I prefer to delegate staff or functional authority to a subordinate?

9. Do I prefer to exercise a considerable amount of direct control through use of such methods as directives or do I prefer to control by using methods such as advice and information?

10. How do I perceive the relative importance of support and structure as components of good leadership?

role ambiguity that exists because of a lack of clearly designated roles, responsibilities, and authority.

While all social workers have management styles that can be seen in the way they approach the functions of management, our management styles can and should change over time. They change naturally as we learn from experience and as we rethink our attitudes and perceptions of people and of situations. However, we also should try to stretch and to grow as managers. The best managers are versatile. For example, they can be tough and authoritarian when needed and they also can be understanding and supportive when required. This gives them some definite advantages over other managers who have a more limited repertoire. The observation that, as a person, we may naturally tend to prefer a more controlling or a more laid-back approach to management does not absolve us from learning to use other approaches.

Managers' Needs and Organizational Needs

It is often very difficult to determine the approach to management that is best for a given situation. In Chapter 10 we discussed how effective managers offer both consideration and structure, and how the best balance of the two depends on such variables as the needs of staff and the needs of the situation. But, where do the needs of the manager factor into the equation? Managers need to be able to plan, staff, organize, control, lead, and perform other management tasks. This need is very important and cannot be ignored. If it is, problems can result. For example, a manager who provides too much consideration and insufficient structure may find it difficult to exercise control over staff behaviors when control is necessary.

Other problems can result when managers' own personal needs influence the ways they approach the job of manager. There are a number of ways that this can occur. We are social beings. We all desire to have others respond emotionally to us in certain ways (see Figure 12.3). Thus we act in ways that promote these responses. As long as the response is desirable for the organization, this can be good. For example, as was noted earlier, effective managers act in ways that staff learn to trust them, have confidence in them and perceive them as fair. However, certain other types of actions on the part of managers that are designed to meet their needs can promote emotional responses that are dysfunctional in organizations. For example, some managers seem to have a strong need to be feared and seek to gratify it in the workplace. They use intimidation, unpredictable "tirades," public criticism, or sarcastic put-downs to generate fear among staff. They often see nothing wrong with this, rationalizing that managers need to be respected. But they fail to recognize that fear is not the same as respect and should not be confused with it.

Respect, of course, is good. It results naturally when, over time, a manager develops a reputation for being competent, but also for being fair, trustworthy, and so forth. Respect makes the manager's job easier. For example, people are more likely to do their best work or to comply with the wishes of a manager who they respect rather than one who lacks

FIGURE 12.3 *What Managers May Seek from Subordinates*

Need	How Achieved	Consequences	Desirability
To Be Feared	intimidation, rage ridicule	emotional duress immobilization	undesirable
To Be Respected	competence trust, fairness	dedication loyalty	high
To Be Liked	respect personality traits	loyalty pleasant work climate	desirable, not necessary
To Be Loved	may be unachievable in the work place personal relationships	loss of respect, pity	undesirable

respect. Thus it is good for the organization. In contrast, fear of a manager is not good for the organization. It immobilizes people, inhibits communication, and causes staff to work under emotional duress. Managers who create a work environment that seems like a "reign of terror" are operating out of their needs, not that of the organization. They are little more than tyrants.

Another nearly opposite need, the need to be loved, can also cause major problems when managers attempt to gratify it through their actions in the workplace. Again, a narrow but important distinction between two emotions is helpful here. In the same way that respect and fear are very different and have very different consequences for the work environment, being liked as a manager and being loved are quite different. While not absolutely necessary in all cases (some people, for whatever reason, will always choose to dislike us), being liked by the majority of one's subordinates certainly makes the job of manager much easier. Being liked entails, among other things, being perceived as "a good person" who shares the same professional values and is a considerate, understanding boss. Staff members are likely to give their best efforts for a manager who they like. Liking promotes respect and vice versa. They are complementary and very closely related.

Being loved is, of course, a basic need of human beings. However, it is best gratified through family and friends. Being loved by one's subordinates is both unnecessary and, perhaps, impossible given the power differential that exists. Managers perceived as always trying to be loved are likely to be ridiculed or even pitied. Thus efforts to be loved by staff can dissolve respect rather than promote it.

The management style adopted by managers may include various acts of kindness. There is no reason why such actions as occasionally providing refreshments for staff meetings, sending thank you notes to staff for a job well done, or offering assistance to a staff member at a time of crisis should be perceived as an indication that the manager is unduly "needy." Such actions, often characteristic of a nurturing style of management, can be very effective for boosting staff morale, breaking down unnecessary boundaries, and promoting teamwork. So long as these are the reasons for them (and not the manager's need to be loved) and others perceive that to be the case, there is no problem. A note of warning is appropriate, however. Because the manager is in a position of power, staff members are unlikely to complain about a nurturing management style, even if it is unwanted and makes them uncomfortable. Some people just want to do their job and to not have that kind of relationship with the manager. They should be encouraged to express this and their wishes should also be respected. Effective managers stay in touch with the needs of others, and know when to "back off." To impose a nurturing relationship on all staff, whether they desire it or not, can be just another form of tyranny.

There is yet another way that managers sometimes cause problems by confusing their needs with those of staff or of the organization. It is particularly common among managers who have held management positions for a while (perhaps, too long) and who have become overly identified with the organization. It involves a logical fallacy. Senior managers, especially those who have had a number of successes and have been praised and rewarded for them by board members or higher-level managers, often start to believe that anything that can result in more success for them, must be good for the organization. They may rationalize that they have a broader perspective on situations (as managers do) and access to information not available to others. Therefore, their perceptions of what the organization needs (which just happens to be what *they* need or want) are always correct. Their successes gradually cause them to rely less and less on subordinates for input. They lose touch with the needs and preferences of others. An "I know what is best for them" attitude can develop. Opposition becomes less frequent over time. Staff may be fearful of opposing the manager who may skillfully prevent an organized rebellion through a combination of "divide and conquer," intimidation and "buy-offs."

What is wrong with a knowledgeable, experienced manager making most important decisions with little or no input from staff? For one thing, it can result in bad decisions, since no manager is infallible or has access to all needed information. But a paternalistic approach to management that may be perceived as self-serving is also just not effective. It does not promote desirable teamwork and an organizational climate conducive to the staff's "ownership" of their work that is so important to organizational functioning.[10] Staff will not do their best work when they believe that they are merely working to pursue the manager's own personal agenda.

Effective managers recognize their own needs but do not attempt to gratify them through their relationships with staff. They also work to remain humble and avoid behaviors that are (or can be misinterpreted as) elitist or self-serving and, thus, not in the best interest of the organization.

Becoming a Better Manager

Regardless of the line that they occupy on an organizational chart, social workers who are successful in their management roles learn to think like a manager and to take on the personal identity of a manager. Unless they make conscious efforts to continue to develop and to grow as managers, they can easily slip in and out of their manager's role every day, perform the functions of the manager, but never really perform them comfortably or particularly well.

The best managers are lifelong learners. They are never content with their current knowledge and skills, always seeking to improve. This sounds like hard work, but it gets easier as it becomes a natural, comfortable approach to one's work. One well-known writer, Peter Drucker, has made the observation that "it takes more energy to improve from incompetence to mediocrity than to improve from first-rate performance to excellence."[11]

The best managers remain sensitive to themselves and how they are performing as managers. They regularly (at least daily) evaluate their work, identifying what seems to have worked and what has not been effective. Another author, Topolov, also points out the importance of knowing ourselves physically, for example, knowing what time of day we do our best work and when we should avoid making important decisions or when we have become too tired and need to quit for the day.[12] These practices help us to set and maintain high standards as managers.

What else can social workers do to become better managers and to more closely identify with management? For one thing, they can read and remain current on new theory and developments within the field of management. They can subscribe to and read one or more journals (within social work and/or in related fields such as business) and can even make their own contributions to knowledge by conducting research on social work management and writing articles for publication.

Association with other managers also helps us to think and to feel more like managers. This can occur informally in semi-social situations. It can also take place at seminars and symposia that provide knowledge and skills to new and experienced managers. Some managers have chosen to set up groups consisting of other managers and themselves who regularly get together to discuss topics of management relevance over lunch or at other convenient times. The group members (frequently from a variety of organizations) learn from each other at the same time that they form valuable managers' networks.

Management is an integral part of social work practice. With reasonable effort and determination, it can also become an exciting and a gratifying activity for the social worker.

Summary

In this chapter we built upon some of the insights developed in earlier discussions. We attempted to complete the reader's understanding of management within human service organizations by examining some of the stresses that social workers in the role of manager often report.

We warned against the danger of making a hasty decision when the offer of a position with increased management responsibilities is made. We looked at some of the enticements that frequently lure social workers into management positions and why they are insufficient in themselves to guarantee either happiness or success. It was emphasized that it is not the desire to become a manager but the desire to do the job of the manager that is an important prerequisite to success in the role of manager.

The reader was reminded that there are often many ways to approach the tasks of management. The importance of developing a management style consistent with one's personality was stressed. The relationship between a manager's own intra-personal needs and those of the organization received special attention.

Finally, it was emphasized that becoming a successful manager at any level requires a certain management "mind set" and a commitment. One must learn to think like a manager and to take actions that will promote the development of an identity as a manager. Becoming and remaining a successful manager is a career-long activity.

Endnotes

1. S. Martin, "Women in Social Work: A Study of Their Perceptions of Power in Organizations." Ph.D. Dissertation, The University of South Carolina, Columbia, SC, 1995.

2. R. Weinbach, "Meeting a Supervisory Responsibility: Shared Evaluation of Supervisory Potential," *The Clinical Supervisor*, 10 (2), (1992): 195–209.

3. R. Scurfield, "Clinician to Administrator: Difficult Role Transition?," *Social Work*, 26 (1981): 498.

4. A. Kadushin, *Supervision in Social Work* (New York: Columbia University Press, 1985), p. 300.

5. B. Gummer, *The Politics of Social Administration* (Englewood Cliffs, NJ: Prentice Hall, 1990), pp. 29–48.

6. C. Hayes, "What Do Managers Do? A Critical Review," *Journal of Management Studies*, 23 (1) (1986): 104.

7. Alvin M. Gouldner, *Patterns of Industrial Bureaucracy* (Glencoe, IL: Free Press, 1954), p. 79.

8. D. Champagne and R. Hogan, "Personal Style Inventory," *The 1980 Annual Handbook for Group Facilitators* (University Associates, 1981).

9. J. Kotin and M. Sharaf, "Management Succession and Administrative Style," *Psychiatry,* 30 (1967): 237–248.

10. See, e.g., J. Belasco and R. Stayer, *The Flight of the Buffalo* (New York: Warner Books, 1993), pp. 59–64.

11. Peter F. Drucker, "Managing Oneself," *Harvard Business Review* (March–April, 1999): 67.

12. B. Topolov, *The Art and Skill of Working with People* (New York: MJF Books, 1997), pp. 293–294.

Index